INSTRUCTOR AND ADJUNCT SUPPORT MANUAL

to accompany

INTERMEDIATE ALGEBRA
TENTH EDITION

Marvin L. Bittinger

Indiana University Purdue University Indianapolis

PEARSON

Addison
Wesley

Boston San Francisco New York
London Toronto Sydney Tokyo Singapore Madrid
Mexico City Munich Paris Cape Town Hong Kong Montreal

Reproduced by Pearson Addison-Wesley from electronic files supplied by the author.

Copyright © 2007 Pearson Education, Inc.
Publishing as Pearson Addison-Wesley, 75 Arlington Street, Boston, MA 02116.

ISBN   0-321-30581-7

1 2 3 4 5 6 BB 09 08 07 06

CONTENTS

INTRODUCTION

Dear Faculty:

The Bittinger book team at Pearson Addison-Wesley is very excited that you will be using *Intermediate Algebra*, Tenth Edition. We know that whether you are teaching this course for the first time or the tenth time, you will face many challenges, including how to prepare for class, how to make the most effective use of your class time, how to present the material to your students in a manner that will make sense to them, how best to assess your students, and the list goes on.

This manual is designed to make your job easier. Inside these pages are words of advice from experienced instructors, general and content-specific teaching tips, a list of the objectives covered within *Intermediate Algebra*, descriptions of both student and instructor supplements that accompany this text, and a list of valuable resources provided by your fellow instructors.

We would like to thank the following professors for sharing their advice and teaching tips. This manual would not be what it is without their valuable contribution.

David P. Bell, *MSSM, Professor of Mathematics, Florida Community College at Jacksonville*

Chris Bendixen, *Lake Michigan College*

Sandy Berry, *Mathematics Department Chair, Hinds Community College – Vicksburg Campus*

Deanna L. Dick, *Alvin Community College*

Kathleen C. Ebert, *Alfred State College*

Rosa Kavanaugh, *Division Chair/Instructor of Mathematics, Ozarks Technical Community College*

Susan M. Leland, *Instructor, Montana Tech*

Michael Montaño, *Riverside Community College*

Nancy Ressler, *Professor of Mathematics, Oakton Community College*

Tomesa Smith, *EdD, Wallace State Community College*

Sharon Testone, *PhD, Professor of Mathematics, Onondaga Community College*

Roy D. West, *Robeson Community College*

Rebecca E. Wyatt-Semple, *Mathematics Instructor, Nash Community College*

It is also important to know that you have a very valuable resource available to you in your Pearson Addison-Wesley sales representative. If you do not know your representative, you can locate him/her by logging on to www.aw.com/replocator and typing in your zip code. Please feel free to contact your representative if you have any questions relating to our text or if you need additional supplements. Of course, you can always contact us directly at math@aw.com.

 In addition, the Addison-Wesley Math Adjunct Support Center, staffed by qualified mathematics instructors with over 50 years of combined experience at both the community college and university level, provides assistance for faculty. Support is provided in the areas of suggested syllabus consultation, tips on using materials packaged with your book, book-specific content assistance, and teaching suggestions including advice on classroom strategies. For more information, visit www.aw-bc.com/tutorcenter/math-adjunct.html.

We know that teaching this course can be challenging. We hope that this and the other resources we have provided will help to minimize the amount of time it takes you to meet those challenges.

Good luck in your endeavors!

The Bittinger book team

Dear Adjunct Faculty and Mentors:

My purpose in writing this introduction is to encourage both adjunct instructors and those responsible for guiding them to use the Instructor and Adjunct Support Manual. Adjunct faculty are playing an increasingly larger role in colleges and universities. At my institution adjunct faculty teach over 50% of the mathematics courses. In addition the adjunct's job is more challenging today than ever before. Some are hired on very short notice. Many drive from school to school, leaving them with very little preparation time. Still others receive little or no mentoring. With this confluence of an expanded role and increased difficulties, there comes a growing need to provide adjunct faculty with the support materials to help them meet a variety of challenges. The Instructor and Adjunct Support Manual is an invaluable resource in this regard.

This supplement has been developed by instructors for instructors. Virtually every element of the manual is the result of thoughtful comments and suggestions from adjunct faculty and their mentors. The offered recommendations address the challenges and concerns that adjunct faculty experience. Proposed topics range from the practical, such as items to be included in a syllabus in Sample Syllabi, to the probing, such as the most effective way to teach a particular concept in Teaching Tips Correlated to Textbook Sections. Other topics include General, First-Time Advice, Extra Practice Exercises, and Helpful Tips for Using Supplements and Technology. As a result of faculty involvement, an extremely useful resource has been developed for all those engaged in the adjunct experience.

Whether you are an adjunct instructor or a supervisor of adjunct faculty, I hope my words will motivate you to use the tools found in this support manual. Developed by teachers for teachers and dealing with a variety of topics pertinent to the adjunct experience, I believe you will find the Instructor and Adjunct Support Manual a wonderful addition to the support materials published by Pearson Addison-Wesley.

Have a great semester!

John M. Samoylo
Mathematics Department Co-coordinator
Delaware County Community College

GENERAL, FIRST-TIME ADVICE

We asked the contributing professors for words of advice to instructors who are teaching this course for the first time or for the first time in a long while. Their responses can be found on the following pages.

David P. Bell, *Florida Community College at Jacksonville*

1. So, you are considering teaching Intermediate Algebra in college for the first time! Before you even consider the syllabus, let's try to get a picture of your students. The most challenging students will be those who are essentially, totally unprepared for college. These students went through high school attending class at least some of the time and waiting for the teacher to provide all the required topics and knowledge in class. These students rarely if ever studied or did homework. That certainly was a negative beginning wasn't it. The fact is, if you prepare for these students, you will save time and effort on your part and more importantly for the students who do come prepared for college. For many of these students, you are their first and most important link to college level mathematics. These students need to be taught good study habits. They need to learn the value of timely performance of homework assignments and they need to learn to read the algebra textbook before each lesson. You still want to try mission impossible? That's great. Let's get started.

2. You will want to speak with an experienced faculty member and discuss just how and where to get started with the course. Many of those I work with use the review chapter to set the stage for the concept of student responsibility and ownership of their success. The Bittinger Intermediate Algebra text provides an excellent review of basic algebra in Chapter R. I skim the material in this chapter and stress the importance of this being review material. I state, "If the material and concepts in chapter R are new to you, or you do not remember any of them, stop, think, and come see me or visit a counselor. You may be in the wrong class! If the material is familiar, but you have not used it for some time, you have until the next class when we will test your knowledge of this material. You and I need to know if you have areas requiring extra review. Now is the time to make certain that you have every chance for success in the class!" Please don't use this statement as a class opener. You must try to gain some of the students' trust before you can be this honest with them.

3. I've set the stage and given you some disheartening details. Armed with this knowledge, you now set up the first class. You will see every expression on the faces of these students the first day of class, from fear to outright boredom, as you enter the classroom. This is your chance to get their attention and make that first impression. DO NOT pull out a stack of syllabi and start going over the details and requirements. Take this opportunity to open a discussion between the students and yourself. I have a group sheet that I pass out to get things started that includes room for four students and some general information. Notice that I have not mentioned algebra. The questions include: Why this college?; Where are you from?; What do you do?; What program are you in?; What do you expect from this class?; and e-mail and phone numbers. I then have the students break into groups and find students who reside in the same general area. This increases the chance that they will get together later to study. I give them plenty of time to gather the information knowing that they will each be introducing someone else in the class. The fear of math is now gone because I just told them that they each have to stand and introduce someone they most likely never met before. The icebreaker gives you the opportunity to get the roll and a feel for the class. Once the introductions are over, I introduce myself in the same format and we get down to business. Did I mention attendance? You can not overstress the need to read and understand the syllabus (the syllabus must contain all data pertinent to class management and student success for this course.) and the need to get started NOW! Did I mention

attendance? You should mention attendance as a requirement as often as you can stand it. I use the rest of this first session to review topics from the review chapter. This is the last time I will cover this material in class, but Stress the need to visit you during office hours or visit school tutors if available. I require each student to send me an e-mail from their school provided e-mail account. Did I mention attendance? These students are very mobile and the e-mails, addresses, and phone numbers they provide the first week of class change rapidly. Their school e-mail does not change. Thus, you will be able to contact them should they not show up for class. The underlying theme you must get out and repeat often is that to be successful, they will need to read, do homework and study. The more ways you find to get this message out, the better.

4. You should be able to procure an example of an elementary algebra final exam. You can provide this test to the students with a key and allow them to test themselves to see whether they are ready for this class. You may want to use the test as a quiz score or bonus just to emphasize to the student how important this material is. The important thing to keep in mind is "Now is the best time to remediate or relearn lost elementary algebra concepts." I have found that students who are made aware of possible problem areas will rise to the occasion and seek help early to increase their chances of success.

5. Once the first meeting is over, you always want to begin the day with something to make them think. I use quizzes, group problems, specific homework problems and anything else that I can to try to get their attention early. If they know the first few minutes are important, they will be less apt to be tardy. I try not to present the very examples that are in the text. If they read the textbook, presenting these often will create boredom that you do not want. I look for examples similar to those presented in the textbook. This provides the students with ample resources to complete the homework. Speaking of homework, try to assign mostly questions that have the answers in the textbook. Students can check the accuracy of their efforts. Some instructors collect homework so that the student sees a need to actually do it. I find that the students often just copy the solutions manual and turn it in as their own work. The contrast between the first test results and the homework is often a fantastic learning tool for the student. Spend a few minutes each day covering homework questions, but you control that time.

Students would rather spend all day on homework than the new lesson.

6. Tests are the primary measurement tool you have to gauge student learning and comprehension. Create the test so that it checks understanding of the topics you chose to cover. I focus on open response and applications questions. Build the test so that the better students finish early. Set a time limit. These students need to learn time management and there is no time like the present. Speaking of time management, you might also want to talk about overall semester load, work, family, study time, etc and see if there really is time to get it all done. The websites: http://www.askjeeves.com and http://www.pruplemath.com have excellent interactive study skills and time management routines and assistance.

7. Timely return of test results is a must. Occasionally you will have students who score low for a number of silly errors. Let them know that they could have done much better if they had been a bit more careful. They like knowing that you care enough to notice.

8. The comprehensive final exam is your last chance to see if you have prepared these students well for college algebra or the next course in the sequence at your college. I often offer to replace each student's lowest test score with the final exam score. It provides a bit of extra motivation and if the student does well on the final, I can rest assured that they are as ready for college algebra as I can get them.

9. Throughout the course, try to use the class leaders to assist and motivate the students who are struggling. Everyone benefits from this exchange and the students get a sense of teamwork for their efforts.

10. Finally, on those occasions where you have given your best lecture with your best definitions and you know the students should understand, but you see confusion in their eyes, you may get frustrated. The frustration comes from the belief that these students should have benefited from your presentation. Do your best to hide that frustration. The students will pick up on it very quickly and interpret that frustration as a personal issue. They feel you are frustrated with them and we know the frustration is directed at yourself. If you slip, just explain to the class your honesty with them will be a benefit later. Above all, keep an eye out for that light. You will see students suddenly perk up and profess "I see it now." It is so much fun seeing these people of all ages, colors, creeds, races, religions, etc. turn into knowledge-hungry students, and they pay you too.

Best of luck.

Chris Bendixen, *Lake Michigan College*

1. Generally the first day of class is one of the most important classes in the semester, not for the mathematical material, but for the "how to succeed" materials. The students' need the syllabus for the first class meeting. Go over the syllabus in great detail, stressing that this is a contract between you (instructor) and them (students). Explain to the students how much material is generally covered in each class period. Thus, if they miss a class, they know about how much was covered. Do not talk in a dry monotone voice for the entire class. You need the students' attention. Show enthusiasm in your teaching. Make it appear that this is the best subject ever.

2. Next item is the class roster. Go over the roster, trying to correctly pronounce all students names.

3. I like to tell the students on day one that everybody has a 100% in the class, now. It is up to you (the student) to maintain this grade. To maintain the grade, you should do the following:

   - Read the material before the material has been covered. It may not make sense at this point, but when the instructor goes over it, you will recognize the terminology. Also, after the material has been covered in class, go back over the reading. Amazingly, a lot more of the material will make sense.

   - To be truly successful in math, you must do homework, homework, homework—as soon as the material has been covered. Do not wait until the day before the exam to work on the problems, stay on top of it. Related to this is odd answers are generally listed in the back part of the book. Tell the students to check the problems, and, if the answer is not correct, rework it until it is correct. DO not give up after the first attempt.

   - Next, tell the students to take advantage of all the supplemental materials, such as: MATH-XL, InterAct Math, student solutions manuals, and additional internet math resources.

   - I try to get the students involved in study groups with their peers. I volunteer to attend the initial meeting of the study group. After that, they are on their own.

   - Always refresh yourself on prior materials. Math is a building block subject, you must be on top of all aspects of it throughout the entire course.

   - Finally give the students a study guide for the exams. I personally give the students a sample exam. I also post the sample exam on the school's BlackBoard site.

4. I tell the class about special policies, like:
   - Attendance policy
   - Late exam policy
   - Cell phone policy (this is a must) make the students turn off their cell phonse before class. If they go off during class, penalize the student. Cell phones are very disruptive to the flow of the class.
   - Grading policy
   - When to expect exams

Sandy Berry, *Hinds Community College*

"What do you teach?" Throughout my 35-year career I have been asked that question many times. My response is that I try to teach **students** about mathematics. A teacher's focus should be on their students first. Treat each student with the utmost respect. Take time to get to know your students as people. Learn their names as soon as possible. Call them by name often. Remember what it was like the first time you were a student in a course that you knew would be difficult for you. Try to help your students understand that your purpose is to help them learn mathematics.

Individual learning styles or learning modes—visual, auditory, and/or kinesthetic—play an important role in student understanding and performance. Some students learn best through seeing problems worked out, others through hearing a thorough explanation, and others by engaging in hands-on activities. Most successful students utilize more than one mode of learning. It is important that you as an instructor become aware of your own learning and teaching styles and work at developing techniques of presenting material that will address all learning styles.

Working through problems carefully and completely on the board while carefully telling students what you are doing and thinking will serve to accommodate most learners. Incorporating hands-on activities for kinesthetic learners will require some inventiveness on the part of the instructor. Brain research shows that learners will not develop appropriate neural networks for remembering how to do math problems without **doing** them and doing them correctly. So take time in class to let your students practice what you are demonstrating. Give them immediate feedback and help them correct their mistakes. Continually search for better ways of communicating with your students.

Deanna L. Dick, *Alvin Community College*

1. Try to remember to stick to a schedule, approximately 50 minutes per section in the textbook.

2. Always allow more time for rational expressions and word problems.

3. Use fractions daily in class and the students will become much less afraid of them and will be more successful with them. Just be prepared—they may never like them!

4. Allow at most one-fourth of the class period for questions, and then move on to new material. Students are great at wasting time if they can get away with it and teachers are bad about wanting to answer all the questions. Make them come to your office hours. One-on-one explanations are always better anyway. If a class is persistent, answer the questions and then give the lecture in the last 10 minutes of class. They will never play the stall game again!

5. Try to point out when a problem requires previously learned material to finish solving it.

   Example: When working a problem like Exercise 34 in Section 5.5 (a rational equation) remind the students that they learned how to solve the resulting equation in Section 4.8. Sometimes it is hard for students to tie the sections together and to see how one problem relates to another.

6. On word problems—make your students identify the variable **in words**. Tell them to be specific. If they don't know what they are looking for, it will be difficult for them to come up with equations they can solve to find it!

   Example: $x = \neq$ of bull-riders in Cheyenne, Wyoming

   This is more descriptive than $x = \#$ men, which could mean bull-riders or just citizens of the city. This is especially important when you are dealing with systems of equations that may talk about both ideas.

7. Have the students do the reviews and chapter tests when studying for their test.

8. Remember, most developmental math students don't read the textbook, though they should always be encouraged to do so. Therefore, helpful hints come primarily from the instructor. If the text gives a good hint, make sure you also give it in your lecture. Otherwise they may never see it.

9. Don't work the examples in the textbook. No college student wants to be read to. That is why they spent so much money on the textbook! Give them new examples to supplement what is in the text.

10. Don't panic or get upset if you make a mistake on a problem or get stuck on one. It happens to everyone eventually and can actually be encouraging to your students. Students love to correct their teachers, and the fact that they caught the mistake builds their confidence. Also, they remember when they get stuck at home that we got stuck in class, which can make it a little less frustrating. After all, if we can solve a problem that gives us trouble with a little more time and thought, then that may be all they need as well.

11. Show your students how to use technology to check your results, but recognize that they will never understand it if they don't learn to do it by hand.

12. My first semester teaching, I taught a class that was almost all word problems, "finite math." It was an 8 A.M. class and I am not a morning person. I had a wonderful student who always asked questions and his favorite thing to ask was why I set up the problem this way instead of his way, and why his equation didn't work. Usually, I would erase the correct equation and write his in its place. As students often find out, sometimes it is harder to troubleshoot an equation than to start again from scratch. I wasted a lot of time, and confused students by focusing on the wrong equation. As a first-time teacher I quickly learned to do the problem correctly in class, and trouble-shoot their homework after class.

Kathleen C. Ebert, *Alfred State College*

I value five basic things in all my classes and here is my advice.

1. When you teach a course for the first few times, plan out the entire semester ahead. Additionally, until you get it down pat include many extra review days at the end. I am student centered and students always need much more time on a topic than I

think. I can't always plan which topics they will struggle on or be sick during.

2. Summarize at the beginning of each class (what you've covered recently) and at the end of class (what we did today). It helps students see the big picture of how it all relates and comes together.

3. At the end of class I put 2–5 problems on the board (or on a handout) for them to work on before they leave. I walk around so I know who needs help and who doesn't; they can work together. Engaging the student is key.

4. I do not collect homework regularly but I do make sure they review for tests. I collect (or look through their notebooks) their review assignments and I count it as a quiz or homework grade.

5. Last but not least, I always make my students do test corrections. I do not believe in adding points to their tests for it but I do count them as a quiz grade (percent corrected for all problems they got wrong). I make them do these on a separate sheet of paper or on a new test (this makes it easier for me to grade). They can go to the lab, come to me, or find a friend that can help. They are able to continue to hand these in until all are correct. Often I make them write a sentence about why they got each one wrong. One other thing I occasionally do is offer extra credit. For extra credit, students complete a section in the book that we did not cover. They have to read the section, take good notes (that they could teach from), do the odd problems (showing all work), and cither present the information or take a quiz on it, or both. Some how they find time. They practice all the important stuff, reading a math text, taking their own notes, learning for understanding. I usually wait with this offer until they start asking "is there anything I can do…" Depending on how much they do, and how well determines how much credit I give them.

Rosa Kavanaugh, *Ozarks Technical College*

1. Since this is the second-level course in the traditional algebra sequence, students should have a basic familiarity with the introductory concepts of algebra. However, almost all students bring into this course a number of deficiencies in those basic concepts. And those students who are marginally placed into the course have some major holes in their understanding of the foundations of algebra. Part of what the instructor should be attempting to do in this course is to help students to identify and fill holes in their foundations as well as to learn the content that is new in this course.

2. The instructor who is familiar with common errors and misunderstandings can be more effective in helping the students to be successful in repairing and building upon this foundation. The text is a good reference for addressing many of these common errors. An instructor who chooses to include a discussion of such an error in the classroom should be very careful about what is written on the board. If the topic is avoiding "improper cancellation" in fractions, the instructor should either be careful to write

$$\frac{x^2 + 4x + 3}{x + 3} = \frac{x + 4x + 1}{x + 1}$$

Wrong!

as the author does in Chapter 5 or should tell students to put down their pencils and simply watch. If the lesson is being presented on a dry-erase board, this is a very appropriate time to use a red marker for emphasis.

3. Mathematical language and notation are foreign and confusing for students who are seeing algebra for the first time. Much of the mathematical language has meaning in the more familiar English language. Although developmental mathematics students also have weak language skills, we can help them identify words by associating them with the English language. These associations can help our students make the connections that will give the mathematical language more meaning to them. A good example is the word "distribute." This is a good time to encourage some discussion of the meaning of the word in common everyday language and then make the connections to the specific mathematical meaning.

4. Perhaps the most troublesome counterexample to the notion that mathematical language has meaning in the English language is in the words "term" and "factor." In the English language, these words do not have the same specific meaning that they do in mathematics. When we say, "These were factors in our decision," that does not mean that those factors were multiplied. When we say, "These were the terms of our agreement." that does not mean that the terms were added. Yet these same words have those very precise meaning in mathematics. In the English language we use the word term in a very generic way. The word term should be used very deliberately and precisely in the mathematics classroom.

5. Students often confuse problem types on exams. One reason is that they tend to overlook the instruc-

tions as they do homework since all of the problems in a section tend to be the same type. I believe that the instructor should not only emphasize the meaning of the instructions but also write the instructions as part of the example. Students in developmental mathematics classes tend to include in their notes much of what is written on the board, but little of the words that the instructor says, but does not write. Thus it is important that the instructor not only say, "Solve" but also write:

"Solve $3x + 5 = 5(x - 1)$."

This kind of emphasis helps students avoid common confusion such as the difference between solve and simplify.

6. Mathematics instructors themselves must model good mathematical notation. One of my notation "pet peeves" is improper use of equal signs. Occasionally, adjunct faculty insert errant equal signs as they perform intermediate steps of a problem.

7. Another more subtle but, I believe, equally serious error is the omission of equals signs between simplification steps. Perhaps one of the most common occurrences of this is in the demonstration of the factoring process. For example, I observe a number of faculty who write a factoring problem as:

$$3x^4 - 12y^4$$
$$3\left(x^4 - 4y^4\right)$$
$$3\left(x^2 + 2y^2\right)\left(x^2 - 2y^2\right)$$

Omitting the equal signs between the steps is not only mathematically unsound but also eliminates the rationale for checking the result of a factoring problem by redistributing because they should be **equal**.

8. Correct mathematical language can also be an issue. Some instructors say "LCM" when they mean "LCD." Another common error is confusion of "expression" and "equation." If we are to convince our student that mathematics is a precise discipline with precise language, our own language must also model such precision.

9. Students often have difficulty memorizing formulae. Whenever there are formulae that students need to memorize, I give them a strategy for memorizing the formulae as they do their homework. I tell them that each time they use the formula, it is important that they write the formula first and then substitute the given info. Many students tend instead merely to write the result after substitution and miss the learning benefits of the writing process. I explain that the

repeated writing of the original formula as they use it actually helps them to remember it.

10. Instructors should be prepared not only to describe to students what the process is but also to explain why the process works. This may not be an issue for some students but is particularly important to many adult learners. They may have heard the rules before but did not buy into the validity of the process. This stumbling block is sometimes an impediment to further learning in the course. Instructors need to be willing to provide such explanations during class if time permits. For example, some students never saw the validity of the rules for operations with signed numbers. Others are still confused about why division by zero is undefined. Settling these kinds of questions allows students to progress in topics where they were confused in the past.

11. The text contains a good introduction to the benefits of students' recognizing and using the learning objectives of each section. One other use of these objectives that we recommend to students is in preparing for exams. So many students at this level have never learned how to study. They tend to believe that the way to prepare for an exam is to work all of the several hundred problems assigned for homework. We find Bittinger's a, b, c,…coding of learning objectives very helpful in helping students to identify that they do not have to rework all of the problems in a given section but should instead concentrate on one from each objective to identify areas of strength and weakness. Then they understand that if they have difficulty, they can return to the discussion correlating to that objective in the section/chapter.

Susan Leland, *Montana Tech*

Using silly, catchy phrases helps students to remember common pitfalls and procedures in algebra. Some examples follow:

1. Bells and whistles: as in "Bells and whistles should go off in your mind every time you see a negative sign in front of parentheses! Change every sign inside." This can be used for many other situations also, such as putting a 6 sign in front of any square root radical inserted into an equation. I have students come back to see me two and three years after being in my class and they say they still hear "bells and whistles" when doing math.

2. The rules never change: as in "This equation has fractions in it—but the rules never change." Keep properties, theorems, procedures, and rules very generic so that they fit every conceivable situation. Students at this level need to do problems the same way every time. Try to avoid showing several different ways to do any one type of problem—that just confuses many intermediate algebra students. Those students who already know another way to approach a given problem should be allowed to use a different, but correct, method, but don't burden the rest of the class with more than one method.

3. Details, details, details: as in missing signs, incorrect arithmetic, and copying problems incorrectly. If you can get students to concentrate on all the details, grades improve! My students hear me say this at least a million times in a semester—at least according to them!

4. Set the dumpster on fire, as in the following joke. A mathematician decided he wanted to change jobs. He went to the fire chief and said, "Chief, I'd like to become a fireman!" The fire chief said, "Great! I need to give you a little test." The chief took the mathematician into the alley where there was a dumpster, a hose on the ground, and a water spigot. The chief said to the mathematician, "What would you do if you came out here and found the dumpster on fire?" The mathematician immediately said, "I'd hook the hose up to the spigot, turn the water on, and put out the fire." The chief said, "Great! You'll make a super fireman! Now, what would you do if you came out here and found the dumpster wasn't on fire?" The mathematician thought for a moment, then brightened and said, "I'd set it on fire!" The chief said, "What? That's terrible! Why in the world would you set the dumpster on fire?" The mathematician replied, "Because then I would have reduced it to a problem I already know how to solve!"

   This joke is applicable to so many topics in algebra, especially equation solving. Every equation in the book—systems, quadratic, rational, radical— eventually "reduces" to a linear equation, something we already know how to solve after Chapter One! So, "set the dumpster on fire" and get to a problem we already know how to do!

Michael Montaño, *Riverside Community College*

1. Eye contact with your audience is essential when you are delivering a lecture.

2. When a class does not reply to a question, do not be too anxious and proceed to answer the question yourself. Use the "dead air" time to your advantage. A classroom does not need to be dynamic at all times. Silence allows students some time to organize and collect their thoughts.

3. Definitions are very important. Make sure that students understand every aspect of the definition.

4. Pattern recognition is a very powerful technique in the teaching of mathematics. Fitting the problem to the same format as the rule can be very useful.

Nancy Ressler, *Oakton Community College*

1. The student *grapevine* is healthy and flourishing! If you habitually modify due dates for homework, exams, quizzes, projects and content presentation, students will expect that if they miss any of the above it is acceptable because you *probably* were going to make *another* change anyway. The matter of fairness is prominent. Adjusting for one student means that it is necessary to *adjust* for others. By doing so, you will have *twice* the course duties that are necessary for a seasoned educator.

2. Additionally, if you **only** address course expectations on the first class meeting, word will "get out" and *future* first class meetings will not be well attended since students will expect only a friendly discussion! They rationalize; they *can read* the syllabus by themselves later! On the first class meeting bring a tablet and sharpened pencils (usually each division or cluster office has supplies for faculty) for those students that have brought no supplies. Provide each with a pencil and a few sheets of paper as you **begin your course lecture on day ONE!** Ensuring good habits by a content focus on day ONE also allows students to experience your teaching methodology and style.

3. Students will complain about the amount of course content in most math courses. Faculty MUST prepare the students for success in future courses. This can only be achieved by covering **all** of the content described by the department's generic syllabus. You are hired to teach the class…not to cater to those that are better or less prepared. Individualized help can be provided during your office hours *if* a reasonable answer still leaves the student confused or *if* a better prepared student has future/later content questions.

4. Encourage students to visit with tutors. In high school *needy* students or the labeled *nerds* frequented tutoring. In college, the bright and astute

attend tutoring. The difference between A's and B's and B's and C's become apparent by tutor visits. Invite a college tutor to talk to your classes. Once the students meet the people they will be working with during the course it is easier for them to make the tutoring appointment!

Tomesa Smith, *Wallace State Community College*

Fifteen years ago I began my teaching career at a community college. Considering the typically diverse nature of community college students, I decided to have students fill out an index card of information on the first day of class. On the card, I asked for:

Name (how it will be written on test papers, first and last); Student Number; Major; Phone (in case calculators, purses, books, etc. are left in the room); Email; Family; Job (approximate number of hours worked and approximate times); Math history (high school and college); Goal for class

Through the years, I have changed the format some, but I continue to utilize the cards because they have proven to be very helpful. While students complete their cards in class, I tell them some information about myself. After taking up the cards, I call roll by them immediately. This helps me to begin connecting faces with names and to ask for correct pronunciation if needed. I note these things on the card and then use the set as a deck of cards throughout the term. I call roll by them, assign groups by them, and document absences or unusual circumstances on them. I think students appreciate that I strive to learn their names, that I am concerned about them when they are absent, and that I want them to achieve their goals.

I suppose through the years, I have incorporated other strategies that have become equally routine to me. I've always tried to start class on time. How can I expect students to be on time if I'm not? I also try to utilize every minute of class time. I never want students to leave my classroom feeling as though we could have accomplished more. Being organized is half the battle. I think students respect a teacher who is prepared and enthusiastic about each topic. I also try to foster respect in the classroom. I give students my attention when they are talking to me and expect them to give me their attention when I am talking to them. Often students will say that they did not want to ask a question because it was dumb. No questions are dumb ones, so I try to encourage students to ask me about anything they do not understand.

Aside from the actual lecturing and learning in the classroom, I have found that these tips have helped me to become a better instructor through the years. To teach a subject seems the best way to learn it, so repetition will help with the subject matter. To help with everything else, be prepared, punctual, respectful, cheerful, and willing to make adjustments along the way. If you can do these things, you are destined to be a great teacher.

Sharon Testone, *Onondaga Community College*

1. Students enrolled in an intermediate algebra course at the community college level are often students who have just completed a developmental beginning algebra course or they are students who have had intermediate algebra in high school and just need to refresh their skills. These two groups of students are very different from each other. The former beginning algebra students may be struggling with this new material. Meanwhile, the students who just need a refresher may be bored with the material. It is the instructor's role to meet the needs of these diverse groups.

2. Group work can help to alleviate the problem of diverse abilities in an intermediate algebra course. The instructor should form the groups by including a mixture of students who never have had intermediate algebra and students who are just reviewing the material. This method will provide an avenue for students to truly help each other. Be sure to have individual students or a representative from the group show you at least one completed problem before the end of the class period. (Another alternative is to have a group representative put the solution on the board.) This technique helps to assure that students will be able to do their homework.

3. An important time management tip is to count the number of class periods, subtract the number of "testing days" and subtract at least two class periods for review at the end of the semester. This result is the number of instructional periods. Divide the number of instructional periods into the number of sections that need to be taught. This result gives the approximate number of sections that need to be taught each class period. This simple calculation will help new faculty avoid the pitfall of moving too quickly or too slowly through the course. Additionally, the faculty member will most likely complete all topics in the syllabus and not omit any essential material.

4. Always be on time to class and always end the class on time. Our students have very busy schedules and faculty needs to respect that fact.

5. Always be prepared for class and always hand back graded homework, quizzes, and tests the very next class period.

6. Before teaching the course for the first time, ask your department chairperson what the prerequisites are for this course. This information will assist you in gauging what knowledge the students should have when entering your classroom. They may not be completely prepared, but you will know what skills they are expected to possess and you will not spend much time reteaching material from the previous course. Additionally, determine what course(s) your students will enroll in after completing your course. Be sure that you prepare the students for those courses, but don't teach the topics from them.

7. Often intermediate algebra students do not complete their homework assignments and this leads to failure. One option is to require that students complete homework assignments in a separate notebook. On test days instructors can review the notebook (without actually grading it) to determine if students are completing their assignments. Another option is to collect homework daily or randomly and grade it.

8. Giving a five-minute quiz after reviewing homework questions at the beginning of the class period is often helpful for new instructors. The quiz results will let both the students and the instructor know how they are doing. If the whole class fails a quiz, then most likely the instructor needs to make improvements.

9. Prepare handouts with matching overheads or Power Point slides. Students at this level are often not good note takers and have difficulty listening and writing at the same time. Handouts that include key concepts, one or two worked-out examples, and two or three problems for the students to complete immediately are very useful.

10. Be sure to assign the synthesis problems in each chapter as group work. These problems are a little more challenging and they help the students increase their level of understanding.

Roy West, *Robeson Community College*

Remember that the material being taught is developmental. A lot of times college instructors feel that most students just need some extra practice and they will catch on. This may be true for some classes. You as an instructor need to feel them out. I personally have found that nothing replaces working problems for them in class and showing the various situations that can occur. The responsible student will get the practice they need when they do the homework problems themselves at home. Use your class time wisely.

Rebecca Wyatt-Semple, *Nash Community College*

I Wish They Had Told Me…

Rule 1: For all instructors, whether full-time or adjunct: There is never enough time! Prioritize your schedule so that you don't get overwhelmed. If you come into class too tired to function, your value as an instructor will be minimal at best. Take care of yourself so that you will be able to take care of the students entrusted to you. We encourage students to set priorities in order to get their work done, so practice what you preach.

Rule 2: You'll work harder than any of your students. You'll have to be creative in presentations, develop interesting assignments, challenge the most gifted students, and help the least gifted. You will be many things to your students, but you are not their buddy. You are a professional who should be clearly concerned with each student's welfare and progression in education.

Rule 3: Use the text, and the supplementary items that are available, to your best advantage. Bittinger texts are extremely well written with excellent Study Tips for students, generous margins and margin exercises (Yes! Encourage students to write in their books), Chapter Summaries, Practice Tests, warnings and cautions, and Cumulative Reviews. Students can teach themselves from this text, especially if they take advantage of the Learning Resources such as the *Student's Solutions Manual*, videotapes, InterAct Math® Tutorial Web site, the Addison-Wesley Math Tutor Center, and the on-line help available through MyMathLab and MathXL®.

Rule 4: The first week of class is critical. Set the pace of the course and let students know what is expected of them. Put your rules in writing and give them out with the course syllabus. The first day of class is the best time to have the students fill out an index card with information you may need: name, student ID number, e-mail, phone number, areas of interest, and intended major. Collect the cards and review them before the next scheduled meeting of the class. Try to learn the students' names as quickly as possible. Use the index cards in selecting problems to use in class and homework. For example, if you know that your class has a number of students interested in the sciences of medicine, problems can be selected to reflect their interest.

Rule 5: Know your school or department's policy on calculators in the classroom and their use on tests and exams. Find out which calculators are recommended for your course and which, if any, are banned. Talk to instructors who teach the courses following yours to see what calculator skills they expect students to have upon entry into their classes, and be certain that your students develop these skills before the end of the course. It is effective to split tests and exams in two parts: Part A covers basic concepts with minimal calculations and no calculators allowed, and Part B emphasizes problems in which the use of calculators would be beneficial.

Rule 6: If you assign homework, you'll have to grade homework. Students need a great deal of practice. You don't need to become bogged down in grading homework. Grade approximately one-fourth of the homework problems by random selection, or by some method of selection of your own. Students will not know ahead of time which problems are to be graded, and are responsible for all problems assigned. Let students know that you are practicing sampling, an acceptable statistical technique. If you fail to grade homework, or fail to give some incentive for doing it, most students will not do the practice necessary to internalize concepts. Let students know from day one what your policy on homework will be, and stick to your policy.

Rule 7: Use proper mathematical notation, draw neat graphs, and label the axes appropriately. Do what you want your students to do. Set high standards for your work and hold your students to these standards. It is far easier to develop good habits than to break bad habits. Being skilled in the reading and use of proper notation will allow your students to advance to higher levels of mathematics, read, and understand the texts.

Rule 8: Most students do not know how to read math texts. Teach them. Structure assignments so that they must read the text, make use of examples, and write brief discussions. Assign discussion problems as well as calculation problems. Have students "teach" a section to the class. Give group assignments in which a student must explain concepts to others in his group. Bittinger's math texts always have an abundance of discussion problems.

Rule 9: Prepare yourself for the question: "When will I ever need to know this stuff?" Make a mental list of situations that require algebraic thought. At the beginning of each chapter, think of ways the concepts of that chapter may be encountered in the "real world." If you can't think of many examples, do a little research or talk to other instructors in the math area or in other departments.

Rule 10: Multiple-choice tests should be used with caution. They are easy to grade, but you should not fall into the trap of always testing in this manner. Multiple-choice tests do not always reveal what students actually know, nor do they require critical thinking skills. Students, by their own admission, do a great deal of guessing. Mix multiple-choice questions with questions requiring that students show their work and thought processes.

SAMPLE SYLLABI

Provided by:

    Chris Bendixen, *Lake Michigan College*

    Kathleen C. Ebert, *Alfred State College*

    Nancy Ressler, *Oakton Community College*

Lake Michigan College
COURSE SYLLABUS
Division of Liberal Arts and General Studies

I.   Coure Identification

Instructor: Chris Bendixen

Office: C 222 - D

Office Hours: as posted on door; other times by appointment.

Phone Numbers: Email address:

Course: Intermediate Algebra, Math 101

Section:

Time & Place:

Credit Hours: Four (4)

Prerequisites: MATH 125/high school alg. passed with C or better

II.   Textbooks and/or Equipment/Supplies

Required Items: *Intermediate Algebra*, 9th ed., by Bittinger and the *Student's Solution Manual* for the above.

A <u>Scientific Calculator</u> is required for this course. as a minimum it should have parentheses, and be able to perform powers, roots, and logarithms Preferably, the calculator should be a graphing calculator like TI83 plus, TI 84, TI86. I will use the TI83 plus.

III.   Course Description from the Catalog

Course Description: This course is designed to provide students with sufficient algebraic knowledge and skills for success in subsequent mathematics and science courses. the study includes a brief review of the four fundamental operations, sets and the real number system, factoring, fractions, linear and fractional equations and inequalities, functions and their graphs, systems of equations, determinants and Cramer's rule, exponents and radicals, quadratic equations and logarithms.

Course Aims: Upon successful completion of this course the student should be familiar with factoring, solving linear and fractional equations and inequalities, the concept of function, systems of equations, determinants and Cramer's rule, exponents and radicals, quadratic equations, and logarithms.

IV.   Goals and Objectives

See Appendix A.

V.   Writing Across the Curriculum

The tests must be written neatly, clearly, and be coherently organized. **You must show enough steps to indicate an understanding of the processes used.**

VI. Grading Criteria and Requirements

Student Evaluation: Periodic tests will be given. Tests are given after the completion of each designated study unit (generally 2–4 sections, or an entire chapter). Problems will be selected, at the discretion of the instructor, for this purpose. The problems are selected that demonstrate critical thinking skills You will find it helpful to do the problems sections in the chapter. Answers to odd problems are in the back of your text; the solution manual has complete solutions for these problems. On all tests you must show how you obtained your answers. **An answer alone is worth nothing or almost nothing.**

Study Time: You need to study at least 2 hours for every hour in class. Just as one cannot learn to swim by merely watching someone else, you cannot learn mathematics without doing it yourself. If you do not have enough time to study, you had best drop the course while you still have time to get a refund. Most students find it helpful to form study groups. Get to know your fellow students in the class and find compatible students with whom to study. You will find the class more enjoyable and easier to understand, if you do.

Computation: At the conclusion of the semester you will have accumulated the following percentages:

Quizzes	10%
Tests:	65%
Final Exam:	20%
Homework	5%

Homework: Homework assignments will be given at the beginning of each section. ALL WORK MUST BE SHOWN WHERE APPROPRIAT. Answers to odd-numbered exercises are in the back of the book. Answers to all margin exercises and practice tests are also in the back of the book. Homework will be assigned over material and then turned in on the next class period at the beginning of the class. Homework will now constitute 5% of the final grade. It is important that the student completes the homework, and turns the homework in on time. Late homework will not be accepted. The students' grade for the homework will be based on the total number of homeworks turned in. If a student misses a homework, then the student cannot achieve the highest percent for the homework grade.

Quizzes: Expect one quiz every week. The quiz will relate to the previous class materials. Also, the problems will come directly from homework problems. The total for all the quizzes is worth the equivalent to one unit exam. It is important to keep on top of the material covered in class. Quizzes will be given at the end of the class (the last 20 minutes).

Pace: Expect at least two sections of the book to be covered during a class period.

VII. Grading Scale

Each grading unit will be calculated as an integer percentage. Your final grade for the semester will be determined using the following scale:

90–100	A	Excellent
80–89	B	Good
70–79	C	Fair
60–69	D	Passing, but deficient
0–59	E	Failing

VIII. Make-up Policy

Late Work: There will be **no** make-up tests. In exceptional cases, you may be able to make arrangements to take a test early, but **never late**. If you miss more than one test, you have a bigger problem that needs to be addressed. You should consider seeing a college counselor for this.

IX. Attendance Policy/Withdrawal Policy

Attendance: STUDENTS ARE EXPECTED TO ATTEND ALL SCHEDULED CLASS SESSIONS

> *You are expected to read the text, do all assigned problems, and attend class. Tests are based on the lectures, may cover material not in the text, and may cover problems not in the homework. As a result, attendance is necessary for good performance. Future employers use attendance records to decide upon the reliability of your work.*
>
> *Some instructors have a tendency to cover related material that is not in your book. You are responsible for this material as well as the material that is in your book. **You have been warned!***

See the college catalog for attendance/withdrawal policies/ A student finding it necessary to withdraw form class MUST file with the Records and Registration Office. DON'T JUST STOP COMING TO CLASS; PLEASE FILL OUT A DROP SLIP IF YOU ARE NOT ABLE TO FINISH THE CLASS.

Mindful of the diverse student body that Lake Michigan College serves, and the varied belied systems that its students represent, the College will make a reasonable effort to accommodate students who need to be excused from classes for the observance of religious holidays. This policy does not apply to students who knowingly register for classes scheduled to meet on days that consistently conflict with their day of worship, e.g., a student who signs up for Saturday classes when the student normally worships on Saturday.

NOTE: Modern technology like beepers, cell phones, pagers are to be shut off during class. These devices can be disruptive to the flow of the class.

Withdrawal: Students must initiate withdrawal from a class by completing the required forms available in the Records & Registration Office through the 12th week of the Fall & Winter semesters. Once officially withdrawn from a course, students will be assigned a grade of a "W". Beyond this point in the semester, withdrawing students are to be assigned a grade by the instructor.

X.   Assignment Schedule

Generally allow 3 days to cover a chapter. However, some chapters will be covered quicker, and some will be covered slower than that pace.

Course Outline:

Chapter R:	*Review of Basic Algebra*
Chapter One	*Solving equations and Inequalities*
Chapter Two:	*Graphs, Functions , and Applications*
Chapter Three:	*Systems of Equations*
Chapter Four:	*Polynomials and Polynomial Functions*
Chapter Seven:	*Quadratic Equations*
Chapter Five:	*Rational Expressions and Equations*
Chapter Six:	*Radical Expressions and Equations*

Class Activities: The format employed in this class is lecture-discussion. Student participation is expected. Remember: It is better to ask a stupid question than remain silent and unenlightened.

Appendix A

Goals & Objectives: Upon completion of the course the student should be able to:

A. Perform real number computations
  1. Translate between word expressions and algebraic expressions
  2. Evaluate algebraic expressions when numbers are specified as letters
  3. Perform operations on real numbers and use signed expressions correctly
  4. Understand and use the properties of real numbers to
    a. simplify expressions containing parentheses
    b. multiply and factor expressions
  5. Use exponential notation to
    a. rewrite expressions with (without) integer exponents
    b. multiply and divide
    c. raise a power to a power

B. Solve linear equations and inequalities of one variable
  1. Use the addition and multiplication principles, separately and together, to solve equations and inequalities
  2. Solve literal equations for a specified expression
  3. Graph simple (single) inequalities on a number line
  4. Use set operations to create and solve compound inequalities
  5. Graph compound inequalities on a number line
  6. Use absolute value in solving equations and inequalities

C. Graph equations and inequalities of two variables
  1. Plot points in a plane given their coordinates
  2. Recognize equations corresponding to lines (linear equations)
  3. Determine the slope and all intercepts (x- and y-intercepts) of a line given its equation
  4. Determine whether a given point satisfies a given linear equation (inequality)
  5. Solve for the equation of, and graph, a line (including horizontal and vertical lines) given
    a. slope and a point on the line (could be the x- or y-intercept)
    b. two points on the line (could be the x- and y-intercepts)
    c. a point and the equation of a line it is parallel (perpendicular) to
  6. Graph inequalities in two variables using the
    a. line-point method
    b. double-number-line (double-inequality) method

D. Solve systems of linear equations (inequalities) of two or more variables
  1. Determine whether a given point satisfies a specified system of linear equations (inequalities)
  2. Determine whether a given system of linear equations (inequalities) is
    a. consistent or inconsistent
    b. dependent or independent
  3. Evaluate second and third order determinants
  4. Solve systems of linear equations by
    a. graphing (two variables only)
    b. the substitution method
    c. the elimination method
    d. Cramer's rule
  5. Graph systems of linear inequalities of two variables

E. Understand properties of polynomials and perform calculations using them
   1. Determine the degree and leading (trailing) coefficient (term) of a polynomial
   2. Arrange a polynomial in ascending (descending) powers of a given variable
   3. Add (Subtract) polynomials and determine their additive inverse (opposite)
   4. Evaluate polynomials at a point and apply this method to functions
   5. Multiply
      a. a polynomial by a monomial
      b. two binomials (FOIL)
      c. two polynomials (distributive law)
      d. an expression by itself
      e. together the sum and difference of two expressions
   6. Factor a polynomial
      a. whose terms have a common factor (could be a negative common factor)
      b. that is a trinomial
      c. by grouping terms
   7. Recognize, and factor, special-product polynomials, including
      a. the difference of squares (one may be multi-termed)
      b. a trinomial square
      c. the sum (difference) of two cubes
   8. Divide two polynomials
      a. using Euclid's algorithm for long division—divisor could be a monomial or multi-termed
      b. using Horner's algorithm for synthetic substitution (synthetic division) — divisor must be linear with leading coefficient of one

F. Perform calculations involving rational [fractional] expressions and solve fractional equations
   1. Multiply (Divide) fractional [rational] expressions
   2. Find lowest common multiple (LCM) of two polynomials to
      a. express all fractional expressions with their lowest common denominator (LCD)
      b. add (subtract) two fractional expressions
      c. determine forbidden values for the expression—cannot divide by zero
   3. Solve fractional equations (including fractional literal equations)
   4. Simplify complex fractional expressions
      a. determine **all** forbidden values
      b. using
         i. top-bottom-flip method
         ii. total-common-denominator method
   5. Understand the difference among direct, inverse [indirect], and joint [multiple] variation
   6. Solve problems involving variation and determine the coefficient [constant] of variation
   7. Find the equation of variation for a given type of variation from initial conditions

G. Perform calculations involving radicals, fractional exponents, and complex numbers; solve equations
   1. Understand radical expressions
      a. identify the index and the radicand
      b. understand principle root and when it applies
      c. determine if a value is rational or irrational
   2. Multiply and divide radicals having the same index or different indices

3. Simplify radical expressions
   a. to add (subtract) them
   b. after a multiplication (division)
4. Rational numerators and/or denominators of fractional radical expressions
5. Use rational [fractional] exponents to
   a. convert between radical and exponential expressions
   b. lower the index of a radical expression
   c. handle nested radicals
   d. multiply radicals of different indices
6. Solve radical equations involving one or more radical expressions
7. Use imaginary and complex numbers in expressions, including
   a. finding the modulus [norm, "absolute value"]
   b. calculate the powers of i
   c. using the four fundamental operations $+$, $-$, $\times$, $\div$
   d. finding complex conjugates [Hermitians]

H. Solve quadratic and quasi-quadratic equations
   1. Solve quadratic equations
      a. by factoring
      b. by completing the square
      c. using the quadratic formula
   2. Evaluate the discriminant to
      a. understand the nature of the roots (real, non-real)
      b. determine the number of x-intercepts
   3. Convert quasi-quadratics into quadratics and solve equations involving them
   4. Solve radical equations that become quadratic
   5. Graph parabolas, finding
      a. the vertex and the axis [line] of symmetry
      b. the vertex form of the parabola's equation

I. Understand the properties of exponential and logarithmic functions
   1. Illustrate the properties of inverse functions both algebraically and graphically [geometrically]
   2. Graph exponential (logarithmic) functions of any base
   3. Convert equations from logarithmic to exponential form and back
   4. Find logarithms to any base both exactly (change of base formula) and using a calculator
   5. Solve exponential (logarithmic) equations

J. Find enjoyment in the study of mathematics

MATH 2003 — INTERMEDIATE ALGEBRA

ALFRED STATE COLLEGE

FALL 2005

Professor:
Office: SDC 329
Phone:

Math Tutoring Lab: SDC 102
Phone:

Time	Monday	Tuesday	Wednesday	Thursday	Friday
9:00 AM					
10:00 AM					
11:00 AM	Math 2003 SDC 109		Math 2003 SDC 109		Math 2003 SDC 109
12:00					
1:00 PM					
2:00 PM	Math 2003 SDC 138		Math 2003 SDC 138		Math 2003 SDC 138
3:00 PM	Trig Math 2043		Trig Math 2043		
4:00 PM					

Required materials:

Text: *Intermediate Algebra*, Bittinger, 9th edition; Addison-Wesley Publishing Company.
3-ring binder/notebook

Catalog Description:

This course is intended to be a continuation of the study of algebra, concentrating in the area of polynomials. Students taking this course have a knowledge of basic linear algebra, but do not have a sufficient background to attempt College Algebra. Topics to be covered include: Exponents and Polynomials, Factoring, Solving Quadratic Equations, Rational Expressions, Rational Functions. This course should prepare students to enter College Algebra, Math 1033.

Course Objective:

We will cover the better part of chapters 4–7, and other topics if time permits.
At the end of Math 2003 the student should be able to:
1. Add, subtract, multiply, divide polynomials;
2. Factor algebraic expressions;
3. Use factoring to perform operations with fractions and simplify the results;
4. Solve quadratic equations;
5. Apply the basic concepts of operations involving radicals and rational expressions; and
6. Be able to identify and evaluate simple relations and functions.
7. ____ (*insert other topic objectives here*) _____
8. ____ (*insert other topic objectives here*) _____

Evaluation:

The following is a tentative form of evaluation, subject to minor changes.

Chapter Tests (4)	45%
Weekly Quizzes (~10) and Test Corrections (4) Portfolio Check (1)	30%
Class Participation/Attendance	5%
Final Exam	20%

Chapter Tests   Each of the chapters will have a Test, with time set aside for review. You MUST notify me in ADVANCE if you will be missing a Test—otherwise you will receive a zero.

Weekly Quizzes   There will be approximately 8 quizzes. Additional quizzes may be given—the top eight grades will be counted. These may or may not be announced. They will be 5-10 minutes in length. They will <u>often</u> come directly from your homework or class notes, and often open notebook (NOTEBOOK only). Doing homework consistently will be extremely beneficial. ABSOLUTELY NO missed quizzes can be made up. NO MAKEUPS !

Test Corrections   You will be required to hand in test corrections. These must be done on a SEPARATE sheet of paper, all work shown, for any problem with points taken off. These will be graded on neatness, and accuracy. They will count equivalent to a quiz.

Portfolio   Your notebook may be checked once. It is required that you keep a 3-ring notebook. This will contain all *handouts* (syllabus, in class worksheets, etc), *notes, homework*—and it will be neat and organized.

Class Participation/Attendance   During each class we will be doing problems, individually or in groups. Participation in these will count for this grade. Therefore, if you are absent, physically or mentally, you will receive a zero for the day.

Final Exam   You will have one cumulative final exam <u>during final exam week</u>. Date and time to be announces

MATH LAB ... SDC 102 ... 4261

YOU ARE ENCOURAGED TO USE THE MATH TUTOR LAB SERVICES.

YOU SHOULD PLAN TO DO YOUR HOMEWORK IN THE LAB—THERE WILL BE A PROCTOR THERE TO ASSIST YOU AS/IF YOU HAVE A QUESTION, OR IF YOU GET STUCK. SCHEDULE TIME FOR THIS JUST LIKE YOU SCHEDULE A CLASS - for example: MWF at 1

COME TO THE MATH LAB TO DO YOUR HOMEWORK ALONE OR WITH OTHERS.

YOU SHOULD GO TO SDC ROOM 102 AS SOON AS POSSIBLE TO SIGN UP FOR TUTORING. AS INCENTIVE, IF YOU SPEND 10 HOURS IN TUTORING, EVERY ADDITIONAL HOUR WILL BE A POINT ADDED TO YOUR TEST AVERAGE. KEEP TRACK OF THESE HOURS. THIS MUST BE QUALITY TUTORING TIME.

PLEASE GET HELP EARLY, DO NOT WAIT UNTIL THE LAST MINUTE. TAKE ADVANTAGE OF THE FREE SERVICES AVAILABLE TO YOU.

I WILL ALSO ENCOURAGE YOU TO WORK IN GROUPS. IF POSSIBLE I WILL FIND A GROUP STUDY LEADER. SEE ME IF YOU ARE INTERESTED.

OAKTON COMMUNITY COLLEGE
GENERIC COURSE SYLLABUS

I.   Course Prefix: MAT
Course Number: 120
Course Name: Intermediate Algebra
Credit: 4
Lecture: 4
Lab: 0

I.   Prerequisite
MAT 052 (or an appropriate score on the OCC Mathematics Assessment Test) and MAT 053 (or geometry proficiency). MAT 053 and MAT 120 may be taken concurrently.

III.   Course (Catalog) Description
This course covers real and complex numbers, exponents, polynomials, radicals, first and second degree equations, system of equations, inequalities, rational expressions and logarithms.

IV.   Course Objectives
    A.   Demonstrate an understanding of the real numbers and their properties.
    B.   Extend the basic operations and factoring with polynomials.
    C.   Extend the basic operations of rational expressions.
    D.   Solve first and second degree equations and inequalities in one variable.
    E.   Perform the basic operations of complex numbers.
    F.   Demonstrate the ability to use the definitions and laws of exponents, roots and radicals.
    G.   Graph equations and inequalities in two variables.
    H.   Solve systems of equations and inequalities.
    I.   Demonstrate an understanding of functions.
    J.   Apply concepts and techniques to problem solving.

V.   Academic Integrity
Students and employees at Oakton Community College are required to demonstrate academic integrity and follow Oakton's Code of Academic Conduct. This code prohibits:
  • cheating,
  • plagiarism (turning in work not written by you, or lacking proper citation),
  • falsification and fabrication (lying or distorting the truth),
  • helping others to cheat,
  • unauthorized changes on official documents,
  • pretending to be someone else or having someone else pretend to be you,
  • making or accepting bribes, special favors, or threats, and
  • any other behavior that violates academic integrity.

There are serious consequences to violations of the academic integrity policy. Oakton's policies and procedures provide students a fair hearing if a complaint is made against you. If you are found to have violated the policy, the minimum penalty is failure on the assignment and, a disciplinary record will be established and kept on file in the office of the Vice President for Student Affairs for a period of 3 years.
Details of the Code of Academic Conduct can be found in the Student Handbook.

VI. Outline of Topics

A. Real Numbers
   1. Properties
   2. Operations
   3. Real number system

B. Solving Equations and Inequalities in One Variable
   1. Solving linear equations
   2. Formulas
   3. Solving linear inequalities
   4. Compound inequalities
   5. Absolute value equations and inequalities
   6. Applications

C. Graphing Equations and Inequalities in Two Variables
   1. Rectangular coordinate system
   2. Distance, midpoint and slope formula
   3. Graphing
   4. Slope-intercept and point-slope formulas
   5. Parallel and perpendicular lines
   6. Graphing inequalities
   7. Graphing circles with center at origin
   8. Applications

D. Systems of Equations and Inequalities
   1. Graphical solution
   2. Algebraic solutions (elimination and substitution)
   3. Solution of systems with three variables
   4. Nonlinear equations
   5. Systems of inequalities
   6. Applications

E. Polynomials
   1. Basic operations
   2. Long division and synthetic division
   3. Special products
   4. Factoring
   5. Using factoring to solve equations
   6. Applications

F. Rational Expressions
   1. Simplifying
   2. Basic operations
   3. Complex rational expressions
   4. Solving equations with rational expressions
   5. Formulas
   6. Variation
   7. Applications

G. Exponents, Roots and Radicals
   1. Laws of exponents
   2. Scientific notation
   3. Rational exponents
   4. Simplifying radical expressions
   5. Operations with radical expressions
   6. Rationalizing denominators
   7. Solving equations with radical expressions
   8. Applications

    H.   Complex Numbers
        1.   Definition
        2.   Simplifying powers of i
        3.   Basic operations
    I.   Quadratic Equations and Inequalities
        1.   Solving by factoring
        2.   Solving by completing the square
        3.   Solving by use of quadratic formula
        4.   Formulas
        5.   Algebraic solutions of nonlinear systems
        6.   Solving nonlinear inequalities
        7.   Applications
    J.   Functions
        1.   Definition
        2.   Function notation
        3.   Graphing linear and quadratic functions
        4.   Applications
    K.   Suggested optional topics: exponential and logarithm functions and equations.

VII. Methods of Instruction:

(To be completed by instructor)

Methods of presentation can include lectures, discussion, demonstration, experimentation, audio-visual, group work, and regularly assigned homework. Calculators / computers will be used when appropriate.

VIII. Course Practices Required:

(To be completed by instructor)

IX. Instructional Materials:

Required Textbook: *Intermediate Algebra* by Marvin L. Bittinger, 9th Edition, Addison-Wesley, 2003.

IX. Methods of Evaluating Student Progress:

(To be determined and announced by instructor)

Evaluation methods can include assignments, quizzes, chapter or major tests, individual or group   projects, computer assignments and/or a final examination.

XI. Other Course Information:

Individual instructors will establish and announce specific policies regarding attendance, due dates and make-up work, incomplete grades, etc.

If you have a documented learning, psychological, or physical disability you may be entitled to reasonable academic accommodations or services. To request accommodations or services, contact the ASSIST office in Instructional Support Services. All students are expected to fulfill essential course requirements. The College will not waive any essential skill or requirement of a course or degree program.

Effective beginning term: Fall 2000   Ending term: _____
                                   (term) (year)   (term) (year)

Syllabus prepared by: Chair: N. Ressler; R. Diprizio; P. Boisvert; A. Legere; C. Murphy;
                              S. Stock   Date: ____

Reviewed by Dept/Program Chair: R. Maglio   Date: 4/99

Approved by Dean: E. Garcia   Date: 4/99

TEACHING TIPS CORRELATED TO TEXTBOOK SECTIONS

Following is a listing of the objectives included in the Intermediate Algebra *text, as well as specific teaching tips provided by the contributing professors.*

 R) **Review of Basic Algebra**

SECTION TITLES AND OBJECTIVES

Part 1 OPERATIONS

R.1 The Set of Real Numbers

Use roster and set-builder notation to name sets, and distinguish among various kinds of real numbers ● Determine which of two real numbers is greater and indicate which, using $<$ and $>$; given an inequality like $a < b$, write another inequality with the same meaning; and determine whether an inequality like $-2 \leq 3$ or $4 > 5$ is true ● Graph inequalities on a number line ● Find the absolute value of a real number

R.2 Operations with Real Numbers

Add real numbers ● Find the opposite, or additive inverse, of a number ● Subtract real numbers ● Multiply real numbers ● Divide real numbers

R.3 Exponential Notation and Order of Operations

Rewrite expressions with whole-number exponents, and evaluate exponential expressions ● Rewrite expressions with or without negative integers as exponents ● Simplify expressions using the rules for order of operations

Part 2 MANIPULATIONS

R.4 Introduction to Algebraic Expressions

Translate a phrase to an algebraic expression ● Evaluate an algebraic expression by substitution

R.5 Equivalent Algebraic Expressions

Determine whether two expressions are equivalent by completing a table of values ● Find equivalent fraction expressions by multiplying by 1, and simplify fraction expressions ● Use the commutative and the associative laws to find equivalent expressions ● Use the distributive laws to find equivalent expressions by multiplying and factoring

R.6 Simplifying Algebraic Expressions

Simplify an expression by collecting like terms ● Simplify an expression by removing parentheses and collecting like terms

R.7 Properties of Exponents and Scientific Notation

Use exponential notation in multiplication and division ● Use exponential notation in raising a power to a power, and in raising a product or a quotient to a power ● Convert between decimal notation and scientific notation and use scientific notation with multiplication and division

TEACHING TIPS

Although the material in chapter R is prerequisite material to this course, you will find a wide range of under-standing with reference to the material. I sometimes offer a separate review class on the review material for those interested in relearning the material. Many of the students have allowed time to elapse between their last algebra class and this one. Although the class is not part of the course, it does help to retrieve lost knowledge. During the review you will often find students who know little or no algebra. This is a placement issue that colleagues around the country have encountered. Recommend to these students that they visit a counselor and consider taking a lower level mathematics course to prepare for success.

Try to test the class in the first or second week on these prerequisite skills. You want to establish an understanding of the strengths and weaknesses of these students as well as allowing them to see the same thing. I often find that showing a student they need to work on a topic is so much better than telling them. If you ask a student about elementary algebra, they have seen it, had it and know it. They will tell you they don't need to waste time taking it again. Please keep in mind the fact that Chapter R is not a comprehensive review of elementary algebra. One could almost argue that it contains only basic mathematics.

David P. Bell,
Florida Community College at Jacksonville

◆ ◆ ◆

The review material in this chapter is very, very basic. Intermediate algebra students definitely should have an understanding of this material. Since there is so much to cover in an intermediate algebra course, I would just assign the Chapter R test on pp. 73–74.

Based on the results of that test, I would give each student a list of sections in Chapter R that he or she should review independently. The only topic that I might review briefly would be negative exponents and scientific notation.

Sharon Testone,
Onondaga Community College

◆ ◆ ◆

Most students need to review Chapter R, but most course outlines do not allow time for a lengthy review. Here are four methods to squeeze in the needed re-examination of basic numerical and algebraic skills students should have when beginning an intermediate algebra course. All four methods get the students actively involved from day one, and put the responsibility of the review on the students.

Method 1: Assignment for the first class: Students must read Chapter R and **write down** the concepts, sections, and prob-lems that they would like explained at the next class meeting. At the second meeting of the class, take up these written requests, order them to match the sections on Chapter R, and explain **only those written requests.** If students still have questions at the end of class, arrange to meet with them outside of class, or direct them to a tutorial center, if your school has one. Encourage students with remaining questions to form study groups and review Chapter R together.

Method 2: On the first day of class, assign the chapter test for Chapter R. Have students check and grade their own papers by dividing the number correct by the total number of problems on the test (63). The answers to both odd and even numbered problems are given in the back of the book. On the second day of class, have students write a summary of how they feel they did on the test, and hand in the summary with their "grade" at the top. Encourage (or require) all students who scored below 80% (or you set the percent) to do further review either in the text, or view videotapes, or use other resources that may be available.

Method 3: The first assignment is to read Chapter R and prepare a test (you decide how many questions) with a sepa-rate answer key showing all the work. The problems used from Chapter R may not be those for which there are answers in the book or in the *Student's Solutions Manual.* On the second meeting of the class, collect the tests and answer keys, then redistribute them so that no student has his or her own test. (For those stu-dents who were not in attendance for the first class, or who failed to do the assignment, have a test pre-pared, but no answer key for them. Those students will have to take the teacher-prepared test.) The students who prepared tests and answer keys will "correct" the answer keys of the student-made test they were given, and "grade" the test. Tests will then be turned in to the instructor. Each test should be signed by the test maker and the grader. After looking over the results of this testing exercise, the instructor will have a fair idea which students need more review than class time allows, and refer those students to the proper tutorial services available. (This method works best in a small class.)

Method 4: Divide the class into small groups and assign several sections of Chapter R to each group. Each group is responsible for preparing a discussion and review for the entire class on its assigned sections. One group's assigned sections can be all the "Calculator Corner" sections in Chapter R. Another group can be responsible for all "Study Tips." During the second class meeting, each group presents its "review." This may take more than one class meeting.

Rebecca Wyatt-Semple,
Nash Community College

Section R.1

Using parentheses and brackets instead of the open and closed dot when graphing linear inequalities eases the transition to interval notation later on.

Susan Leland,
Montana Tech

◆ ◆ ◆

For many, the study of the Real Number System is *boring.* Students need to be reminded that passing a *Rules of the Road* Exam is necessary to drive a vehicle. Therefore, understanding (and passing) the properties of the Real Number System is necessary to navigate through math!

Nancy Ressler,
Oakton Community College

◆ ◆ ◆

When describing the sets of numbers, I use these examples. Think of **natural numbers** as the way that a child naturally learns to count. They start with one, then two, then three, etc. Remember the **whole numbers** by the long o sound in the whole. That o (or zero) means that it is included in the set of natural numbers and they are together given a new name, the **whole numbers.** The **integers** are the negative and positive whole numbers. Rational and fractional sound so much alike, almost like they rhyme, that it is easy to remember that they go together. **Rational numbers** include integers, fractions, and decimals that either terminate or repeat. **Irrational numbers** are those unusual types that cannot be written as a terminating decimal, repeating decimal, or as a quotient of integers. **Real numbers** are all of these categories put together. They are, for the most part, the ones you can work with on a calculator.

The greater than or less than symbol itself can provide a clue as to which way a student should shade a number line when graphing inequalities. If the variable is on the left-hand side, think of the inequality symbol as the point of an arrow. That arrow indicates which way the number line should be shaded from the initial number, located on the opposite side of the variable. Remember that this only works if the variable is on the left-hand side. If it is not, manipulate the inequality by reversing sides and then if it is not, write an equivalent inequality with the variable on the left-hand side.

Tomesa Smith,
Wallace State Community College

Section R.2

Many colleges do not allow the use of calculators and graphing calculators until Intermediate Algebra. Consequently, many of your students will not have much experience with the calculators. There is also debate on the benefits of using calculators for tasks the student cannot perform manually. Again, talk to experienced faculty about the issue. Many students have difficulty with fractions and decimals. They understand the topics, but are plagued with a variety of simple, silly errors. The use of a calculator can help here by allowing the student to concentrate on the new topics rather than basic math mechanics. I teach the procedures for calculation using fractions and how to retrieve fractional answers from the calculator. I also like to take a few order-of-operations questions like #49 and 65 in R.3 page 32, work them out by hand, and show just how useful the calculator can be.

David P. Bell,
Florida Community College at Jacksonville

◆ ◆ ◆

Very little time needs to be spent on multiplication and division of integers. Spend your time on addition and subtraction. Emphasize the addition rules - point out to your class that every subtraction problem becomes an addition problem and uses those same rules.

On page 19, point out the three ways a negative sign can be used in a fraction -in the numerator, in the denominator, or out in front. This becomes important when dealing with slope.

Susan Leland,
Montana Tech

◆ ◆ ◆

When demonstrating the rules for multiplying and dividing integers, I have students count the number of negative signs in the problem. If there is an odd number of negative signs, the answer is negative. If there is an even number of negative signs, the answer is positive.

Tomesa Smith,
Wallace State Community College

Section R.3

Students tend to do long "order of operation" problems any way that makes them easier! Tell students that they cannot make up their own rules—even if their way is easier—their answer will be wrong more times than not.

Susan Leland,
Montana Tech

◆ ◆ ◆

Without expertise in exponential notation, students will not succeed in future chemistry, biology or math courses. Review non-positive exponents (pages 26, 27), read and discuss Exercise 25 (page 29).

Nancy Ressler,
Oakton Community College

Section R.4

Stress the difference between the terms: evaluate and solve. Students often translate evaluate into some elaborate algebraic solution scheme. It is simply "Plug n' Chug."

Haste makes waste. Take the time to substitute the values into the expression, and then solve it. I find that students are often in a hurry and do the substitution in their heads and consequently confuse themselves and the answer.

David P. Bell,
Florida Community College at Jacksonville

◆ ◆ ◆

The text contains a good list of key words on page 36. Example 1 addresses the confusion caused by the phrase "less than." I use the analogy of translating from one language to another. I note that, in translating from English to another language, it is not enough to merely translate word for word in the original order. Usually there is at least one student who has learned a foreign language and can verify my statement. I explain that in translation between languages there are rules of order to learn. In mathematics, the phrase "less than" changes the order so "5 less than x" becomes "$x - 5$."

Rosa Kavanaugh,
Ozarks Technical College

◆ ◆ ◆

Word problems are very frightening to students. Deciding which operations are called for seems to be the biggest obstacle. Use the idea of translation from the language of English to the language of math. The Key Words table serves as their dictionary. Refer to it often.

Susan Leland,
Montana Tech

Section R.6

The algebraic properties and laws are often overlooked by the students and any expression with parentheses becomes an example of the Associative Law. Try the following: $7 + (3 + 5) = 7 + (5 + 3)$. Practice, practice, practice.

David P. Bell,
Florida Community College at Jacksonville

◆ ◆ ◆

In simplifying nested symbols of grouping, many students tend to remove all symbols of grouping before combining any like terms. I have seen only a few who have been successful in doing this. They usually make errors because of the sheer size of the resulting expression. I demonstrate the preferred procedure: "Remove Innermost Symbols of Grouping" then "Combine Like Terms." In fact, I label each step repeating the acronyms: RISG and CLT. Usually most of the class is looking rather bored by this time. I ask them whether this is a difficult process and they say it is not. Then I ask them to work Margin Exercise 29 on page 53. I circulate around the class and check their work. I can give some extra attention to any that may be having particular difficulty and help others find minor errors. Removing parentheses preceded by a negative sign continues to be a stumbling block for a number of algebra students. The author states on page 51 that this operation may be considered as multiplication by negative one. For many students this needs to be emphasized.

Of course, there are copying errors and various sign errors. Inappropriate distribution is another common type of error. Sometimes this is caused by a missing right-end symbol of grouping to close the group. Some students treat those right-end symbols as decorative rather than functional. It may be instructive to contrast the meaning of $3(2x - 5y) + 7z$ with $3(2x - 5y + 7z)$ and the ambiguous form $3(2x - 5y + 7z)$.

Usually only several of the students get the correct answer the first time. I close the session with a discussion of why so few people were able to get the right answer the first time if this is not a difficult process. They usually attribute this to careless errors. Then I explain to them that what they are doing here is not merely algebra, that they are training their minds to take a set of rather simple rules and apply them carefully to obtain a correct result. I admit that most of them will never be asked to simplify an algebraic expression after they graduate. But I ask how many believe that they will not be expected to take a given procedure and follow it carefully to get a correct result. I have never had a student who believes that! This seems to convince them that what they are learning in this course is not merely algebra but life skills. After that, I rarely am asked the question, "Why do we have to learn this?"

Rosa Kavanaugh,
Ozarks Technical College

Section R.7

The properties of exponents are basic to understanding most of the rest of the course. Emphasize this importance to the students. Provide many and varied examples for homework.

David P. Bell,
Florida Community College at Jacksonville

◆ ◆ ◆

I do believe that students need to see the development of at least the Product Rule so that they know that it follows from the basic definition of exponential notation. They also need to know that the rule is not a conspiracy designed by mathematicians to make their lives more difficult but actually serves to make mathematical operations easier. Would they really want to multiply using the definition of exponential notation? The rule that continues to be most troublesome for students is the one for negative exponents. If there seems to be considerable confusion about why this rule is true, it may be productive to return to the development of it with a comparison such as:

$$\frac{x^3}{x^7} = x^{3-7} = x^{-4}$$

and

$$\frac{x^3}{x^7} = \frac{x \cdot x \cdot x}{x \cdot x \cdot x \cdot x \cdot x \cdot x \cdot x}$$

$$= \frac{1}{x \cdot x \cdot x \cdot x}$$

Sometimes this overwhelmed students in basic algebra so that they never really "bought in" to the rule. At the intermediate algebra level they are often more prepared to receive it.

Students need to know that because the laws of exponents are consistent, there may be several orders of steps that will produce the same correct result. Some students are more successful writing

$$\frac{y^2}{y^{-9}} = \frac{y^2 \cdot y^9}{1} = y^{2+9} = y^{11}$$

rather than subtracting the negative exponents. I also recommend that if they raise a product/quotient to a power that they simplify, if possible, inside the parentheses first.

There seem to be several recurring errors. Students are not careful to learn precise English versions of the laws of exponents. They tend to write on their papers (and say): "When you multiply you add" rather than "When you multiply powers of the same base, you add exponents." Similar difficulties arise in problems with negative coefficients and negative exponents. When they simplify

$$\left(\frac{-3x^{-5}}{y^{-4}}\right)^2$$

they remember to multiply the exponents but tend to also multiply the 2 by -3. This is a good time to remind them that the -3 does have an exponent of 1; thus the 2 should be multiplied by 1 to yield

$$\frac{\left(-3\right)^2 x^{-10}}{y^{-8}}.$$

A rule that I quote to my students and they seem to find meaningful in this section is, "A factor can be moved between the numerator and the denominator by changing the sign of the exponent." An emphasis on factors and exponents vs. coefficients seems to correct many misunderstandings in these problem types.

Rosa Kavanaugh,
Ozarks Technical College

◆ ◆ ◆

As a hint to remember what to do with exponents that are raised to exponents, I have students notice the piece of parenthesis between the two exponents. Since parentheses normally indicate a multiplication process, it reminds students to multiply the exponents. This, I explain, is the basis of the power rule for exponents.

Tomesa Smith,
Wallace State Community College

Solving Linear Equations and Inequalities

SECTION TITLES AND OBJECTIVES

1.1 Solving Equations
Determine whether a given number is a solution of a given equation • Solve equations using the addition principle • Solve equations using the multiplication principle • Solve equations using the addition and multiplication principles together, removing parentheses where appropriate

1.2 Formulas and Applications
Evaluate formulas and solve a formula for a specified letter

1.3 Applications and Problem Solving
Solve applied problems by translating to equations • Solve basic motion problems

1.4 Sets, Inequalities, and Interval Notation
Determine whether a given number is a solution of an inequality • Write interval notation for the solution set or graph of an inequality • Solve an inequality using the addition and multiplication principles and then graph the inequality • Solve applied problems by translating to inequalities

1.5 Intersections, Unions, and Compound Inequalities
Find the intersection of two sets. Solve and graph conjunctions of inequalities • Find the union of two sets. Solve and graph disjunctions of inequalities • Solve applied problems involving conjunctions and disjunctions of inequalities

1.6 Absolute-Value Equations and Inequalities
Simplify expressions containing absolute-value symbols • Find the distance between two points on a number line • Solve equations with absolute-value expressions • Solve equations with two absolute-value expressions • Solve inequalities with absolute-value expressions

TEACHING TIPS

If a student is to master this chapter, the word "solve" must have meaning. This is a good opportunity to connect the mathematical word to the common English word. We hear about "solving a mystery" in a variety of situations. (e.g. "Who robbed the bank?") The meaning is that there is something that we don't know. In algebra, when we are asked to: "Solve $3x + 5 = 5(x - 1)$" we should realize that there is a "mystery" (i.e. "What is x?"). Students who grasp this can understand that there is a goal and can recognize when they have reached it.

Rosa Kavanaugh,
Ozarks Technical College

◆ ◆ ◆

I consider this the most important chapter in the book. Every subsequent chapter involves equations and they all reduce to linear equations. Extra help sessions and worksheets can benefit students who are struggling. Going the extra mile with linear equations pays great dividends later in the course.

Susan Leland,
Montana Tech

◆ ◆ ◆

Students often have trouble determining the solution set for absolute value inequalities. I have the students treat the inequality as an equation and determine the two "starting" points. I then have them choose a test point from three locations. One test point is less than the smaller number, one test point is between the two numbers and the third test point is greater than the larger number. The students can then see where the inequality would be true or false. After shading the correct regions and showing the arrows when appropriate, the students can "read" the solution set from their graph.

Sections 1.1 and 1.2 should be reviewed quite quickly. I would spend the majority of time working with the formulas because students always have problems solving for one variable in terms of other variables. A technique I use is to solve both of these problems simultaneously showing their relationship to each other: $6 = 2x + 3$ and $b = ax + c$.

Sharon Testone,
Onondaga Community College

◆ ◆ ◆

Reading will be the basis of many students' problems, whether it's failure to read instructions or jumping into working exercises before reading through the discussion and examples in the text. Applied problems, a.k.a. word problems, seem to stymie the majority of students. A considerable part of their difficulty in this area is that they do not read the problem enough times to be able to distinguish what is given or known from what is being asked, and what, if anything, can be ignored as a red herring. It will pay off in the long run if extra time is spent on applied problems in all chapters, but especially in Chapter 1. Instruct students who are having difficulties with word problems how to read for necessary information and how to identify superfluous information.

This text has an outstanding selection of applied problems in all chapters. Use them!! Require students to use the five steps for problem solving (page 99) and show their work. In stating the final answer to the word problems, require a complete sentence with proper units of measure. Remind students to reread the problem to be certain they have answered all the questions asked in the problem, and check to see if their answer(s) make sense in the context of the problem.

Rebecca Wyatt-Semple,
Nash Community College

Section 1.1

Since the students have seen this material before, they tend to rush and make unnecessary errors. Stress the importance of taking things one step at a time. And always answer the question with an equation. $X = 5$, not (5) or $\underline{5}$ or $\{5\}$.

David P. Bell,
Florida Community College at Jacksonville

Section 1.2

When using a formula to answer a question, the most common error is made when substituting numbers into the equation. This is especially true when the number substituted is a negative number. Stress care and process. Substitute the numbers into the equation as an entire step. Then you can begin to solve the problem.

David P. Bell,
Florida Community College at Jacksonville

◆ ◆ ◆

Formulas are challenging at all levels of math; students have programmed themselves into *believing* applications and literal equations are difficult! Illustrate and discuss "patterns in math".

Nancy Ressler,
Oakton Community College

◆ ◆ ◆

When introducing formulas, I ask students to call out any formulas they recall from previous courses. I then use the formulas they called out to base my discussion of how a formula is like a recipe and what it means to solve for a particular variable.

Tomesa Smith,
Wallace State Community College

Section 1.3

Students are convinced at an early age that applications are too tough to conquer and they give up before they even try. I have given tests with a separate page of application problems and most students never even dirtied the page. I often hear students in mathematics for liberal arts classes say that "I am just going to teach elementary school, so I don't need this math stuff!" It takes me some time to calm down. Unfortunately, this attitude exists out there and for many of your students, this mentality was thrust upon them _8_ or more years ago. You must be consistent. Read the examples, build the models, set up the equations in words and then substitute the values, build tables, etc. These students really need the repetition, and if there was any section of the text where you might consider spending a bit of extra time, this is it. Your task is to turn application problems into just another math problem.

David P. Bell,
Florida Community College at Jacksonville

◆ ◆ ◆

Students have difficulty labeling the unknowns in an application where there is more than one unknown, but it is desirable to write an equation with only one unknown. The rule of thumb that has seemed to help many students is: "Choose the primary unknown to be the one about which you have the least information." Thus for Example 6 in Section 1.3, the primary unknown is the first angle since there is information given about the other two angles.

Rosa Kavanaugh,
Ozarks Technical College

◆ ◆ ◆

Defining a variable is crucial in problem solving. Require students to make this their first line in a solution. ($x =$ length of wire, etc) This gives them one of the three tools they need to set up an equation, the other two tools being the operations (using the "Key Words" chart in Chapter R) and the numbers in the problem. Without the proper tools, a job cannot be completed. The tool most students forget about is defining the variable.

Susan Leland,
Montana Tech

◆ ◆ ◆

<u>R</u>eally <u>f</u>un and <u>e</u>xciting <u>s</u>tuff, <u>**check**</u> it out! The underlined "r" stands for read, which is the first step in solving an applied problem. Each problem should be read completely. I always refer to the classic trick test that has a long paragraph of directions and then says if you do something like write your name in answer blank #25, you will make a 100 for reading all the directions. The next letter, "f," stands for familiarize, which is the next step in working an applied problem. You must be familiar enough with the problem to know if you need a formula, drawing, or conversion to work the problem out to completion. The "a" stands for assign in the process of assigning a variable to an expression. The "e" in exciting stands for the equation that is formed to solve the problem. By utilizing the variable expressions to set up the equation, a mechanism for solving is formed. "S" stands for that solving process where the unknown is discovered. This forms the basis of discovering what other variables can be equal to in the problem. Hopefully the last word in my phrase is obvious. "Check" means to check the solutions with the wording of the problem. The main thing to check is that the given solutions are consistent with the wording. I caution students not to just check the results with their equation because their equation could be set up incorrectly or yield a number that is not an answer to the original problem.

Tomesa Smith,
Wallace State Community College

◆ ◆ ◆

Applied problems are an essential topic. Often students pass an Intermediate Algebra course, but are then unable to apply those concepts to chemistry, economics, or other fields of study. Instructors should spend at least two class periods on this section.

Sharon Testone,
Onondaga Community College

Section 1.4

Stress consistency in setting up Absolute Value Equalities and Inequalities.

Always begin the same way. If $|x| = a$, then $x = a$ or $x = -a$.

If $|x| < a$, then $x < a$ or $x > -a$ which can be written $-a < x < a$.

If $|x| > a$, then $x > a$ or $x < -a$.

If the students can remember the starting point, they can get to the end. I stress the importance of checking answers to catch errors. Additionally, I like to inject a bit of levity by bestowing algebraic logic to the class. In an example where $|x| = -5$, we discuss the concept of logic. Since absolute value by definition is a positive value, it cannot be negative. Thus, this example has no logical solution.

Have each student raise their right hand and pronounce "You now possess Algebraic Logic." This will usually get a chuckle from a few. At any time where algebraic logic might help and the students miss this step simply ask them to raise their right hand. At times I have even heard students help each other by making the same statement.

David P. Bell,
Florida Community College at Jacksonville

❖ ❖ ❖

In solving inequalities, students seem to change the sign of the inequality in the step following that in which they divide by the negative number. Of course, that means that the preceding step is an untrue inequality. Unfortunately, I have observed a number of instructors who have done exactly the same thing when working examples in class. This is one of the areas in which instructors must be especially careful to avoid an incorrect mathematical procedure.

The author states in Example 14 of Section 1.4 that a linear inequality may be solved with the variable on the left or right of the inequality. I warn students that each approach has its advantages and disadvantages. If the final coefficient of the unknown on the left side is a negative number, there is the potential error of forgetting to change the sign when dividing by the negative number. However, if they avoid that hazard by solving for the unknown on the right side, they are more likely to incorrectly graph the solution on the number line. I recommend that if they do solve for the unknown on the right side they rewrite the inequality with the unknown on the left side before graphing.

Rosa Kavanaugh,
Ozarks Technical College

❖ ❖ ❖

Solving inequalities can be taught immediately after Section 1.1 if you put off the applications until later.

Susan Leland,
Montana Tech

❖ ❖ ❖

Many students will be *at a first time* learning (and understanding) for sets and interval notation.

Nancy Ressler,
Oakton Community College

❖ ❖ ❖

When graphing inequalities on a number line, I demonstrate that the inequality symbol can be treated like the point of an arrow indicating which direction to shade. This only works if the variable is on the left-hand side. If it is not, I go through the process of manipulating it to get it over to the left-hand side. Hopefully, students can tell which way to shade regardless of the position of the variable, but this technique can serve as a checking mechanism or a working procedure.

Tomesa Smith,
Wallace State Community College

❖ ❖ ❖

In Section 1.4, require students to use all forms of inequality notation: set notation, interval notation, and number line graphs. Reinforce the caution in the text concerning what happens to the inequality sign when multiplying (or dividing) by a negative number.

Rebecca Wyatt-Semple,
Nash Community College

Section 1.5

Since our classrooms are all equipped with dry-erase boards, I consider colored markers to be the key to successful demonstration of unions and intersections of sets. Colored chalk would serve the same purpose on a chalkboard. If set A is colored purple on the number line and set B is colored green on the same number line, to identify the intersection of sets I simply ask, "What part of the number line is colored both purple and green?" I also recommend that students do this assignment in colored pencils or markers.

Rosa Kavanaugh,
Ozarks Technical College

Section 1.6

Remind and demonstrate *absolute value* as distance and the *solution value* of the variable. Graphs are useful visual tools. This will require more time than other sections of the chapter.

Nancy Ressler,
Oakton Community College

◆ ◆ ◆

With absolute value inequalities, I have discovered a way to help students determine if an intersection or union is needed to solve a problem. Treating the inequality symbol as an arrow, I have students determine if the arrow is pointing toward or away from the absolute value bars. If the symbol is pointing away, a union is necessary. If it is pointing toward, then an intersection is needed.

Tomesa Smith,
Wallace State Community College

◆ ◆ ◆

Be prepared to spend time on Section 1.6. Absolute value equations and inequalities give quite a few students trouble. Part of their trouble can be traced to their failure to comprehend the importance of and and or in Section 1.5, and how these two concepts relate to intersection and union of sets.

Rebecca Wyatt-Semple,
Nash Community College

Graphs, Functions, and Applications

TEACHING TIPS

Do not skimp on Chapter 2. Being well grounded in the concepts of this chapter will be of immense benefit to students in math, the sciences, statistics, psychology, economics; the list is endless. Graphs are a key method for presenting information in many fields. The idea of functions is the foundation for much of the math that follows in this course.

This chapter is a good place to get the liberal arts student who is stuck taking a math course involved. Some students may not be outstanding as number and variable pushers, but may find interest in researching the history of graphing on the Cartesian plane, and the life and times of Rene Descartes. It is amazing how the simple idea of the *xy*-coordinate system revolutionized mathematics.

Rebecca Wyatt-Semple,
Nash Community College

Section 2.1

Show the importance of the *x*-intercepts and the *y*-intercepts for plotting equations of the form $ax + by = c$. Additionally, if the equation is in the form $y = mx + b$ slope intercept form, then select the *x*'s and do a table of values (pick a negative, a positive and 0), plot the ordered pairs, connect the points.

Chris Bendixen,
Lake Michigan College

◆ ◆ ◆

One of the most common errors in plotting points is interchanging the x- and y-coordinates. If time and the class-room permit, it is helpful to ask students to plot one or two points on their papers before leaving class. This allows the instructor to identify and redirect students who have a tendency to make this mistake.

Rosa Kavanaugh,
Ozarks Technical College

◆ ◆ ◆

Emphasize that one ordered pair = one plotted point. Some students plot the x coordinate on the x-axis and the y coordinate on the y-axis and think they are done.

Susan Leland,
Montana Tech

. ◆ ◆ ◆

When introducing or reviewing the process of plotting ordered pairs, I often mention that the process is similar to the game of *Battleship*. It uses a grid that locates points by an association between a letter and a number, such as B-2. Players then use these coordinates to hide ships while opponents guess their location. The same process is used when reading a road map. Points of interest and cities are located by using a letter-number combination found in the legend. Users then match up the letter and number to find the approximate area of the desired site. Plotting points in algebra is the same process as each of these references except that algebraic graphing utilizes two numbers instead of a letter and number combination. These numbers are called ordered pairs because they reflect alphabetical order with the two axes, the x and the y. The first number listed represents the x value, whereas the second one listed reflects the y value.

Tomesa Smith,
Wallace State Community College

◆ ◆ ◆

This section contains primarily review material and instructors should not spend much time on these topics. The only material that may be new to your students are graphs of nonlinear functions. These are revisited in Precalculus courses; therefore, they should be only introduced.

Sharon Testone,
Onondaga Community College

Section 2.2

For this section, show the basic shapes for quadratic, cubic, absolute value functions. Emphasize the vertical line test for functions. Create a good linear function problem, like a population model for the city where you are living. Predict the population in the year "2012".

Chris Bendixen,
Lake Michigan College

◆ ◆ ◆

Function notation is especially troublesome to students since they have heard from the beginning of algebra that "parentheses mean multiply." Now we are faced with the challenge that parentheses can also mean something else. I remind them that this also true in the English language. The word "well" has one meaning in the phrase "dig a well" and another in "feeling well today." In fact we can use both words in the same sentence, "He was not feeling well when he dug the well." Students see that this would be a very difficult issue for someone just learning the English language. But it is clear that the meaning in each case is determined by context and usage. I explain to them that they are facing a similar situation. The students see both meanings of parentheses in the same equation.

For example, given $f(x) = 5x - 4x^2$, then $f(3) = 5(3) - 4(3)^2$.

They will need to analyze context and usage carefully when they see the parentheses notation.

Rosa Kavanaugh,
Ozarks Technical College

◆ ◆ ◆

Students understand the concept of function better if they are shown what a function <u>is not</u>.

Susan Leland,
Montana Tech

◆ ◆ ◆

The concept of function will be new for most students and it often proves to be difficult for them to understand. Functions are introduced on page 174 of the text with the equation "$y = 2x - 3$". This is the time to explain why this is a function and to show students that it can be written as $f(x) = 2x - 3$, with $f(x)$ replacing the y. If students are exposed to this notion from the beginning of this topic, it helps their understanding of functions.

Sharon Testone,
Onondaga Community College

Section 2.3

For the domain, begin with the most elementary definition of domain and range: domain is the set of 1st elements of ordered pairs, and the range is the set of 2nd elements of the ordered pairs, where no two 1st elements are the same.

Next, discuss division by zero and how it affects the domain of functions. I like to do a calculator exercise: "what happens when $x \rightarrow 0$ for a function like $1/x$, begin with a number like $x = 1$, then continue the problem with the value of x getting smaller and smaller, to determine if the student can observe what happens when x gets infinitesimally close to zero. The function gets huge.

Chris Bendixen,
Lake Michigan College

◆ ◆ ◆

In Example 2 of Section 2.3, the author refers to the domain as the curve's shadow or the projection on the x-axis. A similar explanation that has seemed to be meaningful to my students is, "If all of the points on the curve fell down and landed on the x-axis, what part of the x-axis would be covered by those points?" (In the case where part of the curve is below the x-axis, I have to instead refer to the points "falling up" to the x-axis.) This explanation can be used again to find range of a function.

Rosa Kavanaugh,
Ozarks Technical College

◆ ◆ ◆

Students may or may not have experienced functions in Beginning Algebra. You must embellish and reinforce functions; simple examples with questions completed during class time work well.

Nancy Ressler,
Oakton Community College

Section 2.4

Explain the simplicity of positive and negative slopes: Positive rise from left to right, negative slopes fall from left to right. Also, draw pictures of points. Illustrate the carpenter's definition of slope, rise to run.

Chris Bendixen,
Lake Michigan College

◆ ◆ ◆

My students have always found it very confusing to be given two options for graphing using slope-intercept (i.e. either up and right or down and left for positive slope). They seem to be more confident if they don't have to make that choice. I recommend that they avoid the potential confusion by moving up or down from the y-intercept depending on whether the sign of the slope is positive or negative. Then they can **always move over to the right.** I explain to them that the fraction does in fact give them instructions for doing this. For example, I ask them to read the fraction $-\frac{3}{5}$. They say "negative three-fifths" or "negative three over five." The second wording then tells them how to move from the y-intercept if they replace the word "negative" by "down" when they read it: **"down three, over five."** By the same convention, a slope of $\frac{1}{4}$ instructs them to move **"up one, over four."** Students seem to find this explanation very helpful.

Rosa Kavanaugh,
Ozarks Technical College

◆ ◆ ◆

Emphasize the subtraction signs in the slope formula. Students tend to leave them out when the second coordinate they use is negative.

Susan Leland,
Montana Tech

◆ ◆ ◆

Proportional thinking is a weakness for many students, reinforce "what" slope means with simple references to applications and graphs. (2.4 and 2.5 continuity is important)

Nancy Ressler,
Oakton Community College

◆ ◆ ◆

Use the Calculator Corners to explore both linear and nonlinear functions, but also require that students draw simple graphs "by hand." Demand neat graphs and that axes be labeled appropriately. Draw attention to the fact that axes are not always labeled x and y.

Rebecca Wyatt-Semple,
Nash Community College

Section 2.5

Revisit the first exposure to graphing where the intercepts were introduced to graph equations of the form $ax + by = c$.

Chris Bendixen,
Lake Michigan College

◆ ◆ ◆

Require students to write intercepts as ordered pairs. This helps them to avoid the common error of combing the two into one point.

Example: $x + y = 4$.

If you allow $x = 4$ for the x intercept and $y = 4$ for the y intercept, some students will graph one point $-(4, 4)$.

Perpendicular lines have slopes that are opposites and reciprocals—students sometimes think that only one of those requirements needs to be satisfied to have perpendicular lines.

Susan Leland,
Montana Tech

Section 2.6

The author gives two ways to write an equation of a line. The first is the point-slope equation and the second is the slope-intercept equation. I prefer the second method because the students know $y = mx + b$ and are not required to learn another formula.

If two points are given, they can find the slope and then substitute the slope and either point into the equation to find b. Once they have the values for m and b, they can write the equation of the line. I often begin the lesson by giving a value for m and a value for b and ask the students to write the equation of the line. I then give them a value for b and a point and finally two points. By using the same method each time, the students begin to understand the concept.

Sharon Testone,
Onondaga Community College

Systems of Equations

TEACHING TIPS

Treat Chapter 3 as a continuation of Chapter 2. In this chapter students can use their graphing skills to find solutions to problems in two variables and two equations. Make assignments so that students get a balance between drawing graphs by hand, and estimating solutions to systems of equations using the graphing calculator. For best results with the graphing calculators, instruct students to use the intersect feature, if their calculators have this feature, rather than TRACE alone.

Emphasize that the algebraic techniques developed in this chapter produce exact results, while the graphing technique sometimes produces only good *approximations*.

Assign applied problems in two variables, and some with three variables. Select some systems that do not have solutions, as well as those that have an infinite number of solutions.

Rebecca Wyatt-Semple,
Nash Community College

Section 3.1

It is essential for the students to understand that solutions to systems of equations must make all equations true. Be sure they understand that graphically solutions are points of intersection. It is relatively easy to verify solutions with the aid of graphing calculators. Demonstrate the use of the calculator, but do not give them all of the graphing calculator secrets for solving.

Chris Bendixen,
Lake Michigan College

◆ ◆ ◆

When solving a system graphically it is helpful to emphasize to students that there are two different lines representing two different equations by writing and graphing each in a different color (either using colored chalk, dry erase markers, or transparency pens) or different type lines on the graphing calculator. Otherwise students seem to get lost in which intercept or slope corresponds to each equation. The solution of the system is then simply where the two different colored lines intersect.

Rosa Kavanaugh,
Ozarks Technical College

◆ ◆ ◆

Students' graphing tends to be inaccurate and this inaccuracy is magnified when graphing systems. With the availability of graphing calculators, Section 3.1 can be just briefly mentioned when time does not allow full coverage. However, students should be shown the three possible cases—intersecting, parallel, and the same line. These cases can be referred to when solutions are found in Section 3.2.

Susan Leland,
Montana Tech

◆ ◆ ◆

The emphasis in this section should be on using the $f(x)$ and $g(x)$ notations and the definitions of consistent and inconsistent systems. Example 2 on page 247 uses function notation and Example 3 on pp. 247-248 demonstrates consistent and inconsistent systems. Additionally, they include the terms independent and dependent. Most of my students have not seen this terminology.

Sharon Testone,
Onondaga Community College

Section 3.2

It is essential to get the students started in the right direction. If one of the equations has coefficients of "1" or "−1", then have the students solve that equation for that variable. Then substitute the result into the other equation. I like to challenge the students to try the problem the most difficult way. Last but not least, insist that the students check both equations to see if the result is indeed a solution.

Chris Bendixen,
Lake Michigan College

◆ ◆ ◆

Since Section 3.2 may be the first time that many students have seen an algebraic substitution, I try to help them attach meaning to the word "substitution." I ask for examples of "substitution" outside the classroom. The most common answer is player substitutions in sports; I also mention recipe substitutions. I ask students to explain what a "substitution" means, and we usually agree that it means a replacement, one taking the place of another. This seems to help them understand the mechanics of the algebraic substitution. It may also be helpful to mention that the purpose of the substitution is to simplify the problem from an unfamiliar type of two equations containing two unknowns to a very familiar single equation with one unknown.

Rosa Kavanaugh,
Ozarks Technical College

◆ ◆ ◆

Students need to learn the wise choice in solving for one of the variables. Point out that choosing a variable with a coefficient of 1 makes the problem much easier.

Susan Leland,
Montana Tech

Section 3.3

Point out that solving by elimination simply means that by adding and or subtracting multiples of each equation, you are reducing the system of two equations to an easier system of one equation and one unknown. You may need to refresh the students regarding how to solve such an equation. They forget very fast. Once they have eliminated one of the variables, then it is essential that they substitute that number into the other equation to solve for the other variable.

Chris Bendixen,
Lake Michigan College

◆ ◆ ◆

Some students think that only one method—the "correct" one—can be used to solve any given system. After covering this section, present several systems to the class and have them decide whether substitution or elimination is the method to use. Choose some systems that are obviously solved more easily using a particular method, and choose some systems that could be solved equally easily either way.

Susan Leland,
Montana Tech

Section 3.4

Although I am not an artist, I do attempt to draw "pictionary-type" illustrations of mixture problems and motion problems. It seems to help visual learners to grasp these concepts. Box-like containers, boats, cars and airplanes supplemented with directional arrows can be effective aids to completing the necessary tables. In the tables for mixture problems, I recommend only two rows, each representing a quantity that will be added. I use percents to label the headings but not as a separate row since the percents are not additive.

Rosa Kavanaugh,
Ozarks Technical College

◆ ◆ ◆

Courses after Intermediate Algebra focus on applications. It is necessary for students to have experience in setting-up and thinking about word problems prior to entering future courses.

Nancy Ressler,
Oakton Community College

Section 3.5

At this time in the course, I introduce the students to matrix representation of 3 equations and 3 unknowns. It seems tedious to write down all the variables for the problems. After the students feel comfortable with the notation, I then cover Cramer's Rule first. I insist that the students learn different ways of solving systems.

Chris Bendixen,
Lake Michigan College

◆ ◆ ◆

The successful solution of a system of three equations in three unknowns requires that the student both understand the strategy and organize the process. As the author notes in Example 1 on page 283, a common strategic error is eliminating a different variable in obtaining the second equation with two unknowns. This warning is an important one. There are various ways to arrange the equations, but students need to see the importance of attention to detail. You may want to warn them that some of the most common errors are miscopying an equation or neglecting to multiply all terms when multiplying an equation by a constant.

Rosa Kavanaugh,
Ozarks Technical College

◆ ◆ ◆

Systems of equations (3 × 3's), important to support future courses.

Nancy Ressler,
Oakton Community College

◆ ◆ ◆

When solving systems of equations in three variables, explain that the goal is to reduce the number of equations and the number of variables. This is accomplished stepwise by first reducing the number of equations to two and the number of variables to two. Once students have completed that step, they can now use their knowledge of solving two equations in two unknowns to find the solution. These problems may seem overwhelming to students, but they are less intimidated if they are shown that this method is closely related to what they know. Finally, they must check their result in all three equations. I often give points on a test for showing the check.

Sharon Testone,
Onondaga Community College

Section 3.7

Graphing inequalities with different color shadings for each line graphed is important. Spend time on this!

Nancy Ressler,
Oakton Community College

◆ ◆ ◆

When graphing linear inequalities, the test point becomes crucial to the correct shading of the graph. I normally encourage students to use (0, 0) unless it is on or very near the graphed line. Sometimes we do not use a straight edge to form our line so it might be slightly off from where it actually should be. For this reason, we might accidentally think that our line does not go through the origin when it actually does. So, if it is near, stay clear, and pick some other easy test point, such as (1, 1). Students shouldn't pick a complicated test point with fractions, negatives, or such, when a nice whole number will suffice. If the selected test point is true in the original inequality, the test point side of the line should be shaded. If it is false, the opposite side of the line should be shaded.

Tomesa Smith,
Wallace State Community College

◆ ◆ ◆

After covering systems of linear inequalities, if there is time, introduce several simple linear programming problems so that students recognize that there is a practical use for all this shading-on-shading they have done.

Rebecca Wyatt-Semple,
Nash Community College

Section 3.8

Break-even points and points of equilibrium in Section 3.8 give students real life applications for systems of equations. If any students have had these concepts in other courses such as business or economics, you may want to let them explain how the presentations in their other courses differ from the presentation in this text.

Rebecca Wyatt-Semple,
Nash Community College

Polynomials and Polynomial Functions

SECTION TITLES AND OBJECTIVES

4.1 Introduction to Polynomials and Polynomial Functions

Identify the degree of each term and the degree of a polynomial; identify terms, coefficients, monomials, binomials, and trinomials; arrange polynomials in ascending or descending order; and identify the leading term, the leading coefficient, and the constant term ● Evaluate a polynomial function for given inputs ● Collect like terms in a polynomial and add polynomials ● Find the opposite of a polynomial and subtract polynomials

4.2 Multiplication of Polynomials

Multiply any two polynomials ● Use the FOIL method to multiply two binomials ● Use a rule to square a binomial ● Use a rule to multiply a sum and a difference of the same two terms ● For functions f described by second-degree polynomials, find and simplify notation like $f(a + h)$ and $f(a + h) - f(a)$

4.3 Introduction to Factoring

Factor polynomials whose terms have a common factor ● Factor certain polynomials with four terms by grouping

4.4 Factoring Trinomials: $x^2 + bx + c$

Factor trinomials of the type $x^2 + bx + c$

4.5 Factoring Trinomials: $ax^2 + bx + c, a \neq 1$

Factor trinomials of the type $ax^2 + bx + c, a \neq 1$, by the FOIL method ● Factor trinomials of the type $ax^2 + bx + c, a \neq 1$, by the ac-method

4.6 Special Factoring

Factor trinomial squares ● Factor differences of squares ● Factor certain polynomials with four terms by grouping and possibly using the factoring of a trinomial square or the difference of squares ● Factor sums and differences of cubes

4.7 Factoring: A General Strategy

Factor polynomials completely using any of the methods considered in this chapter

4.8 Applications of Polynomial Equations and Functions

Solve quadratic and other polynomial equations by first factoring and then using the principle of zero products ● Solve applied problems involving quadratic and other polynomial equations that can be solved by factoring

TEACHING TIPS

Sections 4.3–4.7 Factoring Techniques. Emphasize the name given to each type of factoring explored. As you introduce a new type of factoring, include a few of the previously discussed types in the assignments that follow. Continually ask your students to name the factoring technique that should be used for a particular problem. Stress patterns. Help your students recognize the similarities and differences in special factoring patterns.

Sandy Berry,
Hinds Community College

◆ ◆ ◆

Use the following form of pattern recognition followed by various examples using this format:

$$(a + b)^2 = a^2 + 2ab + b^2$$
$$\Rightarrow \left(1^{st} + 2^{nd}\right) = \left(1^{st}\right)^2 + 2\left(1^{st}\right)\left(2^{nd}\right) + \left(2^{nd}\right)$$

Michael Montaño,
Riverside Community College

◆ ◆ ◆

Encourage students to use the Study Tip on page 363. It applies to instructors as well as to students. Taking many small steps gets us where we need to be.

Factoring is fundamental! Don't skimp here. We learn to factor polynomials by factoring polynomials. There is no other way. Assign problems requiring all the factor patterns introduced in this chapter. Have the students prepare a 3" × 5" card with the patterns and an example of each. As they work through this chapter, they can move it along as a bookmark. Having all the patterns on one card helps with memorizing. Whether or not the card will be allowed on tests will be left to the instructor.

Rebecca Wyatt-Semple,
Nash Community College

Section 4.1

Emphasize the importance of removing parenthesis. Removing the parenthesis with a "+" sign has no effect on the signs of the terms. However, "−" sign before the parenthesis changes "all" terms to the opposite signs.

Regarding calculator usage, create some fairly complex polynomial functions and have the students input the functions using the function mode. Choose several positive and negative x values to evaluate the functions.

Chris Bendixen,
Lake Michigan College

◆ ◆ ◆

This section does not require a lot of time. Teach the vocabulary and then point out that the addition and subtraction follows the same rules as in Chapter R (the rules never change!)—combine like terms by adding their **coefficients** only. The exponents do not change when adding and subtracting like terms.

Susan Leland,
Montana Tech

◆ ◆ ◆

Stress that $(a \pm b)^2 \neq a^2 \pm b^2$. In other words, do not distribute exponents.

Michael Montaño,
Riverside Community College

Section 4.2

Reintroduce the distributive property. Begin with a monomial times a monomial. Refresh the students on the properties of exponents. Next, multiply a binomial by a binomial. Generally, the students will not remember the distributive property method for this product. I suggest that you do these problems by FOILing. Try to have the students recognize the resulting middle term.

Introduce special products: perfect squares, difference of squares, and cubes. Generally the students do not appreciate the shortcut formula for these special products. However, the special products for cubes may be necessary for the students to remember. I break these down into pieces. That is: the formula for $(x - y)^3 = x^3 - 3x^2y + 3xy^2 - y^3$, I have the student determine each of the four pieces of the product, then put the result together.

Chris Bendixen,
Lake Michigan College

◆ ◆ ◆

Stress to your students that with addition and subtraction of polynomials only the coefficients change, but with multiplication, the variable part may also change. Immediately reinforce this idea with some quick examples:

$$(2x - 3)(5x + 1)$$
$$= 10x^2 + 2x - 15x - 3$$
$$= 10x^2 - 13x - 3$$

Unfortunately students tend to get the addition/subtraction rules confused. Often I will write the following example on the board and ask them to tell me what is wrong with it.

$$(2x - 3)(5x + 1)$$
$$= 10x^2 + 2x - 15x - 3$$
$$= 10x^2 - 13x - 3$$
$$= -3x^4 - 3$$

Deanna L. Dick,
Alvin Community College

◆ ◆ ◆

When presenting Section 4.2 in class I define the sum and difference of the same two terms as "conjugates." We have found that is a good way to first introduce the terminology that students will need in order to rationalize denominators of radical expressions and to divide complex numbers.

Rosa Kavanaugh,
Ozarks Technical College

◆ ◆ ◆

Do NOT spend too much time on multiplication and beginning factoring as this is review.

Nancy Ressler,
Oakton Community College

Section 4.3

For this section, the most important topic is factoring by grouping. This concept is the basis for the grouping number (ac) method of factoring trinomials.

Chris Bendixen,
Lake Michigan College

◆ ◆ ◆

The problems in this section are like the answers in Section 4.2. The answers are like the multiplication problems in Section 4.2. Students are just "undoing" a multiplication problem that someone already did.

Emphasize that an instruction to "Factor" means the answer must be a multiplication problem. A good way for students to recognize that they have a multiplication problem and not an addition or subtraction problem is that all plus and minus signs must be inside parentheses. This is a crucial point in Chapter 5-prepare your class well.

Susan Leland,
Montana Tech

◆ ◆ ◆

To avoid potential sign trouble when using grouping as a factoring technique, I have a little hint that I describe. After the first two terms have been factored by finding a common factor, I check the last sign in the original polynomial against the sign that has just been written down in parentheses. If the two signs agree, factor out a positive factor from the next two terms. If the two checked terms disagree, factor out a negative from the next two terms.

Tomesa Smith,
Wallace State Community College

Section 4.4

Students catch on to this factoring section so quickly that they sometimes stop thinking about watching their signs and checking their answers. After the class starts giving quick correct answers several times in a row, give them the problem (or one similar) to the following: $x^2 + 7x - 12$. Most of your students will give you the answer: $(x + 4)(x + 3)$.

If you wait a minute or two, quickly the students will start to check their answer. Once they see it is prime, and that they almost gave an incorrect answer, they will start checking again. This is a great way to teach them to slow down and to emphasize the benefits of checking their answers.

Deanna L. Dick,
Alvin Community College

Section 4.5

I find that the foiling method (guess method) is confusing for the students. The alternative method (*ac*-method) is much more structured. I do not cover the FOIL method any more. It is key that the students first factor out the GCF from the trinomial. Then apply the *ac*-method i.e., two numbers that multiply to the *ac* (I call this the grouping number, *gn*), and add up to the *b* term. Then rewrite the *bx* term as the sum of the other factors. Finally, factor by grouping.

This works for special products (perfect squares, difference of squares). For difference of squares, the *bx* term is 0.

Chris Bendixen,
Lake Michigan College

◆   ◆   ◆

The *ac*-method of factoring trinomials takes all the guesswork out of factoring. Many students prefer this method—it's the one I teach. However, students who have had algebra before, usually have used the FOIL method. If they do this well, let them continue to use it.

Susan Leland,
Montana Tech

◆   ◆   ◆

The first five sections of this chapter contain material that the students should know, but have most likely forgotten. A review may be all that is needed here, with major emphasis placed on later sections, so as not to spend too much time on these sections and, therefore, be unable to complete the course.

Sharon Testone,
Onondaga Community College

◆   ◆   ◆

In Section 4.5, stress that the greatest common factor must be factored out first. Then when looking for the correct combination to produce the middle term, do not waste time trying binomials that have common factors. The author stresses this in Example 2, but this is the one part students fail to consider. It greatly reduces the time to arrive at the correct factorization.

Roy West,
Robeson Community College

Section 4.6

I like to give drills for this section. First, the students need to recognize perfect square-terms. I will write on the board the first and the last term of a perfect square and ask the students to tell me the middle term. Double the square roots of the first and the last.

Chris Bendixen,
Lake Michigan College

◆   ◆   ◆

Make your students memorize the special products before you start factoring. If you drill the special products into their heads, they will recognize those problems when you start factoring. I have students that often factor $4x^2 - 25$ before I finish writing it down!

Deanna L. Dick,
Alvin Community College

◆ ◆ ◆

SUMS and DIFFERENCES of Cubes are new for most and will require quality time. Other factoring is *review*; therefore, be time-efficient!

Nancy Ressler,
Oakton Community College

◆ ◆ ◆

The only new topic in this section is factoring the sum or differences of cubes. It is important to compare this factoring with the difference of squares and to remind students that they may not be able to factor the sum of squares.

On page 375 the author gives the formulas for factoring sums or differences of cubes. My students have been unable to learn and retain these formulas. Instead of asking the students to learn them, I use the method shown in Example 17 on page 375 with a few more hints added for the students: The sign found in the binomial term always matches the original problem. The sign of the second term of the trinomial is always opposite of the sign found in the original problem. The last term of the trinomial is always positive. Finally, I encourage students to multiply the binomial times the trinomial as a check.

Sharon Testone,
Onondaga Community College

◆ ◆ ◆

Discuss the advantages and disadvantages of both the "FOIL method" and the "*ac*-method" of factoring. When *a*, *b*, and *c* are small, both methods work fine. But as *a*, *b*, and *c* get larger, the "*ac*-method" becomes more difficult.

Roy West,
Robeson Community College

Section 4.7

I rearrange the factoring sections in this chapter to present the topics in the order that they are given in the Strategy For Factoring on page 383. I identify this factoring process by the numbers:

- Number 1 is "Always, always, always remove common factors first."

- Number 2 is for 2 terms: "First look for difference of two squares; if none, then look for a sum or difference of cubes."

- Number 3 is for 3 terms: "Look for a trinomial square; if none, trial and error."

- Number 4 is for 4 terms: "Try factoring by grouping."

- Number 5 is "Last, look to see whether any of the factors can be factored again."

I do not mention the check in this process because I would consider it optional.

This process differs from that of an introductory algebra course by the inclusion of factorization of sums and differences of cubes. This topic provides an opportunity to discuss the question, "How do you distinguish between a square and a cube?" The table of numerical cubes on page 375 is a good beginning for the discussion. Then we consider powers of variables such as x^8, y^9 and z^6. This is a good opportunity to revisit the exponent rule for raising a power to a power. I attempt to lead the class to the conclusion that the exponent of a square is an even number while the exponent of a cube is a multiple of three. This does take a little extra class time, but I believe that it lays an important foundation for the work that will be done in finding roots in Chapter 6. This discussion and the above strategy also provide students with the direction to completely factor Example 20 on page 376. Because both exponents are both even numbers and multiples of three, the expression is both a difference of squares and a difference of cubes. A student could question which approach to follow if the author's strategy did not clearly state, "Try factoring as a difference of squares first."

Rosa Kavanaugh,
Ozarks Technical College

◆ ◆ ◆

This section is essential. Students need to be able to look at a polynomial and determine which factoring approach to use because they will need this skill while working with both rational and radical expressions in the next two chapters. The strategy given on page 383 is excellent. Students should use that strategy as their guide when completing this section.

Sharon Testone,
Onondaga Community College

Section 4.8

Finding the domain of a particular function is a topic of continual importance throughout mathematics. Example 7 on page 391 and the companion exercises are very important. Stress the fact that the excluded values are being eliminated to avoid the existence of zero in the denominator because zero in the denominator would cause the expression to be undefined.

Sandy Berry,
Hinds Community College

◆ ◆ ◆

Stress the fact that you must get zero on one side of the equation **before** you factor, and that each quadratic equation has two possible answers. Two problems I always include when teaching are:

a) $5x^2 = 10x$
b) $x(x - 2) = 3$

On the first one, they always divide both sides by $5x$ and end up with only one answer, which is a big problem—there should be TWO!

With the second problem, they try to set each factor equal to 3. I often let them work it, but let them know when they give me the wrong answer. After these two problems, they quickly start following the steps I write on the board. When asked what to do first they even answer (often as a class), "Get zero on one side of the equation."

Deanna L. Dick,
Alvin Community College

◆ ◆ ◆

When the student learns to solve quadratic equations by factoring there is often a tendency to confuse "factor" with "solve." Some students solve the equation by factoring the trinomial but not setting it equal to zero. Then they cannot proceed to the solutions. Other students instead attempt to "solve" an algebraic expression by setting it equal to zero. Some such errors may be avoided by contrasting the problems "Solve $x^2 - 3x - 4 = 0$" and "Factor $x^2 - 3x - 4$." This is a good opportunity to reinforce the distinction between solving an equation and factoring an expression. In general, if we can identify common errors and address the misconceptions, we can help our students to be more successful.

Be sure to include an example in which the leading coefficient is not one. It is important for students to be confident in dealing with a constant such as the 3 in $3(x - 4)(2x - 1) = 0$. Some feel that they should set the 3 equal to zero. Others who divide the equation by 3, either before or after factoring, usually can't explain why in the equation $x^2 = 7x$ they should not divide by x. This provides an opportunity to remind students that they can divide both sides of an equation by any nonzero number. But of course, the variable x does not qualify since it could be equal to zero.

Rosa Kavanaugh,
Ozarks Technical College

◆ ◆ ◆

Emphasize that factoring is a tool we use to solve problems. Solving polynomial equations by factoring and using the Principle of Zero Products is a clear use of the tool of factoring. Assign a good number of applied problems from Section 4.8, and review the concept of functions, domain, and range. The graphing calculator is useful in this section.

Rebecca Wyatt-Semple,
Nash Community College

Rational Expressions, Equations, and Functions

TEACHING TIPS

Read Study Tips with and/or to your students. The majority of the students never look at this feature. The Time Management study tip (page 468) is especially helpful.

Michael Montaño,
Riverside Community College

◆ ◆ ◆

For my intermediate algebra students, this chapter represents totally new material. I try to relate this chapter to what we know about fractions in general and then incorporate polynomials into the problems.

Sharon Testone,
Onondaga Community College

◆ ◆ ◆

Explain to students why the numerator and denominator are usually left in a factored form even though the instructions say to simplify. In early chapters this would have implied to carry out the multiplication. (Note: The expression is more useful to us in its factored form when solving equations.)

Roy West,
Robeson Community College

◆ ◆ ◆

This chapter usually requires extra time. Traditionally this entire chapter is naturally difficult for students who have not committed the factor patterns to memory, but have lived in hope that factoring would go away.

Introduce *rational expressions* as old friends also known as *fractions*. All the things we learned in fifth and sixth grade about fractions are true of these expressions. The operations performed on rational expressions are familiar ones: simplifying, multiplying, dividing, adding, and subtracting. The only thing different is that we must remember that division by zero is undefined. We have to keep an eye on the denominators and restrict the variables so that denominators cannot be equal to zero. Review why division by zero is undefined. Then ask students what should we know about x in expressions such as

$$\frac{(3x - 4)}{x + 6}?$$

Rebecca Wyatt-Semple,
Nash Community College

Section 5.1

Students have a tendency to forget what has been taught to them in the past. It is essential to remind them how to multiply, divide, add and subtract fractions. Next apply this to simple expressions that have an obvious like factor that can be canceled. Then build on this concept. A major problem that I have with some students is: they want to have a LCD when multiplying and dividing.

For rational expressions you need to remind the students that functions are not defined when the denominator of the rational expression is zero. Thus, the domain of the function is going to be all the other values of x.

Chris Bendixen,
Lake Michigan College

◆ ◆ ◆

When working with rational expressions, I usually start with a numerical problem and work my way quickly up to an algebraic expression. Consider the fraction $\frac{12}{16}$. I review what they learned in fourth grade (i.e. $\frac{12}{16} = \frac{4 \cdot 3}{4 \cdot 4} = \frac{3}{4}$. I stress the fact that the numerator and denominator both need to be factored **before** simplifying the fraction. Also, I point out that we can't cancel the terms, and therefore when faced with a problem like $\frac{x + 4}{x - 5}$ I tell them "I don't want to see **anyone** give me the answer $-\frac{4}{5}$! Remember x is a term and we can only cancel factors." The more you review that idea, the better off your students will be, although you will still see a lot of inappropriately canceled terms!

Deanna L. Dick,
Alvin Community College

◆ ◆ ◆

The author addresses the concept of canceling on page 416. I tell students, "Cancel means divide by common factors." I have found that if I continue to repeat this simple definition throughout the course, it helps to explain the common errors of "illegal canceling" of rational expressions in Chapter 5. Some students are confused by similarities in the terminology "cross-canceling," "multiplying straight across," and "cross multiplying." This chapter is a good time to clarify the terminology and make the following distinctions:

- "multiplying straight across" is the way that some people describe multiplication of fractions, that is multiplying the numerators and multiplying the denominators.

- "cross canceling" is sometimes used to describe the process of simplification by "removing factors of one." It is important to distinguish that this can be done whenever the same factor appears in the numerator **and** denominator of a fraction (or product of fractions.)

- "cross multiplying" is one way to describe the fact that when one fraction is **equal** to another fraction there is a relationship between the products of the numerator of each and the denominator of the other. A much better way to describe this is by using the term "cross products," as Dr. Bittinger does. But a number of students use the less precise terminology and need help with clarification.

Students have difficulty seeing the difference between dealing with opposites when they simplify a fraction (removing a factor of 1) and finding a common denominator involving opposites. The author addresses this in the explanation preceding Example 13 in Section 5.1. I sometimes generalize it as: "Whenever you have **opposites as factors in the numerator and denominator of the same fraction,** you can replace that combination by a factor of negative one." Then if a pair of **opposites is in the denominators of different fractions being added or subtracted,** the common denominator will contain only one of the pair. The other of the pair can be converted to the first by multiplying that fraction by

$$\frac{(-1)}{(-1)}.$$

Fractions intimidate so many students. It is difficult but important to convince them that an **equation with fractions** is actually easier to deal with than an **expression with fractions.** They need to be convinced that the first step in solving an equation with fractions is to clear the fractions. If they have mastered this in Chapter 1, then they will find the rational equations in Chapter 5 much less difficult. After students learn to clear fractions when solving fractional equations, they sometimes also try to clear fractions when simplifying rational expressions. The author's table "Are You Calculating or Solving?" on page 457 is a valuable reference on this topic. Another form of the question might be, "Will you keep fractions or clear fractions?"

Rosa Kavanaugh,
Ozarks Technical College

◆ ◆ ◆

Teach your class the mantra "Factor, then cancel," or "If you can't factor, you can't cancel." One of the biggest mistakes math students make is to cancel terms instead of factors. See the caution on page 416. You will fight this mistake constantly.

Susan Leland,
Montana Tech

◆ ◆ ◆

In Section 5.1 remember to explain why we need to consider only factors of the denominator in determining where a rational expression is not defined.

Roy West,
Robeson Community College

◆ ◆ ◆

Warn students about the error in simplifying shown in the Caution box on page 416. Make up a silly penalty that students must pay each time they simplify incorrectly and hold them to paying the penalty. It will make a positive, lasting impression.

Rebecca Wyatt-Semple,
Nash Community College

Section 5.2

The major problem that I have had with this section is for expressions like: $\frac{3}{x} + \frac{5}{x-1}$, some of the students simply say that the LCD is $x - 1$. They will then subtract "1" from the "3" and from the x to get $\frac{7}{x-1}$.

When subtracting rational expressions students have a tendency to forget to distribute the "$-$" sign through the parenthesis.

If the denominators differ by a factor of -1, then choose to multiply the first expression by $\frac{-1}{-1}$ when subtracting. This causes less confusion. Not as many negative signs to worry about in this type of problem.

Chris Bendixen,
Lake Michigan College

◆ ◆ ◆

Work more subtraction problems than addition. Students always have trouble remembering to distribute the sign, especially with rational expressions. Teaching them to use parenthesis in the numerator while combining fractions can help your students remember.

$$\frac{4}{x - 1} - \frac{3}{x + 2}$$

$$= \frac{(4x + 8) - (3x - 3)}{(x - 1)(x + 2)}$$

$$= \frac{4x + 8 - 3x - 3}{(x - 1)(x + 2)}$$

$$= \frac{x + 11}{(x - 1)(x + 2)}$$

Another problem that my students have is they try to simplify the fractions right after they get a common denominator. Something that can help them stop this is to let them work a problem on their own. Walk around and look at what they get. Then ask them how many ended up with the original problem they started with. After that, they are more likely to make a note to themselves that with addition/subtraction of rational expressions you simplify at the end of the problem (just the opposite of multiplication).

Deanna L. Dick,
Alvin Community College

◆ ◆ ◆

Splitting this section into at least three days of instruction seems to help students.

- Day 1 Just find LCDs, lots and lots of them.

- Day 2 Do very simple addition and subtraction problems, using and pointing out the same steps every time.

- Day 3 Attack the more complicated (don't call them harder!) problems, using and pointing out the same steps as used the day before.

Emphasize Step 3 on page 428—students forget to multiply out the numerators and combine like terms and they get lost at that step. Point out that they should not cancel until they have done everything they possibly can to the numerator.

Susan Leland,
Montana Tech

◆ ◆ ◆

When adding rational expressions and finding LCDs, I use a technique called the "cover-up" routine. In it, students find an LCD in factored form and then must convert each rational expression to a new one utilizing the LCD. To aid in this conversion, students can "cover up" the factors in the LCD that already exist in the rational expression and what's left uncovered gets multiplied by the old numerator and becomes the new numerator. This "cover-up" method works with addition and subtraction as long as an LCD is needed or the denominators are different.

Tomesa Smith,
Wallace State Community College

◆ ◆ ◆

The students have trouble subtracting rational expressions because they do not distribute the negative sign appropriately. They especially have trouble if one denominator is the opposite of the other. Example:

$$\frac{5}{x} - \frac{6}{-x}.$$

There are many ways to approach this problem, but often it helps to demonstrate that $\frac{-1}{2} = \frac{1}{-2} = -\frac{1}{2}$, and then the students can just bring the negative sign to the fraction bar.

$$\frac{5}{x} - -\frac{6}{x} = \frac{5}{x} + \frac{6}{x} = \frac{11}{x}$$

Sharon Testone,
Onondaga Community College

◆ ◆ ◆

In Section 5.2 work some numerical examples of addition and subtraction to remind students how to add and subtract rational expressions. Keep one example in one corner of the board to refer back to when students ask, "What do I do next?"

Roy West,
Robeson Community College

Section 5.3

When dividing a polynomial by a monomial (where one of the terms of the polynomial is the same as the monomial), a common tendency is that the students forget to include the "1" in the quotient. They simply omit it.

When dividing a polynomial with missing terms by a binomial, remind the student that all terms have to be represented. I tell them to put 0's for the missing terms. This is like place markers (or dummy variables).

Chris Bendixen,
Lake Michigan College

◆ ◆ ◆

This topic is new for most students. Introduce polynomial division by comparing it to the division algorithm in arithmetic (non-Americans may not be familiar with it, since they utilize a different yet similar approach for division).

Nancy Ressler,
Oakton Community College

◆ ◆ ◆

After dividing the first term of the divisor into its dividend and placing its quotient above the long division bar, the quotient is multiplied back by the divisor. Following this process, I use this expression: "Draw a line and change the signs of everything above the line." The changed signs are circled to serve as reminders to use the changed signs in an addition process. This way, students do not have to remember to keep up with mental subtraction—by distributing the negative and adding the terms, the subtraction part is bypassed.

Tomesa Smith,
Wallace State Community College

◆ ◆ ◆

Long division of polynomials may cause problems because some students have never been required to use long division with numbers. Calculators introduced too soon in elementary school cause many problems later. Now is later. If students are not familiar with the division algorithm, they'll be lost in Section 5.3.

Rebecca Wyatt-Semple,
Nash Community College

Section 5.4

I introduce complex rational expressions as "fractions within fractions" and show several numerical examples before the algebraic examples.

We review division of a single fraction by a single fraction

$$\frac{\dfrac{2}{3}}{\dfrac{5}{7}}$$

Then I present a problem that many of them may have never considered:

$$\frac{\dfrac{1}{2} + \dfrac{1}{3}}{1 + \dfrac{1}{4}}$$

I demonstrate the author's Method 2 then Method 1 for simplifying this complex numerical fraction. Students usually express a preference for Method 2, but I do allow the option of using either method. Words to the wise regarding common points of confusion and sources of error:

- If both the numerator and denominator of the complex expression have only one term, Method 2 will usually be less involved.

- In Method 2, the LCDs of the numerator and denominator are found separately and need not be the same

- In Method 1, the numerator and denominator must both be multiplied by the LCM of all secondary denominators in the expression.

- The author clearly shows distribution of the LCM onto each term. Some students attempt to do this step mentally and perform some incorrect cancellation in the process.

Rosa Kavanaugh,
Ozarks Technical College

◆ ◆ ◆

With complex fractions, I think that Method 2 in the text works the best (page 446). You are just using concepts that they know. You are combining the fractions in the numerator and fractions in the denominator. Finally, you are multiplying the numerator by the reciprocal of the denominator. Students have trouble clearing fractions as required in Method 1.

Sharon Testone,
Onondaga Community College

Section 5.5

Give them an example of a rational equation that has no solution (i.e. results in a zero in the denominator). In fact, after that problem I have them start writing next to each problem the numbers that result in a zero in the denominators (the possible extraneous solutions that would have to be thrown out). Although the "no solution" problems still catch them, not as many are being caught!

Deanna L. Dick,
Alvin Community College

◆ ◆ ◆

When finished with this section, show the difference between rational equations and adding/subtracting rational expressions. Start an equation, then an addition problem, an equation, then an addition problem, etc., until they can tell you the correct procedure each time. Students forget that they can get rid of the denominators right away in rational equations, but cannot do so in addition or subtraction problems. This is a major stumbling block.

Susan Leland,
Montana Tech

◆ ◆ ◆

Recognition of the type of problem is essential. We have a running dialogue in class regarding Rational Equations:

Professor: "What type of equation do we have?" **Class:** "Rational Equation."

Professor: "What do we do with Rational Equations?" **Class:** "We clear the fractions."

Professor: "How do we clear the fractions?" **Class:** "We multiply each term on both sides of the equation by the LCD."

In this manner we learn the rules and involve the class.

Michael Montaño,
Riverside Community College

Section 5.6

I have students remember the way to set up work problems by describing them as "one over the first thing's time plus one over the second thing's time, etc., equals one over the total time." This description makes the set-up of these types of problems easier to remember.

Tomesa Smith,
Wallace State Community College

◆ ◆ ◆

Proportions are a terrific problem-solving tool in so many areas. In Section 5.6, be certain that students practice recognition of situations in which proportions would be the solution method of choice. However, only direct proportions are covered in this text. You may want to give examples of inverse proportions and how to recognize the type of proportion required by the wording of problems. When students reach the section on variation (5.8), they will have had an introduction to the concept of "inverse."

Rebecca Wyatt-Semple,
Nash Community College

Section 5.7

The skills taught in this section have significance in many diverse fields of study. Students need to be able to manipulate formulas applicable to different disciplines, from physics to business. One technique for isolating a particular variable in a formula is to write the variable intended for isolation in red and then circling that variable in red as well. The other letters in the formula should be considered as ordinary numbers and the circled red letter as the only "variable" in the formula. This helps students focus their attention on that particular "variable" in considering 1) where is the "variable?" 2) what has been done to the "variable?" and 3) how would you undo what has been done to the "variable?" Colored chalk or colored markers make the presentation of this technique more effective.

Sandy Berry,
Hinds Community College

◆ ◆ ◆

Some students tend to believe that they have solved for P in the equation

$$P = A - Prt$$

I explain that the formula should give a definition for P. When we define a word in English, we do not use the word in its own definition. For example, in a biology class, a student could not use the word "photosynthesis" in a definition of "photosynthesis." Thus we cannot use the symbol P in the definition of P.

Rosa Kavanaugh,
Ozarks Technical College

Section 5.8

I love the variation section! A great way to get them to understand the equations and relationships given for direct, inverse, and joint variation is to talk about weight! For direct variation I ask them what they could increase or decrease that would have the same effect on their weight. They **all** come up with food. Then I focus on why some people can eat the same amounts and gain different amounts of weight. You might even bring in some nutrition labels off of various foods. When asked to explain that they answer, metabolism! That makes it easy to introduce the proportionality constant k. The equation $w = kd$ follows naturally.

Then I can introduce inverse variation by asking what we would increase/decrease in our life to decrease/increase our weight respectively. Again, they all come up with exercise. Now we can write the equation $w = \frac{k}{e}$. For joint variation I remind them that any plan for weight control should involve both diet and exercise. This gives a joint variation equation of $w = \frac{kd}{e}$.

Deanna L. Dick,
Alvin Community College

◆ ◆ ◆

This topic is very important because, nationally, students are weak in proportional thinking.

Nancy Ressler,
Oakton Community College

Radical Expressions, Equations, and Functions

SECTION TITLES AND OBJECTIVES

6.1   Radical Expressions and Functions

Find principal square roots and their opposites, approximate square roots, find outputs of square-root functions, graph square-root functions, and find the domains of square-root functions ● Simplify radical expressions with perfect-square radicands ● Find cube roots, simplifying certain expressions, and find outputs of cube-root functions ● Simplify expressions involving odd and even roots

6.2   Rational Numbers as Exponents

Write expressions with or without rational exponents, and simplify, if possible ● Write expressions without negative exponents, and simplify, if possible ● Use the laws of exponents with rational exponents ● Use rational exponents to simplify radical expressions

6.3   Simplifying Radical Expressions

Multiply and simplify radical expressions ● Divide and simplify radical expressions

6.4   Addition, Subtraction, and More Multiplication

Add or subtract with radical notation and simplify ● Multiply expressions involving radicals in which some factors contain more than one term

6.5   More on Division of Radical Expressions

Rationalize the denominator of a radical expression having one term in the denominator ● Rationalize the denominator of a radical expressions having two terms in the denominator

6.6   Solving Radical Equations

Solve radical equations with one radical term ● Solve radical equations with two radical terms ● Solve applied problems involving radical equations

6.7   Applications Involving Powers and Roots

Solve applied problems involving the Pythagorean theorem and powers and roots

6.8   The Complex Numbers

Express imaginary numbers as bi, where b is a nonzero real number, and complex numbers as $a + bi$, where a and b are real numbers ● Add and subtract complex numbers ● Multiply complex numbers ● Write expressions involving powers of i in the form $a + bi$ ● Find conjugates of complex numbers and divide complex numbers ● Determine whether a given complex number is a solution of an equation

TEACHING TIPS

Section 6.1

Review all the perfect squares, perfect cubes, and perfect fourth powers.

Remind the student that radicals, of even index powers, are only defined when the radical expressions are greater than or equal to zero. For odd index powers, the radicals are defined for all real numbers.

If evaluating radical functions, first find the domain of the function.

Chris Bendixen,
Lake Michigan College

◆ ◆ ◆

I believe that students connect more meaning with radicals if they are encouraged to do some decimal approximations before they consult their calculators. When asking for an approximation of $\sqrt{38}$, students to approximate **before** they perform the operations on their calculators. With a little direction, they usually predict an answer between 6.1 and 6.3. This helps them to develop some number sense.

Students tend to make some common careless errors in writing radicals. They sometimes forget to write the index of the radical. I emphasize that if the index does not appear, it is understood to be two. I encourage them from the beginning to develop the habit of considering the index whenever they write a radical. Another common careless error is shortening the overbar so that $\sqrt{5xy}$ appears as $\sqrt{5}xy$. Students need to be warned that the overbar must extend fully over any quantity that is to be considered as part of the radicand.

Rosa Kavanaugh,
Ozarks Technical College

◆ ◆ ◆

Stress that when x/y is used as an exponent, the denominator y is the index of the radical while the numerator x is the power to which the base is raised.

Michael Montaño,
Riverside Community College

Section 6.2

Make the students convert any expression raised to a negative power immediately to avoid sign errors.

Example: $5^{-3} = \dfrac{1}{5^3} = \dfrac{1}{125}$ not $5^{-3} = -125$.

Repeat over and over that the negative exponent means that number is in the denominator and that it has nothing to do with the sign of the number. For some reason they really fight this idea.

Deanna L. Dick,
Alvin Community College

◆ ◆ ◆

Before attempting to work with rational exponents, you must review the rules for integer exponents. These laws are listed on page 510 of the text. For each of the 5 rules, show an example with integer exponents and then an example with rational exponents. This method should help students apply what they know to another situation.

Sharon Testone,
Onondaga Community College

Section 6.3

It is important when simplifying radicals to separate the perfect powers. For example: simplify $\sqrt{96x^3y^5}$ the perfect squares are $16x^2y^4$, isolate these under the radical, then the other part of the radical is the left overs. Rewrite as: $\sqrt{16x^2y^4 \cdot 6xy}$, the $6xy$ are the left overs, they will stay under the radical.

Chris Bendixen,
Lake Michigan College

◆ ◆ ◆

Have students make, or give them, a list of perfect squares and cubes. The list should go from 0^2 to 15^2 and 0^3 to 10^3. You might even get daring and try to get them to learn 0^4 to 5^4. If you have them learn the list they will have a much easier time simplifying radicals. It is surprising how few students know the perfect square and cube roots! Memorization is **not** a sinful educational habit!

Deanna L. Dick,
Alvin Community College

◆ ◆ ◆

The author simplifies radicals by factoring. One of my students "discovered" an algorithm for this simplification, and a number of others have preferred it when I present it as an option.

To simplify Example 12 on page 517

- Write the factored form of the radicand in exponential form

$$\sqrt[3]{16a^7b^{11}} = \sqrt[3]{2^4a^7b^{11}}$$

- Perform a long division of each exponent by the index 3

$$3\overline{)4} \quad R1 \qquad 3\overline{)4}^{\,2} \quad R2 \qquad 3\overline{)4}^{\,3} \quad R3$$

- In each case the dividend is the power of the base multiplied by the simplified radical and the remainder is the power of the base in the simplified radicand

$$2^1a^2b^3 \qquad \sqrt[3]{2^1a^1b^2} = 2a^2b^3 \quad \sqrt[3]{2ab^2}$$

This provides an opportunity to review expressing radicals using rational exponents and the laws of exponents.

Rosa Kavanaugh,
Ozarks Technical College

◆ ◆ ◆

Review a list of perfect squares and cubes before doing Section 6.3. Students need to be able to recognize them quickly as factors in the radicand.

Roy West,
Robeson Community College

Section 6.4

Remind students that radicals may not appear as like terms until they are simplified. Once simplified, they can quickly be added or subtracted. A great example is something like $\sqrt{45} - \sqrt{20}$. Often students will say it won't give $\sqrt{25} = 5$ as their answer. It is a nice neat solution, but it's wrong. They did **not** combine like terms. Instead we need to emphasize always **simplify the radicals first**. Then we'll get $3\sqrt{5} - 2\sqrt{5} = \sqrt{5}$.

Deanna L. Dick,
Alvin Community College

◆ ◆ ◆

In Sections 6.3 and 6.4, my students have found the following rules helpful:

- The only rule for adding and subtracting in all of algebra is "combine like terms." The author's definition of "like radical terms" on page 524 addresses this well and merits emphasis.

- When multiplying and dividing, the factors outside the radical stay outside and the factors inside the radical stay inside (except, of course, in the simplification process.) This seems to help students with the distribution in multiplying radical expressions and also answer most questions about division such as why in the form

$$\frac{\sqrt{96}}{2\sqrt{3}}$$

the 96 can be divided by 3 but not by 2 and after simplification to

$$\frac{\sqrt{32}}{2}$$

the 32 cannot be divided by 2 but simplified to

$$\frac{4\sqrt{2}}{2}$$

in which the 4 can be divided by the 2 in the denominator.

Rosa Kavanaugh,
Ozarks Technical College

Section 6.5

Students always have problems rationalizing denominators. They have difficulty distinguishing between the following types of problems.

Example: Rationalize $\dfrac{3}{\sqrt{x} + 5}$ vs. Rationalize $\dfrac{3}{\sqrt{x + 5}}$

I try to distinguish between the two by saying the operation sign is "trapped" and has to remain or it is "free" and it has to change.

Sharon Testone,
Onondaga Community College

Section 6.6

When working out solutions, remember the rule from earlier, check your answers. Answers may be extraneous. Mathematically, you can do the problem correctly, but in the end, check the answer.

Chris Bendixen,
Lake Michigan College

◆ ◆ ◆

In solving equations, it is often desirable to simplify by dividing each term on both sides of the equation by some number. However, dividing both sides of an equation by an expression containing a variable might cause one to lose a solution. In a situation such as

$$x + 1 = 2\sqrt{x + 1}$$
$$(x + 1)^2 = \left(2\sqrt{x + 1}\right)^2$$
$$(x + 1)(x + 1) = 4(x + 1)$$

students are tempted to divide both sides of the equation by the common factor $x + 1$ which causes the loss of the solution $x = -1$.

Similarly, multiplying both sides of an equation by an expression containing a variable or raising both sides of an equation to some power other than 1, can introduce extraneous roots. Consequently, checking each potential root in the original equation is imperative.

Sandy Berry,
Hinds Community College

◆ ◆ ◆

When solving a radical equation such as $\sqrt{x + 7} = x - 5$ students often square all terms rather than **both sides** of the equation. Since there is a binomial on the right side, FOIL is required, but most students try to distribute the power instead. I often do several of these types of examples, and in the last 5-10 minutes of class make them do one on their own. If they do it correctly, they get to go. Otherwise, they have to stay until they correct it and show me the correct answer(s). If they have to stay after class, they usually don't forget to use FOIL.

Deanna L. Dick,
Alvin Community College

◆ ◆ ◆

Correctly squaring the binomials involved is probably the most common difficulty that students have with solving equations with radicals. It is tempting to encourage them to write the factors twice and then use the FOIL method. This is not efficient for students in the long run. Almost all of them are continuing to a higher-level mathematics course. Continuing to use this step is a crutch that hinders them as they attempt to progress. I tell them that they are not ready for the next course unless they can square the binomial quickly using its rule. This does not seem to be an objective that is emphasized in many high schools, and students are reluctant to advance to this higher level thinking skill.

> Rosa Kavanaugh,
> *Ozarks Technical College*

◆ ◆ ◆

Be sure to check possible solutions when solving a radical equation after squaring both sides of the equation since extraneous roots may be formed in this process.

> Michael Montaño,
> *Riverside Community College*

◆ ◆ ◆

In Section 6.6 while solving equations with two radicals, it is generally easier to solve if you isolate the most complicated looking radical first.

> Roy West,
> *Robeson Community College*

Section 6.8

Evaluating higher powers of *i* often proves difficult for many students. An alternate method that utilizes the cyclical nature of the powers of *i* involves dividing the **power of *i*** by 4 and examining the remainder of that division.

The cycle of powers of *i*

$$i^1 = i$$
$$i^2 = -1$$
$$i^3 = -i$$
$$i^4 = 1$$

For instance $i^{75} = i^3 = -i$, because 3 is the remainder when 75 is divided by 4, meaning that i^{75} is equivalent to i^3 which is equal to $-i$.

> Sandy Berry,
> *Hinds Community College*

◆ ◆ ◆

Remind students that $i = \sqrt{-1}$ and therefore *i* cannot be left in the denominator of a fraction (no radicals may be left in the denominator of a rational expression). Emphasize that we are rationalizing the denominator, and therefore the techniques we learned before with radicals (Chapter 5) still apply.

> Deanna L. Dick,
> *Alvin Community College*

◆ ◆ ◆

A good way to teach operations involving complex numbers is to compare $(5 + 2i)$ and $(3 - 4i)$ to $(5 + 2x)$ and $(3 - 4x)$. They can be added, subtracted or multiplied just like any other binomial. The main difference occurs when we leave x^2 alone, but i^2 becomes (-1) and then the problem can be simplified further.

> Sharon Testone,
> *Onondaga Community College*

Quadratic Equations and Functions

SECTION TITLES AND OBJECTIVES

7.1 The Basics of Solving Quadratic Equations
Solve quadratic equations using the principle of square roots and find the x-intercepts of the graph of a related function ● Solve quadratic equations by completing the square ● Solve applied problems using quadratic equations

7.2 The Quadratic Formula
Solve quadratic equations using the quadratic formula, and approximate solutions using a calculator

7.3 Applications Involving Quadratic Equations
Solve applied problems involving quadratic equations ● Solve a formula for a given letter

7.4 More on Quadratic Equations
Determine the nature of the solutions of a quadratic equation ● Write a quadratic equation having two numbers specified as solutions ● Solve equations that are quadratic in form

7.5 Graphing $f(x) = a(x - h)^2 + k$
Graph quadratic functions of the type $f(x) = ax^2$ and then label the vertex and the line of symmetry ● Graph quadratic functions of the type $f(x) = a(x - h)^2$ and then label the vertex and the line of symmetry ● Graph quadratic functions of the type $f(x) = a(x - h)^2 + k$, finding the vertex, the line of symmetry, and the maximum or minimum y-value

7.6 Graphing $f(x) = ax^2 + bx + c$
For a quadratic function, find the vertex, the line of symmetry, and the maximum or minimum value, and graph the function ● Find the intercepts of a quadratic function

7.7 Mathematical Modeling with Quadratic Functions
Solve maximum - minimum problems involving quadratic functions ● Fit a quadratic function to a set of data to form a mathematical model, and solve related applied problems

7.8 Polynomial and Rational Inequalities
Solve quadratic and other polynomial inequalities ● Solve rational inequalities

TEACHING TIPS

Section 7.1

I begin this section similar to the approach used in the textbook I take a factorable trinomial and solve it by factoring, much as we have already done. We look at the graph and I get the students to agree that the x-intercepts are the solutions. Then I choose a parabola with real roots, that is not factorable like $x^2 - 3x - 12$, and show that there are two real roots and consider how we might get the solutions.

Students almost always understand the principle of square roots, but can rarely do the calculations even after seeing several examples. Make the students perform the steps and be deliberate. I use several polynomials that are factorable to teach this concept. I then foil them out to a quadratic. Going back and forth sets up an understanding for later.

Completing the square when fractions are involved is always interesting. Have the students concentrate on the mechanics and use the fraction capabilities of the calculator. If the first degree coefficient is 7/2, there is almost always a desire to make $(7/2)/2 = 7$. Rather than spend the time re-teaching basic math, get the students to use their calculators to help.

David P. Bell,
Florida Community College at Jacksonville

◆ ◆ ◆

For most students the method of completing the square is the most difficult method to master for solving quadratic equations. Completing the square is an alternate method for solving quadratic equations. In layman language:

1. Write the equation in the form $ax^2 + bx = c$.. In other words, collect the variable terms on the left and the constant term on the right side of the equation.

2. Divide each term on both sides of the equation by the coefficient of x^2, namely a.

3. Determine what number should be added to the left side of the equation in order to make that side a perfect square trinomial. That value can be determined by finding the value of

$$[1/2 \text{ (the coefficient of } x)]^2.$$

This quantity must be added to both sides of the equation.

4. Factor the perfect square on the left side of the equation.

5. The equation is now in the form of $(\text{something})^2 = a$ number.

6. Take the square root of both sides of the equation in order to finish the solution.

Sandy Berry,
Hinds Community College

❖ ❖ ❖

This is a long section and completing the square is difficult for students. Therefore, it may help your students to do a few completing the square problems when covering 7.1, and then review the process with a few more problems when covering 7.2 (the quadratic formula) since this section goes very quickly.

Deanna L. Dick,
Alvin Community College

❖ ❖ ❖

Showing the graph of a quadratic function is needed to demonstrate that solving for x really means finding the x-intercepts. This is demonstrated nicely on page 574 of the text. Often students find values for x by factoring and solving, but they have no idea what those values mean.

Sharon Testone,
Onondaga Community College

❖ ❖ ❖

Be sure not to skip the material on solving equations by completing the square, even though the quadratic formula is much easier. Completing the square will be necessary while working with conics to write an equation, given in general form, in standard form.

Roy West,
Robeson Community College

Section 7.2

Have the students close their textbooks and put down their pencils. Begin with the generic form of a quadratic and have them guide you through completing the square. Once you have solved the equation, you can discuss the results and the fact that this is in the text.

David P. Bell,
Florida Community College at Jacksonville

❖ ❖ ❖

After I have introduced the quadratic formula, I remind students of the strategy for memorizing the formula as they do their homework. I tell them that each time they use the formula, it is important that they write the formula **first** and then substitute the given information. Many students tend instead merely to write the result after substitution and miss the learning benefits of the writing process. I explain that the repeated writing of the original formula as they use it actually helps them to remember it.

In addition to the development in the text, I try to help my students make additional connections to the formula for the x-coordinate of the vertex by using the quadratic formula to find the x-intercepts of the graph of the function. I choose a function with irrational real zeros and approximate and graph them. We discuss the symmetry and note that the x-coordinate of the vertex is midway between those two zeros that were determined from the quadratic formula as

$$\frac{-2}{2a} \pm \frac{\sqrt{\text{something}}}{2a}.$$

I point out to students that this x-coordinate of the vertex was the $\frac{-b}{2a}$ and that this is not really a new formula for them to memorize since it is already imbedded in the quadratic formula that they already know.

Rosa Kavanaugh,
Ozarks Technical College

◆ ◆ ◆

Students often write the quadratic formula without extending the fraction bar under the $-b$. I always say "$-b$ plus or minus the square root of (b squared $- 4ac$) ALL OVER $2a$."

When using the quadratic formula, students often forget to put the trinomial in descending order.

Sharon Testone,
Onondaga Community College

◆ ◆ ◆

Be sure to develop the quadratic formula by completing the square on $ax^2 + bx + c = 0$ to show that the quadratic formula is derived by completing the square and to show that it does not take a math wizard to derive valuable math formulas.

Roy West,
Robeson Community College

Section 7.3

Work a **lot** of word problems. Tell students to read the problem before they start trying to write equations. Ask them for input and **explain** why their answers are correct or incorrect. Don't let them just sit there and make you do the word problems. If they help you to translate it to an equation in class, they will feel more confident at home by themselves.

Deanna L. Dick,
Alvin Community College

Section 7.4

I hand out a sheet with six or seven quadratics. Some have two real solutions, an example has one real solution, and the rest have no real solutions. I ask the students to calculate the value of the discriminant without labeling it as such. Once they have the numbers, we graph each equation and discuss what we see. Usually at least one student will make the connection between the reading and what we have just done.

David P. Bell,
Florida Community College at Jacksonville

◆ ◆ ◆

When using the substitution method for solving equations that are quadratic in form, make sure your students use a letter that is **different** than the variable in the original equation. Otherwise they may forget to replace their substitution for the original expression and finish solving the original equation. Also remind them that if the original equation involves either a fraction, or a radical there may be an extraneous solution that must be thrown out. Checking their answers in the original problem solves both problems.

Deanna L. Dick,
Alvin Community College

Section 7.5

Have the students graph $y = x^2$ and graph it on their graphing calculator. Add and subtract values from x^2 and discuss the relationship before moving to and trying values in $(x - h)^2$ format and then combine. The students can derive the general form of a parabola on their own and have a better understanding of what is happening. If you have a method of projecting this evolution on the board with something like an emulator, that's even better.

David P. Bell,
Florida Community College at Jacksonville

◆ ◆ ◆

Point out the summary on page 621 on shortcuts for graphing the equation $f(x) = a\left(x - h\right)^2 + k$. Stress that the vertex is (h, k) and draw attention to the sign change for the number "h" inside the function.

Deanna L. Dick,
Alvin Community College

◆ ◆ ◆

Important to illustrate with a hand sketched graph the vertex, line of symmetry, and orientation; this short cut is quick to identify all of the above.

Nancy Ressler,
Oakton Community College

Section 7.6

Re-visit completing the square and the look of the quadratic at the point where the students have just added the value to both sides of the equation. Take the next step and rewrite it as a perfect square equal to a constant. Subtract the constant from both sides of the equation and discuss what you see now.

David P. Bell,
Florida Community College at Jacksonville

Section 7.7

I like to take a relatively simple business equation like $-x^2 + 30x - 120$ and have the class graph it. Then we begin a discussion about why we start losing money at approximately 25 or 26 units. find the discussion lends a relevance to what we are doing and the students are less suspicious of the new process.

David P. Bell,
Florida Community College at Jacksonville

◆ ◆ ◆

Work problems like Exercise 6 on page 647 so that students realize that a standard formula can be modified to fit a given set of circumstances. Instead of using the perimeter formula of $P = 2l + 2w$, it and use the equation $P = l + 3w$ to calculate perimeter. Students often resist modifying formulas to fit the problem; instead they try to change the problem to fit the formula.

Deanna L. Dick,
Alvin Community College

◆ ◆ ◆

Basic motion problems tend to be especially intimidating to students. I share with them an acronym that one of my students noticed a number of years ago.

"**d**istance **i**s **r**ate multiplied by **t**ime" can be abbreviated as dirt.

Since the author's examples and all of the basic exercises for solving nonlinear inequalities contain no repeated linear factors, some more observant students may note that all of the signs have alternated. Some may question the necessity of the calculations for all intervals when they could just calculate one and alternate to determine the signs of the others. The instructor may want to be prepared with a counterexample such as Exercises 56 and 57 in the Synthesis exercises on page 659.

Rosa Kavanaugh,
Ozarks Technical College

Exponential and Logarithmic Functions

SECTION TITLES AND OBJECTIVES

8.1 Exponential Functions
Graph exponential equations and functions ● Graph exponential equations in which x and y have been interchanged ● Solve applied problems involving applications of exponential functions and their graphs

8.2 Inverse and Composite Functions
Find the inverse of a relation if it is described as a set of ordered pairs or as an equation ● Given a function, determine whether it is one-to-one and has an inverse that is a function ● Find a formula for the inverse of a function, if it exists, and graph inverse relations and functions ● Find the composition of functions and express certain functions as a composition of functions ● Determine whether a function is an inverse by checking its composition with the original function

8.3 Logarithmic Functions
Graph logarithmic functions ● Convert from exponential equations to logarithmic equations and from logarithmic equations to exponential equations ● Solve logarithmic equations ● Find common logarithms on a calculator

8.4 Properties of Logarithmic Functions
Express the logarithm of a product as a sum of logarithms, and conversely ● Express the logarithm of a power as a product.   ● Express the logarithm of a quotient as a difference of logarithms, and conversely ● Convert from logarithms of products, quotients, and powers to expressions in terms of individual logarithms, and conversely ● Simplify expressions of the type $\log_a a^k$

8.5 Natural Logarithmic Functions
Find logarithms or powers, base e, using a calculator ● Use the change-of-base formula to find logarithms to bases other than e or 10 ● Graph exponential and logarithmic functions, base e

8.6 Solving Exponential and Logarithmic Equations
Solve exponential equations ● Solve logarithmic equations

8.7 Mathematical Modeling with Exponential and Logarithmic Functions
Solve applied problems involving logarithmic functions ● Solve applied problems involving exponential functions

TEACHING TIPS

Quick graphing tip for students: if the exponent is an algebraic expression, find where it equals zero and pick values larger and smaller than that value to get a good quick plot.

Example: $f(x) = 3^{x-4}$

$$x - 4 = 0 \Rightarrow x = 4$$

Therefore let x equal: 2, 3, 4, 5, and 6.

Deanna L. Dick,
Alvin Community College

◆ ◆ ◆

Use graphing calculators and/or projection screens for working problems and verifying solutions. Graphing calculators are especially effective in this chapter.

In all chapters, you never have to work the problem in the same form as given by the author. Rearrange terms and form to fit your particular situation.

Michael Montaño,
Riverside Community College

◆ ◆ ◆

Try the following problem at the beginning of the chapter to create interest in exponential equations.

Ask: If you could fold a piece of notebook paper fifty times about how high would it reach?

Allow students in the class to guess. Most will say a few inches; some will be bold and say a few feet. All will be shocked to see that it would reach past the sun. Show how it fits the pattern of an exponential expression.

Folds	Thickness in terms of sheets of paper
1	2
2	4
3	8
4	16
n	2^n

Therefore 50 folds would represent a thickness of 2^{50} sheets of paper. Multiply this by the thickness of 1 piece of notebook paper (about 1/250th of an inch). Then converting to miles will yield about 71,000,000 miles. Note: The average distance to the sun is about 93,000,000 miles.

Roy West,
Robeson Community College

Section 8.1

Students typically find this chapter difficult. When I teach logs I try to ease into it by reviewing other function families (2.1, 2.2) using something like the "visualizing for success" worksheet. I also review the basics of exponents (R.7, 6.2). This review gives students direction, context, and confidence before beginning.

Kathleen C. Ebert,
Alfred State College

◆ ◆ ◆

Use transformations and translations to graph exponential functions. It is a cleaner method than the roster method.

Michael Montaño,
Riverside Community College

Section 8.2

When teaching composition of functions $f \cdot g$ make sure that they understand the notation means composition, not multiplication. Review that multiplication would be represented as $f \cdot g$ or fg. Also the first function is what you are substituting **into** and the second function is what you are substituting **in**.

Deanna L. Dick,
Alvin Community College

◆ ◆ ◆

The only way I have been able to be successful in this chapter is to spend additional time (for both inverse and composites) helping students visualize the relationships. Students need the diagrams for composites (and/or colored markers). They need extra practice and repetition on these topics. It helps for them to see it as a pattern.

Kathleen C. Ebert,
Alfred State College

◆ ◆ ◆

Students seem to be able to accept the explanation of the inverse function as a "reverse." The example I have used is that if my son drove me to work this morning because he wanted to use my car today, what directions would he use to return home? If we turned left onto National Avenue from Sunset, he would need to turn right onto Sunset from National Avenue on the way home. This also gives me an opportunity to plant the idea of a one-to-one function since we could have followed Campbell to Central, but he could not reverse that path since Campbell is a one-way street north of Grand.

> Rosa Kavanaugh,
> *Ozarks Technical College*

◆ ◆ ◆

The introduction of the inverse (antilog) log function is helpful in changing from exponential to logarithmic form and vice versa.

> Michael Montaño,
> *Riverside Community College*

◆ ◆ ◆

Rewriting the equation as an inverse is *not usually required* in Intermediate Algebra (keep a close eye on the syllabus); Example 2 on page 668 is excellent to discuss with the class.

> Nancy Ressler,
> *Oakton Community College*

Section 8.3

Section 8.1 teaches the student about the special features of the graphs of exponential equations and Section 8.2 develops the inverse relationship between exponential equations and logarithmic equations. These previously learned relationships allow the student to sketch the graph of any logarithmic equation by reflecting the related exponential equation about the line $y = x$ since exponential and logarithmic functions are inverses of each other.

> Sandy Berry,
> *Hinds Community College*

◆ ◆ ◆

Having students rewrite the logarithmic functions as exponential equations will give them more practice rewriting the logarithmic equations before they are solving them in 8.6. They need that practice. It also makes it easier for them to substitute values to come up with points for a graph.

> Deanna L. Dick,
> *Alvin Community College*

◆ ◆ ◆

The author notes just before Example 2 on page 725 that logarithms are useful when there is a variable in the exponent. I use this as a motivational idea to develop the concept of the logarithm. In Section 8.3, I would ask the class to solve $10^x = 5$. They quickly realize that they cannot solve it using the algebraic tools that they have. I ask them to tell me in English how they would describe x in the equation. They usually say (with varying degrees of coaching), "x is the power of the base 10 that gives 5." We translate the English sentence to mathematical symbols and develop the logarithmic form.

I do not ask students to memorize the relationships converting between exponential and logarithmic equations. Instead I emphasize the form of each equation and the position of the base and the exponent in each type of equation as the author does in his examples on page 701. I have also begun to name the "other number" in the logarithmic equation as the "argument" (of the logarithm). Students seem comfortable with this, and those who will continue to higher-level mathematics courses will already be familiar with the terminology.

Another advantage of using this terminology is that when we cover the properties of logarithms, I can make the statement, "The only way that you can change an argument is by using one of these properties." This seems to help students to avoid some of the more common errors such as attempting to "distribute logs."

> Rosa Kavanaugh,
> *Ozarks Technical College*

◆ ◆ ◆

A perfect opportunity to revisit functions and their importance, don't overkill, just enough. This concept is new for most students.

Nancy Ressler,
Oakton Community College

Section 8.4

Remember to connect the properties of logarithms to the properties of exponents as the proof does on page 709.

Roy West,
Robeson Community College

Section 8.5

The number *e* seems to be especially intimidating to many students. At this level (and this near to the end of the course) there is little possibility of their appreciating a development of the definition of *e*. My approach is simply to ask what the symbol π means. The first answer is 3.14, but they later realize that is an approximation that is acceptable in many cases. If I ask for a more precise answer, they refer to their calculators. Sometimes a student remembers the definition of circumference divided by diameter. I explain to them that they can use π without knowing the definition by remembering 3.14 or consulting their calculators for a more precise approximation. I compare *e* to π in those same ways: there is a precise definition that they do not need to remember to use it and that they should remember 2.718 and consult their calculators for a more precise approximation. After this we proceed to using the calculator.

Rosa Kavanaugh,
Ozarks Technical College

Section 8.6

Something I tell my students, that they seem to remember, is that as a general rule of thumb, we can solve exponential equations by rewriting them as logarithmic equations (take the "log" or "ln" of both sides), and we can solve logarithmic equations by rewriting them as exponential equations. Just remind them to combine the logarithms and write them as one logarithm before changing it to an exponential equation.

Deanna L. Dick,
Alvin Community College

◆ ◆ ◆

Throughout this section, I stress exact versus approximate. I require exercises to be done with and without a calculator—in class, on homework, and on the test. I really want them to know how to identify what method to use to solve or simplify so we practice that. Often my directions are very specific (use a particular method, or leave all answers exact). I quiz on "what method would you use" or "what relationship do you see". If they see more than one method/relationship I know they are in good shape. When I give homework we look through the problems to identify the method (the first step). I find that this helps.

Kathleen C. Ebert,
Alfred State College

Section 8.7

Make a point of telling your students where they will encounter similar word problems—chemistry, biology, financial fields, etc. Try to give the word problems relevance and stir up some interest, even if it means a little research on your part.

If the students get interested in the word problems they will try harder to work them out.

Deanna L. Dick,
Alvin Community College

◆ ◆ ◆

This section is one of the most important sections in this chapter. Reviewing the exponential and logarithmic functions prior to presenting real world applications is very beneficial to the students. Many students enrolled in an intermediate algebra course have majors such as chemistry, physics, biology, business, or economics. These problems demonstrate to the students the relevancy of exponential and logarithmic functions.

Sharon Testone,
Onondaga Community College

◆ ◆ ◆

Make sure students are required to learn the properties in this chapter. Knowing them reveals to the student how to work the problems.

Roy West,
Robeson Community College

9 Conic Sections

TEACHING TIPS

Section 9.1

The function values of a quadratic equation all follow a certain pattern. Knowledge of that pattern provides a simple but elegant manner for sketching the graph of any quadratic function. If you examine a chart for some of the values of the quadratic equation $y = x^2$, the pattern is revealed.

Change in x	Values of x	Values of y	Change in y
	0	0	
1	1	1	1
1	2	4	3
1	3	9	5
1	4	16	7
1	5	25	9

For each change of 1 in the value of x, the changes in the value of y present a pattern of odd natural numbers: 1, 3, 5, 7... This pattern of changes in the y values may be utilized to easily sketch the graph of any quadratic equation which is expressed in the form $y = a(x - h)^2 + k$.

The graph of the quadratic equation will be a parabola with the features:

Vertex of the parabola (h, k).

If $a > 0$, the curve will open upward.

If $a < 0$, the curve will open downward.

The value of a also determines the rate at which the parabola will rise or fall.

The basic quadratic equation $y = x^2$ can be sketched by starting at the vertex and plotting addition points by moving

Over 1 (change in x) and up 1 (change in y)

Over 1 and up 3

Over 1 and up 5

Over 1 and up 7

and so on.

Then, if $a = 2$ the curve can be drawn by starting at the vertex and plotting points by moving

Over 1 (change in x) and up

2×1 (change in y)

Over 1 and up 2×3

Over 1 and up 2×5

Over 1 and up 2×7

Which causes the curve to rise twice as fast as the usual parabola.

Sandy Berry,
Hinds Community College

◆ ◆ ◆

Since this is the first section where our parabolas are not functions, make sure to give plenty of examples of parabolas quadratic with respect to y. Show students that the variable raised to the second power is the variable involved in the equation for the line of symmetry. Knowing the line of symmetry tells them whether the graph opens up or down, or right or left since it runs in the same direction as the graph.

Deanna L. Dick,
Alvin Community College

◆ ◆ ◆

I think identification is important. When I teach conics, I begin the chapter with..."here are four more types of graphs (circle, parabola, ellipse, hyperbola) each has a specific equation form." I present all four right up front. I make a copy of the cone cross sections (9.1, p758) with a table/column under each and give it as a handout. As we go along we add the identifying equation and characteristics of each section to the handout. Having it in one place at the end of the chapter helps. Again, I like to use the "Visualizing for Success" worksheet and create some others of my own.

Kathleen C. Ebert,
Alfred State College

◆ ◆ ◆

The distance formula can be nicely developed by working a numerical example on a blank transparency placed over a coordinate grid. Students can count the spaces to find the vertical and horizontal distances. Then the grid can be removed so students will need to construct a way to find those same distances using the coordinate values. I believe this helps them to make connections to the formula.

Rosa Kavanaugh,
Ozarks Technical College

◆ ◆ ◆

Use several real world applications for a conic. Example: headlights, amphitheaters, whispering galleries, etc.

Use the definition of the circle and the distance formula to derive the equation for a circle.

Michael Montaño,
Riverside Community College

Section 9.2

For Sections 9.2 and 9.3, share with students the quick way to determine whether an equation is a circle, an ellipse, or a hyperbola. Signs and coefficients are the same on the squared terms of the circle; signs, but not coefficients, are the same on the squared terms of the ellipse; and signs are different on the squared terms of the hyperbola. If the students know what the graph will look like in the end, they are more likely to graph it correctly and not draw an ellipse when it should be a hyperbola.

Deanna L. Dick,
Alvin Community College

◆ ◆ ◆

Before I begin to develop the equation for the ellipse, I ask students to pair up and provide each team with a piece of string about twelve inches long. I direct them to tie two knots, one near each end, and place the knots along the line that runs lengthwise through the center of the paper. Then I show them how one person should hold the knots in place while the other stretches the string taut to draw the ellipse. I ask them to repeat the process on a second piece of paper. Each member of the team then has an ellipse to label. This is one of the few ways that I have found to involve kinesthetic learners in the construction of this level of mathematics.

Rosa Kavanaugh,
Ozarks Technical College

◆ ◆ ◆

Use a string and two fixed points (vertices) to draw an ellipse and use the drawing to establish the relationship between a, b and c in the formula for an ellipse.

Michael Montaño,
Riverside Community College

Section 9.4

Have students tell you the possible number of solutions by looking at the basic graphs of the equations and how they may or may not intersect. This gives the students a visual of what to expect in the way of answers to the problem, and it gives them more practice determining the type of graph given by each equation. The more you can review material from previous sections the better it is for your students!

Deanna L. Dick,
Alvin Community College

◆ ◆ ◆

When solving a nonlinear system of equations, I instruct students to substitute the value that they find for the first unknown into the "simpler" of the two original equations. This not only makes the process easier but also means that if one of those equations was linear and the other quadratic they will not obtain two values for the second unknown, one of which would be extraneous.

When I make a change of variables such as the author does in Example 5 on page 790, I make a change of color on the board. This helps students to understand what has been done and is a good reminder to change back to the original variable/color to solve the original equation.

Rosa Kavanaugh,
Ozarks Technical College

◆ ◆ ◆

Page 797 presents a super review of properties and formulas, it serves as a good overview of what to expect in an algebraic sequential course.

Nancy Ressler,
Oakton Community College

◆ ◆ ◆

Solutions to nonlinear systems of equations can be demonstrated by using the graphing calculator. Many problems can be completed in a relatively short time period by using the graphing calculator. I believe that students should be asked to graph a few nonlinear equations using traditional methods, but the calculator should be introduced quite early in this section.

Sharon Testone,
Onondaga Community College

COMMENTS FROM STUDENTS

Mathematics suggestions from students in a college level transfer class.
Submitted by Nancy Ressler, Oakton Community College

Michelle S.:

Upon thinking back on my most successful math courses I have discovered the following techniques were most helpful:

- During my Introduction to Calculus class in high school the instructor had pre-assembled packets for each chapter. Upon the start of a new chapter he would pass them out to every student. It was your choice whether or not to use it. Inside this packet were the main concepts from the chapter and spaces with sample problems. We would discuss the topics, and do the sample problems within the packet. When it came time to complete the homework it was a piece of cake because we had all of the relevant information in one place. It was always great to look back at a similar example we had gone over in class.

- Give group quizzes, not open-note quizzes. Group quizzes are great because you get the opportunity to learn from your classmates. Sometimes, as good as the teacher may be, a few students may have a hard time understanding some topics. If you are hit with a quiz, it is a lot of pressure. So sometimes teachers make it open-note; well, what if your notes don't mean anything to you? Sometimes it is easier to understand if a friend/classmate explains it to you.

- Homework: don't assign a lot, because people will not do it. If you assign way too much homework, the students do not do or even in some cases attempt it. Give a reasonable amount because then you know they'll at least try it out. Homework is great for practice.

- Give study guides before tests. Math is a really touchy subject for a lot of people. More times than not, students will be overwhelmed with tests. There are often times when we don't know what to expect from the teacher in terms of tests. Are you giving partial credit? Is it multiple-choice? We don't know what the material always is, and we may miss a part.

If you give us a sample test (study guide) at least we know what to expect, and to focus most of our attention on.

- Extra credit is key. "Extra" means it's an option. If you're doing well in a class, you don't need to do extra credit work, but if you're struggling, it helps so much. You have to do work, but you're going that extra step, so why not be rewarded for it?

- Organize office hours/times to meet with students. Make sure that you specify times outside of the classroom when you can help students if they need it. Sometimes students are embarrassed to ask questions in front of the entire class, or just don't understand a problem, as many times as they attempt it.

Nick T.:

Here are some helpful hints from a student's point of view.

First off, math books with the answers in the back are essential. Allowing a student to check his work saves a lot of time, effort and frustration. Also, it can make some problems easier to work out by knowing the answer first. There have been a few times this year that I, by knowing the answer, could work my way backwards through the problem, and figure out the concepts simply. By checking your work you can be assured that you have done the problems correctly.

Second, I think it's hard for some students to keep up with all the math terms. Keeping explanations simple and using language that everyone can understand will help the students learn the material better. And instead of just showing students an equation and saying, here's the equation, now solve the problem, the teacher should plug numbers into the equation and explain where those numbers came from. Show as many examples in class as you possibly can of any type of problem students might see on the homework. The more examples a student sees the quicker he can pick up on the material. Some students, such as myself, cannot understand the book's explanation for the life of them, especially some of those crazy materials. Students like that rely solely on what they are taught in class; that is why I think that maximizing examples is extremely important. Also, make sure that there are ample tutors around to help students outside of class. There have been three times this year when I have gone to the tutoring center and none of the "finite" math tutors could help me with what I needed help with. People that aren't as math-minded heavily rely on tutors and in-class explanations. As long as the teacher can keep explanations simple and clear and show plenty of examples, then the class should roll by smoothly. I hope this has offered some kind of help.

Rahil M.:

My math teacher in high school showed us this information which I thought would be great for any teacher.

1. Thou shall accept the challenge of teaching math and educate thyself in every way so that students will learn.

2. Thou shall recognize that some students fear or dislike math and be compassionate and understanding when teaching.

3. Thou shall convey to students that their self worth is unrelated to their math skills.

4. Thou shall adapt teaching strategies to meet the different learning styles of students.

5. Thou shall respect all student questions as you would have them respect yours.

6. Thou shall pursue the response of "I still don't understand" through different avenues until there is understanding.

7. Thou shall not ask a class "Do you understand?" Instead, thou shall determine what each student knows and does not know, and address student problems individually.

8. Thou shall identify students in need of extra help and make certain they get it.

9. Thou shall actively involve students in class, assign daily homework, and quiz frequently, knowing that student discipline comes from teacher discipline.

10. Though they may at times seem few, thou shall count thy blessings.

Adam S.:

As a student in math, I find it very useful to do the problems as a class. When the teacher gives the whole class a problem to do and then, using class participation, he/she solves it on the board, it is a great way to learn. The reason I feel that this is so great a learning tool is that it keeps the class involved, and it puts the teacher at the student's pace so that he/she can realize whether or not the students actually understood the material.

I have had teachers in the past who have ignored this method and merely done the problems on the board. They usually end up going at a pace far ahead of most of the students in the class and they have no perception of whether or not the students are actually learning the material.

I really like the open forum previously described, and while I don't think it necessary to use the entire class period I think some time should be devoted to this teaching style, especially in math where many students can fall behind very quickly.

Also I find the internet homework on CourseCompass™ to be very useful in helping me learn the material, and I hope to see this type of program in all my classes soon.

INDEX OF STUDY TIPS

With page references to Bittinger's Intermediate Algebra, *Tenth Edition*

To the Instructor:

The study tips that follow can be used in a variety of ways other than in the order they arise in the books. Admittedly, we would like all students to have mastered these skills before they start our courses, but this is often not the case.

One way to use these study tips is by category. For example, when you are about to give a test, review all the tips on test taking with your students. When you sense that students are not using their time wisely, you might cover all the suggestions on time management. Keep in mind that each tip may not work for each student, but certainly every student will gain something from these suggestions. Good luck!

EXTRA PRACTICE EXERCISES

Extra Practice 1
Addition And Subtraction Of Real Numbers
Use after Section R.2

EXAMPLES: Add.

$$\text{a)} \quad 5 + 9 = 14$$
$$-5 + 9 = 4$$

$$\text{b)} \quad 5 + (-9) = -4$$
$$-5 + (-9) = -14$$

$$\text{c)} \quad -\frac{5}{8} + \frac{2}{3} = -\frac{15}{24} + \frac{16}{24} = \frac{1}{24}$$
$$6.7 + (-8.1) = -1.4$$

Add.

1. $-4 + (-5) =$ _____

2. $-7 + 6 =$ _____

3. $8 + (-3) =$ _____

4. $-8 + 8 =$ _____

5. $-11 + (-17) =$ _____

6. $-15 + 3 =$ _____

7. $-6 + 15 =$ _____

8. $5 + (-7) =$ _____

9. $18 + (-3) =$ _____

10. $-9 + (-19) =$ _____

11. $-9 + 2 =$ _____

12. $6 + (-7) =$ _____

13. $-3 + (-1) =$ _____

14. $-4 + (-4) =$ _____

15. $18 + (-15) =$ _____

16. $-15 + 4 =$ _____

17. $-7 + 19 =$ _____

18. $16 + (-9) =$ _____

19. $24 + (-11) =$ _____

20. $-5 + 6 =$ _____

21. $-3 + (-9) =$ _____

22. $12 + (-7) =$ _____

23. $-7 + 14 =$ _____

24. $-2 + (-5) =$ _____

25. $-21 + 21 =$ _____

26. $-8 + 2 =$ _____

27. $9 + (-11) =$ _____

28. $-5 + (-11) =$ _____

29. $-\dfrac{3}{4} + \left(-\dfrac{2}{5}\right) =$ _____

30. $\dfrac{7}{8} + \left(-\dfrac{3}{4}\right) =$ _____

31. $-\dfrac{5}{12} + \dfrac{2}{3} =$ _____

32. $-\dfrac{1}{5} + \left(-\dfrac{1}{3}\right) =$ _____

33. $\dfrac{7}{9} + \left(-\dfrac{1}{4}\right) =$ _____

34. $-\dfrac{1}{2} + \dfrac{5}{7} =$ _____

35. $-9.5 + 4.3 =$ _____

36. $-8.7 + 15.2 =$ _____

37. $-3.1 + (-6.8) =$ _____

38. $15.6 + (-19.2) =$ _____

39. $-7.5 + 9.1 =$ _____

40. $-6.5 + (-9.9) =$ _____

EXAMPLES: Subtract.

$$6 - 9 = 6 + (-9) = -3$$

$$-6 - 9 = -6 + (-9) = -15$$

$$6 - (-9) = 6 + 9 = 15$$

$$-6 - (-9) = -6 + 9 = 3$$

$$-\dfrac{2}{3} - \dfrac{4}{5} = -\dfrac{10}{15} + \left(-\dfrac{12}{15}\right) = -\dfrac{22}{15}$$

$$6.9 - (-5.2) = 6.9 + 5.2 = 12.1$$

Subtract.

41. $-6 - 10 =$ _____

42. $-7 - (-7) =$ _____

43. $15 - (-3) =$ _____

44. $6 - 11 =$ _____

45. $-9 - 12 =$ _____

46. $-8 - (-15) =$ _____

47. $3 - 8 =$ _____

48. $-7 - 3 =$ _____

49. $-5 - (-6) =$ _____

50. $1 - (-13) =$ _____

51. $-7 - (-4) =$ _____

52. $-8 - 2 =$ _____

53. $9 - (-2) =$ _____

54. $-19 - (-6) =$ _____

55. $7 - 16 =$ _____

56. $15 - 3 =$ _____

57. $-15 - 4 =$ _____

58. $5 - (-8) =$ _____

59. $-9 - (-7) =$ _____

60. $6 - 11 =$ _____

61. $5 - (-6) =$ _____

62. $-15 - (-7) =$ _____

63. $3 - 15 =$ _____

64. $6 - (-8) =$ _____

65. $-2 - 6 =$ _____

66. $17 - 21 =$ _____

67. $19 - (-4) =$ _____

68. $-6 - (-12) =$ _____

69. $\dfrac{5}{8} - \dfrac{1}{2} =$ _____

70. $-\dfrac{3}{4} - \dfrac{2}{3} =$ _____

71. $-\dfrac{9}{10} - \left(-\dfrac{3}{4}\right) =$ _____

72. $-\dfrac{1}{5} - \dfrac{1}{6} =$ _____

73. $\dfrac{7}{12} - \left(-\dfrac{2}{5}\right) =$ _____

74. $-\dfrac{5}{9} - \left(-\dfrac{5}{6}\right) =$ _____

75. $7.8 - (-13.2) =$ _____

76. $-4.1 - 16.3 =$ _____

77. $8.7 - 12.4 =$ _____

78. $-8.2 - (-5.5) =$ _____

79. $-5.3 - 1.8 =$ _____

80. $6.9 - (-3.4) =$ _____

Extra Practice 2
Multiplication and Division of Real Numbers
Use after Section R.2

EXAMPLES: Multiply.

    a) $5 \cdot 6 = 30$ b) $5 \cdot (-6) = -30$ c) $-\dfrac{5}{8} \cdot \left(\dfrac{2}{3}\right) = -\dfrac{10}{24} = -\dfrac{5}{12}$

           $-5 \cdot 6 = -30$ $-5 \cdot (-6) = 30$ $(-3.5) \cdot (-7.9) = 27.65$

Multiply.

1. $-7 \cdot 3 =$ _____

2. $9 \cdot (-8) =$ _____

3. $-11 \cdot 4 =$ _____

4. $-7 \cdot (-4) =$ _____

5. $16 \cdot (-4) =$ _____

6. $-13 \cdot (-11) =$ _____

7. $-21 \cdot 5 =$ _____

8. $10 \cdot (-2) =$ _____

9. $-6 \cdot 5 =$ _____

10. $20 \cdot (-9) =$ _____

11. $-8 \cdot (-13) =$ _____

12. $-3 \cdot (-11) =$ _____

13. $-19 \cdot 5 =$ _____

14. $-15 \cdot 12 =$ _____

15. $16 \cdot (-9) =$ _____

16. $-7 \cdot (-15) =$ _____

17. $4 \cdot (-12) =$ _____

18. $-9 \cdot 12 =$ _____

19. $-3 \cdot (-27) =$ _____

20. $15 \cdot (-8) =$ _____

21. $-19 \cdot (-3) =$ _____

22. $-15 \cdot (-9) =$ _____

23. $17 \cdot (-5) =$ _____

24. $-24 \cdot 7 =$ _____

25. $\dfrac{2}{3} \cdot \left(-\dfrac{6}{7}\right) =$ _____

26. $-\dfrac{5}{8} \cdot \dfrac{10}{9} =$ _____

27. $-\dfrac{4}{5} \cdot \left(-\dfrac{15}{16}\right) =$ _____

28. $\dfrac{7}{10} \cdot \left(-\dfrac{5}{14}\right) =$ _____

29. $-\dfrac{16}{3} \cdot \dfrac{9}{8} =$ _____

30. $-\dfrac{3}{4} \cdot \left(-\dfrac{16}{27}\right) =$ _____

31. $(0.8) \cdot (-0.9) =$ _____   32. $-4.5 \times 6.8 =$ _____

33. $-9 \cdot (-7.3) =$ _____   34. $(1.5) \cdot (-5.8) =$ _____

35. $-3.7 \times 6.6 =$ _____   36. $(-8.3) \cdot (-4.6) =$ _____

EXAMPLES: Divide.

a) $15 \div 3 = 5$ b) $15 \div (-3) = -5$ c) $-\dfrac{7}{8} \div \left(-\dfrac{3}{2}\right) = -\dfrac{7}{8} \cdot \left(-\dfrac{2}{3}\right) = \dfrac{14}{24} = \dfrac{7}{12}$

$-15 \div 3 = -5$ $-15 \div (-3) = 5$ $-8.4 \div 2.1 = -4$

Divide.

37. $75 \div 5 =$ _____   38. $-78 \div 3 =$ _____

39. $413 \div (-7) =$ _____   40. $-300 \div (-12) =$ _____

41. $-126 \div 21 =$ _____   42. $-595 \div (-5) =$ _____

43. $270 \div (-15) =$ _____   44. $-156 \div 26 =$ _____

45. $275 \div (-11) =$ _____   46. $-270 \div (-30) =$ _____

47. $-95 \div 19 =$ _____   48. $-168 \div (-14) =$ _____

49. $-576 \div 32 =$ _____   50. $39 \div 13 =$ _____

51. $-198 \div (-18) =$ _____   52. $320 \div (-16) =$ _____

53. $-384 \div 24 =$ _____   54. $-152 \div 19 =$ _____

55. $-336 \div (-21) =$ _____   56. $-195 \div 13 =$ _____

57. $-288 \div (-9) =$ _____   58. $-160 \div (-32) =$ _____

59. $-135 \div 15 =$ _____   60. $-153 \div (-51) =$ _____

61. $\dfrac{3}{4} \div \left(-\dfrac{5}{2}\right) =$ _____   62. $-\dfrac{5}{8} \div \dfrac{9}{16} =$ _____

63. $-\dfrac{8}{9} \div \left(-\dfrac{2}{27}\right) =$ _____   64. $\dfrac{5}{7} \div \left(-\dfrac{10}{21}\right) =$ _____

65. $-\dfrac{5}{4} \div \dfrac{5}{4} =$ _____   66. $-\dfrac{2}{3} \div \left(-\dfrac{8}{9}\right) =$ _____

67. $15.5 \div 3.1 =$ _____   68. $-9.9 \div 3.3 =$ _____

69. $-21.5 \div (-4.3) =$ _____   70. $14.4 \div (-1.2) =$ _____

71. $-5.234 \div (0.5) =$ _____   72. $-34.84 \div 6.7 =$ _____

Extra Practice 3
Order of Operations
Use after Section R.3

EXAMPLE: Simplify.

$$\frac{2^2 - 3 \cdot 4 + 7}{5 - 2^2 \cdot 3 + 6} = \frac{4 - 3 \cdot 4 + 7}{5 - 4 \cdot 3 + 6}$$
$$= \frac{4 - 12 + 7}{5 - 12 + 6}$$
$$= \frac{-1}{-1}$$
$$= 1$$

1. $2^3 - 3^2 =$ _____

2. $2 \cdot 3 - 4 \cdot 2 + 7 =$ _____

3. $5(-1) + 6(-2) =$ _____

4. $(-2)(3) - (-1)(7) - (-2) =$ _____

5. $3 + 2^2 - 16 \cdot 3^2 =$ _____

6. $6 + (3 - 4) - 2 =$ _____

7. $6 + 3 - (4 - 2) =$ _____

8. $3^2 - 8 \cdot 2 + 7^2 - 35 =$ _____

9. $-4\left(2^3\right) - 6 =$ _____

10. $\left(8 - 2\right)^2 =$ _____

11. $\left(4 - 6\right)^2 =$ _____

12. $4 - 6^2 =$ _____

13. $[32 \div (-4)] \div 2 =$ _____

14. $32 \div [(-4) \div 2] =$ _____

15. $\dfrac{4 - 3^2}{8^2 + 2} =$ _____

16. $\dfrac{7^2 - 8^2 + 1^3}{2^3 + 3^2 - 2^3} =$ _____

17. $\dfrac{2(8 + 3) - 4(7 + 2)}{5(6 - 1) - 3(8 - 6)} =$ _____

18. $\dfrac{3.2(2 - 4) + 6}{4.9 - 3(6 + 1)} =$ _____

19. $\dfrac{8 - 4^2 + 3 \cdot 5}{4 \cdot 2 - 3^2 + 9} =$ _____

20. $\dfrac{2 \cdot 3 - 4 \cdot 5 + 6}{-20 \div (-5) \div 8} =$ _____

21. $5 + 10 - 3^2 =$ _____

22. $6 \cdot 4 + 5^2 - 11 =$ _____

23. $7 \cdot (2 + 3) - 21 =$ _____

24. $(5 + 7) \div 2^2 =$ _____

25. $5^2 - 4^2 + 3 \cdot 2 =$ _____

26. $8 \cdot 9 - 6^2 + 4 =$ _____

27. $9^2 - (20 + 11) =$ _____

28. $(2 + 3) \cdot 10^2 + 5^2 =$ _____

29. $3 \cdot (30 + 4) - 7^2 =$ _____

30. $(1 + 5) \cdot 5 - 7 \cdot 4 =$ _____

31. $0 \cdot 15^2 \cdot (400 + 21) \div 19^2 =$ _____

32. $0 \cdot 1^2 \cdot (59 + 92) + 5 =$ _____

33. $6 \cdot \left(5 + 0\right)^2 =$ _____

34. $(7 - 7) \cdot 33^2 \div (45 + 3)^2 =$ _____

35. $49 \div 7^2 \cdot (531 + 4) =$ _____

36. $(232 + 18) \div 250 + 3 \cdot 33 =$ _____

37. $\dfrac{5 \cdot 30}{15} - (3 + 3) =$ _____

38. $\dfrac{(10 + 14) \cdot 200}{10^2} =$ _____

39. $\dfrac{10 \cdot (25 + 7)}{(5 + 3)^2} =$ _____

40. $\dfrac{25 \cdot (6 + 7) - 5^2}{(6 + 7)^2 - 19} =$ _____

41. $3 \cdot 4 \div (1 + 2) \div 5 =$ _____

42. $(9 + 6) \cdot 3 \div (24 + 6) =$ _____

43. $\left(1^6 + 13\right) \cdot 2 \div 7^2 =$ _____

44. $\left(8^2 - 2^2\right) \div 80 =$ _____

Extra Practice 4
Using the Distributive Laws
Use after Section R.5

Multiply using the distributive law.

EXAMPLE: $8(6x - 4) = 8 \cdot 6x - 8 \cdot 4 = 48x - 32$

Multiply.

1. $7(n - 4) =$ _____

2. $5(x + 6) =$ _____

3. $-2(x - 7) =$ _____

4. $-9(y + 10) =$ _____

5. $-4(a + 3b) =$ _____

6. $10(2x - 3y) =$ _____

7. $-5(x + 2y - 6) =$ _____

8. $8(5x + 4y - 12) =$ _____

9. $9(2a - b + 3) =$ _____

10. $-7(-3p - 15q + 14) =$ _____

11. $3(-6r + 15t - 21) =$ _____

12. $20(-6a - 10b + 9) =$ _____

Factoring is the reverse of multiplying. To factor, we can use the distributive laws in reverse.

EXAMPLE: $3x + 27y - 6 = 3 \cdot x + 3 \cdot 9y - 3 \cdot 2 = 3(x + 9y - 2)$

Factor.

13. $6x - 6 =$ _____

14. $8x + 24 =$ _____

15. $4x - 28 =$ _____

16. $5y - 30 =$ _____

17. $7x + 7 =$ _____

18. $9x - 63 =$ _____

19. $48 - 8x =$ _____

20. $55 - 11x =$ _____

21. $6a + 9 =$ _____

22. $14x - 49 =$ _____

23. $10y + 15 =$ _____

24. $18a - 30 =$ _____

25. $50x - 70 =$ _____

26. $32x + 24 =$ _____

27. $6x + 30 - 36a =$ _____

28. $15x + 45y - 15 =$ _____

29. $bx - 3by + 6b =$ _____

30. $ax - 5a - ay =$ _____

31. $6x + 9y - 24 =$ _____

32. $25x - 15y + 75 =$ _____

Extra Practice 5
Simplifying Algebraic Expressions
Use after Section R.6

EXAMPLE: Simplify. $-(3x + 2y - 8) = -3x - 2y + 8$

Simplify.

1. $-(x^2 - 2x + 5) =$ _____
2. $-(3x - 4y + 7) =$ _____
3. $-(2a + 3b + 4c) =$ _____
4. $-(-3a + 2b - c) =$ _____
5. $-(3x + 7) + 2 =$ _____
6. $2 - (4x - 8) =$ _____
7. $2y - (3y - 4) =$ _____
8. $-4y - (3x - 7y) =$ _____
9. $5y - (4x + 7y) - 2x =$ _____
10. $3a - (2a + 4b) - 6b =$ _____

EXAMPLE: Simplify. $2\{[3(x - 2) + 4] + 5[x - 3]\} = 2\{[3x - 6 + 4] + 5x - 15\}$

$$= 2\{3x - 2 + 5x - 15\}$$

$$= 2\{8x - 17\}$$

$$= 16x - 34$$

11. $3[4x - 7] + 5 =$ _____
12. $8[2 - 3x] - 5 =$ _____
13. $[4x - 3(x - 1) + 6] =$ _____
14. $[6x - 2(3x - 6) + 8] =$ _____
15. $2[3(2x - 1) + 7] =$ _____
16. $-8[2(3x + 4) - 2x] =$ _____
17. $[7(x - 3) + 4] - [6(3x - 2) + x] =$ _____
18. $[2(3x - 1) + 5] - [7(x + 4) - 8] =$ _____
19. $3\{[6(x - 4) + 2] - [3x + 2]\} =$ _____
20. $2\{[3(x - 6) + 1] - 4[3(x - 2) - 3]\} =$ _____

Extra Practice 6
Solving Equations Using the Addition and Multiplication Principles
Use after Section 1.1

Solve.

1. $x + 37 = 98$ _____
2. $y - 53 = 141$ _____
3. $59 + a = -123$ _____
4. $-72 + t = -40$ _____
5. $-55 = x + 32$ _____
6. $a + \dfrac{5}{6} = -\dfrac{1}{2}$ _____
7. $\dfrac{3}{4} + x = \dfrac{7}{8}$ _____
8. $y - 3\dfrac{1}{2} = -2\dfrac{2}{3}$ _____
9. $48x = -192$ _____
10. $-25a = -200$ _____
11. $-15y = 96$ _____
12. $-\dfrac{1}{3}x = 48$ _____
13. $\dfrac{3}{2}r = -\dfrac{4}{5}$ _____
14. $x - 56 = -42$ _____

15. $15 - y = 33$ _____

16. $51 - x = -133$ _____

17. $-31t = -93$ _____

18. $-53 + a = 65$ _____

19. $-\frac{5}{3}b = -\frac{1}{6}$ _____

20. $58x = -145$ _____

21. $-89 = -27 - a$ _____

22. $\frac{x}{4} = -45$ _____

23. $\frac{r}{-3} = \frac{1}{3}$ _____

24. $\frac{11}{2}y = -3\frac{2}{3}$ _____

25. $t + \frac{5}{8} = -\frac{3}{4}$ _____

26. $\frac{b}{-5} = 11$ _____

27. $-\frac{7}{8}t = -\frac{7}{8}$ _____

28. $3x + 5x = 48$ _____

29. $18x - 12x = -96$ _____

30. $3y - 13y = 50$ _____

31. $9t - 16t = -49$ _____

32. $5a - 4 = 26$ _____

33. $8r + 16 = -48$ _____

34. $-10x - 41 = 69$ _____

35. $11b = 45 - 4b$ _____

36. $9z + \frac{1}{2}z = 38$ _____

37. $x + 58 = 135$ _____

38. $62y = -558$ _____

39. $3a + 4a - 3 = 11$ _____

40. $6x + 5 - 2x = -19$ _____

41. $9r + 3r - 5 = 25$ _____

42. $3x + 2 = 2x - 6$ _____

43. $5z - 4 = 4z - 3$ _____

44. $4y + 2y - 7 = 3y + 11$ _____

45. $3t - 5 = 7t + t - 15$ _____

46. $6x + 5x - 4 = 2x - 8$ _____

47. $\frac{1}{2}x + \frac{1}{3}x = \frac{1}{6}x - 5$ _____

48. $\frac{2}{3}y - \frac{5}{4}y + 8 = -\frac{11}{12}y - 4$ _____

49. $\frac{z}{-5} = -15$ _____

50. $\frac{t}{2} = -33$ _____

51. $\frac{h}{13} = 0$ _____

52. $-2y + 7 = 7$ _____

53. $5x - 4 = 4x - 4$ _____

54. $-3462a = 0$ _____

Extra Practice 7
Solving Formulas
Use after Section 1.2

EXAMPLE: Solve for a.

$$P = 2a + 3b + 4c$$
$$P - 3b - 4c = 2a$$
$$\frac{P - 3b - 4c}{2} = a$$

Solve for the given letter.

1. $A = p + prt$ for r _____

2. $A = p + prt$ for t _____

3. $V = lwh$ for l _____

4. $V = lwh$ for h _____

5. $A = \frac{1}{2}d_1d_2$ for d_1 _____

6. $A = \frac{1}{2}d_1d_2$ for d_2 _____

7. $y = mx + b$ for m _____

8. $y = mx + b$ for b _____

9. $p = \dfrac{100a}{t}$ for a _____

10. $y = \dfrac{kx}{z}$ for x _____

11. $A = 2\pi r$ for π _____

12. $V = \pi r^2 h$ for h _____

Extra Practice 8
Solving Problems
Use after Section 1.3

Solve.

1. When 6 is added to three times a number, the result is 30. Find the number. _____

2. When you double a number and then add 20, you get $\dfrac{4}{3}$ of the original number. Find the number. _____

3. The perimeter of a rectangle is 52 cm. The length is 8 cm greater than the width. Find the width and length. _____

4. The perimeter of a rectangle is 78 m. The width is 7 m less than the length. Find the length and width. _____

5. The sum of three consecutive even integers is 150. Find the integers. _____

6. The sum of three consecutive odd integers is 261. Find the integers. _____

7. A 20-ft board is cut into three pieces. The second piece is three times as long as the first. The third piece is twice as long as the second. Find the lengths of the pieces. _____

8. A 450-m fence is divided into three sections. The second section is twice as long as the first. The third section is three times as long as the second. Find the lengths of the sections. _____

9. The second angle of a triangle is three times as large as the first. The third angle is 20° larger than the sum of the first two. Find the measures of the angles. _____

10. The second angle of a triangle is twice as large as the first. The third angle is 50° less than the second. Find the measures of the angles. _____

11. The cost of renting a car is $18 per day plus 16¢ per mile. Matt pays $214 for a three-day rental. How many miles did he drive? _____

12. Thirteen less than twice a number is seventeen more than half the number. What is the number? _____

Extra Practice 9
Solving Inequalities
Use after Section 1.4

EXAMPLES: Solve.

a) $5x - 9 > 6$
    $5x > 15$
    $x > 3$

    The solution set is $\{x | x > 3\}$.

b) $4x + 3 \le 7x + 9$
    $-3x \le 6$
    $x \ge -2$

    The solution set is $\{x | x \ge -2\}$.

Solve.

1. $y + 3 > 9$ _____

2. $x - 7 \ge -3$ _____

3. $5x < 35$ _____

4. $3a + 2 \geq 8$ _____

5. $8x + 3 < 7x + 4$ _____

6. $-9y > 63$ _____

7. $5x - 9 \geq 2$ _____

8. $3x + 4 \leq -2$ _____

9. $10y - 7 > -2y + 17$ _____

10. $3t - 1 \leq 8t + 24$ _____

11. $\frac{3}{4}x < 7$ _____

12. $8y - 7 > 3 - 2y$ _____

13. $6y + 5 \geq 4y + 7$ _____

14. $2m - 1 \geq 5m - 7$ _____

15. $5 + 6x > 9 - x$ _____

16. $10x + 7 \leq 7x - 5$ _____

17. $3x + 1 < 16$ _____

18. $5x - 4 > 21$ _____

19. $8y - 11 \geq 7y + 2$ _____

20. $3m - 4 < 7m - 16$ _____

21. $-3x \leq \frac{1}{4}$ _____

22. $\frac{3}{2}y > -6$ _____

23. $x + 2 \geq 3x - 4$ _____

24. $7x < 2x + 15$ _____

25. $x - \frac{1}{2} > \frac{1}{3}$ _____

26. $y + \frac{2}{3} \leq \frac{5}{6}$ _____

27. $15 - 3x > 4x - 13$ _____

28. $-2 < 5x + 8 - 3x$ _____

29. $17 < 5 - 4y$ _____

30. $31 > 7 - 6y$ _____

Extra Practice 10
Absolute-Value Equations and Inequalities
Use after Section 1.6

EXAMPLES: Solve.

a) $|3x - 5| = 16$
    $3x - 5 = -16 \ or \ 3x - 5 = 16$
    $3x = -11 \ or \ 3x = 21$
    $x = -\frac{11}{3} \ or \ x = 7$

   The solution set is $\left\{ -\frac{11}{3}, 7 \right\}$.

b) $|3x - 5| \leq 16$
    $-16 \leq 3x - 5 \leq 16$
    $-11 \leq 3x \leq 21$
    $-\frac{11}{3} \leq x \leq 7$

   The solution set is $\left\{ x \mid -\frac{11}{3} \leq x \leq 7 \right\}$.

c) $|3x - 5| > 16$

    $3x - 5 < -16 \ or \ 3x - 5 > 16$
    $3x < -11 \ or \ 3x > 21$
    $x < -\frac{11}{3} \ or \ x > 7$

   The solution set is $\left\{ x \mid x < -\frac{11}{3} \ or \ x > 7. \right\}$

Solve.

1. $|8x - 3| > 21$ _____

2. $|y - 2| \leq 7$ _____

3. $|5x + 8| < 23$ _____

4. $|9 - 2x| = 5$ _____

5. $|x| = 4$ _____

6. $\left|\frac{1}{2}y - 3\right| \geq 3$ _____

7. $|y + 9| \leq 2$ _____

8. $\left|y + \frac{1}{3}\right| > \frac{4}{3}$ _____

9. $|-4x + 3| > 13$ _____

10. $\left|\frac{5}{8}x\right| < 10$ _____

11. $|10y - 1.3| = 4.7$ _____

12. $|9 - 4x| \geq 15$ _____

13. $|x + 9| > 17$ _____

14. $\left|\frac{3}{4} + x\right| = \frac{1}{4}$ _____

15. $|9 - y| > 11$ _____

16. $|y| \leq \frac{1}{5}$ _____

17. $\left|\frac{3}{7}y\right| > \frac{3}{7}$ _____

18. $|3 - x| = 2$ _____

19. $|5x - 2| \geq 15$ _____

20. $|17 - 4x| < 23$ _____

21. $|y - 3| = 51$ _____

22. $|19 - x| > 19$ _____

23. $|8x - 3| \leq 5$ _____

24. $|2y - 9| < 15$ _____

25. $|y| > 9$ _____

26. $\left|3y - \frac{5}{9}\right| \leq \frac{4}{9}$ _____

27. $|8 - 3y| < 35$ _____

28. $|0.2x + 0.5| \geq 0.9$ _____

29. $\left|x - \frac{2}{9}\right| \geq \frac{4}{9}$ _____

30. $|34 - 4y| \leq 14$ _____

Extra Practice 11
Graphing Linear Equations
Use after Section 2.1

EXAMPLE: Graph. $y = x - 2$

x	y	(x, y)
	$y = x - 2$	
-2	-4	$(-2, -4)$
-1	-3	$(-1, -3)$
0	-2	$(0, -2)$
1	-1	$(1, -1)$
2	0	$(2, 0)$

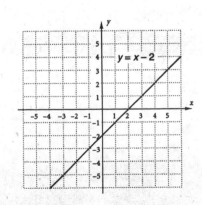

1. $y = 3x + 1$

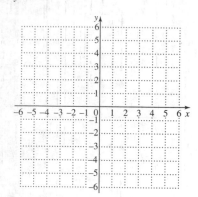

2. $y = 2x - 3$

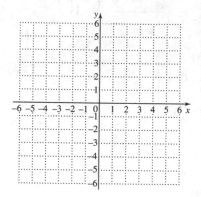

3. $y = x + 4$

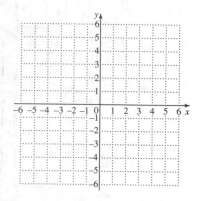

4. $y = -3x + 2$

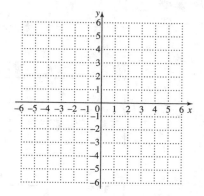

5. $y = \dfrac{3}{2}x + 2$

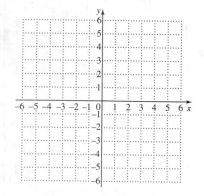

6. $y = -x$

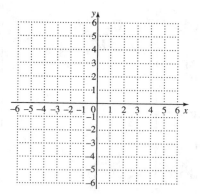

7. $y = x + 5$

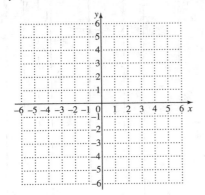

8. $y = -3x - 1$

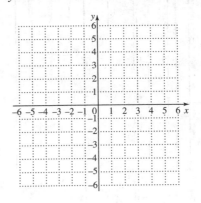

9. $y = 5 - x$

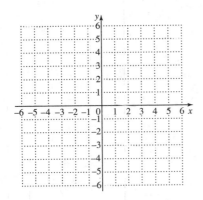

10. $y = \dfrac{2}{3}x - 1$

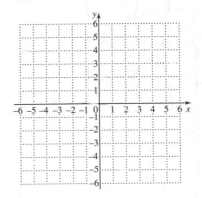

11. $y = 3x - 2$

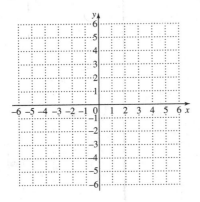

12. $y = -4 - x$

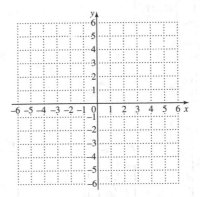

13. $y = -3x$

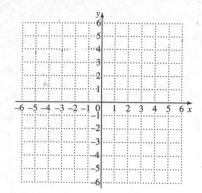

14. $y = 2x + 3$

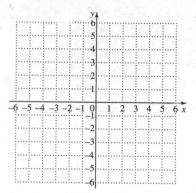

15. $y = \dfrac{1}{3}x + 2$

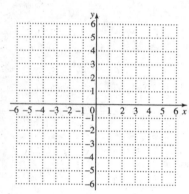

16. $y = 5x - 4$

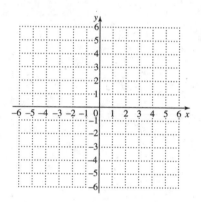

Extra Practice 12
Finding Function Values
Use after Section 2.2

EXAMPLES.

Given $\quad f(x) = 3x - 7$, find $f(-2)$.
$$f(-2) = 3(-2) - 7 = -6 - 7 = -13$$

Given $\quad f(x) = 2x^2 - 5x + 2$, find $f(0)$.
$$f(0) = 2(0)^2 - 5(0) + 2 = 2 \cdot 0 - 5 \cdot 0 + 2 = 2$$

Given $\quad f(x) = x^3 + 7x - 1$, find $f(3a)$.
$$f(3a) = (3a)^3 + 7(3a) - 1 = 27a^3 + 21a - 1$$

Find the function values.

1. $f(x) = 2x + 5$

    a) $f(-2) =$ _____

    b) $f(-8) =$ _____

    c) $f(0) =$ _____

    d) $f(1.2) =$ _____

2. $g(t) = t^2 - 5$

    a) $g(0) =$ _____

    b) $g(7) =$ _____

    c) $g(-9) =$ _____

    d) $g(-1.4) =$ _____

e) $f\left(\dfrac{3}{4}\right) =$ _____

e) $g\left(\dfrac{2}{3}\right) =$ _____

3. $h(x) = -22$

   a) $h(-11) =$ _____

   b) $h(-1.6) =$ _____

   c) $h(0) =$ _____

   d) $h(15) =$ _____

   e) $h(209) =$ _____

4. $f(x) = |x| - 8$

   a) $f(-19) =$ _____

   b) $f(-1) =$ _____

   c) $f(0) =$ _____

   d) $f(18) =$ _____

   e) $f(100) =$ _____

5. $g(t) = |t - 2|$

   a) $g(7) =$ _____

   b) $g(-5) =$ _____

   c) $g(-30) =$ _____

   d) $g(400) =$ _____

   e) $g(a + 1) =$ _____

6. $f(x) = 2x^3 - x$

   a) $f(0) =$ _____

   b) $f(4) =$ _____

   c) $f(-3) =$ _____

   d) $f(4a) =$ _____

   e) $f(-10) =$ _____

Extra Practice 13
Finding Domain and Range
Use after Section 2.3

The solutions of an equation in two different variables consist of a set of ordered pairs. The <u>domain</u> is the set of all first coordinates and the <u>range</u> is the set of all second coordinates.

Find the domain and the range of each of the following functions.

1.

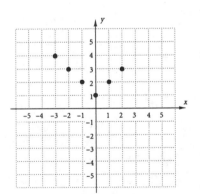

Domain:

Range:

2.

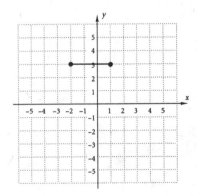

Domain:

Range:

3.

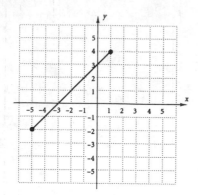

Domain:
Range:

4.

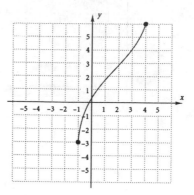

Domain:
Range:

5.

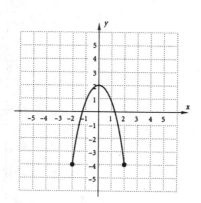

Domain:
Range:

6.

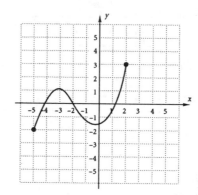

Domain:
Range:

Find the domain.

7. $f(x) = \dfrac{5}{x - 2}$

8. $f(x) = 3 - 2x$

9. $f(x) = x^2 - 4$

10. $f(x) = \dfrac{4}{6x - 5}$

11. $f(x) = \dfrac{x - 1}{2x + 3}$

12. $f(x) = |x| + 1$

13. $f(x) = |x - 3|$

14. $f(x) = \dfrac{-7}{3 + x}$

15. $f(x) = x^2 - 4x - 5$

Extra Practice 14
More on Graphing Linear Equations
Use after Section 2.5

EXAMPLES: Graph.

a) $3x - 2y = 6$

To find the y-intercept, let $x = 0$.
Then solve for y:
$$3 \cdot 0 - 2y = 6$$
$$-2y = 6$$
$$y = -3$$

Thus $(0, -3)$ is the y-intercept.
Plot both intercepts and a third point $(4, 3)$ as a check.

To find the let x-intercept, let $y = 0$.
Then solve for x:
$$3x - 2 \cdot 0 = 6$$
$$3x = 6$$
$$x = 2$$

Thus $(2, 0)$ is the x-intercept.

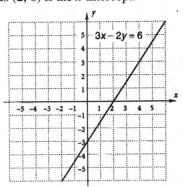

b) $y = -3$

x	y	(x, y)
	$y = -3$	
-2	-3	$(-2, -3)$
0	-3	$(0, -3)$
4	-3	$(4, -3)$

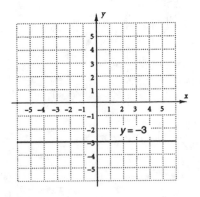

c) $x = 4$

x	y	(x, y)
$x = 4$		
4	-2	$(4, -2)$
4	0	$(4, 0)$
4	3	$(4, 3)$

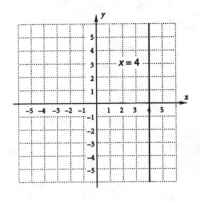

Graph.

1. $3x + 6y = 12$

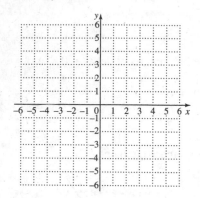

2. $2x - 5y = 10$

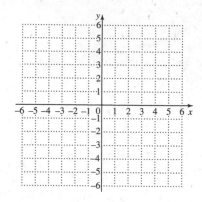

3. $x - 3y = 6$

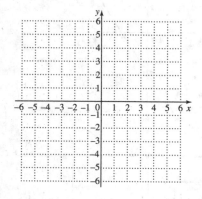

4. $y = 2$

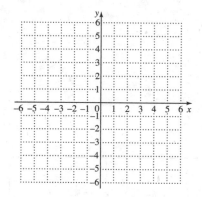

5. $y = 3x + 1$

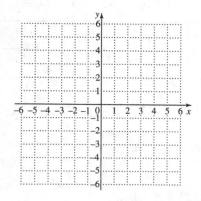

6. $4x + 2y = 8$

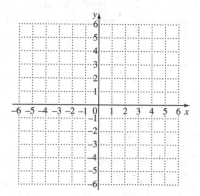

7. $x - y = 3$

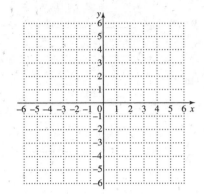

8. $x = -1$

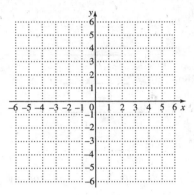

9. $5x + 3y = 15$

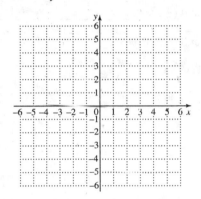

Extra Practice 15
Slope and Equations of Lines
Use after Section 2.6

EXAMPLES:

a) Find a slope-intercept equation for the line with slope 2 that contains $(0, 5)$.

$y = mx + b$ The slope-intercept equation.

$y = 2x + 5$ Substitute 2 for m and 5 for b.

b) Find an equation of a line that contains the points $(5, -2)$ and $(-2, 1)$.

$$m = \frac{1 - (-2)}{-2 - 5} = \frac{3}{-7} = -\frac{3}{7}$$ First find the slope.

$$y - (-2) = -\frac{3}{7}(x - 5)$$ Use the point-slope equation and substitute $-\frac{3}{7}$ for m, 5 for x_1, and -2 for y_1.

$$y + 2 = -\frac{3}{7}x + \frac{15}{7}$$ (We could just as easily have substituted -2 for x_1 and 1 for y_1.)

$$y = -\frac{3}{7}x + \frac{15}{7} - \frac{14}{7}$$

$$y = -\frac{3}{7}x + \frac{1}{7}$$

We could also use the slope-intercept equation. See Section 2.6 for an example.

Find an equation of the line containing the given point and having the given slope.

1. $(4, -3), m = -1$ _____

2. $(-5, -6), m = 2$ _____

3. $(-7, 2), m = 3$ _____

4. $(3, 5), m = -2$ _____

5. $(6, -2), m = -3$ _____

6. $(5, -2), m = 2$ _____

7. $(7, 0), m = 4$ _____

8. $(0, 9), m = -2$ _____

9. $(5, -1), m = \dfrac{1}{5}$ _____

10. $(-3, -2), m = \dfrac{1}{4}$ _____

Find an equation of the line that contains the given pair of points

11. $(1, 5)$ and $(4, 2)$ _____

12. $(-4, 2)$ and $(1, -3)$ _____

13. $(-5, -3)$ and $(1, -1)$ _____

14. $(0, 3)$ and $(-2, 6)$ _____

15. $(-8, 3)$ and $(-4, 1)$ _____

16. $(6, 2)$ and $(-3, 0)$ _____

17. $(1, 3)$ and $(4, 6)$ _____

18. $(3, -4)$ and $(-3, 4)$ _____

19. $(-7, 4)$ and $(-4, 7)$ _____

20. $(9, -5)$ and $(7, 7)$ _____

Extra Practice 16
Solving Systems of Linear Equations
Use after Sections 3.2 and 3.3

EXAMPLES:

 a) Solve using the substitution method: $5x - 2y = 4,$
$$y = 5 - x.$$

Substitute $5 - x$ for y.

$5x - 2y = 4$

$5x - 2(5 - x) = 4$

$5x - 10 + 2x = 4$

$7x = 14$

$x = 2$

Then substitute 2 for x and solve for y.

$y = 5 - x$

$y = 5 - 2$

$y = 3$ The solution is $(2, 3)$.

 b) Solve using the elimination method: $2x + 7y = -1,$
$$-x - 2y = 2.$$

Multiply the second equation by 2 and then add.

$2x + 7y = -1$

$\underline{-2x - 4y = 4}$

$3y = 3$

$y = 1$

Then substitute 1 for y and solve for x.

$2x + 7y = -1$

$2x + 7 \cdot 1 = -1$

$2x + 7 = -1$

$2x = -8$

$x = -4$ The solution is $(-4, 1)$.

Solve.

1. $4x + 3y = 1,$
$x = 1 - y$ _____

2. $2x - y = 6,$
$-x + y = -1$ _____

3. $6x - y = 3,$
$4x - 2y = -2$ _____

4. $2x + 3y = 7,$
$x = 1 - 4y$ _____

5. $2x + 3y = 6,$
   $x - 3y = -15$ _____

6. $7x - 5y = 4,$
   $y = 3x - 4$ _____

7. $2y - 5x = -1,$
   $x = 2y + 5$ _____

8. $4x + 3y = 1,$
   $3x + 5y = -13$ _____

9. $6x - 5y = 3,$
   $4x + 3y = 21$ _____

10. $x + y = 4,$
    $3x + 4y = 10$ _____

11. $-3x + y = 2,$
    $7x - 8y = 1$ _____

12. $7x + 2y = 2,$
    $x - 2y = 14$ _____

13. $9y - 2x = -7,$
    $x - 3y = 5$ _____

14. $3x - 5y = 8,$
    $4x - 7y = 12$ _____

15. $5x + 2y = 12,$
    $3x - 4y = 2$ _____

16. $x + 4y = 7,$
    $3x + 7y = 6$ _____

17. $5x - 8y = 25,$
    $-x + 4y = -7$ _____

18. $0.5x + 2y = 9,$
    $4x - 1.5y = 2$ _____

19. $8x - 6y = 0,$
    $x + 9y = \dfrac{13}{4}$ _____

20. $\dfrac{2}{3}x + \dfrac{1}{4}y = 18,$
    $\dfrac{1}{6}x - \dfrac{3}{8}y = -6$ _____

Extra Practice 17
Solving Problems Using Systems of Equations
Use after Sections 3.2 and 3.3

EXAMPLE: The sum of two numbers is 95. One number is 16 less than twice the other. Find the numbers.

We let x represent one number and y represent the other number.

We solve the following system.
$x + y = 95,$
$x = 2y - 16.$

Using the substitution method, we substitute $2y - 16$ for x.

$x + y = 95$ Then substitute 37 for y and solve for x.
$(2y - 16) + y = 95$ $x = 2y - 16$
$3y - 16 = 95$ $x = 2 \cdot 37 - 16$
$3y = 111$ $x = 58$
$y = 37$ One number is 58, the other is 37.

This system could also have been solved using the elimination method.

$$x + y = 95$$
$$\begin{array}{c} x + y = 95 \\ x = 2y - 16 \end{array} \text{ or } \begin{array}{c} x + y = 95 \\ x - 2y = -16 \end{array} \text{ or } \begin{array}{c} \underline{-x + 2y = 16} \\ 3y = 111 \\ y = 37 \end{array}$$

Then substitute 37 for y and solve for x.

Solve.

1. Find two numbers whose sum is 49 and whose difference is 13. _____

2. Two angles are supplementary. One angle is 60° more than twice the other. Find the angles.
   _____

3. Two angles are complementary. Their difference is 36°. Find the angles. _____

4. The perimeter of a rectangle is 160 cm. The length is 4 cm less than three times the width. Find the length and the width. _____

5. The sum of two numbers is −11. Twice the first number minus the second is 32. Find the numbers. _____

6. The difference between two numbers is 14. Twice the smaller is 7 more than the larger. What are the numbers? _____

7. The perimeter of a lot is 84 ft. The length exceeds the width by 16 feet. Find the length and the width. _____

8. The sum of a certain number and a second number is 21. The second number minus the first number is −57. Find the numbers. _____

9. The perimeter of a rectangular field is 110 feet. The length is 7 feet more than twice the width. Find the dimensions. _____

10. Two angles are complementary. One angle is 10° less than three times the other. Find the measures of the angles. _____

Extra Practice 18
Total Value, Mixture, and Motion Problems
Use after Section 3.4

See Section 3.4 for examples.

1. There were 239 people at a concert. Admission was $15 each for adults and $5.50 each for children. The receipts were $2758.50. How many adults and how many children attended?

   _____

2. A chemist has one solution that is 20% acid and a second that is 65% acid. How many gallons of each should be mixed together to get 120 gallons of a solution that is 50% acid?

   _____

3. The Calhouns generate one-and-a-half times as much trash as their neighbors, the Millers. Together, the two households produce 15 bags of trash each month. How much trash does each household produce? _____

4. The Candy Shack has 20 lb of mixed white and dark chocolates worth $7.50 per pound. White chocolates alone sell for $8.00 per pound and dark chocolates sell for $6.00 per pound. How many pounds of each are in the mixture? _____

5. A collection of quarters and nickels is worth $3.70. There are 22 coins in all. How many of each are there? _____

6. Two investments are made totaling $16,000. For a certain year, these investments yield $970 in simple interest. Part of the $16,000 is invested at 5% and the rest at 7%. How much is invested at 7%?

   _____

7. One night a theater sold 548 movie tickets. An adult's ticket costs $6.50, and a child's ticket costs $3.50. In all, $2881 was taken in. How many of each kind of ticket were sold?

   _____

8. A train leaves town traveling north at 40 km/h. Two hours later another train leaves on a parallel track and travels north at 45 km/h. How far from town will the second train overtake the first?

   _____

9. Two cars leave town at the same time going in opposite directions. One travels at 50 mph, and the other travels at 60 mph. In how many hours will they be 495 miles apart?

   _____

10. A boat traveled for two hours downstream with a 5 km/h current. The return trip against the same current took four hours. Find the speed of the boat in still water. _____

11. An airplane flew for three hours with a 30-mph tail wind. The return flight against the same wind took $3\frac{1}{2}$ hours. Find the speed of the airplane in still air. _____

12. A canoeist paddled two hours with a 3 km/h current to a fishing site. The return trip against the same current took six hours. Find the speed of the canoe in still water. _____

13. A train leaves Smithville and travels south at a speed of 60 mph. Three hours later, a second train leaves on a parallel track and travels south at 90mph. How far from the station will they meet?

   _____

14. A small boat took 2 hr to make a trip downstream with a 4-mph current. The return trip against the same current took 3 hr. Find the speed of the boat in still water. _____

Extra Practice 19
Addition and Subtraction of Polynomials
Use after Section 4.1

EXAMPLES:

$$\text{Add.} \quad \left(2x^2 - 3x + 4\right) + \left(8x^2 - 7x - 6\right) = 2x^2 - 3x + 4 + 8x^2 - 7x - 6$$
$$= \left(2 + 8\right)x^2 + (-3 - 7)x + (4 - 6)$$
$$= 10x^2 - 10x - 2$$

$$\text{Add.} \quad \begin{array}{r} 3x^2 + 3x - 7 \\ 4x^2 - 2x + 8 \\ \hline 7x^2 + x + 1 \end{array}$$

Add.

1. $(2x - 3) + (4x - 2) =$ _____

2. $(3x + 7) + (5x - 4) =$ _____

3. $\left(6x^2 + 2\right) + \left(3x^2 - 4x + 5\right) =$ _____

4. $(2x - 3) + \left(5x^2 - 4x + 2\right) =$ _____

5. $\left(4x^2 + 2x\right) + \left(5x^2 - 3x\right) =$ _____

6. $\left(7x^2 - 3x + 2\right) + \left(3x - 2x^2 + 8\right) =$ _____

7. $\left(4x^5 - 3x^3 + 2x^2 - 1\right) + \left(5x^4 - 7x^3 + 3x + 1\right) = $ _____

8. $\left(1 + 2x^2 - 3x^3 + 5x^4\right) + \left(3x^2 - 3x^3 + 7x^4 - 2x\right) = $ _____

9. $4x^2 + 7x - 8$
$3x^2 + 2x + 3$
$\underline{x^2 + 5}$

10. $7x^2 - 8x + 7$
$7x + 5$
$\underline{-2x^2 + 3x}$

EXAMPLES:

Subtract. $\quad \left(5x^2 - 7x + 2\right) - \left(3x^2 - 2x + 3\right) = 5x^2 - 7x + 2 - 3x^2 + 2x - 3$

$$= 2x^2 - 5x - 1$$

$4x^4 - 3x^2 + 5x - 1$
Subtract. $\underline{2x^4 + 4x - 8}$
$2x^4 - 3x^2 + x + 7$

Subtract.

11. $(4x + 3) - (7x - 5) = $ _____

12. $(-3x - 5) - (-7x - 4) = $ _____

13. $\left(5x^2 - 3x + 2\right) - \left(2x^2 + 7x + 5\right) = $ _____

14. $\left(5x^3 - 3x + 1\right) - \left(-2x^3 + x^2 - 4\right) = $ _____

15. $\left(1 - 2x + 5x^2\right) - \left(2 - 6x + 2x^2\right) = $ _____

16. $\left(5 - 3x^2\right) - \left(4x^2 - 2x + 7\right) = $ _____

17. $\left(4x^3 - 7x^2 + 2x - 1\right) - \left(8x^3 - 3x^2 + 5x - 2\right) = $ _____

18. $\left(8x^5 - 4x + 5\right) - \left(3x^4 + 2x - 7\right) = $ _____

19. $5x^2 - 3x + 2$
$\underline{4x^2 + 7x - 5}$

20. $8x^3 + 2x - 3$
$\underline{4x^3 - 2x^2 + 8}$

Extra Practice 20
Multiplication of Polynomials
Use after Section 4.2

EXAMPLES:

Multiply. $\qquad \left(4x^2\right)(2xy) = 8x^3y$

$$4x(3x - 5) = 12x^2 - 20x$$
$$(5x + 2)(x + 3) = 5x(x + 3) + 2(x + 3)$$
$$= 5x^2 + 15x + 2x + 6$$
$$= 5x^2 + 17x + 6$$

$$(4x - 3)\left(x^2 + 2x - 1\right) = 4x\left(x^2 + 2x - 1\right) - 3\left(x^2 + 2x - 1\right)$$
$$= 4x^3 + 8x^2 - 4x - 3x^2 - 6x + 3$$
$$= 4x^3 + 5x^2 - 10x + 3$$

Multiply.

1. $(3x^2)(5x^3) = $ _____

2. $(4x^4)(-3x^2) = $ _____

3. $(8y^3)(-4y^5) = $ _____

4. $(2z)(-3z)(4z^5) = $ _____

5. $3x(4x - 7) = $ _____

6. $5x(-2x + 9) = $ _____

7. $8x^3(4x^2 + 3x + 2) = $ _____

8. $-9x^2(3x^3 + 7x - 2) = $ _____

9. $(x + 3)(x + 5) = $ _____

10. $(7x + 6)(2x + 3) = $ _____

11. $(5x + 8)(2x + 1) = $ _____

12. $(x - 3)(x - 5) = $ _____

13. $(3x - 7)(x - 1) = $ _____

14. $(6x - 2)(7x - 6) = $ _____

15. $(x^2 - 1)(x + 3) = $ _____

16. $(2x + 4)(x^2 - 8) = $ _____

17. $(x - 5)(x^2 + 3x - 4) = $ _____

18. $(x + 2)(x^2 - 7x - 2) = $ _____

19. $(x + 4)(x^3 - 3x^2 + 4x - 5) = $ _____

20. $(x^2 + 3x + 7)(x^2 - 2x + 4) = $ _____

21. $x^2 - 6x + 4$
    $x^2 + 3x + 2$

22. $x^2 - 8x + 5$
    $x^2 - 2x - 3$

Extra Practice 21
Factoring Polynomials
Use after Sections 4.3 – 4.7

EXAMPLES:
   Factor completely.
   a) $4x^3 + 12x^2 - 8x = 4x(x^2 + 3x - 2)$

   b) $5x^3 - 3x^2 + 20x - 12 = x^2(5x - 3) + 4(5x - 3) = (5x - 3)(x^2 + 4)$

   c) $x^2 + 2x - 35 = (x + 7)(x - 5)$

   d) $3x^2 - 5x - 2 = (3x + 1)(x - 2)$

   e) $x^2 - 18x + 81 = (x - 9)^2$

   f) $4x^2 - 25y^2 = (2x + 5y)(2x - 5y)$

Factor.

1. $x^2 - 6x - 16 = $ _____

2. $4y^2 + 7y - 2 = $ _____

3. $5a^3 - 25a^2 + 15a = $ _____

4. $9x^2 - 16 = $ _____

5. $x^2 - 64 = $ _____

6. $a^2 + 12a + 27 = $ _____

7. $6x^2 + 12x + 6 = $ _____

8. $x^3 + 2x^2 - 5x - 10 = $ _____

9. $x^2 - 10x + 21 = $ _____

10. $12x^5 - 6x^3 + 3x^2 = $ _____

11. $6y^2 - 54 = $ _____

12. $4y^2 - 17y - 15 = $ _____

13. $6x^2 - 7x + 2 =$ _____

14. $5x^2 - 5 =$ _____

15. $y^5 + 3y^3 + 4y^2 + 12 =$ _____

16. $x^2 - 7x - 18 =$ _____

17. $x^2 - 8x + 16 =$ _____

18. $a^2 - 9a + 14 =$ _____

19. $49x^2 - 1 =$ _____

20. $8x^4 - 4x^3 + 12x^2 =$ _____

21. $y^2 + 10y + 25 =$ _____

22. $3a^2 + 12a - 3 =$ _____

23. $x^4 - 81 =$ _____

24. $9y^2 - 12y + 4 =$ _____

25. $a^2 + 11a + 30 =$ _____

26. $8t^2 + 2t - 3 =$ _____

27. $75x^2 - 30x + 3 =$ _____

28. $3t^2 - 8t - 3 =$ _____

29. $x^2 + 3x + 8x + 24 =$ _____

30. $y^2 - 22y + 121 =$ _____

31. $x^2 - 2x - 3 =$ _____

32. $4x^2 - 24x + 36 =$ _____

33. $y^2 - 6y + 5 =$ _____

34. $25t^2 - 4 =$ _____

35. $14x^3 - 7x^2 + 21x =$ _____

36. $9x^2 + 42x + 49 =$ _____

37. $9x^2 - 81 =$ _____

38. $12x^2 + 4x - 5 =$ _____

39. $49a^2 - 28a + 4 =$ _____

40. $8x^2 - 29x - 12 =$ _____

Extra Practice 22
Solving Problems Using Quadratic Equations
Use after Section 4.8

EXAMPLE:

Three times the square of a number plus five times that number is 2. Find the number.

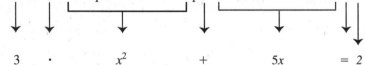

Three times the square of a number plus five times that number is 2.

$$3 \quad \cdot \quad x^2 \quad + \quad 5x \quad = 2$$

Solve:
$$3x^2 + 5x = 2$$
$$3x^2 + 5x - 2 = 0$$
$$(3x - 1)(x + 2) = 0$$

$$x = \frac{1}{3} \text{ and } x = -2$$

The values $\frac{1}{3}$ and -2 check in the original problem. There are two numbers, $\frac{1}{3}$ and -2.

Solve.

1. If you subtract a number from twice its square, the result is 3. Find all such numbers.

   _____

2. If 6 is added to the square of a number, the result is 22. Find all such numbers.

   _____

3. Five more than the square of a number is six times the number. Find all such numbers.
   _____

4. Twenty more than the square of a number is twelve times the number. Find all such numbers.
   _____

5. The product of the page numbers on two facing pages of a book is 600. Find the page numbers.
   _____

6. The product of two positive consecutive even integers is 224. Find the integers.
   _____

7. Two more than a number times five less than that number is 18. Find all such numbers.
   _____

8. The length of a rectangle is 8 cm greater than the width. The area of the rectangle is 105 cm². Find the width and the length. _____

9. The area of a square is 45 more than the perimeter. Find the length of a side.
   _____

10. The height of a triangle is 6 m less than the base. The area is 56 m². Find the height and the base.
    _____

11. The base of a triangle is 8 cm greater than the height. The area of the triangle is 120 cm². Find the height and the base. _____

12. The sum of the squares of two consecutive odd whole numbers is 202. Find the numbers.
    _____

Extra Practice 23
Addition and Subtraction of Rational Expressions
Use after Section 5.2

EXAMPLE:

Do this calculation.

$$\frac{5x}{x^2 - 3x - 4} - \frac{2x}{x^2 - 6x + 8}$$

$$= \frac{5x}{(x - 4)(x + 1)} - \frac{2x}{(x - 4)(x - 2)}, \text{LCM} = (x - 4)(x - 2)(x + 1)$$

$$= \frac{5x}{(x - 4)(x + 1)} \cdot \frac{x - 2}{x - 2} - \frac{2x}{(x - 4)(x - 2)} \cdot \frac{x + 1}{x + 1}$$

$$= \frac{5x(x - 2) - 2x(x + 1)}{(x - 4)(x - 2)(x + 1)}$$

$$= \frac{5x^2 - 10x - 2x^2 - 2x}{(x - 4)(x - 2)(x + 1)}$$

$$= \frac{3x^2 - 12x}{(x - 4)(x - 2)(x + 1)}$$

$$= \frac{3x(x - 4)}{(x - 4)(x - 2)(x + 1)}$$

$$= \frac{3x}{(x - 2)(x + 1)}$$

Add or subtract. Simplify.

1. $\dfrac{x-1}{x+3} + \dfrac{x+7}{x+3}$ _____

2. $\dfrac{x-1}{x+6} + \dfrac{x+3}{x-2}$ _____

3. $\dfrac{a^2}{a-4} + \dfrac{16}{4-a}$ _____

4. $\dfrac{4y}{y^2-y-2} - \dfrac{5y}{y^2+y-6}$ _____

5. $\dfrac{3x+2}{x-1} - \dfrac{x+5}{x-1}$ _____

6. $\dfrac{4}{a+2} + \dfrac{a+1}{a^2-4} - \dfrac{3}{a-2}$ _____

7. $\dfrac{y-5}{3y+9} - \dfrac{y+1}{2y+6}$ _____

8. $\dfrac{5}{a} + \dfrac{3}{-a}$ _____

9. $\dfrac{x+1}{x^2-7x+10} + \dfrac{3}{x^2-x-2}$ _____

10. $\dfrac{b-3}{b^2-9} + \dfrac{b+3}{b^2+6b+9}$ _____

11. $\dfrac{a-5}{a^2-5a} + \dfrac{a+5}{a^2-25}$ _____

12. $\dfrac{y+7}{y^2-49} - \dfrac{3y+1}{49-y^2}$ _____

13. $\dfrac{x+2}{x^2+x} - \dfrac{1}{x} + \dfrac{3}{x+1}$ _____

14. $\dfrac{b+3}{2b+6} - \dfrac{2}{3b}$ _____

15. $\dfrac{5x}{x+2} - \dfrac{x}{x-1} + \dfrac{3}{x^2+x-2}$ _____

16. $\dfrac{5}{x^2+3x} - \dfrac{4}{x^2-x-12}$ _____

17. $\dfrac{a}{1-a} + \dfrac{3a}{a+1} - \dfrac{5}{a^2-1}$ _____

18. $\dfrac{8x+4}{2x^2-9x-5} + \dfrac{x-1}{x-5}$ _____

19. $\dfrac{y-5}{6y} - \dfrac{4y+1}{y}$ _____

20. $\dfrac{9x}{x^2-81} + \dfrac{3x}{x+9}$ _____

Extra Practice 24
Division of Polynomials
Use after Section 5.3

EXAMPLES:
  Divide.

  a) $\left(15x^6 - 10x^4 + 35x^3\right) \div 5x^3$

$$\dfrac{15x^6 - 10x^4 + 35x^3}{5x^3}$$
$$= \dfrac{15x^6}{5x^3} - \dfrac{10x^4}{5x^3} + \dfrac{35x^3}{5x^3}$$
$$= 3x^3 - 2x + 7$$

  Answer: $3x^3 - 2x + 7$

b) $\left(x^4 - 2x^2 + 5x - 6\right) \div (x + 2)$

$$
\begin{array}{r}
x^3 - 2x^2 + 2x + 1 \\
x + 2 \overline{)x^4 + 0x^3 - 2x^2 + 5x - 6} \\
\underline{x^4 + 2x^3} \\
-2x^3 - 2x^2 \\
\underline{-2x^3 - 4x^2} \\
2x^2 + 5x \\
\underline{2x^2 + 4x} \\
x - 6 \\
\underline{x + 2} \\
-8
\end{array}
$$

Answer: $\quad x^3 - 2x^2 + 2x + 1, \text{R} - 8, \text{ or } x^3 - 2x^2 + 2x + 1 + \dfrac{-8}{x + 2}$

We could also use synthetic division in Example (b). See Section 5.3 for an example.

Divide.

1. $\dfrac{32x^4 - 4x^2}{8} = $ _____

2. $\dfrac{3x^5 + 30x^3 + 18x}{6} = $ _____

3. $\dfrac{y - 4y^2 + y^4}{y} = $ _____

4. $\dfrac{27x^8 - 15x^4 + 3x^2}{x^2} = $ _____

5. $\left(25x^7 - 20x^4 + 15x^2\right) \div \left(-5x^2\right) = $ _____

6. $\left(36y^5 + 27y^4 - 18y^3\right) \div \left(9y^2\right) = $ _____

7. $\dfrac{8r^2s^2 + 10rs^3 - 6r^2s}{-2rs} = $ _____

8. $\dfrac{7x^3y^2 - 21x^2y + 35x^3y^4}{7x^2y} = $ _____

9. $\left(x^2 + 3x - 28\right) \div (x - 4) = $ _____

10. $\left(x^2 - 16x + 64\right) \div (x - 8) = $ _____

11. $\dfrac{x^2 - 81}{x + 9} = $ _____

12. $\dfrac{x^2 - 121}{x - 11} = $ _____

13. $\left(x^2 + 7x + 15\right) \div (x - 5) = $ _____

14. $\left(x^2 + 12x - 18\right) \div (x - 3) =$ _____

15. $\dfrac{10x^3 - 11x^2 + 19x + 10}{5x + 2} =$ _____

16. $\dfrac{12x^3 - 16x^2 - 27x + 36}{3x - 4} =$ _____

17. $\left(x^4 - 2x^2 + 3\right) \div (x - 1) =$ _____

18. $\left(x^4 + 5x^2 + 2\right) \div (x + 2) =$ _____

19. $\left(x^6 - 5x^3 - 36\right) \div \left(x^3 + 4\right) =$ _____

20. $\left(x^6 + 2x^3 - 10\right) \div \left(x^3 - 2\right) =$ _____

21. $\left(x^4 - 81\right) \div (x + 3) =$ _____

22. $\left(x^3 - 64\right) \div (x - 4) =$ _____

23. $\left(a^3 - 5a^2 + 25a - 125\right) \div (a - 5) =$ _____

24. $\left(a^3 - 5a^2 + 25a - 125\right) \div (a + 5) =$ _____

Extra Practice 25
Simplifying Complex Rational Expressions
Use after Section 5.4

EXAMPLE:

Simplify.

$$\frac{3 - \frac{1}{x}}{9 - \frac{1}{x^2}} = \frac{3 - \frac{1}{x}}{9 - \frac{1}{x^2}} \cdot \frac{x^2}{x^2} \qquad \text{or} \qquad \frac{3 - \frac{1}{x}}{9 - \frac{1}{x^2}} = \frac{3 \cdot \frac{x}{x} - \frac{1}{x}}{9 \cdot \frac{x^2}{x^2} - \frac{1}{x^2}}$$

$$= \frac{3 \cdot x^2 - \frac{1}{x} \cdot x^2}{9 \cdot x^2 - \frac{1}{x^2} \cdot x^2} \qquad\qquad = \frac{\dfrac{3x - 1}{x}}{\dfrac{9x^2 - 1}{x^2}}$$

$$= \frac{3x^2 - x}{9x^2 - 1} \qquad\qquad\qquad = \frac{3x - 1}{x} \cdot \frac{x^2}{9x^2 - 1}$$

$$= \frac{x(3x - 1)}{(3x - 1)(3x + 1)} \qquad\qquad = \frac{3x - 1}{x} \cdot \frac{x^2}{(3x - 1)(3x + 1)}$$

$$= \frac{x}{3x + 1} \qquad\qquad\qquad = \frac{x}{3x + 1}$$

Simplify.

1. $\dfrac{1 + \dfrac{4}{9}}{1 - \dfrac{2}{3}}$ _____

2. $\dfrac{\dfrac{8}{27} - 8}{\dfrac{1}{3} + 1}$ _____

3. $\dfrac{\frac{1}{x} + 4}{\frac{1}{x} - 2}$ _____

4. $\dfrac{\frac{4}{a} + a}{\frac{a}{4} + a}$ _____

5. $\dfrac{\frac{1}{x} - 1}{\frac{1}{x} - 2}$ _____

6. $\dfrac{\frac{3}{y} + \frac{2}{3y}}{y + \frac{y}{3}}$ _____

7. $\dfrac{1 - \frac{1}{x}}{1 - \frac{1}{x^2}}$ _____

8. $\dfrac{4 - \frac{1}{x}}{\frac{4}{x}}$ _____

9. $\dfrac{\frac{a}{a + b}}{\frac{a^2}{a^2 - b^2}}$ _____

10. $\dfrac{\frac{1}{x} + \frac{1}{y}}{\frac{x}{y} - \frac{y}{x}}$ _____

11. $\dfrac{\frac{4}{m} + \frac{3}{m^3}}{\frac{2}{m^2} - \frac{5}{m}}$ _____

12. $\dfrac{\frac{3}{4x^3} - \frac{1}{2x}}{\frac{3}{2x} + \frac{5}{4x^3}}$ _____

13. $\dfrac{\frac{1}{8} - \frac{1}{y}}{\frac{8 - y}{8}}$ _____

14. $\dfrac{9 - \frac{4}{x^4}}{3x + \frac{2}{x}}$ _____

15. $\dfrac{\frac{a - 4}{a^3}}{\frac{2}{a} - \frac{8}{a^2}}$ _____

16. $\dfrac{\frac{4}{x^2 y} + \frac{3}{xy^2}}{\frac{2}{xy^3} + \frac{1}{x^2 y}}$ _____

Extra Practice 26
Solving Rational Equations
Use after Section 5.5

EXAMPLE:

Solve. $\dfrac{5}{x + 2} = \dfrac{3}{x}$

The LCM is $x(x + 2)$, $\qquad x(x + 2)\left(\dfrac{5}{x + 2}\right) = x(x + 2)\left(\dfrac{3}{x}\right)$

$$5x = 3(x + 2)$$
$$5x = 3x + 6$$
$$2x = 6$$
$$x = 3$$

Check: $\dfrac{5}{x + 2} = \dfrac{3}{x}$

$\dfrac{5}{3 + 2}$	$\dfrac{3}{3}$
$\dfrac{5}{5}$	1
1	TRUE

The solution is 3.

Solve.

1. $\dfrac{4}{x-1} = \dfrac{5}{x}$ _____

2. $\dfrac{x-3}{x+2} = \dfrac{4}{5}$ _____

3. $\dfrac{5}{x} = \dfrac{4}{x} + \dfrac{1}{2}$ _____

4. $\dfrac{1}{3} - \dfrac{3}{4} = \dfrac{x}{12}$ _____

5. $\dfrac{4}{3x} + \dfrac{2}{x} = \dfrac{2}{3}$ _____

6. $\dfrac{8}{x-5} = \dfrac{2}{x+5}$ _____

7. $\dfrac{x-7}{x+3} = \dfrac{2x}{x+3}$ _____

8. $\dfrac{y-1}{4} - \dfrac{y+1}{10} = 1$ _____

9. $\dfrac{a+3}{a} = 5$ _____

10. $b - \dfrac{3}{b} = 2$ _____

11. $\dfrac{1}{x} - \dfrac{4}{x} + \dfrac{5}{x} = \dfrac{1}{4}$ _____

12. $\dfrac{x-2}{x+2} = \dfrac{x+10}{x}$ _____

13. $x + \dfrac{5}{x} = 6$ _____

14. $\dfrac{2x}{x-6} - \dfrac{1}{x+6} = \dfrac{27}{x^2-36}$ _____

15. $\dfrac{x-2}{x} = 4 - \dfrac{x+4}{x-3}$ _____

16. $\dfrac{2x+1}{5x-3} = \dfrac{5x+1}{6x-2}$ _____

17. $\dfrac{2x-1}{5} - \dfrac{x+2}{15} = 1$ _____

18. $\dfrac{x+3}{x-1} = \dfrac{x+2}{x-3}$ _____

Extra Practice 27

Solving Problems and Proportions

Use after Section 5.6

EXAMPLE:

A number plus five times its reciprocal is -6. Find the number.

A number plus five times its reciprocal is -6.

$$x \quad + \quad 5 \quad \cdot \quad \dfrac{1}{x} \quad = -6$$

Solve: $x + 5 \cdot \dfrac{1}{x} = -6$

$$x\left(x + \dfrac{5}{x}\right) = x(-6) \qquad \text{Multiplying by the LCD, } x, \text{ on both sides.}$$
$$x^2 + 5 = -6x$$
$$x^2 + 6x + 5 = 0$$
$$(x+5)(x+1) = 0$$
$$x = -5 \text{ or } x = -1$$

The values -5 and -1 check in the original problem. The solutions are -5 and -1.

Solve.

1. A number minus three times its reciprocal is 2. Find the number. _____

2. The sum of a number and twice its reciprocal is 3. Find the number. _____

3. It takes Carolyn 4 hr to type a final exam. It takes Elise 3 hr to do the same job. How long would it take them, working together, to do the typing? _____

4. A swimming pool can be filled in 15 hr by pipe A alone and in 24 hr by pipe B alone. How long would it take to fill the pool if both pipes were working? _____

5. One car travels 30 km/h faster than another. In the same time that one travels 200 km, the other goes 320 km. Find their speeds. _____

6. The speed of a freight train is 16 mph slower than the speed of a passenger train. The freight train travels 420 miles in the same time that it takes the passenger train to travel 500 miles. Find the speed of each train. _____

7. William walked 195 km in 12 days. At this rate, how far would he walk in 36 days?

   _____

8. The winner of an election for class president won by a vote of 8 to 5 with 992 votes. How many votes did the loser get? _____

9. Triangles ABC and XYZ are similar. Solve for z if $x = 12$, $a = 10$, and $c = 8$.

   _____

10. Triangles DEF and GHI are similar. Solve for e if $d = 15$, $g = 9$, and $h = 6$.

    _____

11. To determine the number of deer in a game preserve, a game warden catches 415 deer, tags them, and lets them loose. Later, 140 deer are caught; 28 of them are tagged. Estimate the number of deer in the preserve. _____

Extra Practice 28
Multiplying, Dividing, and Simplifying Radical Expressions
Use after Section 6.3

EXAMPLES:

Simplify. Assume that all expressions represent nonnegative numbers.

a) $\sqrt[3]{320x^6y^4z^2}$

$= \sqrt[3]{64 \cdot 5 \cdot x^6 \cdot y^3 \cdot y \cdot z^2}$

$= \sqrt[3]{64x^6y^3}\sqrt[3]{5yz^2}$

$= 4x^2y\sqrt[3]{5yz^2}$

b) $\sqrt[4]{(81a^8b^4)^2}$

$= \left(\sqrt[4]{3^4a^8b^4}\right)^2$

$= (3a^2b)^2$

$= 9a^4b^2$

c) $\sqrt{\dfrac{75y^5}{16x^2}}$

$= \dfrac{\sqrt{75y^5}}{\sqrt{16x^2}}$

$= \dfrac{\sqrt{25y^4 \cdot 3y}}{\sqrt{16x^2}}$

$= \dfrac{5y^2\sqrt{3y}}{4x}$

Simplify. Assume that all expressions represent nonnegative numbers.

1. $\sqrt{20x^3yz^2} =$ _____

2. $\sqrt[3]{128x^4y^2} =$ _____

3.　$\sqrt[4]{a^{16}b^{12}} =$ _____

4.　$\sqrt{\dfrac{49a^3}{b^4}} =$ _____

5.　$\sqrt{45a^3bc^2} =$ _____

6.　$\sqrt{16^3} =$ _____

7.　$\sqrt[3]{\dfrac{16x^5}{y^6}} =$ _____

8.　$\sqrt[4]{64a^7b^{12}} =$ _____

9.　$\sqrt{50a^2b^5} =$ _____

10.　$\sqrt[5]{(32x^{10})^3} =$ _____

11.　$\sqrt{\dfrac{16x^3}{81}} =$ _____

12.　$\sqrt{500x^2yz^{11}} =$ _____

13.　$\sqrt[3]{216^2} =$ _____

14.　$\sqrt[3]{\dfrac{64a^7}{27}} =$ _____

15.　$\sqrt[3]{240x^4y^5} =$ _____

16.　$\sqrt[4]{x^7y^9z^{12}} =$ _____

17.　$\sqrt{\dfrac{24x^3}{25}} =$ _____

18.　$\sqrt[4]{256^3} =$ _____

19.　$\sqrt[5]{(32a^5b^{10})^3} =$ _____

20.　$\sqrt[3]{(54a^3)^2} =$ _____

EXAMPLES:

Assume that all expressions represent nonnegative numbers.

a)　Multiply and simplify.

$$\sqrt{32xy^3}\sqrt{4x^2y^5}$$

$$= \sqrt{128x^3y^8}$$

$$= \sqrt{64 \cdot 2 \cdot x^2 \cdot x \cdot y^8}$$

$$= \sqrt{64x^2y^8}\sqrt{2x}$$

$$= 8xy^4\sqrt{2x}$$

b)　Divide and simplify.

$$\dfrac{\sqrt[3]{56a^5b^{14}}}{\sqrt[3]{7ab^5}}$$

$$= \sqrt[3]{\dfrac{56a^5b^{14}}{7ab^5}}$$

$$= \sqrt[3]{8a^4b^9}$$

$$= \sqrt[3]{8 \cdot a^3 \cdot a \cdot b^9} = 2ab^3\sqrt[3]{a}$$

Multiply or divide and simplify. Assume that all expressions represent nonnegative numbers.

21.　$\sqrt[3]{5(x+2)^2}\sqrt[3]{25(x+2)^2} =$ _____

22.　$\dfrac{\sqrt{32a^5b^3}}{\sqrt{2ab^2}} =$ _____

23.　$\dfrac{6\sqrt{45x^3}}{3\sqrt{5x}} =$ _____

24.　$\sqrt[3]{x^7}\sqrt[3]{64xy^2} =$ _____

25.　$\sqrt{8x^3y}\sqrt{3xy^2} =$ _____

26.　$\dfrac{\sqrt[3]{81a^5b^8}}{\sqrt[3]{3ab^2}} =$ _____

27. $\dfrac{\sqrt[3]{625x^6y^4}}{\sqrt[3]{5xy}} =$ _____

28. $\sqrt{6(x+3)^3}\sqrt{3(x+3)} =$ _____

29. $\sqrt[3]{6^5a^2b}\,\sqrt[3]{6^2ab} =$ _____

30. $\dfrac{\sqrt[3]{27xy^7}}{\sqrt[3]{xy}} =$ _____

31. $\dfrac{9\sqrt[5]{160x^8y^{11}}}{3\sqrt[5]{5xy^2}}$ _____

32. $\sqrt[3]{4(y-3)^2}\,\sqrt[3]{2(y-3)^5} =$ _____

Extra Practice 29
Addition, Subtraction, and More Multiplication with Radicals
Use after Section 6.4

EXAMPLES:

Add or subtract. Simplify by collecting like radical terms, if possible.

a) $\quad 5\sqrt{6} + 8\sqrt{6} = (5+8)\sqrt{6} = 13\sqrt{6}$

b) $\quad 8\sqrt{2} - \sqrt{18} = 8\sqrt{2} - \sqrt{9\cdot 2}$
$$= 8\sqrt{2} - 3\sqrt{2}$$
$$= (8-3)\sqrt{2} = 5\sqrt{2}$$

Multiply.

a) $\quad \sqrt{5}(\sqrt{6} + \sqrt{3}) = \sqrt{5}\cdot\sqrt{6} + \sqrt{5}\cdot\sqrt{3}$
$$= \sqrt{30} + \sqrt{15}$$

b) $\quad (3 + \sqrt{2})(9 + \sqrt{2}) = 3\cdot 9 + 3\cdot\sqrt{2} + \sqrt{2}\cdot 9 + \sqrt{2}\cdot\sqrt{2}$
$$= 27 + 3\sqrt{2} + 9\sqrt{2} + 2$$
$$= 29 + 12\sqrt{2}$$

Add or subtract. Simplify by collecting like radical terms, if possible.

1. $4\sqrt{5} + 6\sqrt{5}$ _____

2. $9\sqrt{3} - 2\sqrt{3}$ _____

3. $3\sqrt{2a} + \sqrt{2a}$ _____

4. $6\sqrt{11} + 2\sqrt{11} + \sqrt{11}$ _____

5. $\sqrt{x} - \sqrt{4x}$ _____

6. $2\sqrt{50} + 8\sqrt{2}$ _____

7. $6\sqrt{12} - 3\sqrt{3}$ _____

8. $\sqrt{80} + \sqrt{20}$ _____

9. $\sqrt{72} - \sqrt{98}$ _____

10. $\sqrt{125} - 3\sqrt{20} + 4\sqrt{45}$ _____

11. $5\sqrt{24} + 2\sqrt{54} - \sqrt{96}$ _____

12. $\sqrt{49a} - 5\sqrt{a} + \sqrt{81a}$ _____

Multiply.

13. $\sqrt{2}\left(\sqrt{7} + \sqrt{5}\right)$ _____

14. $\sqrt{10}\left(\sqrt{3} - \sqrt{2}\right)$ _____

15. $\left(4 + \sqrt{6}\right)\left(3 + \sqrt{6}\right)$ _____

16. $\left(8 - \sqrt{10}\right)\left(5 - \sqrt{10}\right)$ _____

17. $\left(\sqrt{7} + 1\right)\left(\sqrt{7} - 8\right)$ _____

18. $\left(\sqrt{3} + 5\right)\left(\sqrt{3} - 5\right)$ _____

19. $\left(\sqrt{2} - \sqrt{11}\right)\left(\sqrt{2} + \sqrt{11}\right)$ _____

20. $\left(6 + 5\sqrt{3}\right)\left(1 - \sqrt{3}\right)$ _____

21. $\left(2 - \sqrt{6}\right)\left(4 + 3\sqrt{6}\right)$ _____

22. $\left(5 + \sqrt{2}\right)^2$ _____

23. $\left(8 - \sqrt{3}\right)^2$ _____

24. $\left(6 - 2\sqrt{5}\right)^2$ _____

25. $\left(\sqrt{x} + \sqrt{7}\right)^2$ _____

26. $\left(\sqrt{6} - \sqrt{y}\right)^2$ _____

Extra Practice 30
Rationalizing Denominators
Use after Section 6.5

EXAMPLES:
Assume that all expressions represent nonnegative numbers.

a)   Rationalize the denominator.

$$\frac{\sqrt[3]{4x^2}}{\sqrt[3]{2y^5}}$$

$$= \frac{\sqrt[3]{4x^2}}{\sqrt[3]{3y^5}} \cdot \frac{\sqrt[3]{9y}}{\sqrt[3]{9y}}$$

$$= \frac{\sqrt[3]{36x^2y}}{\sqrt[3]{27y^6}}$$

$$= \frac{\sqrt[3]{36x^2y}}{3y^2}$$

b)   Rationalize the denominator.

$$\frac{5}{\sqrt{7} + \sqrt{5}}$$

$$= \frac{5}{\sqrt{7} + \sqrt{5}} \cdot \frac{\sqrt{7} - \sqrt{5}}{\sqrt{7} - \sqrt{5}}$$

$$= \frac{5\sqrt{7} - 5\sqrt{5}}{\left(\sqrt{7}\right)^2 - \left(\sqrt{5}\right)^2}$$

$$= \frac{5\sqrt{7} - 5\sqrt{5}}{7 - 5}$$

$$= \frac{5\sqrt{7} - 5\sqrt{5}}{2}$$

Rationalize the denominator. Assume that all expressions represent nonnegative numbers.

1. $\sqrt{\dfrac{6}{7}} =$ _____

2. $\dfrac{\sqrt{2}}{\sqrt{5}} =$ _____

3. $\sqrt{\dfrac{8x}{3y}} =$ _____

4. $\sqrt{\dfrac{2x}{3y}} =$ _____

5. $\dfrac{\sqrt[3]{3x^2}}{\sqrt[3]{5y^4}} =$ _____

6. $\dfrac{\sqrt[4]{7y^3}}{\sqrt[4]{8x^5}} =$ _____

7. $\dfrac{\sqrt[3]{4x^2}}{\sqrt[3]{5y}} =$ _____

8. $\dfrac{\sqrt[5]{2x^3}}{\sqrt[5]{3y}} =$ _____

9. $\dfrac{\sqrt[3]{3x}}{\sqrt[3]{y}} =$ _____

10. $\sqrt{\dfrac{5y}{3x}} =$ _____

11. $\dfrac{2x}{\sqrt{5y}} =$ _____

12. $\dfrac{3x^2}{\sqrt[3]{2y}} =$ _____

13. $\dfrac{4}{8 - \sqrt{5}} =$ _____

14. $\dfrac{-3\sqrt{5}}{\sqrt{6} - \sqrt{3}} =$ _____

15. $\dfrac{18\sqrt{3}}{\sqrt{3} - \sqrt{7}} =$ _____

16. $\dfrac{2\sqrt{3}}{\sqrt{3x} - \sqrt{2x}} =$ _____

17. $\dfrac{\sqrt{7} - 2\sqrt{3}}{\sqrt{7} - \sqrt{3}} =$ _____

18. $\dfrac{2\sqrt{x} - \sqrt{y}}{\sqrt{x} + \sqrt{y}} =$ _____

19. $\dfrac{\sqrt{7} - 2\sqrt{x}}{\sqrt{7} + \sqrt{x}} =$ _____

20. $\dfrac{2\sqrt{x} - \sqrt{y}}{\sqrt{x} - 3\sqrt{y}} =$ _____

Extra Practice 31
Solving Radical Equations
Use after Section 6.6

EXAMPLE: Solve. $\sqrt{x + 19} - \sqrt{x - 20} = 3$

$$\sqrt{x + 19} = \sqrt{x - 20} + 3$$
$$\left(\sqrt{x + 19}\right)^2 = \left(\sqrt{x - 20} + 3\right)^2$$
$$x + 19 = x - 20 + 6\sqrt{x - 20} + 9$$
$$30 = 6\sqrt{x - 20}$$
$$5 = \sqrt{x - 20}$$
$$5^2 = \left(\sqrt{x - 20}\right)^2$$
$$25 = x - 20$$
$$45 = x$$

The solution is 45.

Check: $\sqrt{x + 19} - \sqrt{x - 20} = 3$

$\sqrt{45 + 19} - \sqrt{45 - 20}$	3
$\sqrt{64} - \sqrt{25}$	
$8 - 5$	
3	TRUE

Solve.

1. $x + 2 = \sqrt{7x + 2}$ _____

2. $\sqrt{x} - 3 = 3$ _____

3. $\sqrt{x + 9} + \sqrt{x + 2} = 7$ _____

4. $y - 5 = \sqrt{y - 3}$ _____

5. $\sqrt{-3x + 4} = 2 - x$ _____

6. $1 - x = \sqrt{-5x + 1}$ _____

7. $\sqrt{a} + 2 = 5$ _____

8. $\sqrt{x - 5} + \sqrt{x + 6} = 11$ _____

9. $\sqrt[3]{x - 1} - 3 = 0$ _____

10. $\sqrt{y + 3} - \sqrt{2y - 8} = 1$ _____

11. $\sqrt{x + 12} - \sqrt{x - 12} = 12$ _____

12. $\sqrt{x + 4} - \sqrt{2x + 9} = -1$ _____

13. $\sqrt{x + 7} + \sqrt{x - 4} = 11$ _____

14. $5 - \sqrt{x} = 1$ _____

15. $\sqrt[3]{4x + 3} + 2 = 5$ _____

16. $\sqrt{x + 9} + \sqrt{x + 4} = 5$ _____

17. $\sqrt{x + 10} + \sqrt{x} = 3$ _____

18. $\sqrt{5x + 3} = \sqrt{3x + 7}$ _____

19. $\sqrt{7x + 8} - \sqrt{41 - 2x} = 3$ _____

20. $\sqrt{10 - 2x} - \sqrt{5x + 16} = 3$ _____

Extra Practice 32
Solving Quadratic Equations Using the Quadratic Formula
Use after Section 7.2

EXAMPLE: Solve $3x^2 - 5x + 1 = 0$ using the quadratic formula.

$$3x^2 - 5x + 1 = 0, a = 3, b = -5, c = 1$$

$$x = \frac{-(-5) \pm \sqrt{(-5)^2 - 4(3)(1))}}{2(3)}$$

$$= \frac{5 \pm \sqrt{25 - 12}}{6} = \frac{5 \pm \sqrt{13}}{6}$$

Quadratic Formula:
$$x = \frac{-b \pm \sqrt{b^2 - 4ac}}{2a}$$

Solve.

1. $x^2 - 3x = 4$ _____

2. $y^2 - 6y = -8$ _____

3. $x^2 = 10x - 25$ _____

4. $2y^2 - 7y - 15 = 0$ _____

5. $x^2 - 36 = 0$ _____

6. $y^2 - 49 = 0$ _____

7. $x^2 - 3x - 3 = 0$ _____

8. $x^2 - 5x - 7 = 0$ _____

9. $y^2 - 8y + 11 = 0$ _____

10. $y^2 + 7y - 1 = 0$ _____

11. $x^2 + 6x + 8 = 4$ _____

12. $x^2 - 3x + 1 = 6$ _____

13. $4x^2 + 7x + 2 = 0$ _____

14. $5x^2 - 3x - 1 = 0$ _____

15. $2x^2 - 3x = 3$ _____

16. $6x^2 + 6x = 8$ _____

17. $4y^2 - 6y - 1 = 0$ _____

18. $2y^2 - 5y = -3$ _____

19. $8x^2 = 200$ _____

20. $9x^2 = 144$ _____

Extra Practice 33
Solving Problems Using Quadratic Equations
Use after Section 7.3

EXAMPLE: Find the length of a diagonal of a square whose sides are 7 m long. Give an exact answer and an approximation to three decimal places.

Let $d =$ length of the diagonal.

Then substitute 7 for a, 7 for b, and d for c in the Pythagorean equation.
$$7^2 + 7^2 = d^2$$
$$49 + 49 = d^2$$
$$98 = d^2$$
$$\sqrt{98} = d$$
$$9.899 \approx d$$

The length of the diagonal is $\sqrt{98}$ m, or approximately 9.899 m.

Solve.

1. Find the length of a diagonal of a square whose sides are 11 cm long. _____

2. Find the length of a diagonal of a rectangle with width 9 cm and length 12 cm.

   _____

3. The width of a rectangle is 5 inches less than its length. The area of the rectangle is 84 in.^{2}. Find the dimensions of the rectangle. _____

4. The hypotenuse of a right triangle is 50 m long. The length of one leg is 10 m longer than the other. Find the length of the shorter leg. _____

5. The length of a rectangle is 4 times the width. The area of the rectangle is 900 in.^{2}. Find the length and the width. _____

6. The hypotenuse of a right triangle is 17 feet. One leg is 7 feet shorter than the other. Find the lengths of the legs. _____

7. The length of a rectangle is 5 inches more than twice the width. The area of the rectangle is 102 in.^{2}. How long is the rectangle? _____

8. The hypotenuse of a right triangle is 26 in. The length of one leg is 14 in. longer than the other. Find the length of the shorter leg. _____

9. The perimeter of a rectangle is 20 inches. The area of the same rectangle is 18 sq. inches. Find the width of the rectangle to the nearest tenth of an inch. _____

10. A landscaper wants to enclose a 90-ft by 120-ft rectangle with a walk of uniform width. He wants to use a supply of crushed rock that will cover 1744 square feet of walk. How wide should he make the walk? _____

11. A boat travels 12 miles upstream and then turns around and travels 12 miles downstream. The total time for both trips is 3 hours. If the stream flows at 1 mph, how fast does the boat travel in still water? Round the answer to the nearest tenth. _____

12. The speed of a boat in still water is 15 km/h. The boat travels 40 km upstream and 40 km downstream in a total time of 6 hr. What is the speed of the stream? _____

Extra Practice 34
Solving Equations Quadratic in Form
Use after Section 7.4

EXAMPLE: Solve. $\left(1 + 3\sqrt{x}\right)^2 - 11(1 + 3\sqrt{x}) + 28 = 0$

Let $u = 1 + 3\sqrt{x}$ and substitute u for $1 + 3\sqrt{x}$.
$$u^2 - 11u + 28 = 0$$
$$(u - 7)(u - 4) = 0$$
$$u - 7 = 0 \quad \text{or} \quad u - 4 = 0$$
$$u = 7 \quad \text{or} \quad u = 4$$

Substitute $1 + 3\sqrt{x}$ for u and solve for x.
$$1 + 3\sqrt{x} = 7 \quad \text{or} \quad 1 + 3\sqrt{x} = 4$$
$$3\sqrt{x} = 6 \quad \text{or} \quad 3\sqrt{x} = 3$$
$$\sqrt{x} = 2 \quad \text{or} \quad \sqrt{x} = 1$$
$$x = 4 \quad \text{or} \quad x = 1$$

Both values check. The solutions are 4 and 1.

Solve.

1. $a - 6\sqrt{a} - 27 = 0$ _____

2. $x^4 - 8x^2 + 12 = 0$ _____

3. $5x^{-2} - 5x^{-1} - 60 = 0$ _____

4. $(3x - 1)^2 + 2(3x - 1) - 15 = 0$ _____

5. $a - 10\sqrt{a} + 9 = 0$ _____

6. $(5 - \sqrt{x})^2 + 5(5 - \sqrt{x}) - 24 = 0$ _____

7. $x^4 - 6x^2 + 8 = 0$ _____

8. $x - 13\sqrt{x} + 36 = 0$ _____

9. $(y^2 - 2y)^2 - 11(y^2 - 2y) + 24 = 0$ _____

10. $x^4 + 4x^2 - 21 = 0$ _____

11. $(x^2 - 5x)^2 - 2(x^2 - 5x) - 24 = 0$ _____

12. $a - 12\sqrt{a} + 20 = 0$ _____

13. $(4x + 2)^2 - 10(4x + 2) + 25 = 0$ _____

14. $(\sqrt{x} - 7)^2 - 13(\sqrt{x} - 7) + 40 = 0$ _____

15. $x^4 - 7x^2 + 12 = 0$ _____

16. $2y^{-2} + 7y^{-1} - 15 = 0$ _____

Extra Practice 35
Graphs of Quadratic Functions
Use after Sections 7.5 and 7.6

See Sections 7.5 and 7.6 for examples.

1. $f(x) = 3x^2$

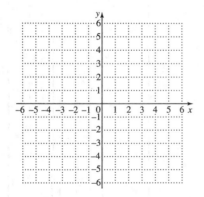

2. $f(x) = (x - 1)^2$

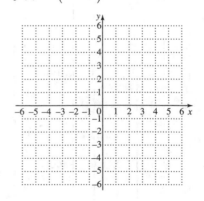

3. $f(x) = (x - 2)^2 + 3$

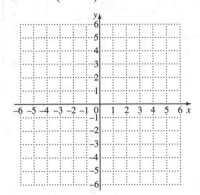

4. $f(x) = 2(x - 3)^2 + 1$

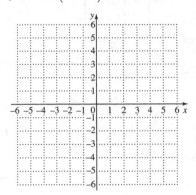

5. $f(x) = x^2 - 6x + 7$

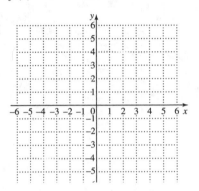

6. $f(x) = -4x^2$

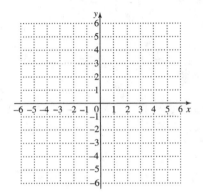

7. $f(x) = x^2 + 4x + 2$

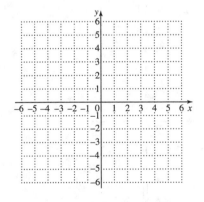

8. $f(x) = 3(x - 1)^2$

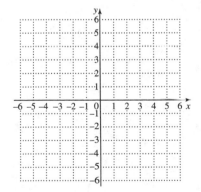

9. $f(x) = -2x^2 - 20x - 47$

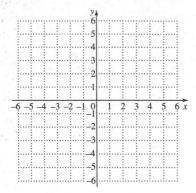

10. $f(x) = (x + 3)^2$

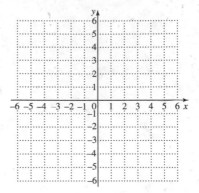

11. $f(x) = -\dfrac{1}{2}x^2$

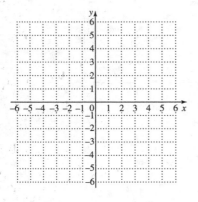

12. $f(x) = (x - 1)^2 - 2$

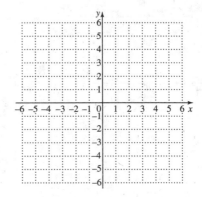

13. $f(x) = 2x^2 - 16x + 29$

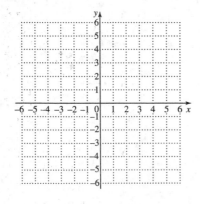

14. $f(x) = 2(x - 1)^2$

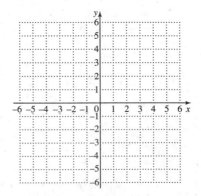

15. $f(x) = (x - 3)^2$

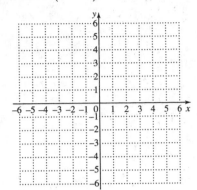

16. $f(x) = 1.5x^2$

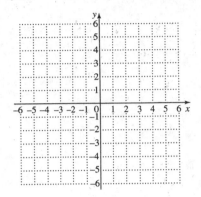

17. $f(x) = -2(x + 3)^2 + 4$

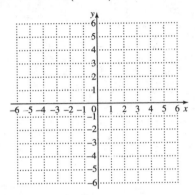

18. $f(x) = x^2 - 2x + 3$

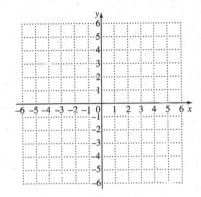

19. $f(x) = (x + 1)^2$

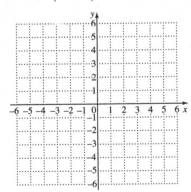

20. $f(x) = (x + 2)^2 - 3$

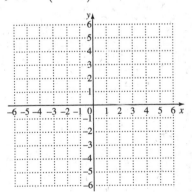

21. $f(x) = -4x^2 + 24x - 35$

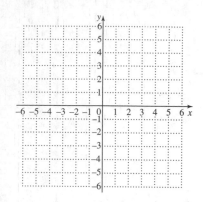

22. $f(x) = -\dfrac{1}{2}(x + 1)^2 + 4$

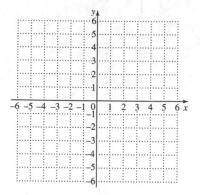

23. $f(x) = -2(x - 1)^2$

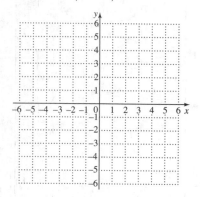

24. $f(x) = -4x^2$

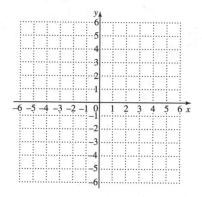

25. $f(x) = x^2 + 6x + 7$

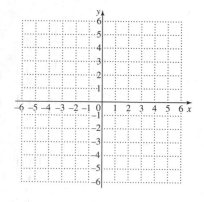

26. $f(x) = -(x + 4)^2$

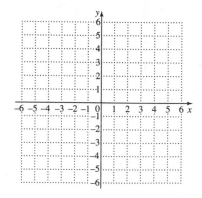

27. $f(x) = 4x^2 - 4x + 1$

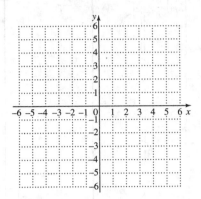

28. $f(x) = \dfrac{1}{3}(x + 3)^2$

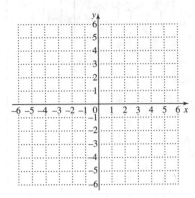

29. $f(x) = -x^2 - 4x - 9$

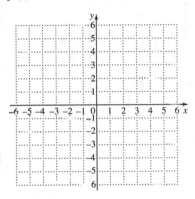

30. $f(x) = 2x^2 - 4x - 3$

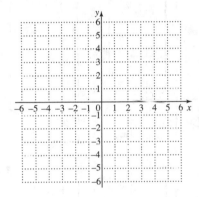

31. $f(x) = (x + 2)^2 - 1$

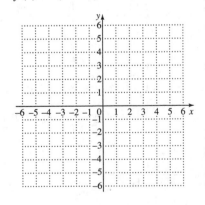

32. $f(x) = -4(x - 1)^2 + 1$

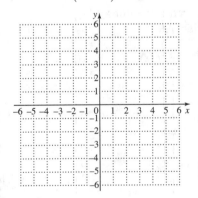

33. $f(x) = \frac{1}{4}(x - 4)^2$

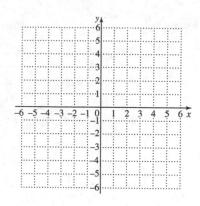

34. $f(x) = -\frac{1}{2}(x + 2)^2$

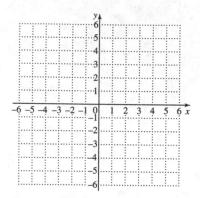

35. $f(x) = x^2 - x + 1$

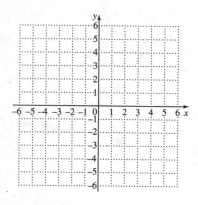

36. $f(x) = -3x^2 - 6x - 1$

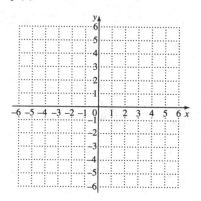

Extra Practice 36
Graphs of Quadratic Functions
Use after Section 7.6

EXAMPLE: Graph $f(x) = x^2 - 2x - 3$.

The *y*-intercept is found by finding $f(0)$. In $f(x) = x^2 - 2x - 3$, the *y*-intercept is $(0, -3)$.

The *x*-intercept(s) are found when $f(x) = 0$. Solve $x^2 - 2x - 3 = 0$ either by factoring or using the quadratic formula.

$$x^2 - 2x - 3 = 0$$
$$(x - 3)(x + 1) = 0$$
$$x = 3 \text{ or } x = -1 \quad \text{The } x\text{-intercepts are } (3, 0) \text{ and } -1, 0).$$

The *x*-coordinate of the vertex is found by using $-\frac{b}{2a}$ from the quadratic equation

$f(x) = ax^2 + bx + c$. The second coordinate of the vertex is found by substituting $-\frac{b}{2a}$ for *x* and computing $f\left(-\frac{b}{2a}\right)$. In $f(x) = x^2 - 2x - 3$, $a = 1$ and $b = -2$.

The *x*-coordinate of the vertex is $-\frac{b}{2a} = -\frac{(-2)}{2(1)} = \frac{2}{2} = 1$

We substitute 1 for *x* to find the second coordinate of the vertex:

$$f(x) = x^2 - 2x - 3 = (1)^2 - 2(1) - 3 = -4.$$

The vertex is $(1, -4)$. The axis of symmetry is $x = 1$.
We can also look at other points on the parabola and then draw a smooth graph.

x	y $f(x) = x^2 - 2x - 3$	$(x, f(x))$
-2	5	$(-2, 5)$
-1	0	$(-1, 0)$
0	-3	$(0, -3)$
1	-4	$(1, -4)$
2	-3	$(2, -3)$

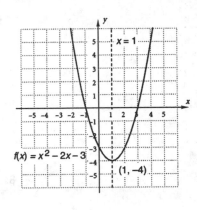

Graph the quadratic function. Find the vertex, the line of symmetry, and the maximum or minimum value.

1. $f(x) = 4x^2$

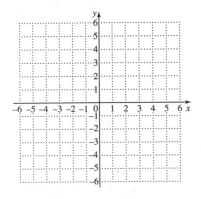

2. $f(x) = x^2 + 3$

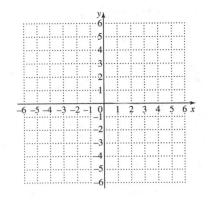

3. $f(x) = -x^2 + 4x$

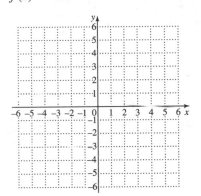

4. $f(x) = x^2 - x - 2$

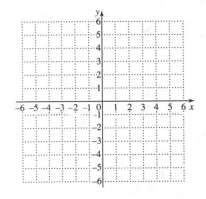

5. $f(x) = x^2 + 4x + 4$

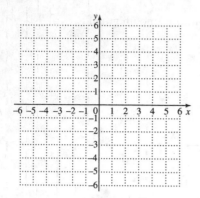

6. $f(x) = -\dfrac{1}{3}x^2$

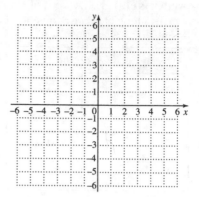

7. $f(x) = -x^2 + 2x + 3$

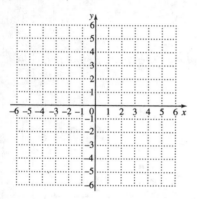

8. $f(x) = 1.5x^2$

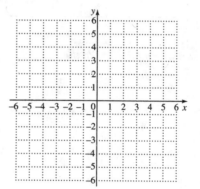

9. $f(x) = 4 - x^2$

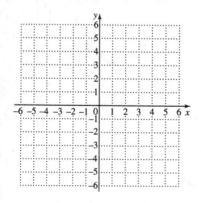

Extra Practice 37
Graphing Exponential and Logarithmic Functions
Use after Sections 8.1 and 8.3

See Sections 8.1 and 8.3 for examples.

Graph.

1. $f(x) = 2^{x-1}$

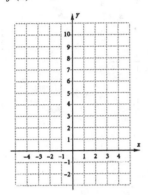

2. $f(x) = 3^x + 2$

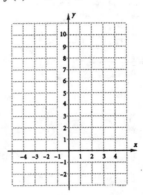

3. $f(x) = 2^x - 4$

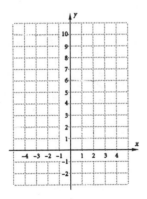

4. $f(x) = 5^{x-3}$

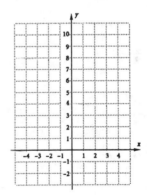

5. $f(x) = 4^{x+1}$

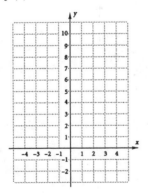

6. $f(x) = 2^x + 1$

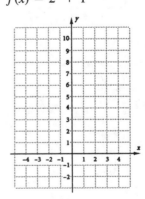

7. $f(x) = \left(\dfrac{1}{2}\right)^x$

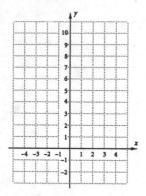

8. $f(x) = 4^{2-x}$

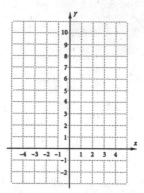

9. $f(x) = 2^{3x-1}$

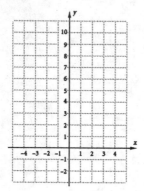

10. $x = 3^y$

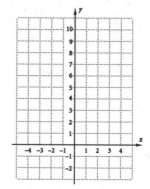

11. $x = \left(\dfrac{1}{3}\right)^y$

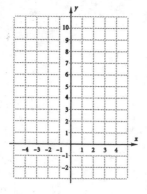

12. $x = \left(\dfrac{3}{4}\right)^y$

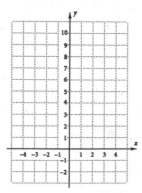

13. $f(x) = \log_3 x$

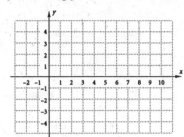

14. $f(x) = \log_5 x$

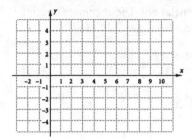

15. $f(x) = \log_{1/2} x$

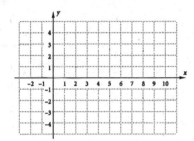

16. $f(x) = \log_{1/4} x$

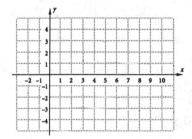

17. $f(x) = \log_2 x$

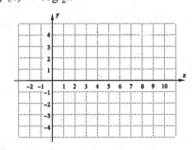

18. $f(x) = \log_{1/3} x$

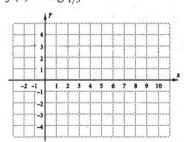

Extra Practice 38
Solving Exponential and Logarithmic Equations
Use after Section 8.6

EXAMPLES. Solve.

a) $7^{x-1} = 343$
    $7^{x-1} = 7^3$
    $x - 1 = 3$

    $x = 4$

b) $6^x = 15$
    $\log 6^x = \log 15$
    $x\log 6 = \log 15$

    $x = \dfrac{\log 15}{\log 6}$

    $x \approx \dfrac{1.1761}{0.7782}$

    $x \approx 1.5113$

c) $e^{-3t} = 0.04$
    $\ln e^{-3t} = \ln 0.04$
    $-3t\ln e = \ln 0.04$

    $-3t = \ln 0.04$

    $t = \dfrac{\ln 0.04}{-3}$

    $t \approx \dfrac{-3.2189}{-3}$

    $t \approx 1.073$

Solve.

1. $3^{5x} = 81$ _____

2. $e^{4t} = 120$ _____

3. $4^x = 6$ _____

4. $6^x = 2$ _____

5. $e^{-2t} = 0.6$ _____

6. $5^{3x+2} = 625$ _____

7. $8^{x+1} = 16$ _____

8. $10^x = 7$ _____

9. $7^x = 1520$ _____

10. $e^{0.04t} = 10$ _____

11. $e^{5t} = 5$ _____

12. $6^x = 7.1$ _____

13. $6^{x+3} = 36$ _____

14. $4^{x-1} = 3$ _____

15. $12^{2x-3} = 16$ _____

16. $10^{5-x} = 1000$ _____

EXAMPLE. Solve: $\log_2(x + 1) - \log_2(x - 1) = 4$

$$\log_2(x + 1) - \log_2(x - 1) = 4$$

$$\log_2\frac{x + 1}{x - 1} = 4$$

$$\frac{x + 1}{x - 1} = 16$$

$$x + 1 = 16x - 16$$

$$17 = 15x$$

$$\frac{17}{15} = x$$

The solution is $\dfrac{17}{15}$.

Check: $\log_2(x + 1) - \log_2(x - 1) = 4$

$$
\begin{array}{c|c}
\log_2\left(\dfrac{17}{15} + 1\right) - \log_2\left(\dfrac{17}{15} - 1\right) & 4 \\
\log_2\dfrac{32}{15} - \log_2\dfrac{2}{15} & \\
\log_2\left(\dfrac{32}{15} \div \dfrac{2}{15}\right) & \\
\log_2 16 & \\
4 &
\end{array}
$$

Solve.

17. $\log x + \log(x + 15) = 2$

_____

18. $\log(x + 2) - \log x = 3$

_____

19. $\log_3(2x - 7) = 4$

20. $\log_5(x - 11) = 2$

_____

_____

21. $\log x + \log(x - 21) = 2$

22. $\log_2(x - 2) + \log_2(x + 2) = 5$

_____

_____

23. $\log(3x + 4) = 1$

24. $\log(x + 33) - \log x = 2$

_____

_____

25. $\log x - \log(x + 5) = -1$

26. $\log_4(x + 3) - \log_4 x = 3$

_____

_____

27. $\log_4(x - 6) + \log_4(x + 6) = 3$

28. $\log_6 x + \log_6(x - 9) = 2$

_____

_____

29. $\log x + \log(x - 0.21) = -2$

30. $\log(x - 48) + \log x = 2$

_____

_____

31. $\log_7 x + \log_7(4x + 21) = 3$

32. $\log_2(5 - x) = 4$

_____

_____

Extra Practice 39
Graphing Circles, Ellipses, and Hyperbolas
Use after Sections 9.1–9.3

EXAMPLES: See Sections 9.1–9.3 for examples.
Graph.

1. $x^2 + y^2 = 16$

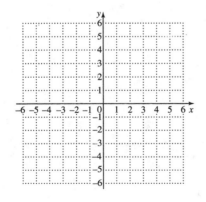

2. $x^2 + y^2 = 36$

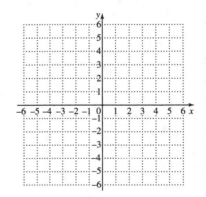

3. $x^2 + y^2 + 2x - 4y - 4 = 0$

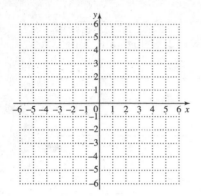

4. $x^2 + y^2 - 8x - 10y + 5 = 0$

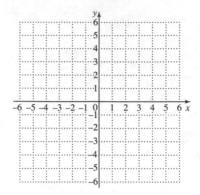

5. $\dfrac{x^2}{36} + \dfrac{y^2}{100} = 1$

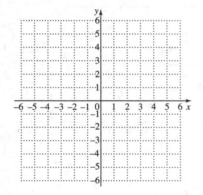

6. $\dfrac{x^2}{49} + \dfrac{y^2}{16} = 1$

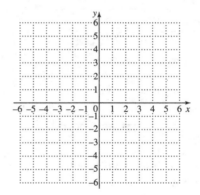

7. $4x^2 + y^2 = 36$

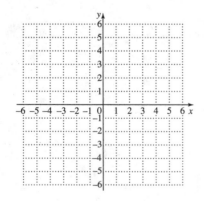

8. $4x^2 + 25y^2 = 100$

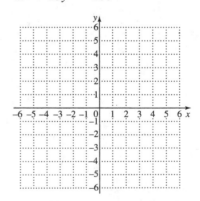

9. $\dfrac{x^2}{36} - \dfrac{y^2}{64} = 1$

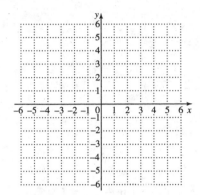

10. $\dfrac{y^2}{81} - \dfrac{x^2}{9} = 1$

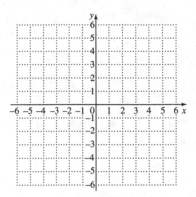

11. $4x^2 - 49y^2 = 196$

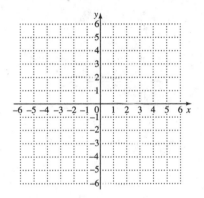

12. $16y^2 - 9x^2 = 144$

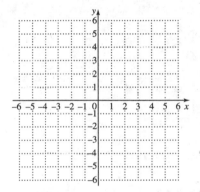

13. $\dfrac{x^2}{64} + y^2 = 1$

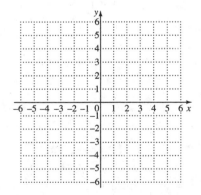

14. $\dfrac{y^2}{25} - \dfrac{x^2}{4} = 1$

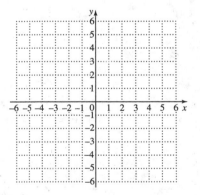

15. $16x^2 - 36y^2 = 144$

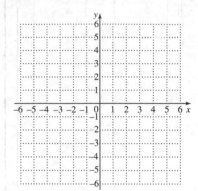

16. $x^2 + y^2 = 81$

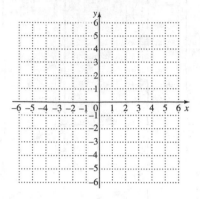

17. $x^2 + 9y^2 = 36$

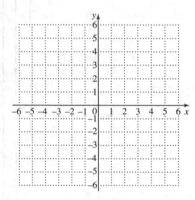

18. $x^2 + y^2 + 6x - 10y - 15 = 0$

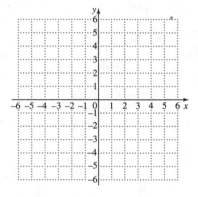

Extra Practice 40
Solving Nonlinear Systems of Equations
Use after Section 9.4

EXAMPLE. Solve:
$$4y^2 = 16 - 3x^2,$$
$$2x^2 = y^2 + 7.$$

$$3x^2 + 4y^2 = 16 \quad \rightarrow \quad 3x^2 + 4y^2 = 16$$
$$2x^2 - y^2 = 7 \quad \rightarrow \quad \underline{8x^2 - 4y^2 = 28} \text{ (Multiplying by 4)}$$
$$11x^2 = 44 \text{ (Adding)}$$
$$x^2 = 4$$
$$x = \pm 2$$

If $x = 2$, $x^2 = 4$, and if $x = -2$, $x^2 = 4$, so substituting 2 or -2 in $2x^2 = y^2 + 7$, we have $2 \cdot 4 = y^2 + 7$

$$1 = y^2$$
$$\pm 1 = y$$

The solutions are $(2, 1)$, $(-2, 1)$, $(2, -1)$, and $(-2, -1)$.

Solve.

1. $x^2 + y^2 = 20,$
     $xy = 8$

2. $x^2 + y^2 = 49,$
     $x^2 - y^2 = 49$

3. $x^2 - 25 = -y^2,$
   $y - x = 1$

   _____

4. $x^2 + y^2 = 82,$
   $xy = -9$

   _____

5. $x^2 + 4y^2 = 16,$
   $2y = 4 - x$

   _____

6. $x^2 + y^2 = 41,$
   $5x - 4y = 0$

   _____

7. $25x^2 + y^2 = 100,$
   $10x + 2y = 20$

   _____

8. $x^2 = 36 - y^2,$
   $x^2 = 36 + y^2$

   _____

9. $y^2 - 3x^2 = 25,$
   $3x^2 + y^2 = 25$

   _____

10. $x^2 + y^2 = 34,$
    $y - x = 2$

    _____

11. $x^2 - y = 8,$
    $x^2 + y^2 = 20$

    _____

12. $x^2 + y^2 = 64,$
    $y^2 = x + 8$

    _____

13. A rectangle has perimeter 170 cm, and the length of a diagonal is 65 cm. What are its dimensions?
    _____

14. The area of a rectangle is $12\sqrt{2}m^2$. The length of a diagonal is $\sqrt{34}m$. Find the dimensions.
    _____

15. The product of two numbers is -44. The sum of their squares is 137. Find the numbers.
    _____

16. The sum of the squares of two positive numbers is 89. Their difference is 3. What are the numbers?
    _____

17. The sum of the squares of two positive integers is 58. Their difference is 4. What are the integers?
    _____

18. The perimeter of a rectangle is 44 m and the area is 105 m^2. What are the dimensions of the rectangle? _____

19. The product of two numbers is $\frac{1}{6}$. The sum of their squares is $\frac{13}{36}$. Find the numbers.
    _____

20. The area of a rectangle is 0.48 cm^2. The length of a diagonal is 1.0 cm. Find the dimensions of the rectangle. _____

EXTRA PRACTICE EXERCISES ANSWERS

Extra Practice 1

1. -9 **2.** -1 **3.** 5 **4.** 0 **5.** -28 **6.** -12 **7.** 9 **8.** -2 **9.** 15 **10.** -28 **11.** -7 **12.** -1 **13.** -4 **14.** -8
15. 3 **16.** -11 **17.** 12 **18.** 7 **19.** 13 **20.** 1 **21.** -12 **22.** 5 **23.** 7 **24.** -7 **25.** 0 **26.** -6 **27.** -2
28. -16 **29.** $-\frac{23}{20}$ **30.** $\frac{1}{8}$ **31.** $\frac{1}{4}$ **32.** $-\frac{8}{15}$ **33.** $\frac{19}{36}$ **34.** $\frac{3}{14}$ **35.** -5.2 **36.** 6.5 **37.** -9.9 **38.** -3.6 **39.** 1.6
40. -16.4 **41.** -16 **42.** 0 **43.** 18 **44.** -5 **45.** -21 **46.** 7 **47.** -5 **48.** -10 **49.** 1 **50.** 14 **51.** -3
52. -10 **53.** 11 **54.** -13 **55.** -9 **56.** 12 **57.** -19 **58.** 13 **59.** -2 **60.** -5 **61.** 11 **62.** -8 **63.** -12
64. 14 **65.** -8 **66.** -4 **67.** 23 **68.** 6 **69.** $\frac{1}{8}$ **70.** $-\frac{17}{12}$ **71.** $-\frac{3}{20}$ **72.** $-\frac{11}{30}$ **73.** $\frac{59}{60}$ **74.** $\frac{5}{18}$ **75.** 21
76. -20.4 **77.** -3.7 **78.** -2.7 **79.** -7.1 **80.** 10.3

Extra Practice 2

1. -21 **2.** -72 **3.** -44 **4.** 28 **5.** -64 **6.** 143 **7.** -105 **8.** -20 **9.** -30 **10.** -180 **11.** 104 **12.** 33
13. -95 **14.** -180 **15.** -144 **16.** 105 **17.** -48 **18.** -108 **19.** 81 **20.** -120 **21.** 57 **22.** 135 **23.** -85
24. -168 **25.** $-\frac{4}{7}$ **26.** $-\frac{25}{36}$ **27.** $\frac{3}{4}$ **28.** $-\frac{1}{4}$ **29.** -6 **30.** $\frac{4}{9}$ **31.** -0.72 **32.** -30.6 **33.** 65.7 **34.** -8.7
35. -24.42 **36.** 38.18 **37.** 15 **38.** -26 **39.** -59 **40.** 25 **41.** -6 **42.** 119 **43.** -18 **44.** -6 **45.** -25
46. 9 **47.** -5 **48.** 12 **49.** -18 **50.** 3 **51.** 11 **52.** -20 **53.** -16 **54.** -8 **55.** 16 **56.** -15 **57.** 32 **58.** 5
59. -9 **60.** 3 **61.** $-\frac{3}{10}$ **62.** $-\frac{10}{9}$ **63.** 12 **64.** $-\frac{3}{2}$ **65.** -1 **66.** $\frac{3}{4}$ **67.** 5 **68.** -3 **69.** 5 **70.** -12
71. -10.468 **72.** -5.2

Extra Practice 3

1. -1 **2.** 5 **3.** -17 **4.** 3 **5.** -137 **6.** 3 **7.** 7 **8.** 7 **9.** -38 **10.** 36 **11.** 4 **12.** -32 **13.** -4 **14.** -16
15. $-\frac{5}{66}$ **16.** $-\frac{14}{9}$ **17.** $-\frac{14}{19}$ **18.** $\frac{4}{161}$ **19.** $\frac{7}{8}$ **20.** -16 **21.** 6 **22.** 38 **23.** 14 **24.** 3 **25.** 15 **26.** 40 **27.** 50
28. 525 **29.** 53 **30.** 2 **31.** 0 **32.** 5 **33.** 150 **34.** 0 **35.** 535 **36.** 100 **37.** 4 **38.** 48 **39.** 5 **40.** 2 **41.** $\frac{4}{5}$
42. $\frac{3}{2}$ **43.** $\frac{4}{7}$ **44.** $\frac{3}{4}$

Extra Practice 4

1. $7n - 28$ **2.** $5x + 30$ **3.** $-2x + 14$ **4.** $-9y - 90$ **5.** $-4a - 12b$ **6.** $20x - 30y$ **7.** $-5x - 10y + 30$
8. $40x + 32y - 96$ **9.** $18a - 9b + 27$ **10.** $21p + 105q - 98$ **11.** $-18r + 45t - 63$
12. $-120a - 200b + 180$ **13.** $6(x - 1)$ **14.** $8(x + 3)$ **15.** $4(x - 7)$ **16.** $5(y - 6)$ **17.** $7(x + 1)$
18. $9(x - 7)$ **19.** $8(6 - x)$ **20.** $11(5 - x)$ **21.** $3(2a + 3)$ **22.** $7(2x - 7)$ **23.** $5(2y + 3)$ **24.** $6(3a - 5)$
25. $10(5x - 7)$ **26.** $8(4x + 3)$ **27.** $6(x + 5 - 6a)$ **28.** $15(x + 3y - 1)$ **29.** $b(x - 3y + 6)$
30. $a(x - 5 - y)$ **31.** $3(2x + 3y - 8)$ **32.** $5(5x - 3y + 15)$

Extra Practice 5

1. $-x^2 + 2x - 5$ **2.** $-3x + 4y - 7$ **3.** $-2a - 3b - 4c$ **4.** $3a - 2b + c$ **5.** $-3x - 5$ **6.** $-4x + 10$
7. $-y + 4$ **8.** $-3x + 3y$ **9.** $-6x - 2y$ **10.** $a - 10b$ **11.** $12x - 16$ **12.** $-24x + 11$ **13.** $x + 9$ **14.** 20
15. $12x + 8$ **16.** $-32x - 64$ **17.** $-12x - 5$ **18.** $-x - 17$ **19.** $9x - 72$ **20.** $-18x + 38$

Extra Practice 6

1. 61 **2.** 194 **3.** -182 **4.** 32 **5.** -87 **6.** $-\dfrac{4}{3}$ **7.** $\dfrac{1}{8}$ **8.** $\dfrac{5}{6}$ **9.** -4 **10.** 8 **11.** $-\dfrac{32}{5}$ **12.** -144 **13.** $-\dfrac{8}{15}$
14. 14 **15.** -18 **16.** 184 **17.** 3 **18.** 118 **19.** $\dfrac{1}{10}$ **20.** $-\dfrac{5}{2}$ **21.** 62 **22.** -180 **23.** -1 **24.** $-\dfrac{2}{3}$ **25.** $-\dfrac{11}{8}$
26. -55 **27.** 1 **28.** 6 **29.** -16 **30.** -5 **31.** 7 **32.** 6 **33.** -8 **34.** -11 **35.** 3 **36.** 4 **37.** 77 **38.** -9 **39.** 2
40. -6 **41.** $\dfrac{5}{2}$ **42.** -8 **43.** 1 **44.** 6 **45.** 2 **46.** $-\dfrac{4}{9}$ **47.** $-\dfrac{15}{2}$ **48.** -36 **49.** 75 **50.** -66 **51.** 0 **52.** 0
53. 0 **54.** 0

Extra Practice 7

1. $r = \dfrac{A - p}{pt}$ **2.** $t = \dfrac{A - p}{pr}$ **3.** $l = \dfrac{V}{wh}$ **4.** $h = \dfrac{V}{lw}$ **5.** $d_1 = \dfrac{2A}{d_2}$ **6.** $d_2 = \dfrac{2A}{d_1}$ **7.** $m = \dfrac{y - b}{x}$
8. $b = y - mx$ **9.** $a = \dfrac{pt}{100}$ **10.** $x = \dfrac{yz}{k}$ **11.** $\pi = \dfrac{A}{2r}$ **12.** $h = \dfrac{V}{\pi r^2}$

Extra Practice 8

1. 8 **2.** -30 **3.** $w = 9\text{cm}; l = 17\text{cm}$ **4.** $w = 16\text{m}; l = 23\text{m}$ **5.** $49, 50, 51$ **6.** $85, 87, 89$ **7.** 2 ft; 6ft; 12ft
8. 50m; 100m; 300m **9.** $20°, 60°, 100°$ **10.** $46°; 92°; 42°$ **11.** 1000 mi **12.** 20

Extra Practice 9

1. $\{y|y > 6\}$ **2.** $\{x|x \geq 4\}$ **3.** $\{x|x < 7\}$ **4.** $\{a|a \geq 2\}$ **5.** $\{x|x < 1\}$ **6.** $\{y|y < -7\}$ **7.** $\left\{x\Big|x \geq \dfrac{11}{5}\right\}$
8. $\{x|x \leq -2\}$ **9.** $\{y|y > 2\}$ **10.** $\{t|t \geq -5\}$ **11.** $\left\{x\Big|x < \dfrac{28}{3}\right\}$ **12.** $\{y|y > 1\}$ **13.** $\{y|y \geq 1\}$
14. $\{m|m \leq 2\}$ **15.** $\left\{x\Big|x > \dfrac{4}{7}\right\}$ **16.** $\{x|x \leq -4\}$ **17.** $\{x|x < 5\}$ **18.** $\{x|x > 5\}$ **19.** $\{y|y \geq 13\}$
20. $\{m|m > 3\}$ **21.** $\left\{x\Big|x \geq -\dfrac{1}{12}\right\}$ **22.** $\{y|y > -4\}$ **23.** $\{x|x \leq 3\}$ **24.** $\{x|x < 3\}$ **25.** $\left\{x\Big|x > \dfrac{5}{6}\right\}$
26. $\left\{y\Big|y \leq \dfrac{1}{6}\right\}$ **27.** $\{x|x < 4\}$ **28.** $\{x|x > -5\}$ **29.** $\{y|y < -3\}$ **30.** $\{y|y > -4\}$

Extra Practice 10

1. $\left\{x \mid x < -\dfrac{9}{4} \text{ or } x > 3\right\}$ **2.** $\{y \mid -5 \le y \le 9\}$ **3.** $\left\{x \mid -\dfrac{31}{5} < x < 3\right\}$ **4.** $\{2, 7\}$ **5.** $\{-4, 4\}$

6. $\{y \mid y \le 0 \text{ or } y \ge 12\}$ **7.** $\{y \mid -11 \le y \le -7\}$ **8.** $\left\{y \mid y < -\dfrac{5}{3} \text{ or } y > 1\right\}$ **9.** $\left\{x \mid x < -\dfrac{5}{2} \text{ or } x > 4\right\}$

10. $\{x \mid -16 < x < 16\}$ **11.** $\{-0.34, 0.6\}$ **12.** $\left\{x \mid x \le -\dfrac{3}{2} \text{ or } x \ge 6\right\}$ **13.** $\{x \mid x < -26 \text{ or } x > 8\}$ **14.**
$\left\{-1, -\dfrac{1}{2}\right\}$ **15.** $\{y \mid y < -2 \text{ or } y > 20\}$ **16.** $\left\{y \mid -\dfrac{1}{5} \le y \le \dfrac{1}{5}\right\}$ **17.** $\{y \mid y < -1 \text{ or } y > 1\}$ **18.** $\{1, 5\}$

19. $\left\{x \mid x \le -\dfrac{13}{5} \text{ or } x \ge \dfrac{17}{5}\right\}$ **20.** $\left\{x \mid -\dfrac{3}{2} < x < 10\right\}$ **21.** $\{-48, 54\}$ **22.** $\{x \mid x < 0 \text{ or } x > 38\}$

23. $\left\{x \mid -\dfrac{1}{4} \le x \le 1\right\}$ **24.** $\{y \mid -3 < y < 12\}$ **25.** $\{y \mid y < -9 \text{ or } y > 9\}$ **26.** $\left\{y \mid \dfrac{1}{27} \le y \le \dfrac{1}{3}\right\}$

27. $\left\{y \mid -9 < y < \dfrac{43}{3}\right\}$ **28.** $\{x \mid x \le -7 \text{ or } x \ge 2\}$ **29.** $\left\{x \mid x \le -\dfrac{2}{9} \text{ or } x \ge \dfrac{2}{3}\right\}$ **30.** $\{y \mid 5 \le y \le 12\}$

Extra Practice 11

1.
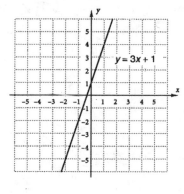

2.
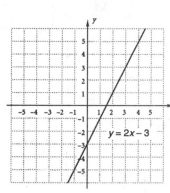

3.
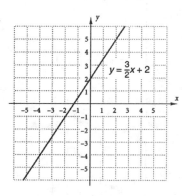

4.
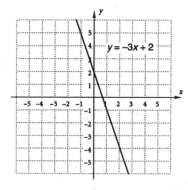

5.
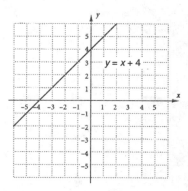

6.
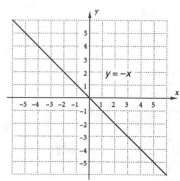

142 Instructor and Adjunct Support Manual   *Intermediate Algebra,* **Tenth Edition**

7.

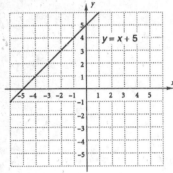

$y = x + 5$

8.

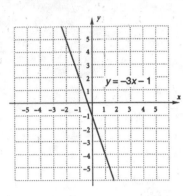

$y = -3x - 1$

9.

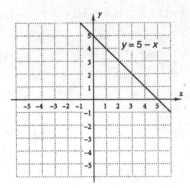

$y = 5 - x$

10.

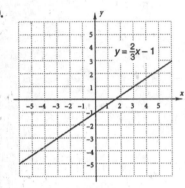

$y = \frac{2}{3}x - 1$

11.

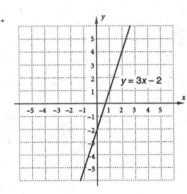

$y = 3x - 2$

12.

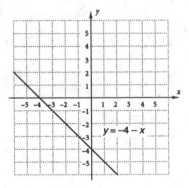

$y = -4 - x$

13.

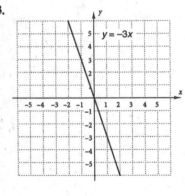

$y = -3x$

14.

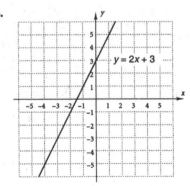

$y = 2x + 3$

15.

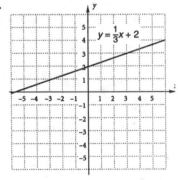

$y = \frac{1}{3}x + 2$

16.

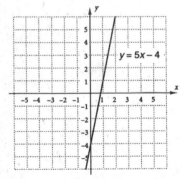

$y = 5x - 4$

Extra Practice 12

1. a) 1 b) -11 c) 5 d) 7.4 e) $\dfrac{13}{2}$ **2.** a) -5 b) 44 c) 76 d) -3.04 e) $-\dfrac{41}{9}$ **3.** a) -22 b) -22 c) -22 d) -22 e) -22

4. a) 11 b) -7 c) -8 d) 10 e)92 **5.** a) 5 b) 7 c) 32 d) 398 e) $|a-1|$ **6.** a) 0 b) 124 c) -51 d) $128a^3-4a$ e) -1990

Extra Practice 13

1. domain = $\{-3, -2, -1, 0, 1, 2\}$; range = $\{4, 3, 2, 1\}$ **2.** domain = $\{x|-2 \le x \le 1\}$; range = $\{3\}$

3. domain = $\{x|-5 \le x \le 1\}$; range = $\{y|-2 \le y \le 4\}$ **4.** domain = $\{x|-1 \le x \le 4\}$;

range = $\{y|-3 \le y \le 6\}$ **5.** domain = $\{x|-2 \le x \le 2\}$; range = $\{y|-4 \le y \le 2\}$

6. domain = $\{x|-5 \le x \le 2\}$; range = $\{y|-2 \le y \le 3\}$ **7.** x is a real number and $x \ne 2$; or

$(-\infty, 2)\bigcup(2, \infty)$ **8.** All real numbers **9.** All real numbers **10.** x is a real number and $x \ne \dfrac{5}{6}$; or

$\left(-\infty, \dfrac{5}{6}\right)\bigcup\left(\dfrac{5}{6}, \infty\right)$ **11.** x is a real number and $x \ne -\dfrac{3}{2}$; or $\left(-\infty, -\dfrac{3}{2}\right)\bigcup\left(-\dfrac{3}{2}, \infty\right)$ **12.** All real num-

bers **13.** All real numbers **14.** x is a real number and $x \ne -3$; or $(-\infty, -3)\bigcup(-3, \infty)$ **15.** All real num-

bers

Extra Practice 14

1.

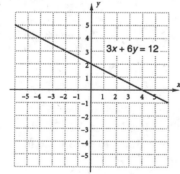

2.

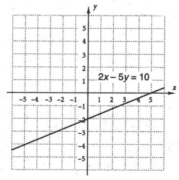

3.

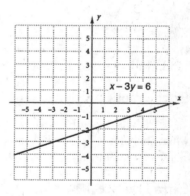

4.

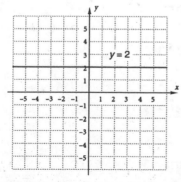

5.

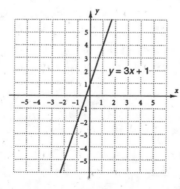

6.

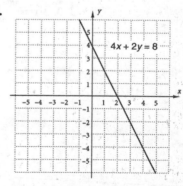

7.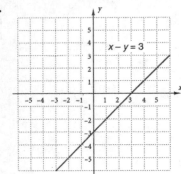

8.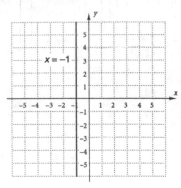

9.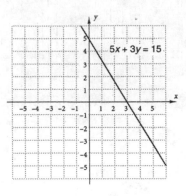

Extra Practice 15

1. $y = -x + 1$ **2.** $y = 2x + 4$ **3.** $y = 3x + 23$ **4.** $y = -2x + 11$ **5.** $y = -3x + 16$ **6.** $y = 2x - 12$

7. $y = 4x - 28$ **8.** $y = -2x + 9$ **9.** $y = \frac{1}{5}x - 2$ **10.** $y = \frac{1}{4}x - \frac{5}{4}$ **11.** $y = -x + 6$ **12.** $y = -x - 2$

13. $y = \frac{1}{3}x - \frac{4}{3}$ **14.** $y = -\frac{3}{2}x + 3$ **15.** $y = -\frac{1}{2}x - 1$ **16.** $y = \frac{2}{9}x + \frac{2}{3}$ **17.** $y = x + 2$ **18.** $y = -\frac{4}{3}x$

19. $y = x + 11$ **20.** $y = -6x + 49$

Extra Practice 16

1. $(-2, 3)$ **2.** $(5, 4)$ **3.** $(1, 3)$ **4.** $(5, -1)$ **5.** $(-3, 4)$ **6.** $(2, 2)$ **7.** $(-1, -3)$ **8.** $(4, -5)$ **9.** $(3, 3)$ **10.** $(6, -2)$

11. $(-1, -1)$ **12.** $(2, -6)$ **13.** $(8, 1)$ **14.** $(-4, -4)$ **15.** $(2, 1)$ **16.** $(-5, 3)$ **17.** $\left(\frac{11}{3}, -\frac{5}{6}\right)$ **18.** $(2, 4)$

19. $\left(\frac{1}{4}, \frac{1}{3}\right)$ **20.** $(18, 24)$

Extra Practice 17

1. 18, 31 **2.** 40°, 140° **3.** 27°, 63° **4.** Length: 59 cm; width: 21 cm **5.** 7, −18 **6.** 21, 35 **7.** Length: 29 ft; width: 13 ft **8.** 39, −18 **9.** Length: 39 ft; width: 16 ft **10.** 25°, 65°

Extra Practice 18

1. 152 adults; 87 children **2.** 40 gal of 20 %; 80 gal of 65% **3.** Calhouns: 9 bags; Millers: 6 bags **4.** 15 lb of white chocolates; 5 lb of dark chocolates **5.** 13 quarters; 9 nickels **6.** $8500 at 7%; $7500 at 5% **7.** 321 adults; 227 children **8.** 720 mi **9.** 4.5 hr **10.** 15 km/h **11.** 390 mph **12.** 6 km/h **13.** 540 mi **14.** 20 mph

Extra Practice 19

1. $6x - 5$ **2.** $8x + 3$ **3.** $9x^2 - 4x + 7$ **4.** $5x^2 - 2x - 1$ **5.** $9x^2 - x$ **6.** $5x^2 + 10$

7. $4x^5 + 5x^4 - 10x^3 + 2x^2 + 3x$ **8.** $12x^4 - 6x^3 + 5x^2 - 2x + 1$ **9.** $8x^2 + 9x$ **10.** $12x^2 - 5x + 12$

11. $-3x + 8$ **12.** $4x - 1$ **13.** $3x^2 - 10x - 3$ **14.** $7x^3 - x^2 - 3x + 5$ **15.** $3x^2 + 4x - 1$

16. $-7x^2 + 2x - 2$ **17.** $-4x^3 - 4x^2 - 3x + 1$ **18.** $8x^5 - 3x^4 - 6x + 12$ **19.** $x^2 - 10x + 7$

20. $4x^3 + 2x^2 + 2x - 11$

Extra Practice 20

1. $15x^5$ **2.** $-12x^6$ **3.** $-32y^8$ **4.** $-24z^7$ **5.** $12x^2 - 21x$ **6.** $-10x^2 + 45x$ **7.** $32x^5 + 24x^4 + 16x^3$
8. $-27x^5 - 63x^3 + 18x^2$ **9.** $x^2 + 8x + 15$ **10.** $14x^2 + 33x + 18$ **11.** $10x^2 + 21x + 8$ **12.** $x^2 - 8x + 15$
13. $3x^2 - 10x + 7$ **14.** $42x^2 - 50x + 12$ **15.** $x^3 + 3x^2 - x - 3$ **16.** $2x^3 + 4x^2 - 16x - 32$
17. $x^3 - 2x^2 - 19x + 20$ **18.** $x^3 - 5x^2 - 16x - 4$ **19.** $x^4 + x^3 - 8x^2 + 11x - 20$
20. $x^4 + x^3 + 5x^2 - 2x + 28$ **21.** $x^4 - 3x^3 - 12x^2 + 8$ **22.** $x^4 - 10x^3 + 18x^2 + 14x - 15$

Extra Practice 21

1. $(x - 8)(x + 2)$ **2.** $(4y - 1)(y + 2)$ **3.** $5a(a^2 - 5a + 3)$ **4.** $(3x + 4)(3x - 4)$
5. $(x + 8)(x - 8)$ **6.** $(a + 9)(a + 3)$ **7.** $6(x + 1)^2$ **8.** $(x^2 - 5)(x + 2)$ **9.** $(x - 7)(x - 3)$
10. $3x^2(4x^3 - 2x + 1)$ **11.** $6(y + 3)(y - 3)$ **12.** $(4y + 3)(y - 5)$ **13.** $(2x - 1)(3x - 2)$
14. $5(x - 1)(x + 1)$ **15.** $(y^2 + 3)(y^3 + 4)$ **16.** $(x - 9)(x + 2)$ **17.** $(x - 4)^2$ **18.** $(a - 7)(a - 2)$
19. $(7x + 1)(7x - 1)$ **20.** $4x^2(2x^2 - x + 3)$ **21.** $(y + 5)^2$ **22.** $3(a^2 + 4a - 1)$
23. $(x^2 + 9)(x + 3)(x - 3)$ **24.** $(3y - 2)^2$ **25.** $(a + 5)(a + 6)$ **26.** $(4t + 3)(2t - 1)$ **27.** $3(5x - 1)^2$
28. $(3t + 1)(t - 3)$ **29.** $(x + 8)(x + 3)$ **30.** $(y - 11)^2$ **31.** $(x - 3)(x + 1)$ **32.** $4(x - 3)^2$
33. $(y - 5)(y - 1)$ **34.** $(5t + 2)(5t - 2)$ **35.** $7x(2x^2 - x + 3)$ **36.** $(3x + 7)^2$ **37.** $9(x + 3)(x - 3)$
38. $(6x + 5)(2x - 1)$ **39.** $(7a - 2)^2$ **40.** $(8x + 3)(x - 4)$

Extra Practice 22

1. $-1, \dfrac{3}{2}$ **2.** $-4, 4$ **3.** $1, 5$ **4.** $2, 10$ **5.** $24, 25$ **6.** $14, 16$ **7.** $-4, 7$ **8.** width: 7 cm, length: 15 cm **9.** 9
10. height: 8 m; base: 14 m **11.** height: 12 cm; base: 20 cm **12.** 9, 11

Extra Practice 23

1. 2 **2.** $\dfrac{2(x^2 + 3x + 10)}{(x - 2)(x + 6)}$ **3.** $a + 4$ **4.** $\dfrac{-y^2 + 7y}{(y - 2)(y + 1)(y + 3)}$ **5.** $\dfrac{2x - 3}{x - 1}$ **6.** $\dfrac{2a - 13}{(a - 2)(a + 2)}$ **7.** $\dfrac{-y - 13}{6(y + 3)}$
8. $\dfrac{2}{a}$ **9.** $\dfrac{x + 7}{(x - 5)(x + 1)}$ **10.** $\dfrac{2}{b + 3}$ **11.** $\dfrac{2a - 5}{a(a - 5)}$ **12.** $\dfrac{4(y + 2)}{(y - 7)(y + 7)}$ **13.** $\dfrac{3x + 1}{x(x + 1)}$ **14.** $\dfrac{3b - 4}{6b}$
15. $\dfrac{4x - 3}{x + 2}$ **16.** $\dfrac{x - 20}{x(x - 4)(x + 3)}$ **17.** $\dfrac{2a^2 - 4a - 5}{(a - 1)(a + 1)}$ **18.** $\dfrac{x + 3}{x - 5}$ **19.** $\dfrac{-23y - 11}{6y}$ **20.** $\dfrac{3x(x - 6)}{(x - 9)(x + 9)}$

Extra Practice 24

1. $4x^4 - \dfrac{1}{2}x^2$ **2.** $\dfrac{1}{2}x^5 + 5x^3 + 3x$ **3.** $1 - 4y + y^3$ **4.** $27x^6 - 15x^2 + 3$ **5.** $-5x^5 + 4x^2 - 3$

6. $4y^3 + 3y^2 - 2y$ **7.** $-4rs - 5s^2 + 3r$ **8.** $xy - 3 + 5xy^3$ **9.** $x + 7$ **10.** $x - 8$ **11.** $x - 9$ **12.** $x + 11$

13. $x + 12 + \dfrac{75}{x - 5}$ **14.** $x + 15 + \dfrac{27}{x - 3}$ **15.** $2x^2 - 3x + 5$ **16.** $4x^2 - 9$ **17.** $x^3 + x^2 - x - 1 + \dfrac{2}{x - 1}$

18. $x^3 - 2x^2 + 9x - 18 + \dfrac{38}{x + 2}$ **19.** $x^3 - 9$ **20.** $x^3 + 4 + \dfrac{-2}{x^3 - 2}$ **21.** $x^3 - 3x^2 + 9x - 27$

22. $x^2 + 4x + 16$ **23.** $a^2 + 25$ **24.** $a^2 - 10a + 75 + \dfrac{-500}{a + 5}$

Extra Practice 25

1. $\frac{13}{3}$ **2.** $-\frac{52}{9}$ **3.** $\frac{1+4x}{1-2x}$ **4.** $\frac{16+4a^2}{5a^2}$ **5.** $\frac{1-x}{1-2x}$ **6.** $\frac{11}{4y^2}$ **7.** $\frac{x}{x+1}$ **8.** $\frac{4x-1}{4}$ **9.** $\frac{a-b}{a}$ **10.** $\frac{1}{x-y}$

11. $\frac{4m^2+3}{2m-5m^2}$ **12.** $\frac{3-2x^2}{6x^2+5}$ **13.** $-\frac{1}{y}$ **14.** $\frac{3x^2-2}{x^3}$ **15.** $\frac{1}{2a}$ **16.** $\frac{4y^2+3xy}{2x+y^2}$

Extra Practice 26

1. 5 **2.** 23 **3.** 2 **4.** -5 **5.** 5 **6.** $-\frac{25}{3}$ **7.** -7 **8.** 9 **9.** $\frac{3}{4}$ **10.** $-1, 3$ **11.** 8 **12.** $-\frac{10}{7}$ **13.** 1, 5 **14.** $-7, \frac{3}{2}$

15. $-\frac{1}{2}, 6$ **16.** $-\frac{1}{13}, 1$ **17.** 4 **18.** -7

Extra Practice 27

1. $-1, 3$ **2.** 1, 2 **3.** $\frac{12}{7}$ hours **4.** $\frac{120}{13}$ hours **5.** 50 km/h, 80 km/h **6.** Freight: 84 mph; Passenger: 100 mph

7. 585 km **8.** 620 **9.** 9.6 **10.** 10 **11.** 2075

Extra Practice 28

1. $2xz\sqrt{5xy}$ **2.** $4x\sqrt[3]{2xy^2}$ **3.** a^4b^3 **4.** $\frac{7a\sqrt{a}}{b^2}$ **5.** $3ac\sqrt{5ab}$ **6.** 64 **7.** $\frac{2x\sqrt[3]{2x^2}}{y^2}$ **8.** $2ab^3\sqrt[4]{4a^3}$ **9.** $5ab^2\sqrt{2b}$

10. $8x^6$ **11.** $\frac{4x\sqrt{x}}{9}$ **12.** $10xz^5\sqrt{5yz}$ **13.** 36 **14.** $\frac{4a^2\sqrt[3]{a}}{3}$ **15.** $2xy\sqrt[3]{30xy^2}$ **16.** $xy^2z^3\sqrt[4]{x^3y}$ **17.** $\frac{2x\sqrt{6x}}{5}$

18. 64 **19.** $8a^3b^6$ **20.** $9a^2\sqrt[3]{4}$ **21.** $5(x+2)\sqrt[3]{x+2}$ **22.** $4a^2\sqrt{b}$ **23.** $6x$ **24.** $4x^2\sqrt[3]{x^2y^2}$ **25.** $2x^2y\sqrt{6y}$

26. $3ab^2\sqrt[3]{a}$ **27.** $5xy\sqrt[3]{x^2}$ **28.** $3(x+3)^2\sqrt{2}$ **29.** $36a\sqrt[3]{6b^2}$ **30.** $3y^2$ **31.** $6xy\sqrt[5]{x^2y^4}$

32. $2(y-3)^2\sqrt[3]{y-3}$

Extra Practice 29

1. $10\sqrt{5}$ **2.** $7\sqrt{3}$ **3.** $4\sqrt{2a}$ **4.** $9\sqrt{11}$ **5.** $-\sqrt{x}$ **6.** $18\sqrt{2}$ **7.** $9\sqrt{3}$ **8.** $6\sqrt{5}$ **9.** $-\sqrt{2}$ **10.** $11\sqrt{5}$
11. $12\sqrt{6}$ **12.** $11\sqrt{a}$ **13.** $\sqrt{14}+\sqrt{10}$ **14.** $\sqrt{30}-2\sqrt{5}$ **15.** $18+7\sqrt{6}$ **16.** $50-13\sqrt{10}$
17. $-1-7\sqrt{7}$ **18.** -22 **19.** -9 **20.** $-9-\sqrt{3}$ **21.** $-10+2\sqrt{6}$ **22.** $27+10\sqrt{2}$ **23.** $67-16\sqrt{3}$
24. $56-24\sqrt{5}$ **25.** $x+2\sqrt{7x}+7$ **26.** $6-2\sqrt{6y}+y$

Extra Practice 30

1. $\frac{\sqrt{42}}{7}$ **2.** $\frac{\sqrt{10}}{5}$ **3.** $\frac{2\sqrt{6xy}}{3y}$ **4.** $\frac{\sqrt{6xy}}{3y}$ **5.** $\frac{\sqrt[3]{75x^2y^2}}{5y^2}$ **6.** $\frac{\sqrt[4]{14x^3y^3}}{2x^2}$ **7.** $\frac{\sqrt[3]{100x^2y^2}}{5y}$ **8.** $\frac{\sqrt[5]{162x^3y^4}}{3y}$

9. $\frac{\sqrt[3]{3xy^2}}{y}$ **10.** $\frac{\sqrt{15xy}}{3x}$ **11.** $\frac{2x\sqrt{5y}}{5y}$ **12.** $\frac{3x^2\sqrt[3]{4y^2}}{2y}$ **13.** $\frac{4(8+\sqrt{5})}{59}$ **14.** $-\sqrt{30}-\sqrt{15}$ **15.** $\frac{9(3+\sqrt{21})}{-2}$,

or $\frac{27+9\sqrt{21}}{-2}$ **16.** $\frac{6\sqrt{x}+2\sqrt{6x}}{x}$ **17.** $\frac{1-\sqrt{21}}{4}$ **18.** $\frac{2x-3\sqrt{xy}+y}{x-y}$ **19.** $\frac{7-3\sqrt{7x}+2x}{7-x}$

20. $\dfrac{2x + 5\sqrt{xy} - 3y}{x - 9y}$

Extra Practice 31

1. 1, 2 **2.** 36 **3.** 7 **4.** 7 **5.** 0, 1 **6.** −3, 0 **7.** 9 **8.** 30 **9.** 28 **10.** 6 **11.** No solution **12.** −4, 0 **13.** 29 **14.** 16 **15.** 6 **16.** 0 **17.** No solution **18.** 2 **19.** 8 **20.** −3

Extra Practice 32

1. −1, 4 **2.** 2, 4 **3.** 5 **4.** $-\dfrac{3}{2}, 5$ **5.** −6, 6 **6.** −7, 7 **7.** $\dfrac{3 \pm \sqrt{21}}{2}$ **8.** $\dfrac{5 \pm \sqrt{53}}{2}$ **9.** $4 \pm \sqrt{5}$

10. $\dfrac{-7 \pm \sqrt{53}}{2}$ **11.** $-3 \pm \sqrt{5}$ **12.** $\dfrac{3 \pm \sqrt{29}}{2}$ **13.** $\dfrac{-7 \pm \sqrt{17}}{8}$ **14.** $\dfrac{3 \pm \sqrt{29}}{10}$ **15.** $\dfrac{3 \pm \sqrt{33}}{4}$

16. $\dfrac{-3 \pm \sqrt{57}}{6}$ **17.** $\dfrac{3 \pm \sqrt{13}}{4}$ **18.** $1, \dfrac{3}{2}$ **19.** −5, 5 **20.** −4, 4

Extra Practice 33

1. $11\sqrt{2}$ cm **2.** 15 cm **3.** 7in. × 12in. **4.** 30 m **5.** $l = 15$ in.; $w = 60$ in. **6.** 8 ft, 15 ft **7.** 17 in. **8.** 10 in. **9.** 2.4 in. **10.** 4 ft **11.** About 8.1 mph **12.** 5 km/h

Extra Practice 34

1. 81 **2.** $\pm\sqrt{2}, \pm\sqrt{6}$ **3.** $-\dfrac{1}{3}, \dfrac{1}{4}$ **4.** $-\dfrac{4}{3}, \dfrac{4}{3}$ **5.** 1, 81 **6.** 4, 169 **7.** $\pm\sqrt{2}, \pm2$ **8.** 16, 81 **9.** −2, −1, 3, 4

10. $\pm\sqrt{3}, \pm i\sqrt{7}$ **11.** −1, 1, 4, 6 **12.** 4, 100 **13.** $\dfrac{3}{4}$ **14.** 144, 225 **15.** $\pm\sqrt{3}, \pm2$ **16.** $-\dfrac{1}{5}, \dfrac{2}{3}$

Extra Practice 35

1.

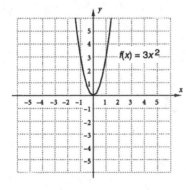

2.

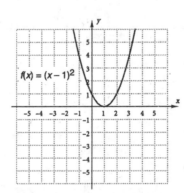

3.

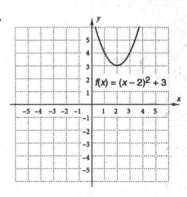

4.

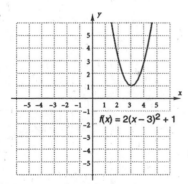

5.

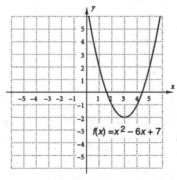

6.

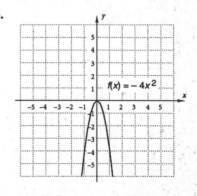

7.

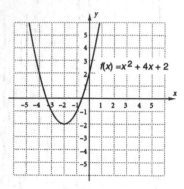

$f(x) = x^2 + 4x + 2$

8.

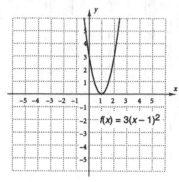

$f(x) = 3(x-1)^2$

9.

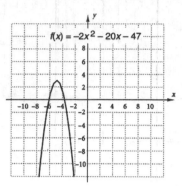

$f(x) = -2x^2 - 20x - 47$

10.

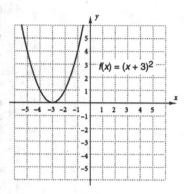

$f(x) = (x+3)^2$

11.

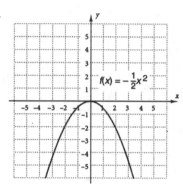

$f(x) = -\frac{1}{2}x^2$

12.

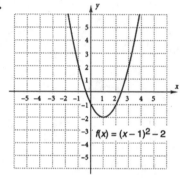

$f(x) = (x-1)^2 - 2$

13.

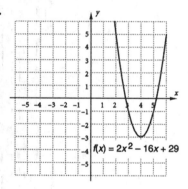

$f(x) = 2x^2 - 16x + 29$

14.

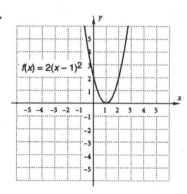

$f(x) = 2(x-1)^2$

15.

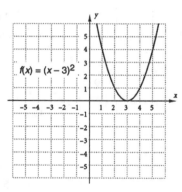

$f(x) = (x-3)^2$

16.

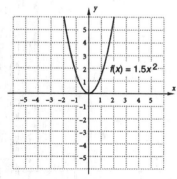

$f(x) = 1.5x^2$

17.

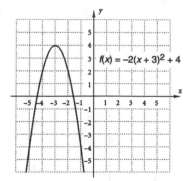

$f(x) = -2(x+3)^2 + 4$

18.

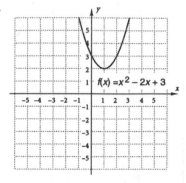

$f(x) = x^2 - 2x + 3$

19.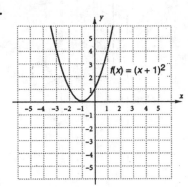

$f(x) = (x + 1)^2$

20.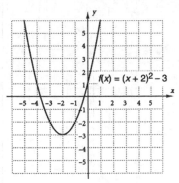

$f(x) = (x + 2)^2 - 3$

21.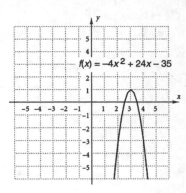

$f(x) = -4x^2 + 24x - 35$

22.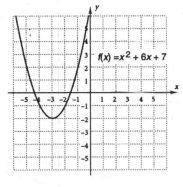

$f(x) = -\frac{1}{2}(x + 1)^2 + 4$

23.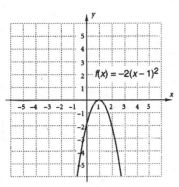

$f(x) = -2(x - 1)^2$

24.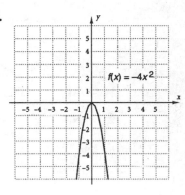

$f(x) = -4x^2$

25.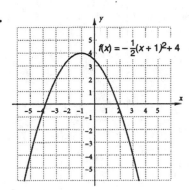

$f(x) = x^2 + 6x + 7$

26.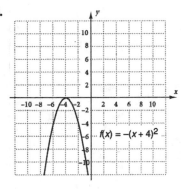

$f(x) = -(x + 4)^2$

27.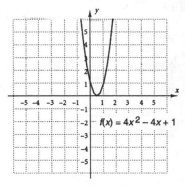

$f(x) = 4x^2 - 4x + 1$

28.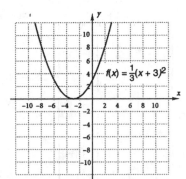

$f(x) = \frac{1}{3}(x + 3)^2$

29.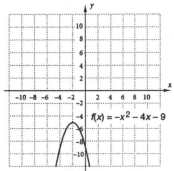

$f(x) = -x^2 - 4x - 9$

30.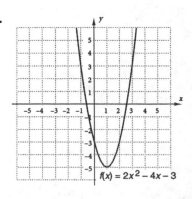

$f(x) = 2x^2 - 4x - 3$

31.

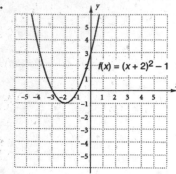

$f(x) = (x + 2)^2 - 1$

32.

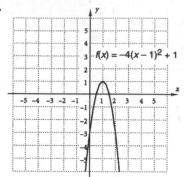

$f(x) = -4(x - 1)^2 + 1$

33.

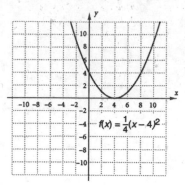

$f(x) = \frac{1}{4}(x - 4)^2$

34.

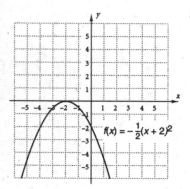

$f(x) = -\frac{1}{2}(x + 2)^2$

35.

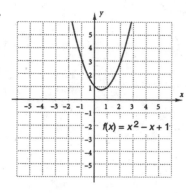

$f(x) = x^2 - x + 1$

36.

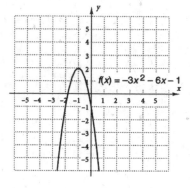

$f(x) = -3x^2 - 6x - 1$

Extra Practice 36

1.

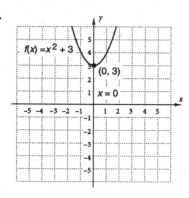

$f(x) = 4x^2$

$(0, 0)$

$x = 0$

2.

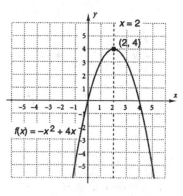

$f(x) = x^2 + 3$

$(0, 3)$

$x = 0$

3.

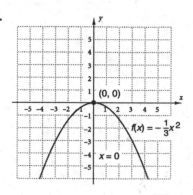

$x = 2$

$(2, 4)$

$f(x) = -x^2 + 4x$

4.

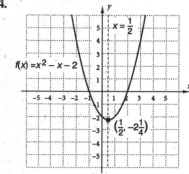

$x = \frac{1}{2}$

$f(x) = x^2 - x - 2$

$\left(\frac{1}{2}, -2\frac{1}{4}\right)$

5.

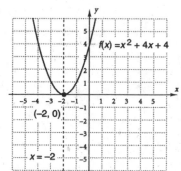

$f(x) = x^2 + 4x + 4$

$(-2, 0)$

$x = -2$

6.

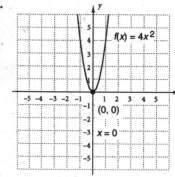

$(0, 0)$

$f(x) = -\frac{1}{3}x^2$

$x = 0$

7.

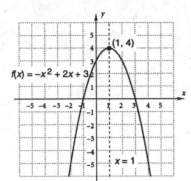

$f(x) = -x^2 + 2x + 3$ (1, 4) $x = 1$

8.

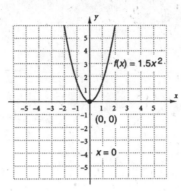

$f(x) = 1.5x^2$ (0, 0) $x = 0$

9.

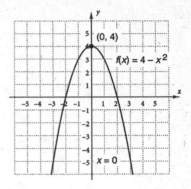

(0, 4) $f(x) = 4 - x^2$ $x = 0$

Extra Practice 37

1.

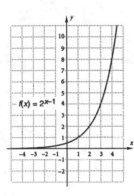

$f(x) = 2^{x-1}$

2.

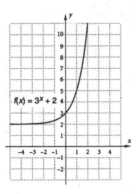

$f(x) = 3^x + 2$

3.

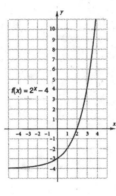

$f(x) = 2^x - 4$

4.

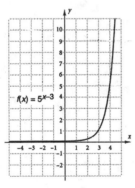

$f(x) = 5^{x-3}$

5.

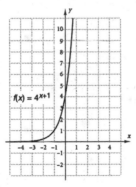

$f(x) = 4^{x+1}$

6.

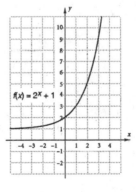

$f(x) = 2^x + 1$

7.

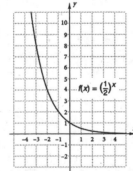

$f(x) = \left(\frac{1}{2}\right)^x$

8.

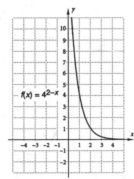

$f(x) = 4^{2-x}$

9.

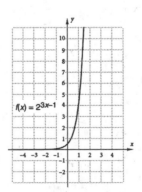

$f(x) = 2^{3x-1}$

10.

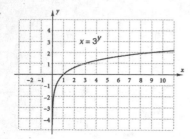

$x = 3^y$

11.

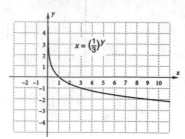

$x = \left(\frac{1}{3}\right)^y$

12.

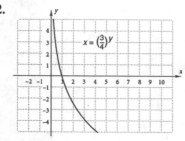

$x = \left(\frac{3}{4}\right)^y$

13.

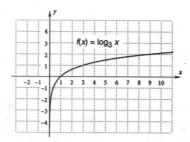

$f(x) = \log_3 x$

14.

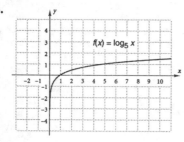

$f(x) = \log_5 x$

15.

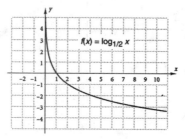

$f(x) = \log_{1/2} x$

16.

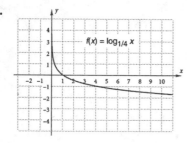

$f(x) = \log_{1/4} x$

17.

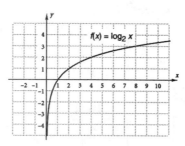

$f(x) = \log_2 x$

18.

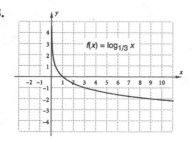

$f(x) = \log_{1/3} x$

Extra Practice 38

1. $\frac{4}{5}$ 2. 1.1969 3. 1.2925 4. 0.3869 5. 0.2554 6. $\frac{2}{3}$ 7. $\frac{1}{3}$ 8. 0.8451 9. 3.7651 10. 57.5646 11. 0.3219

12. 1.0939 13. -1 14. 1.7925 15. 2.0579 16. 2 17. 5 18. $\frac{2}{999}$ 19. 44 20. 36 21. 25 22. 6 23. 2 24. $\frac{1}{3}$

25. $\frac{5}{9}$ 26. $\frac{1}{21}$ 27. 10 28. 12 29. $\frac{1}{4}$ 30. 50 31. 7 32. -11

Extra Practice 39

1.

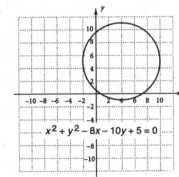

2.

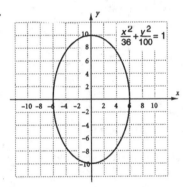

3.

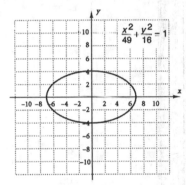

4.

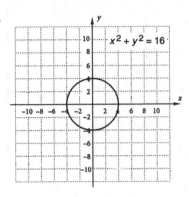

5.

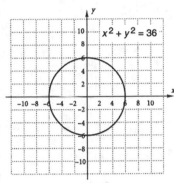

6.

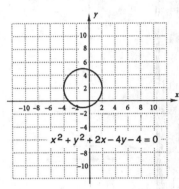

7.

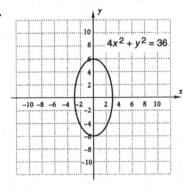

8.

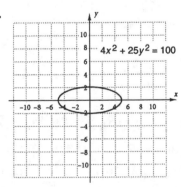

9.

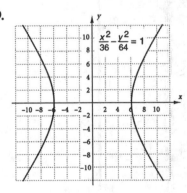

10.

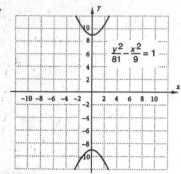

$$\frac{y^2}{81} - \frac{x^2}{9} = 1$$

11.

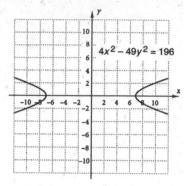

$4x^2 - 49y^2 = 196$

12.

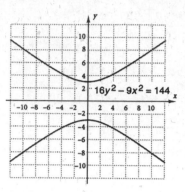

$16y^2 - 9x^2 = 144$

13.

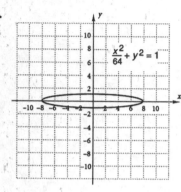

$$\frac{x^2}{64} + y^2 = 1$$

14.

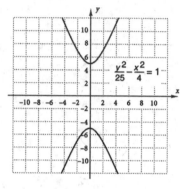

$$\frac{y^2}{25} - \frac{x^2}{4} = 1$$

15.

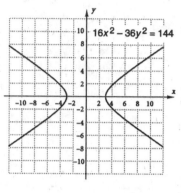

$16x^2 - 36y^2 = 144$

16.

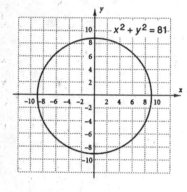

$x^2 + y^2 = 81$

17.

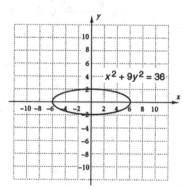

$x^2 + 9y^2 = 36$

18.

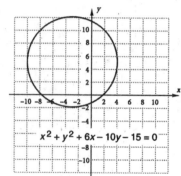

$x^2 + y^2 + 6x - 10y - 15 = 0$

Extra Practice 40

1. $(-4, -2), (-2, -4), (2, 4), (4, 2)$ **2.** $(-7, 0), (7, 0)$ **3.** $(-4, -3), (3, 4)$

4. $(-9, 1), (-1, 9), (9, -1), (1, -9)$ **5.** $(0, 2), (4, 0)$ **6.** $(-4, -5), (4, 5)$ **7.** $(0, 10), (2, 0)$ **8.** $(-6, 0), (6, 0)$

9. $(0, -5), (0, 5)$ **10.** $(-5, -3), (3, 5)$ **11.** $(-2, -4), (2, -4), \left(-\sqrt{11}, 3\right), \left(\sqrt{11}, 3\right)$

12. $(-8, 0), \left(7, -\sqrt{15}\right), \left(7, \sqrt{15}\right)$ **13.** 25 cm by 60 cm **14.** 4 m by $3\sqrt{2}$ m **15.** -4 and 11 or 4 and -11

16. 5 and 8 **17.** 3 and 7 **18.** 7 m by 15 m **19.** $\frac{1}{3}$ and $\frac{1}{2}$ or $-\frac{1}{3}$ and $-\frac{1}{2}$ **20.** 0.6 cm by 0.8 cm

TRANSPARENCY MASTERS

Test Aid: Number Lines

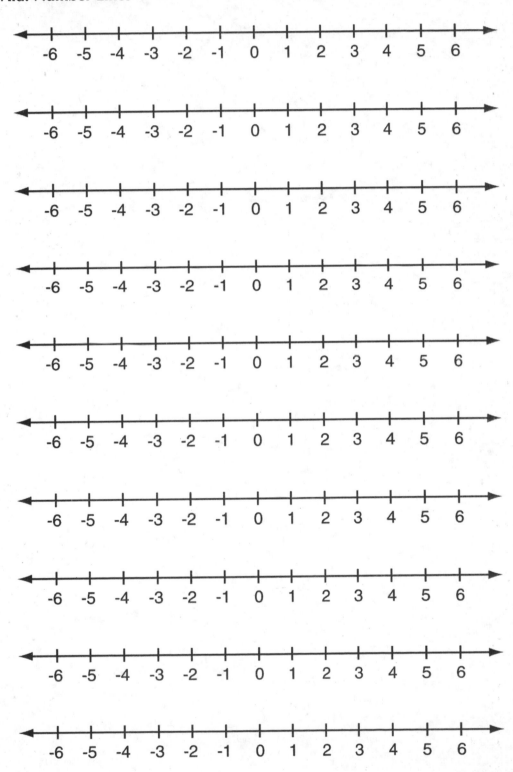

Transparency Master: Number Lines

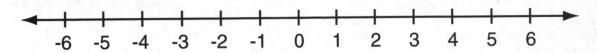

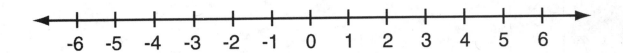

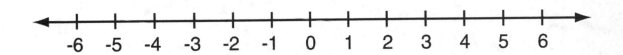

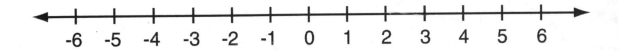

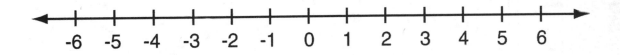

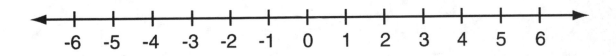

Test Aid: Rectangular Coordinate Grids

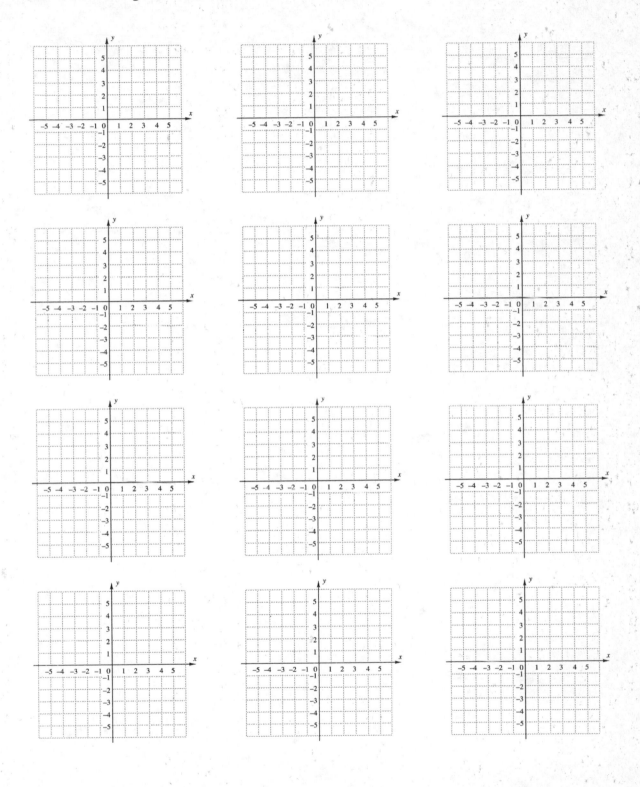

Test Aid: Rectangular Coordinate Grids

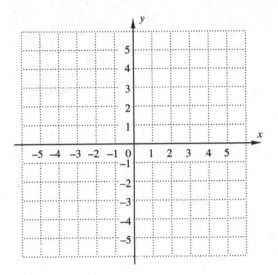

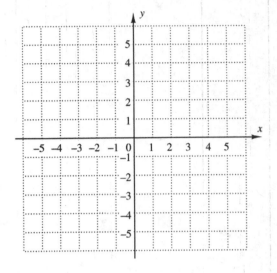

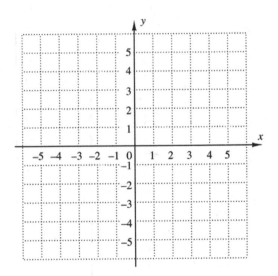

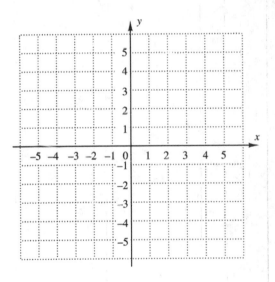

Transparency Master: Rectangular Coordinate Grid

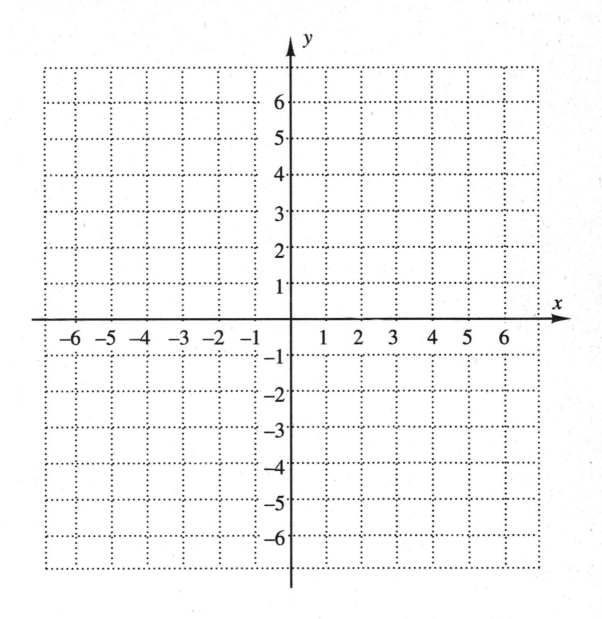

AVAILABLE SUPPLEMENTS

Student Supplements	Instructor Supplements
Student's Solutions Manual (ISBN 0-321-30579-5) • By Judith A. Penna, *Indiana University Purdue University Indianapolis* • Contains completely worked-out solutions with step-by-step annotations for all the odd-numbered exercises in the text, with the exception of the discussion and writing exercises, as well as completely worked-out solutions to all the exercises in the Chapter Reviews, Chapter Tests, and Cumulative Reviews.	**Annotated Instructor's Edition** **(ISBN 0-321-30572-8)** • Includes answers to all exercises printed in blue on the same page as those exercises.
	Instructor's Solutions Manual **(ISBN 0-321-30574-4)** • By Judith A. Penna, *Indiana University Purdue University Indianapolis* • Contains brief solutions to the even-numbered exercises in the exercise sets, answers to all of the Discussion and Writing exercises, and the completely worked-out solutions to all the exercises in the Chapter Reviews, Chapter Tests, and Cumulative Reviews.
Collaborative Learning Activities Manual **(ISBN 0-321-30582-5)** • Features group activities tied to text sections and includes the focus, time estimate, suggested group size and materials, and background notes for each activity. • Available as a stand-alone supplement sold in the bookstore, as a textbook bundle component for students, or as a classroom activity resource for instructors.	**Online Answer Book** • By Judith A. Penna, *Indiana University Purdue University Indianapolis* • Available in electronic form from the instructor resource center. Contact your local Addison-Wesley representative for details. • Contains answers to all the section exercises in the text.
Videotapes (ISBN 0-321-30576-0) • To tie student learning to the pedagogy of the text, lectures are organized by objectives, which are indicated on the screen at the start of each new objective. • Present a series of lectures correlated directly to the content of each section of the text. • Feature an engaging team of instructors who present material in a format that stresses student interaction, often using examples and exercises from the text.	**Printed Test Bank (ISBN 0-321-30570-1)** • By Mark Stevenson, *Oakland Community College, Auburn Hills* • Contains one diagnostic test. • Contains one pretest for each chapter. • Provides 13 new test forms for every chapter and 8 new test forms for the final exam. • For the chapter tests, 5 test forms are modeled after the chapter tests in the text, 3 test forms are organized by topic order following the text objectives, 3 test forms are designed for 50-minute class periods and organized so that each objective in the chapter is covered on one of the tests, and 2 test forms are multiple-choice. Chapter tests also include more challenging synthesis questions. • Contains 2 cumulative tests per chapter beginning with Chapter 2. • For the final exam, 3 test forms are organized by chapter, 3 test forms are organized by question type, and 2 test forms are multiple-choice.
Digital Video Tutor (ISBN 0-321-30580-9) • Complete set of digitized videos (as described above) on CD-ROMs for student use at home or on campus. • Ideal for distance learning or supplemental instruction. • Are available with captioning on request. Contact your local Addison-Wesley representative for details.	

NEW! Work It Out! Chapter Test Video on CD (ISBN 0-321-42264-3)

- Presented by Judith A. Penna and Barbara Johnson
- Provides step-by-step solutions to every exercise in each Chapter Test from the text.
- Helps students prepare for chapter tests and synthesize content.

Math Study Skills for Students Video on CD (ISBN 0-321-29745-8)

- Presented by author Marvin Bittinger
- Designed to help students make better use of their math study time and improve their retention of concepts and procedures taught in classes from basic mathematics through intermediate algebra.
- Through carefully crafted graphics and comprehensive on-camera explanation, focuses on study skills that are commonly overlooked.

Audio Recordings

- By Bill Saler
- Lead students through the material in each section of the text, explaining solution steps to examples, pointing out common errors, and focusing on margin exercises and solutions.
- Audio files are available to download in MP3 format. Contact your local Addison-Wesley representative for details.

Addison-Wesley Math Tutor Center
www.aw-bc.com/tutorcenter

- The Addison-Wesley Math Tutor Center is staffed by qualified mathematics instructors who provide students with tutoring on examples and odd-numbered exercises from the textbook. Tutoring is available via toll-free telephone, toll-free fax, e-mail, or the Internet. White Board technology allows tutors and students to actually see problems worked while they "talk" in real time over the Internet during tutoring sessions.

MathXL® Tutorials on CD (ISBN 0-321-30577-9)

- Provides algorithmically generated practice exercises that correlate at the objective level to the content of the text.
- Includes an example and a guided solution to accompany every exercise and video clips for selected exercises.
- Recognizes student errors and provides feedback; generates printed summaries of students' progress.

NEW! Instructor and Adjunct Support Manual (ISBN 0-321-30581-7)

- Includes Adjunct Support Manual material.
- Features resources and teaching tips designed to help both new and adjunct faculty with course preparation and classroom management.
- Resources include chapter reviews, extra practice sheets, conversion guide, video index, audio index, and transparency masters.
- Also available electronically so course/adjunct coordinators can customize material specific to their schools.

TestGen with Quizmaster (ISBN 0-321-30573-6)

- Enables instructors to build, edit, print, and administer tests.
- Features a computerized bank of questions developed to cover all text objectives.
- Algorithmically based content allows instructors to create multiple but equivalent versions of the same question or test with a click of a button.
- Instructors can also modify test-bank questions or add new questions by using the built-in question editor, which allows users to create graphs, input graphics, and insert math notation, variable numbers, or text.
- Tests can be printed or administered online via the Internet or another network. Quizmaster allows students to take tests on a local area network.
- Available on a dual-platform Windows/Macintosh CD-ROM.

InterAct Math® Tutorial Web site: <u>www.interactmath.com</u>

This open-access Web site provides students with algorithmically generated practice exercises correlated to the textbook for unlimited practice and mastery. Students can go to the Web site, select their textbook, chapter, and section, and retry tutorial exercises for that section as many times as they like with new values each time. Exercises are accompanied by an interactive guided solution that provides helpful feedback for incorrect answers, and students can also view a worked-out sample problem that steps them through an exercise similar to the one they're working on.

MathXL

MathXL® is a powerful online homework, tutorial, and assessment system that uses algorithmically generated exercises correlated at the objective level to your textbook. Instructors can create and assign online homework and tests and can track students' results in MathXL's flexible online gradebook. Students can retry interactive tutorial exercises as many times as they like, with new values each time, for unlimited practice and mastery. They also receive a personalized study plan based on their test results that links directly to exercises for the objectives they need to study and retest. For more information, see page 168.

MyMathLab™

MyMathLab is a complete online course available with this textbook that makes it easy to deliver all or a portion of your course online. MyMathLab offers instructors and students a wide variety of resources, from tutorial exercises and multimedia to automatically graded online homework to flexible course-management tools. Instructors can easily customize MyMathLab to suit their students' needs and help increase their comprehension and success! For more information, see page 169.

Getting Started with MathXL

Overview

MathXL® is a powerful online homework, tutorial, and assessment system tied to Pearson Addison-Wesley and Pearson Prentice Hall textbooks in Mathematics and Statistics. Ideal for use in a lecture, self-paced, or distance-learning course, MathXL diagnoses students' weaknesses and creates a personalized study plan based on their test results. MathXL provides students with unlimited practice using a database of algorithmically-generated exercises correlated to the exercises in their textbook. Each tutorial exercise is accompanied by an interactive guided solution and a sample problem to help students improve their skills independently. Instructors can use MathXL to create online homework assignments, quizzes, and tests that are automatically graded and tracked. Instructors can view and manage all students' homework and test results, study plans, and tutorial work in MathXL's flexible online gradebook.

How to Adopt MathXL

1. **Getting Access**

    If you are interested in using MathXL for one or more of your courses, contact your Addison-Wesley sales representative to request a *MathXL Instructor Access Kit*. (If you are not sure who your sales representative is, go to www.aw-bc.com/replocator.) The access kit provides you with an **instructor access code** for registration.

2. **Registering**

    Registering is an easy process that takes only a few minutes, and you need to register only once, even if you are teaching more than one course with MathXL. Detailed instructions are included in the instructor access kit. As part of the registration process, you select a login name and password that you will use from then on to access your MathXL course. Once you have your instructor access code, go to www.mathxl.com, click the **Register** button, and follow the on-screen instructions to register and log in.

3. **Creating Your MathXL Course**

    Once you've registered, creating your MathXL course is easy! Simply log in at www.mathxl.com, go to the Course Manager, and click Create Course. You will be asked to select the textbook you are using and enter some very basic information about your course. You can create as many courses as you need, and you can customize course coverage to match your syllabus if you wish.

4. **Ordering Books for Your Students**

    To access your MathXL course, each student needs to register in MathXL using a student access code. The easiest way to supply your students with access codes is to order your textbook packaged with the *MathXL Student Access Kit*. Visit the **Books with MathXL** section of the website at www.mathxl.com for a complete list of package ISBNs.

How to Learn More about MathXL

*   To learn more about MathXL, visit our website at www.mathxl.com, or contact your Addison-Wesley sales representative to schedule a demonstration.
*   For detailed instructions on how to register, log in, and set up your first MathXL course, view or print the *Getting Started with MathXL* instructor guide from the **Support** section of the MathXL website at www.mathxl.com.

Getting Started with MyMathLab™

Overview

Powered by CourseCompass™ and MathXL®, MyMathLab is a series of text-specific online courses that accompany Pearson Addison-Wesley and Pearson Prentice Hall textbooks in Mathematics and Statistics. Since 2001, more than one million students at over 1100 colleges and universities have had more success in Math with MyMathLab's dependable and easy-to-use online homework, guided solutions, multimedia, tests, and eBooks. Pearson's premier, proven service teams provide training and support when you need it. And MyMathLab offers the broadest range of titles available for adoption.

When you adopt the MyMathLab course for your textbook, your students can view the textbook pages in electronic form and link to supplemental multimedia resources—such as animations and video clips—directly from the eBook. MyMathLab provides students with algorithmically-generated tutorial exercises correlated to the exercises in their text, and the system generates individualized study plans based on student test results. MyMathLab's powerful homework and test managers and flexible online gradebook make it easy for instructors to create and manage online assignments that are automatically graded, so they can spend less time grading and more time teaching!

How to Adopt MyMathLab

1. **Getting Access**

    If you are interested in using MyMathLab for one or more of your courses, you will need an **instructor access code**. You can receive an instructor access code in one of two ways:
    *   Request a *MyMathLab Instructor Access Kit* from your Addison-Wesley sales representative. To identify your sales representative, go to www.aw-bc.com/replocator.
    *   Request an access code online by visiting the **Getting Started** section of the MyMathLab website at www.mymathlab.com.

2. **Registering**

    MyMathLab courses are accessed through an online learning environment called CourseCompass, so to adopt a MyMathLab course, you need to register in CourseCompass. Registering is an easy process that takes only a few minutes, and you need to register only once, even if you are teaching more than one MyMathLab course. As part of the registration process, you select a login name and password that you will use from then on to access your MyMathLab course. Once you have your instructor access code, go to www.coursecompass.com, click the **Register** button for instructors, and follow the on-screen instructions to register and log in.

3. **Creating Your MyMathLab Course**

    Once you've registered in CourseCompass, creating your MyMathLab course is easy! You will simply be asked to select the course materials for your textbook and enter some very basic information about your course. Approximately one business day later (and often after only an hour or two), you will be notified via e-mail that your course is ready, and you will then be able to log in and begin exploring MyMathLab.

4. **Ordering Books for Your Students**

    To access your MyMathLab course, each student needs to register in CourseCompass using a student access code. The easiest way to supply your students with access codes is to order your textbook packaged with the *MyMathLab Student Access Kit*. Visit the **Books with MyMathLab** section of the website at www.mymathlab.com for a complete list of package ISBNs.

How to Learn More about MyMathLab

*   To learn more about MyMathLab, visit our website at www.mymathlab.com, or contact your Addison-Wesley sales representative to schedule a demonstration.
*   For detailed instructions on how to register, log in, and set up your first MyMathLab course, view or print the *Getting Started with MyMathLab* and *CourseCompass* instructor guide from the **Support** section of the MyMathLab website at www.mymathlab.com.

HELPFUL TIPS FOR USING SUPPLEMENTS AND TECHNOLOGY

David P. Bell, *Florida Community College at Jacksonville*

- MyMathLab has been an inspiration to many of my students. I will discuss it in two forums, self-paced classes and lecture classes.

- My self-paced classes are set up so that students can progress at their own individual pace. There are still lectures, but they are much abbreviated as compared to a traditional lecture class. I would never be able to manage or effectively conduct this type of class without something like MyMathLab. Students can progress faster than usual or take extra time when necessary. Here is how I use the software:

- I set the class up so that homework assignments can be done using the text or the interactive software. Students choose how they prefer to accomplish the work. The big difference is that the MyMathLab software provides an instant response for answers. It allows the student to ask for help by choosing a sample problem completely solved by the software as a demonstration, or a guided solution that makes the student perform each step in the process. Because the problems are algorithmically generated, the students can instantly get a variety of the same type of problems for drill. My classroom is in a computer lab, so everyone has access to computers in class. The college also provides extensive computer access to any student who desires to use computers.

- Many students start the semester working problems from the textbook, see their classmates getting help from the computer and switch to the interactive software during the semester. Many students tell me that when they want to work on their math during strange hours, like early morning when everyone else is sleeping, the software helps to keep them moving forward. While the interactive software is an excellent aid to learning, keep in mind the fact that it will not teach your classes for you. Please note that the problems in the software are identical to those in the

textbook. That way if a student is in section 3.4 of the book and is having difficulty with number 17, they can go to the software and see a similar problem. In fact, they can access the textbook as well as the textbook exercises on-line to go to the very problem.

- Thus far we have only been talking about the interactive practice problems. Students can also access additional worksheets, print them, work them out, and access an answer key to check their work. There are many avenues for practice and drill. Should a student have difficulty with a particular section of the text, they can also access digital videos on-line through MyMathLab. The videos can also be bundled with the textbook. Simply check with your textbook representative. The videos are excellent. Students tell me that they often watch a video over and over until they "get it". This really helps those willing to do what it takes to learn the material.

- MyMathLab is also able to build homework assignments selecting the exact problems you want the students to practice on. The students have access to all the problems through the 'course content' section, but you can designate separate homework. I don't use the prerequisite function in the homework for these classes because of the self-paced nature of the classes, but I will discuss it in the Lecture class discussion.

- You can even generate quizzes and tests for the students to take on-line if you desire to use TestGen. This test generation software is very extensive and useful. If you can't find a problem exactly like the one you want, you can create or modify to your heart's content. Students taking a quiz side-by-side will get different questions or values to their questions because of the algorithmically-generated nature of the questions. They have the opportunity to cheat, but if they do, they end up with the right answer to the wrong question.

- You also have the opportunity to use the TestGen software to make paper tests which can be selected as multiple-choice or open response or a combination of both. Once you have selected questions for a particular test, you can make multiple versions of that test.

■ There is even an electronic copy of the textbook in PDF format for use with MyMathLab. Keep in mind the fact that our students are becoming more and more comfortable and familiar with computers in general.

■ In summary, the software available through MyMathLab is far too extensive for me to cover all the options, but it is easy to learn and use and really makes a difference. Students can pick and choose what they want to use, because students are all different and here is a medium where they can be individuals and still learn what they need to in order to be successful.

■ The traditional class use of MyMathLab is somewhat different. I require that the students purchase the software with their textbook.

■ I usually mirror the homework on-line on the textbook assignments. I often include more problems in the text version than I do in the on-line assignment. Students notice and choose what they think is the easier option. What they don't know is that those who use the on-line interactive homework usually do extra problems of the same type when they are experiencing difficulty, thus actually performing more repetitions. I love this kind of trickery. This is where I often try using prerequisite completion of a section before allowing the next section. This is not an on-line course, so there are limitations and you will always have students who prefer not to use the software. Our students come with a variety of motivational challenges and this software seems to help many become better students.

■ The digital videos are extremely important to students who sat through a lecture but misunderstood the lesson. Students can review the material at their leisure and do often pick up on missed procedures and techniques. I have many students stop by after the course is over and thank me for requiring MyMathLab. They are convinced that without all the help they got from the software they would not have been successful. My primary objective is to provide coordinated tools that give the student the opportunity to pick and choose the method they will use to cover the course and still be successful.

■ The PDF format text allows the student to access the material anytime they can get on-line. I highly recommend that you consider integrating the MyMath-Lab software with your textbook use for assignments. You and your students will benefit.

■ The software even contains power point slide presentations matched to the sections in the text. I like to copy them and then modify them to suit my lecture style. For example, the slides often contain the same example problems that are in the textbook. I like to use similar but different examples to increase the number of examples available to students. It is particularly nice to show a procedure on the screen while we use the steps in that procedure to solve similar examples.

■ I mentioned a few aspects of the TestGen software earlier. You have access to thousands of questions cross-referenced to each and every objective in the text. All the questions have variations you can select at your fingertips. You can generate a number of tests this way. I often generate a test for the class, and simply shuffle the questions and change the number values in the questions for a make-up test. You know the student is receiving the same test this way. I especially like the fact that you can create new problems or import some you already have. When creating questions you even have the option to make them algorithmically-generated as well. Got a class that almost never does what you ask? I give this group a sample or practice test before the actual test accompanied by the answer key. For the actual test, I simply reshuffle the same questions and hand out the test. There will always be a few good students who actually did the practice test. These always get a guilty look on their faces and look up at me. I just wink and nod my head and they proceed to finish the test. Obviously, I do this infrequently, but it is always good for a few grins. Students quickly get the message and some actually increase their homework time and efforts. I have been using TestGen for over eight years and it just keeps getting easier and better.

Chris Bendixen, *Lake Michigan College*

■ In class I will use InterAct Math on occasion. This gives the students an alternative to the same old boring lecture. I will assign problems from this site for the students when the topics are relatively difficult.

■ I encourage the student to do the problems from InterAct Math, particularly if they miss class. The interactmath.com software has a "helpme" solve command. This command forces the student to respond correctly in order to complete the problems.

If a student answers incorrectly to a prompt, the software will give hints.

Sandy Berry, *Hinds Community College*

■ The video series provides a second chance for the student to see and hear another person presenting the material discussed in class. Another advantage of the video series is the capability to stop the tape and replay some portion of the presentation. In addition, the videos are especially useful for students who have had to miss class for some reason.

Deanna L. Dick, *Alvin Community College*

■ **Videos**

I encourage students to view the videos when:

1. They have missed class. Seeing a lecture often helps them more than reading the textbook only.

2. When they are a little unsure about the problems being worked during homework or lecture and would like to see another problem worked, or hear the explanation one more time.

3. If they consistently have trouble with one section, I may have them check out the video and watch it several times as they practice their homework.

■ **Student's Solutions Manual**

I encourage all my students to get a solutions manual and keep it handy when doing their homework. However, I tell them that they should try the problem first, then check their answer. If the answer is not correct they should try to find their mistake. Once they have tried to find the mistake and could not, then they can look at the solutions manual - but only for that problem. Then it is back to trying it on their own again!

■ **Computer Tutorial**

I highly recommend the computer tutorials to my students, especially the younger ones that are comfortable with computers. It provides instruction and practice in one device. Therefore, it is easy for students to switch between practicing and reviewing when necessary. Many students like this, especially when the computer algorithmically creates new problems each time the student works within each section. You just can't beat unlimited practice!

None of these supplements are used in class though. They may use them on their own time, when convenient. Some students use them in our learning lab, while others work at home.

Kathleen C. Ebert, *Alfred State College*

■ The test generator (TestGen) is great! I use it for my daily handout of problems at the end of class and for weekly quizzes. I make sure I expose students to both multiple-choice and open-ended questions. It's very easy to use.

■ Members of my department also use MyMathLab, and make it available to students as much as possible. The first week of class we take students to the lab and go there as much as possible until they get the hang of it. After trying out different ways to use MyMathLab, ranging from required for everything, to optional only, I think a balance works the best. There is still something to be said for paper and pencil, and we still need to be aware of commuter students who don't have readily available technology. Through experimenting, we found that working only with software is not for everyone, so giving students a grading option works. They can use MyMathLab for their homework and have homework count in their grade (since homework aims at mastery they can get a 100% eventually), or they can do homework from the textbook and have a test and quiz only option. We try to encourage as many ways as possible to use MyMathLab. The software is also great if you are able to schedule flexibly, because if you can lecture three days and take students to the computer lab on the fourth, students really do get a good balance. The hybrid/blended (in class/online) environment is very effective for today's college students using technology and this software.

Rosa Kavanaugh, *Ozarks Technical College*

■ The videotapes are probably the resource that our students use most. We suggest that students who have to miss class view the videotapes to try to replace the classroom explanations that they missed.

■ The students who especially appreciate the videos are those who simply can't grasp all of the concepts with the first explanation and need another version. We find a number of students in this course enter with absolutely no background in algebra. When we cover in one semester a course that is presented over a period of one year in high school, we find that the pace is almost overwhelming for many students. They appreciate the opportunity to watch the videos, stop and replay particularly difficult portions, and then watch them again, if necessary.

■ One special way that we have suggested that students use the videos is to watch the video until the instructor presents a problem that he/she plans to work as an example. We recommend that the student copy the problem and pause the video at that point. Then the student can work the problem at his/her own pace. When the problem is completed or the student has reached an impasse, he/she can start the video again and check the work. The instructor's explanation of the problem will provide the student with feedback on his/her work.

Susan Leland, *Montana Tech*

- I always have several students each semester who use MathXL and find the guided solutions very helpful. These are usually students who are struggling and need lots of practice.

- Instructor's Resource Materials: I use the worksheets for many sections in two basic ways: hand them out in class for class work or just for extra practice; put them online to be available for students who desire more practice

- I use TestGen more as a resource for good test problems rather than using it to actually write tests.

Nancy Ressler, *Oakton Community College*

- I begin using the MyMathLab program during the second week of my courses. What MyMathLab does is *helps* to elevate the lecture with a continuing support for each student. All students (those practicing the program) benefit and enjoy learning with this assisted practical 24-7 tutor!

- I use *CourseCompass (*MyMathLab)* for all of my classes. Within the program students can access: guided solutions (interactive steps to problems), videos (instead of a trip to Instructional Media Services to *check out* a video), study plans (no immediate in-person meetings necessary; the program suggests help for cloudy areas) and graded scores on *practice* as well as *for credit* tests.

- Faculty **learning the program:** it isn't necessary to jump into MyMathLab by doing *all* of the great stuff offered. Learn one new thing and do that with each class for a semester, then next semester try by adding another new aspect of the program. A hidden teacher control panel allows the teacher to add, delete or to modify the program without the students realizing that there may be more or less to the program. Pearson Addison-Wesley is wonderful about support and has teachers' frequently asked questions within the program. It is a powerful course support. As you begin to use it you will tweak it to your own style and method!

- If students have problems grasping the content and cannot meet with you during office hours, or with tutors during the time the tutoring center is available, MyMathLab is always available. If students can't sleep at night, if they have time and are near a PC they can get right to work without even looking for their book. Additionally it is a great tool *if you are away* and have found time for yourself within reach of a PC!

- Prior to using MyMathLab I always recommended that my students visit the college's Instructional Media Services and check out/view the videos. With the MyMathLab program study time is more efficient since the videos are already contained in the program.

- I use TestGen for my pencil/paper and electronic testing. You can now *customize* within a small amount of time multiple tests for each unit, stagger the placement of each question, or modify each question with different coefficients!

- I wonder what I did without these two great supports, MyMathLab and TestGen.

Sharon Testone, *Onondaga Community College*

- I teach both in the classroom and on-line. I take my classroom students to the computer lab and show them how to use MathXL® and the CD-ROM videos. I recommend that anyone who has difficulty with a topic review that material by watching the video and then try some practice problems on MathXL®.

- My on-line students are required to watch the digital video tutors as part of the course. I don't believe that I could teach on-line without the videos. Students need to see and hear someone teaching math. They cannot learn the material by reading my "mini-lectures" or by reading the text. My students have told me that they never would have passed without the videos. I encourage my on-line students to use Math-XL® because of the tutorial features. I do not use the on-line testing component. I like MathXL® because it shows examples similar to the homework problems and gives students the option to use the "guided" solutions

- I have developed my own resources for Intermediate Algebra. They include worksheets, self-paced review materials, and handouts of key concepts. I have typed them to look professional by using the equation editor in Microsoft® Word. An icon for the equation editor can be put on the tool bar to make it very easy to insert fractions, radicals, etc. (Click on "Tools" then

"Customize" then "Commands" then "Insert" then scroll down to the "square root icon" that represents "Equation Editor." This icon can be dragged to the tool bar.) I have shown this procedure to at least 12 instructors at my college because they did not know that equation editor exists. It is no longer necessary to hand draw anything on worksheet, quizzes or exams. All materials can look professional.

Roy West, *Robeson Community College*

■ I use TestGen to generate all of my tests. I believe that retesting in developmental courses is very helpful. I retest on all chapters. TestGen allows me to be able to do this. After students take the first test (usually multiple choice) we look at the errors they made and try to fix them. Then they are retested on the material to see how much they have improved. This usually encourages the developmental student to relax a little while taking the test. This would be very difficult to do without TestGen.

■ There are three sources of information that Addison-Wesley provides that are very helpful. The first is MathXL®. It provides students who are computer literate (most are) with sources of instruction, guided practice, or just additional problems to work at home. I use MathXL often in class to get students comfortable in using it, and I also use it to generate examples to do in class. The second is the math videos that accompany the text. I have set up two places on campus where students can go and view the videos on any chapter in the textbook. This is helpful for those who missed a class or who are struggling on a particular topic and need to see some more instruction. The third is the Addison Wesley Math Tutor Center, which is a toll-free number that students can call to get help on any example or odd-numbered problem they are working on. Students are normally shy about calling this source because they are talking to someone live on the phone, but some do use it often.

Rebecca Wyatt-Semple, *Nash Community College*

■ When using texts by Marvin Bittinger, I have found the Printed Test Banks extremely useful.

■ The videotapes for all our math texts are available in our on-campus Curriculum Lab for student use. The tapes that accompany the Bittinger books are excellent. I do not use the tapes in class, but if a student appears to need review, I may make an assignment for that student to view the tapes associated with the nec-

essary review topics. If a student has been absent for several class meetings, the tapes provide one way for that student to catch up. The students who have used the videos have been very positive in their evaluations of them.

■ Software that accompanies our intermediate algebra text is installed in our Student Curriculum Lab. Some students are assigned to use it as part of their class work, other elect to use it to strengthen their skills. However, the majority of students seem to prefer working from the text. This may be because our Student Curriculum Lab is new, and is not very large.

USEFUL OUTSIDE RESOURCES FOR TEACHERS

Texts

Raymond Blum, *Mathamusements,* © 1999, Sterling Publishing Co., Inc. 0806997842

Daniel Chazan. *Beyond Formulas in Mathematics and Teaching: Dynamics of the High School Algebra Classroom,* © 2000, Teachers College Press, Columbia University. 0807739189

C. M. Charles. *Essential Elements of Effective Discipline,* © 2002, Allyn & Bacon. 0201729482

Randy Davidson & Ellen Levitov. *Overcoming Math Anxiety,* Second Edition, © 2000, Addison-Wesley. 0321069188

Barbara Gross Davis, *Tools for Teaching,* © 1993, Jossey-Bass Publishers, San Francisco. 1555425682

John Gullbery, *Mathematics from the Birth of Numbers,* © 1997, WW Norton and Co. 039304002X

Adam Hart-Davis, *Amazing Math Puzzles,* © 1998, Sterling Publishing, Co., Inc. 0806996676

David W. Johnson &Roger T. Johnson. *Meaningful Assessment: A Manageable and Cooperative Process,* © 2002, Allyn & Bacon. 0205327621

Vernon F. Jones & Louise S. Jones. *Comprehensive Classroom Management: Creating Communities of Support and Solving Problems,* Sixth Edition, © 2001, Allyn & Bacon. 0205318509

Liping Ma. *Knowing and Teaching Elementary Mathematics,* © 1999, LEA Publishing.0805829091

Math Spanish Glossary, Second Edition, © 2001, Addison-Wesley. 0201728966

Mathematics Teacher, National Council of Teachers of Mathematics (NCTM) monthly journal.

John Meier, Thomas Rishel {MAA), *Writing in the Teaching and Learning of Mathematics* © 1998, The Library of Congress, The Mathematical Association notes Number 48-86032.

Robert Müller, *The Great Book of Math Teasers,* © 1990, Sterling Publishing Co., Inc. 0806969539

W. James Popham. *Classroom Assessment: What Teachers Need to Know,* Third Edition, © 2002, Allyn & Bacon. 0205333044

Thomas A. Romberg, Editor. *Mathematics Assessment and Evaluation: Imperatives for Mathematics Educators,* © 1992, State University of New York Press. 0791409007

Ruth Stavy & Dina Tirosh. *How Students (Mis-) Understand Science and Mathematics,* © 2000, Teachers College Press, Columbia University. 0807739588

David F. Treagust, Reinders Duit, & Barry J. Fraser, Editors. *Improving Teaching and Learning in Science and Mathematics,* © 1995, Teachers College Press, Columbia University. 0807734799

Carol Vorderman, *Reader's Digest How Math Works,* © 1996, Dorling Kindersley Limited, London. 0762102330

John Webb & Nitsa Movshovitz-Hadar. *One Equals Zero: And Other Mathematical Surprises,* © 1997, Key Curriculum Press. 1559533099

Norman L. Webb, Editor. *Assessment in the Mathematics Classroom,* © 1993, National Council of Teachers of Mathematics. 0873533526

Web Links

www.Algebra.com Help with algebra homework on-line

www.AlgebraHelp.com Math help using technology

www.amatyc.org American Mathematics Association of Two Year Colleges

www.askjeeves.com Phrase your question the way you would in class and you will receive a list of applicable or related topics.

www.aw-bc.com/events Addison-Wesley Workshop Site

www.mathxl.com (see page 168 for more information)

www.coolmath.com Resources for teachers and students. (some pages may require a subscription)

www.education.ti.com Programs, classroom activities, and user manuals for the Texas Instruments calculators.

www.ictcm.org International Conference on Technology in Collegiate Mathematics

http://horizon.unc.edu/TS/ The Technology Source

www.joshhinds.com A motivational and inspirational web site

www.maa.org Mathematics Association of America

www.madeforsuccess.com Chris Widener's site

www.mathnstuff.com Descriptions for some good mathematics manipulatives.

http://mathforum.org/math.topics.html The Math Forum @ Drexel University

http://www.mcli.dist.maricopa.edu/tl/ Teaching and Learning on the Web

www.merlot.org Math applications, worksheets, puzzles, etc.

www.mymathlab.com (see page 169 for more information)

www.nctm.org The National Council of Teachers of Mathematics

www.PurpleMath.com Algebra lessons

http://rubistar.4teachers.org This free website helps teachers to make rubrics.

www.superkids.com Including reviews of educational software

www.umkc.edu/cad/nade National Association for Developmental Education

www.uoregon.edu/~tep/technology/ University of Oregon Teaching Effectiveness Program

CONVERSION GUIDE

This conversion guide is designed to help you adapt your syllabus for Bittinger Intermediate Algebra, *Ninth Edition to Bittinger* Intermediate Algebra, *Tenth Edition by providing a section-by-section cross reference between the two books. Additional revisions and refinements have been made in addition to the changes specified here.*

Sect.	Intermediate Algebra, Ninth Edition	Sect.	Intermediate Algebra, Tenth Edition
R.1	The Set of Real Numbers	R.1	The Set of Real Numbers
R.2	Operations with Real Numbers	R.2	Operations with Real Numbers
R.3	Exponential Notation and Order of Operations	R.3	Exponential Notation and Order of Operations
R.4	Introduction to Algebraic Expressions	R.4	Introduction to Algebraic Expressions
R.5	Equivalent Algebraic Expressions	R.5	Equivalent Algebraic Expressions
R.6	Simplifying Algebraic Expressions	R.6	Simplifying Algebraic Expressions
R.7	Properties of Exponents and Scientific Notation	R.7	Properties of Exponents and Scientific Notation
1.1	Solving Equations	1.1	Solving Equations
1.2	Formulas and Applications	1.2	Formulas and Applications
1.3	Applications and Problem Solving	1.3	Applications and Problem Solving
1.4	Sets, Inequalities, and Interval Notation	1.4	Sets, Inequalities, and Interval Notation
1.5	Intersections, Unions, and Compound Inequalities	1.5	Intersections, Unions, and Compound Inequalities
1.6	Absolute-Value Equations and Inequalities	1.6	Absolute-Value Equations and Inequalities
2.1	Graphs of Equations	2.1	Graphs of Equations
2.2	Functions and Graphs	2.2	Functions and Graphs
2.3	Finding Domain and Range	2.3	Finding Domain and Range
2.4	Linear Functions: Graphs and Slope	2.4	Linear Functions: Graphs and Slope
2.5	More on Graphing Linear Equations	2.5	More on Graphing Linear Equations
2.6	Finding Equations of Lines; Applications	2.6	Finding Equations of Lines; Applications
3.1	Systems of Equations in Two Variables	3.1	Systems of Equations in Two Variables
3.2	Solving by Substitution	3.2	Solving by Substitution
3.3	Solving by Elimination	3.3	Solving by Elimination
3.4	Solving Applied Problems: Two Equations	3.4	Solving Applied Problems: Two Equations
3.5	Systems of Equations in Three Variables	3.5	Systems of Equations in Three Variables
3.6	Solving Applied Problems: Three Equations	3.6	Solving Applied Problems: Three Equations
3.7	Systems of Inequalities in Two Variables	3.7	Systems of Inequalities in Two Variables
3.8	Business and Economics Applications	3.8	Business and Economics Applications
4.1	Introduction to Polynomials and Polynomial Functions	4.1	Introduction to Polynomials and Polynomial Functions
4.2	Multiplication of Polynomials	4.2	Multiplication of Polynomials
4.3	Introduction to Factoring	4.3	Introduction to Factoring
4.4	Factoring Trinomials: $x^2 + bx + c$	4.4	Factoring Trinomials: $x^2 + bx + c$
4.5	Factoring Trinomials: $ax^2 + bx + c, a \neq 1$	4.5	Factoring Trinomials: $ax^2 + bx + c, a \neq 1$

Sect.	Intermediate Algebra, Ninth Edition	Sect.	Intermediate Algebra, Tenth Edition
4.6	Special Factoring	4.6	Special Factoring
4.7	Factoring: A General Strategy	4.7	Factoring: A General Strategy
4.8	Applications of Polynomial Equations and Functions	4.8	Applications of Polynomial Equations and Functions
5.1	Rational Expressions and Functions: Multiplying, Dividing, and Simplifying	5.1	Rational Expressions and Functions: Multiplying, Dividing, and Simplifying
5.2	LCMs, LCDs, Addition, and Subtraction	5.2	LCMs, LCDs, Addition, and Subtraction
5.3	Division of Polynomials	5.3	Division of Polynomials
5.4	Complex Rational Expressions	5.4	Complex Rational Expressions
5.5	Solving Rational Equations	5.5	Solving Rational Equations
5.6	Applications and Proportions	5.6	Applications and Proportions
5.7	Formulas and Applications	5.7	Formulas and Applications
5.8	Variation and Applications	5.8	Variation and Applications
6.1	Radical Expressions and Functions	6.1	Radical Expressions and Functions
6.2	Rational Numbers as Exponents	6.2	Rational Numbers as Exponents
6.3	Simplifying Radical Expressions	6.3	Simplifying Radical Expressions
6.4	Addition, Subtraction, and More Multiplication	6.4	Addition, Subtraction, and More Multiplication
6.5	More on Division of Radical Expressions	6.5	More on Division of Radical Expressions
6.6	Solving Radical Equations	6.6	Solving Radical Equations
6.7	Applications Involving Powers and Roots	6.7	Applications Involving Powers and Roots
6.8	The Complex Numbers	6.8	The Complex Numbers
7.1	The Basics of Solving Quadratic Equations	7.1	The Basics of Solving Quadratic Equations
7.2	The Quadratic Formula	7.2	The Quadratic Formula
7.3	Applications Involving Quadratic Equations	7.3	Applications Involving Quadratic Equations
7.4	More on Quadratic Equations	7.4	More on Quadratic Equations
7.5	Graphing $f(x) = a(x - h)^2 + k$	7.5	Graphing $f(x) = a(x - h)^2 + k$
7.6	Graphing $f(x) = ax^2 + bx + c$	7.6	Graphing $f(x) = ax^2 + bx + c$
7.7	Mathematical Modeling with Quadratic Functions	7.7	Mathematical Modeling with Quadratic Functions
7.8	Polynomial and Rational Inequalities	7.8	Polynomial and Rational Inequalities
8.1	Exponential Functions	8.1	Exponential Functions
8.2	Inverse and Composite Functions	8.2	Inverse and Composite Functions
8.3	Logarithmic Functions	8.3	Logarithmic Functions
8.4	Properties of Logarithmic Functions	8.4	Properties of Logarithmic Functions
8.5	Natural Logarithmic Functions	8.5	Natural Logarithmic Functions
8.6	Solving Exponential and Logarithmic Equations	8.6	Solving Exponential and Logarithmic Equations
8.7	Mathematical Modeling with Exponential and Logarithmic Functions	8.7	Mathematical Modeling with Exponential and Logarithmic Functions
9.1	Parabolas and Circles	9.1	Parabolas and Circles
9.2	Ellipses	9.2	Ellipses
9.3	Hyperbolas	9.3	Hyperbolas
9.4	Nonlinear Systems of Equations	9.4	Nonlinear Systems of Equations
A	Handling Dimension Symbols	A	Handling Dimension Symbols
B	Determinants and Cramer's Rule	B	Determinants and Cramer's Rule
C	Elimination Using Matrices	C	Elimination Using Matrices
D	The Algebra of Functions	D	The Algebra of Functions

VIDEO AND EXERCISE INDEX

VHS Tape	DVT CD	Section	Chapter & Section Titles	Examples from Text Covered	Exercises from Text Covered
		Chapter R	**Review of Basic Algebra**		
1	1	R.1	The Set of Real Numbers	1, 3, 4, 7, 9, 14, 15	1, 3, 5, 41, 43, 51, 53, 57, 59, 63
1	1	R.2	Operations with Real Numbers	1, 2, 7, 11, 12, 16, 19, 24, 38, 39, 46	1, 7, 15, 23, 25, 41, 53, 61, 81, 109
1	1	R.3	Exponential Notation and Order of Operations	5, 13, 22	1, 5, 13, 23, 35, 41, 45, 75, 103
1	1	R.4	Introduction to Algebraic Expressions	1, 7	43
1	1	R.5	Equivalent Algebraic Expressions	3, 5, 6, 13	1, 7, 21, 23, 29, 43, 55
1	1	R.6	Simplifying Algebraic Expressions	11, 23	1, 9, 17, 35, 45, 49, 57
1	1	R.7	Properties of Exponents and Scientific Notation	7, 15, 18, 25	1, 15, 39, 45, 79, 81, 105
		Chapter 1	**Solving Linear Equations and Inequalities**		
2	1	1.1	Solving Equations	1, 3	1, 7, 25, 35, 37, 43, 73
2	1	1.2	Formulas and Applications	5, 6	1, 19
2	1	1.3	Applications and Problem Solving	5, 6	31
2	1	1.4	Sets, Inequalities, and Interval Notation	4	7, 13, 19, 27, 43, 73
2	1	1.5	Intersections, Unions, and Compound Inequalities	1, 4, 6	19, 23, 39, 51
2	1	1.6	Absolute Value Equations and Inequalities	3, 7, 8, 17, 18	7, 9, 23, 27, 61, 79
		Chapter 2	**Graphs, Functions, and Applications**		
3	2	2.1	Graphs of Equations	2, 7	1, 11, 31, 47
3	2	2.2	Functions and Graphs	3, 5, 7, 8	13
3	2	2.3	Finding Domain and Range	1, 5	11, 23
3	2	2.4	Linear Functions: Graphs and Slope	1	7, 15, 27
3	2	2.5	More on Graphing Linear Equations	4	5, 25, 27, 45, 53
3	2	2.6	Finding Equations of Lines; Applications	4	1, 5, 9, 21, 39
		Chapter 3	**Systems of Equations**		
4	2	3.1	Systems of Equations in Two Variables	2	1, 5, 15
4	2	3.2	Solving by Substitution	2, 4	1, 15
4	2	3.3	Solving by Elimination	2, 3	3, 17, 29
4	2	3.4	Solving Applied Problems: Two Equations	2, 5	13
4	2	3.5	Systems of Equations in Three Variables	2	1, 23
4	2	3.6	Solving Applied Problems: Three Equations	1	17, 19
5	2	3.7	Systems of Inequalities in Two Variables	1	13, 15, 41, 43
5	2	3.8	Business and Economics Applications	2	11

VHS Tape	DVT CD	Section	Chapter & Section Titles	Examples from Text Covered	Exercises from Text Covered
		Chapter 4	**Polynomials and Polynomial Functions**		
5	3	4.1	Introduction to Polynomials and Polynomial Functions	4, 10, 12, 13, 14	3, 19, 37
5	3	4.2	Multiplication of Polynomials	4, 5, 6, 21, 23, 24	5, 43, 51, 57, 67, 69
5	3	4.3	Introduction to Factoring	1, 2, 4, 10	33, 37, 43
6	3	4.4	Factoring Trinomials: $x^2 + bx + c$	1, 2, 5, 6, 8	5, 7, 25
6	3	4.5	Factoring Trinomials: $ax^2 + bx + c, a \neq 1$	1, 5	11
6	3	4.6	Special Factoring	1, 14	5, 33, 55, 61, 69, 103
6	3	4.7	Factoring: A General Strategy	3, 5	7, 35, 51
6	3	4.8	Applications of Polynomial Equations and Functions	1, 7	35, 45, 59, 69
		Chapter 5	**Rational Expressions, Equations, and Functions**		
7	3	5.1	Rational Expressions and Functions: Multiplying, Dividing, and Simplifying	4, 11, 13	3, 9, 39, 55
7	3	5.2	LCMs, LCDs, Addition, and Subtraction	2, 7, 14	23, 51, 63
7	3	5.3	Division of Polynomials	none	5, 11, 19, 25
7	3	5.4	Complex Rational Expressions	1, 2	7
7	3	5.5	Solving Rational Equations	4	13, 27, 43
7	3	5.6	Applications and Proportions	1, 6	15
8	3	5.7	Formulas and Applications	2	3, 13
8	3	5.8	Variation and Applications	1, 8	11, 19, 23, 39
		Chapter 6	**Radical Expressions, Equations, and Functions**		
8	4	6.1	Radical Expressions and Functions	9, 14, 36, 43	1, 7, 9, 37, 45, 49, 51, 53
8	4	6.2	Rational Numbers as Exponents	1, 7, 11, 19, 27	1, 15, 31, 43, 55
8	4	6.3	Simplifying Radical Expressions	1, 4	13, 19, 49, 57, 59
8	4	6.4	Addition, Subtraction, and More Multiplication	7, 13	13, 23, 49, 65
8	4	6.5	More on Division of Radical Expressions	1	5, 7, 9, 21, 27, 29
9	4	6.6	Solving Radical Equations	3, 6, 8	11, 17, 53
9	4	6.7	Applications Involving Powers and Roots	none	9, 13, 21, 25
9	4	6.8	The Complex Numbers	5	7, 9, 13, 19, 25, 33, 39, 53, 55, 57, 87, 95
		Chapter 7	**Quadratic Equations and Functions**		
9	4	7.1	The Basics of Solving Quadratic Equations	3, 8	5, 23, 43a
9	4	7.2	The Quadratic Formula	1	5, 29
9	4	7.3	Applications Involving Quadratic Equations	4	31, 33, 41
10	4	7.4	More on Quadratic Equations	none	5, 7, 9, 21, 23, 31, 39, 47
10	4	7.5	Graphing $f(x) = a(x - h)^2 + k$	2	1, 3, 5, 13, 15, 21
10	4	7.6	Graphing $f(x) = ax^2 + bx + c$	1, 4	7
10	4	7.7	Mathematical Modeling with Quadratic Functions	2, 3, 4	3, 31
10	4	7.8	Polynomial and Rational Inequalities	1	15, 25
		Chapter 8	**Exponential and Logarithmic Functions**		
11	5	8.1	Exponential Functions	1, 4, 5	7, 9, 13, 19, 32
11	5	8.2	Inverse and Composite Functions	2, 4, 13	1, 17, 31, 35

VHS Tape	DVT CD	Section	Chapter & Section Titles	Examples from Text Covered	Exercises from Text Covered
11	5	8.3	Logarithmic Functions	9, 12	1, 9, 25, 35, 41, 61, 71, 73
11	5	8.4	Properties of Logarithmic Functions	3, 11, 29	3, 7, 17, 21, 27, 29
11	5	8.5	Natural Logarithmic Functions	8, 10, 14	3, 7, 17, 19, 39
12	5	8.6	Solving Exponential and Logarithmic Equations	1, 2, 5, 7	15, 23, 51
12	5	8.7	Mathematical Modeling with Exponential and Logarithmic Functions	1, 4	5, 25
		Chapter 9	**Conic Sections**		
12	6	9.1	Parabolas and Circles	1, 5, 6	7, 11, 49
12	6	9.2	Ellipses	2, 3	17, 19
12	6	9.3	Hyperbolas	none	5, 11, 15, 19
12	6	9.4	Nonlinear Systems of Equations	3, 4, 6	1

CHAPTER SUMMARIES

Provided by:

Judith A. Penna, *Indiana University Purdue University Indianapolis*

Chapter R Review

Objective [R.1a] Use roster and set-builder notation to name sets, and distinguish among various kinds of real numbers.		
Brief Procedure	Example	Practice Exercises
To use roster notation to name a set, list all the objects in the set.	Use roster notation to name the set of negative integers greater than −5. $\{-4, -3, -2, -1\}$	1. Use roster notation to name the set of positive even integers less than 10. A. $\{2,\ 4,\ 6,\ 8\}$ B. $\{2,\ 4,\ 6,\ 8,\ 10\}$ C. $\{0,\ 2,\ 4,\ 6,\ 8\}$ D. $\{0,\ 2,\ 4,\ 6,\ 8,\ 10\}$
To use set-builder notation to name a set, specify the conditions under which an object is in the set.	Use set-builder notation to name the set of negative integers greater than −5. $\{x\|x$ is a negative integer greater than $-5\}$ This is read "the set of all x such that x is a negative integer greater than −5."	2. Use set-builder notation to name the set of real numbers less than or equal to 12. A. $\{x\|x < 12\}$ B. $\{x\|x \leq 12\}$ C. $\{x\|x \geq 12\}$ D. $\{x\|x < -12\}$
To distinguish among various kinds of real numbers, keep the following in mind. Natural numbers: $\{1,\ 2,\ 3,\ \ldots\}$ Whole numbers: $\{0,\ 1,\ 2,\ 3,\ \ldots\}$ Integers: $\{\ldots,\ -2,\ -1,\ 0,\ 1,\ 2,\ \ldots\}$ Rational numbers: $\left\{\dfrac{p}{q}\middle\| p \text{ and } q \text{ are integers}\right.$ $\left. \text{and } q \neq 0\right\}$ Irrational numbers: Numbers whose decimal representation neither terminates nor repeats. They cannot be represented as the quotient of two integers. Real numbers: $\{x\|x$ is a rational number or x is an irrational number$\}$	Given the numbers -5, $\dfrac{7}{12}$, 2.68, 14, 0, $\sqrt{18}$, $0.212112111\ldots$, and $\sqrt{64}$, name the integers. The numbers in the set of integers are $-5, 14, 0,$ and $\sqrt{64}$. (We include $\sqrt{64}$ because $\sqrt{64} = 8$.)	3. Given the numbers in the example at the left, name the rational numbers. A. -5, $\dfrac{7}{12}$, 2.68, 14, 0, $\sqrt{64}$ B. -5, $\dfrac{7}{12}$, 2.68, 14, 0, $\sqrt{18}$, $\sqrt{64}$ C. -5, $\dfrac{7}{12}$, 2.68, 14, 0, $0.212112111\ldots$, $\sqrt{64}$ D. All of them

Objective [R.1b] Determine which of two real numbers is greater and indicate which, using $<$ or $>$; given an inequality like $a < b$, write another inequality with the same meaning; and determine whether an inequality like $-2 \leq 3$ or $4 > 5$ is true.

Brief Procedure	Example	Practice Exercises
To determine which of two real numbers is greater, consider the relative position of the two numbers on the number line. The one on the left is less than the one on the right. The symbol $<$ means "is less than" and the symbol $>$ means "is greater than."	Use $<$ or $>$ for $\square$ to write a true sentence: $$-7 \,\square\, -10$$ Since -7 is to the right of -10 on the number line, we have $-7 > -10$.	4. Use $<$ or $>$ for $\square$ to write a true sentence: $$-8 \,\square\, 1$$ A. $<$ B. $>$
Given an inequality like $a < b$, write another inequality with the same meaning by interchanging a and b and reversing the direction of the inequality symbol.	Write another inequality with the same meaning as $x > 8$. The inequality $8 < x$ has the same meaning.	5. Write another inequality with the same meaning as $-3 < t$. A. $t < -3$ B. $t > 3$ C. $3 < t$ D. $t > -3$
An inequality like $-2 \leq 3$ is true if either $-2 < 3$ is true or $-2 = 3$ is true. If neither is true, then the inequality is false. To determine whether an inequality like $4 > 5$ is true, determine the relative positions of the numbers on the number line. The one farther to the right is larger.	Determine whether each inequality is true or false. a) $-4 \leq 1$ b) $6 \geq 6$ c) $-10 \geq 2$ a) $-4 \leq 1$ is true since $-4 < 1$ is true. b) $6 \geq 6$ is true since $6 = 6$ is true. c) $-10 \geq 2$ is false since neither $-10 > 2$ nor $-10 = 2$ is true.	6. Determine whether the inequality $-1 \geq -8$ is true or false. A. True B. False

Objective [R.1c] Graph inequalities on the number line.

Brief Procedure	Example	Practice Exercise
Shade all points on the number line that are solutions of the given inequality.	Graph each inequality. a) $x < 1$ b) $x \geq -2$ a) The solutions of $x < 1$ are all numbers less than 1. We shade all points to the left of 1. Use an open circle at 1 to indicate that 1 is not part of the graph. b) The solutions of $x \geq -2$ are all numbers greater than -2 and the number -2 as well. We shade all points to the right of -2, and we use a closed circle at -2 to indicate that -2 is part of the graph. 	7. Graph $x > 2$. A. B. C. D.

Objective [R.1d] Find the absolute value of a real number.

Brief Procedure	Example	Practice Exercise
If the number is negative, make it positive. If the number is positive or zero, leave it alone.	Find $\lvert -4.3 \rvert$. The number is negative, so we make it positive. $\lvert -4.3 \rvert = 4.3$	8. Find $\lvert 59 \rvert$. A. -59 B. 0 C. 59

Objective [R.2a] Add real numbers.

Brief Procedure	Example	Practice Exercise

1. *Positive numbers*: Add the same as arithmetic numbers. The answer is positive.
 2. *Negative numbers*: Add absolute values. The answer is negative.
 3. *A positive and a negative number*: Subtract the smaller absolute value from the larger. Then:
   a) If the positive number has the greater absolute value, the answer is positive.
   b) If the negative number has the greater absolute value, the answer is negative.
   c) If the numbers have the same absolute value, the answer is 0.
 4. *One number is zero*: The sum is the other number.
	Add: $-15 + 9$.
	
	 We have a negative and a positive number. The absolute values are 15 and 9. The difference is 6. The negative number has the larger absolute value, so the answer is negative.
	
	 $-15 + 9 = -6$
		9. Add: $-1.2 + (-3.4)$.
		 A. 4.6
		 B. 2.2
		 C. -2.2
		 D. -4.6

Objective [R.2b] Find the opposite, or additive inverse, of a number.

Brief Procedure	Example	Practice Exercise
The opposite, or additive inverse, of any real number a is the number $-a$ such that $a + (-a) = (-a) + a = 0$. To find the opposite of a number, we change its sign.	Find the opposite of $\dfrac{5}{3}$. The opposite of $\dfrac{5}{3}$ is $-\dfrac{5}{3}$ because $\dfrac{5}{3} + \left(-\dfrac{5}{3} \right) = 0$.	10. Find the opposite of -20. A. -20 B. 0 C. 20

Objective [R.2c] Subtract real numbers.

Brief Procedure	Example	Practice Exercise
For any real numbers a and b, $\quad a - b = a + (-b)$. (To subtract, add the opposite, or additive inverse, of the number being subtracted.)	Subtract: $6 - (-7)$. The opposite of -7 is 7. We change the subtraction to addition and add the opposite. $\quad 6 - (-7) = 6 + 7 = 13$	11. Subtract: $2 - 12$. A. -14 B. -10 C. 10 D. 14

Objective [R.2d] Multiply real numbers.

Brief Procedure	Example	Practice Exercise
a) Multiply the absolute values. b) If the signs are the same, the answer is positive. c) If the signs are different, the answer is negative.	Multiply: $-2.4(3)$. The signs are different, so the answer is negative. $\quad -2.4(3) = -7.2$	12. Multiply: $-7(-9)$. A. -63 B. -16 C. 2 D. 63

Objective [R.2e] Divide real numbers.

Brief Procedure	Example	Practice Exercise
For any real numbers a and b, $b \neq 0$, $\quad a \div b = \dfrac{a}{b} = a \cdot \dfrac{1}{b}$. (To divide, we can multiply by the reciprocal of the divisor.)	Divide: $-\dfrac{1}{3} \div \dfrac{2}{7}$. $-\dfrac{1}{3} \div \dfrac{2}{7} = -\dfrac{1}{3} \cdot \dfrac{7}{2} = -\dfrac{7}{6}$	13. Divide: $-\dfrac{3}{4} \div \left(-\dfrac{5}{11} \right)$. A. $-\dfrac{53}{44}$ B. $-\dfrac{13}{44}$ C. $\dfrac{15}{44}$ D. $\dfrac{33}{20}$

Objective [R.3a] Rewrite expressions with whole-number exponents, and evaluate exponential expressions.

Brief Procedure	Example	Practice Exercises
To rewrite expressions with whole-number exponents, count the number of identical factors. Then make that number the exponent, using the repeated factor as the base.	Write exponential notation for $6 \cdot 6 \cdot 6 \cdot 6$. $\underbrace{6 \cdot 6 \cdot 6 \cdot 6}_{\text{4 factors}} = 6^4$	14. Write exponential notation for $2 \cdot 2 \cdot 2 \cdot 2 \cdot 2$. A. 32 B. $5 \cdot 2$ C. 5^2 D. 2^5
To evaluate exponential expressions, rewrite the exponential expression as a product and compute.	Evaluate: 3^4. $3^4 = 3 \cdot 3 \cdot 3 \cdot 3 = 81$	15. Evaluate: 5^3. A. 15 B. 125 C. 243 D. 625

Objective [R.3b] Rewrite expressions with or without negative integers as exponents.

Brief Procedure	Example	Practice Exercises
For any real number a that is nonzero and any integer n, $\dfrac{1}{a^n} = a^{-n}$.	Rewrite using positive exponents. a) $3x^{-8}$ b) $\dfrac{1}{y^{-2}}$ a) $3x^{-8} = 3 \cdot \dfrac{1}{x^8} = \dfrac{3}{x^8}$ b) $\dfrac{1}{y^{-2}} = y^{-(-2)} = y^2$	16. Rewrite $2n^{-5}$ using a positive exponent. A. $\dfrac{1}{2n^5}$ B. $\dfrac{2}{n^5}$ C. $\dfrac{n^5}{2}$ D. $2n^5$
For any real number a that is nonzero and any integer n, $\dfrac{1}{a^n} = a^{-n}$.	Rewrite $\dfrac{1}{x^3}$ using a negative exponent. $\dfrac{1}{x^3} = x^{-3}$	17. Express $\dfrac{1}{5^4}$ using a negative exponent. A. $\dfrac{1}{5^{-4}}$ B. $\dfrac{1}{(-5)^4}$ C. 5^4 D. 5^{-4}

Objective [R.3c] Simplify expressions using the rules for order of operations.

Brief Procedure	Example	Practice Exercise
1. Do all calculations within grouping symbols before operations outside. 2. Evaluate all exponential expressions. 3. Do all multiplications and divisions in order from left to right. 4. Do all additions and subtractions in order from left to right.	Simplify: $64 \div 4^2 \cdot 3 + (12 - 7)$. $64 \div 4^2 \cdot 3 + (12 - 7)$ $= 64 \div 4^2 \cdot 3 + 5$ $= 64 \div 16 \cdot 3 + 5$ $= 4 \cdot 3 + 5$ $= 12 + 5$ $= 17$	18. Simplify: $9 + (19 - 9)^2 \div 5 \cdot 2$. A. 19 B. 49 C. 121 D. 220

Objective [R.4a] Translate a phrase to an algebraic expression.

Brief Procedure	Example	Practice Exercise
Learn which words translate to certain operation symbols. (See page 33 in the text.) Choose a variable or variables to correspond to the number or numbers involved. It can be helpful to try some numerical examples before writing the algebraic expression.	Translate to an algebraic expression: Four less than some number. Let $n =$ the number. Now if the number were 7, then the translation would be $7 - 4$. Similarly, if the number were 52, then the translation would be $52 - 4$. Thus, we see from these numerical examples, that if the number were n, the translation would be $n - 4$.	19. Translate to an algebraic expression: Three times some number. A. $n + 3$ B. $n - 3$ C. $3 - n$ D. $3n$

Objective [R.4b] Evaluate an algebraic expression by substitution.		
Brief Procedure	Example	Practice Exercise
Substitute for the variable(s) and carry out the resulting calculation.	Evaluate $m - n$ for $m = 29$ and $n = 12$. Substitute 29 for m and 12 for n and carry out the subtraction. $$m - n = 29 - 12 = 17$$	20. Evaluate $\dfrac{x}{y}$ for $x = 72$ and $y = 9$. A. $\dfrac{1}{8}$ B. 8 C. 63 D. 81

Objective [R.5a] Determine whether two expressions are equivalent by completing a table of values.		
Brief Procedure	Example	Practice Exercise
If two expressions have the same value for all allowable replacements, they are equivalent. To determine if this is the case, we can evaluate each expression for some values of the variable and organize the results in a table.	Complete the table by evaluating each expression for the given values. Then determine whether the expressions are equivalent. 		$x + x$	$2x$
$x = -3$		
$x = 0$		
$x = 4$		| We substitute and find the value of each expression. |	$x + x$	$2x$
$x = -3$	-6	-6
$x = 0$	0	0
$x = 4$	8	8 | It appears that the expressions have the same value for all allowable replacements, so they are equivalent.	21. Complete the table by evaluating each expression for the given values. Then determine whether the expressions are equivalent. |	$2(x - 1)$	$2x - 1$
$x = -2$		
$x = 0$		
$x = 3$		| A. Equivalent B. Not equivalent

Objective [R.5b] Find equivalent fraction expressions by multiplying by 1, and simplify fraction expressions.		
Brief Procedure	Example	Practice Exercise
To find an equivalent fractional expression, multiply the fraction by 1 using n/n. If a specific denominator is desired, choose n by determining the number the original denominator should be multiplied by in order to get the desired denominator.	Find a name for $\dfrac{2}{3}$ with a denominator of 12. Since $3 \cdot 4 = 12$, we multiply by $\dfrac{4}{4}$: $$\frac{2}{3} = \frac{2}{3} \cdot \frac{4}{4} = \frac{2 \cdot 4}{3 \cdot 4} = \frac{8}{12}$$	22. Find a name for $\dfrac{3}{4}$ with a denominator of 20. A. $\dfrac{3}{20}$ B. $\dfrac{8}{20}$ C. $\dfrac{15}{20}$ D. $\dfrac{19}{20}$

Objective [R.5b] (continued)

Brief Procedure	Example	Practice Exercise
To simplify a fractional expression, remove a factor of 1 to get the name for the fraction that has the smallest numerator and denominator.	Simplify: $\dfrac{16}{36}$. $$\frac{16}{36} = \frac{4 \cdot 4}{4 \cdot 9} = \frac{4}{4} \cdot \frac{4}{9} = 1 \cdot \frac{4}{9} = \frac{4}{9}$$	23. Simplify: $\dfrac{9}{24}$. A. $\dfrac{1}{6}$ B. $\dfrac{1}{3}$ C. $\dfrac{3}{8}$ D. $\dfrac{9}{8}$

Objective [R.5c] Use the commutative and associative laws to find equivalent expressions.

Brief Procedure	Example	Practice Exercises
The Commutative Laws *Addition* For any numbers a and b, $\quad a + b = b + a$. *Multiplication* For any numbers a and b, $\quad ab = ba$. (We can change the order when adding or when multiplying without affecting the result.)	Use a commutative law to write an equivalent expression. a) $n + 6$ b) xy a) An equivalent expression is $6 + n$, by the commutative law of addition. b) An equivalent expression is yx, by the commutative law of multiplication.	24. Use a commutative law to write an equivalent expression for $8 + a$. A. $a + 8$ B. $8a$ C. $a8$ D. $8 - a$
The Associative Laws *Addition* For any numbers a, b, and c, $\quad a + (b + c) = (a + b) + c$. *Multiplication* For any numbers a, b, and c, $\quad a \cdot (b \cdot c) = (a \cdot b) \cdot c$. (Numbers can be grouped in any manner for addition and for multiplication.)	Use an associative law to write an equivalent expression. a) $(m + n) + 1$ b) $5(st)$ a) An equivalent expression is $m + (n + 1)$, by the associative law of addition. b) An equivalent expression is $(5s)t$, by the associative law of multiplication.	25. Use an associative law to write an equivalent expression for $(4x)y$. A. $y(4x)$ B. $(x4)y$ C. $4(xy)$ D. $y + (4x)$

Objective [R.5d] Use the distributive laws to find equivalent expressions by multiplying and factoring.

Brief Procedure	Example	Practice Exercises
To multiply, use the following: For any numbers a, b, and c, $\quad a(b + c) = ab + ac$ and $\quad a(b - c) = ab - ac$.	Multiply: $5(2x - 3y + z)$. $\quad 5(2x - 3y + z)$ $= 5 \cdot 2x - 5 \cdot 3y + 5 \cdot z$ $= 10x - 15y + 5z$	26. Multiply: $3(x + 4y - 2z)$. A. $3x + 4y - 2z$ B. $3x + 12y + 6z$ C. $3x + 12y - 6z$ D. $3x - 12y - 6z$
To factor, find the largest factor that is common to all the terms of the expression and factor it out.	Factor: $8a + 4b - 12c$. $\quad 8a + 4b - 12c$ $= 4 \cdot 2a + 4 \cdot b - 4 \cdot 3c$ $= 4(2a + b - 3c)$	27. Factor: $36m - 27n + 9p$. A. $3(12m - 9n + 3p)$ B. $36(m - 27n + 9p)$ C. $9(4m - 3n)$ D. $9(4m - 3n + p)$

Objective [R.6a] Simplify expressions by collecting like terms.

Brief Procedure	Example	Practice Exercise
Identify the terms with exactly the same variable, use the distributive laws to factor out the variable, and then simplify.	Collect like terms: $3x - 5y + 8x + y$. $3x - 5y + 8x + y$ $= 3x + 8x - 5y + y$ $= 3x + 8x - 5y + 1 \cdot y$ $= (3 + 8)x + (-5 + 1)y$ $= 11x - 4y$	28. Collect like terms: $6a - 4b - a + 2b$. A. $5a - 2b$ B. $2a + b$ C. $6a - 2b$ D. $5a + 6b$

Objective [R.6b] Simplify an expression by removing parentheses and collecting like terms.

Brief Procedure	Example	Practice Exercise
Use a distributive law to remove parentheses and then collect like terms.	Remove parentheses and simplify: $6x - 2(x - 3y)$. $6x - 2(x - 3y) = 6x - 2x + 6y = 4x + 6y$	29. Remove parentheses and simplify: $3m - n - (2m + 5n)$. A. $m + 4n$ B. $5m + 4n$ C. $m - 4n$ D. $m - 6n$

Objective [R.7a] Use exponential notation in multiplication and division.

Brief Procedure	Example	Practice Exercises
For any number a and any positive integers m and n, $a^m \cdot a^n = a^{m+n}$. (When multiplying with exponential notation, if the bases are the same, keep the base and add the exponents.)	Multiply and simplify: $y^2 \cdot y^6$. $y^2 \cdot y^6 = y^{2+6} = y^8$	30. Multiply and simplify: $x^3 \cdot x^4$. A. x^7 B. $2x^7$ C. x^{12} D. x^{14}
For any nonzero number a and any positive integers m and n, $\dfrac{a^m}{a^n} = a^{m-n}$. (When dividing with exponential notation, if the bases are the same, keep the base and subtract the exponent of the denominator from the exponent of the numerator.)	Divide and simplify: $\dfrac{a^{10}b^4}{a^2 b}$. $\dfrac{a^{10}b^4}{a^2 b} = \dfrac{a^{10}}{a^2} \cdot \dfrac{b^4}{b}$ $= a^{10-2}b^{4-1}$ $= a^8 b^3$	31. Divide and simplify: $\dfrac{x^3 y^7}{x^2 y^4}$. A. y^3 B. xy^3 C. $x^5 y^{11}$ D. $x^6 y^{28}$

Objective [R.7b] Use exponential notation in raising a power to a power and in raising a product or a quotient to a power.

Brief Procedure	Example	Practice Exercises
To raise a power to a power, multiply the exponents. That is, for any real number a and any integers m and n, $$(a^m)^n = a^{mn}.$$	Simplify: $(y^{-3})^2$. $$(y^{-3})^2 = y^{-3 \cdot 2} = y^{-6} = \frac{1}{y^6}$$	32. Simplify: $(b^{-4})^{-3}$. A. $\dfrac{1}{b}$ B. $\dfrac{1}{b^7}$ C. b^7 D. b^{12}
To raise a product to the nth power, raise each factor to the nth power. That is, for any real numbers a and b and any integer n, $$(ab)^n = a^n b^n.$$	Simplify: $(3x^{-4}y^2)^3$. $$(3x^{-4}y^2)^3 = 3^3(x^{-4})^3(y^2)^3$$ $$= 27x^{-12}y^6$$ $$= \frac{27y^6}{x^{12}}$$	33. Simplify: $(8a^3b^{-5})^2$. A. $\dfrac{8a^5}{b^7}$ B. $\dfrac{16a^6}{b^{10}}$ C. $\dfrac{64a^3}{b^5}$ D. $\dfrac{64a^6}{b^{10}}$
To raise a quotient to a power, raise both the numerator and the denominator to the power. That is, for any real numbers a and b, $b \neq 0$, and any integer n, $$\left(\frac{a}{b}\right)^n = \frac{a^n}{b^n}.$$	Simplify: $\left(\dfrac{4}{a^5}\right)^3$. $$\left(\frac{4}{a^5}\right)^3 = \frac{4^3}{(a^5)^3} = \frac{64}{a^{15}}$$	34. Simplify: $\left(\dfrac{y^4}{7}\right)^2$. A. $\dfrac{y^6}{49}$ B. $\dfrac{y^8}{49}$ C. $\dfrac{y^{16}}{49}$ D. $\dfrac{y^8}{7}$

Objective [R.7c] Convert between decimal notation and scientific notation and use scientific notation with multiplication and division.

Brief Procedure	Example	Practice Exercises
To convert from decimal notation to scientific notation, rewrite the number in the form $M \times 10^n$, where n is an integer, $1 \leq M < 10$, and M is expressed in decimal notation. If the original number is large (greater than 1), then n is positive. If it is a small number (less than 1), then n is negative.	Convert 0.00048 to scientific notation. 0.0004. 8 $\llcorner\underline{\quad}\uparrow$ 4 places The number is small, so the exponent is negative. $$0.00048 = 4.8 \times 10^{-4}$$	35. Convert 567,000 to scientific notation. A. 5.67×10^{-5} B. 5.67×10^3 C. 5.67×10^5 D. 567×10^3

Objective [R.7c] (continued)

Brief Procedure	Example	Practice Exercises
Given a number $M \times 10^n$ in scientific notation, convert to decimal notation by moving the decimal point in M n places to the right or left. If the exponent is positive, the number is large, so the decimal point should be moved to the right. If the exponent is negative, the number is small so the decimal point should be moved to the left.	Convert 4.208×10^6 to decimal notation. The exponent is positive, so the number is large. We move the decimal point 6 places to the right. $\qquad$ 4.208000. $\qquad \quad \rule{2cm}{0.4pt}\uparrow$ 6 places $4.208 \times 10^6 = 4,208,000$	36. Convert 3×10^{-4} to decimal notation. A. 0.0003 B. 0.003 C. 3000 D. 30,000
To use scientific notation with multiplication and division, apply the commutative and associative laws and the rules for exponents.	Multiply and express the result in scientific notation: $\qquad (4.2 \times 10^8) \cdot (3.1 \times 10^{-3})$. $\qquad (4.2 \times 10^8) \cdot (3.1 \times 10^{-3})$ $\qquad = (4.2 \cdot 3.1) \times (10^8 \cdot 10^{-3})$ $\qquad = 13.02 \times 10^5$ The answer at this stage is 13.02×10^5, but this is not scientific notation, because 13.02 is not a number between 1 and 10. We convert 13.02 to scientific notation and simplify. $\qquad 13.02 \times 10^5$ $\qquad = (1.302 \times 10) \times 10^5$ $\qquad = 1.302 \times (10 \times 10^5)$ $\qquad = 1.302 \times 10^6$	37. Divide and express the result in scientific notation: $\qquad \dfrac{3.3 \times 10^2}{4.4 \times 10^{-10}}$. A. 0.75×10^{-8} B. 0.75×10^{12} C. 7.5×10^{11} D. 7.5×10^{13}

Chapter 1 Review

Objective [1.1a] Determine whether a given number is a solution of a given equation.

Brief Procedure	Example	Practice Exercise
Substitute the given number in the equation and determine if a true equation results.	Determine whether -3 is a solution of $x + 4 = 1$. $$x + 4 = 1$$ $$\overline{-3 + 4 \ ? \ 1}$$ $$1 \ | \qquad \text{TRUE}$$ Since the left-hand and right-hand sides are the same, we have a true equation so -3 is a solution.	1. Determine whether 5 is a solution of $9x = 42$. A. Yes B. No

Objective [1.1b] Solve equations using the addition principle.

Brief Procedure	Example	Practice Exercise
For any real numbers a, b, and c, $\qquad a = b$ is equivalent to $\qquad a + c = b + c$. Add the same number on both sides of the equation to get the variable alone. Since $a + (-c) = b + (-c)$ is equivalent to $a - c = b - c$, we can also subtract the same number on both sides of the equation.	Solve: $x + 4 = 9$. We subtract 4 on both sides of the equation to get x alone. $$x + 4 = 9$$ $$x + 4 - 4 = 9 - 4$$ $$x + 0 = 5$$ $$x = 5$$ The solution is 5.	2. Solve: $y - 3 = -1$. A. -4 B. -2 C. 2 D. 4

Objective [1.1c] Solve equations using the multiplication principle.

Brief Procedure	Example	Practice Exercise
For any real numbers a, b, and c, $c \neq 0$, $\qquad a = b$ is equivalent to $\qquad a \cdot c = b \cdot c$. Multiply by the same number on both sides of the equation to get the variable alone. For $c \neq 0$, $a \cdot \dfrac{1}{c} = b \cdot \dfrac{1}{c}$ is equivalent to $\dfrac{a}{c} = \dfrac{b}{c}$, so we can also divide by the same number on both sides of the equation.	Solve: $54 = -9y$. We divide by -9 on both sides of the equation to get y alone. $$54 = -9y$$ $$\frac{54}{-9} = \frac{-9y}{-9}$$ $$-6 = 1 \cdot y$$ $$-6 = y$$ The solution is -6.	3. Solve: $6x = -42$. A. 7 B. -7 C. -36 D. -48

Objective [1.1d] Solve equations using the addition and the multiplication principles together, removing parentheses where appropriate.

Brief Procedure	Example	Practice Exercise
First use the addition principle to isolate the term that contains the variable. Then use the multiplication principle to get the variable by itself. If an equation contains parentheses, first use the distributive laws to remove them. Then collect like terms, if necessary, and use the addition and multiplication principles to complete the solution of the equation.	Solve: $8b - 2(3b+1) = 10$. $8b - 2(3b+1) = 10$ $8b - 6b - 2 = 10$ $2b - 2 = 10$ $2b - 2 + 2 = 10 + 2$ $2b = 12$ $\dfrac{2b}{2} = \dfrac{12}{2}$ $b = 6$ The solution is 6.	4. Solve: $3(n-4) = 2(n+1)$. A. -5 B. -2 C. 5 D. 14

Objective [1.2a] Evaluate formulas and solve a formula for a specified letter.

Brief Procedure	Example	Practice Exercises
To evaluate a formula for a given value of the variable, substitute the value for the variable and carry out the resulting calculations.	The formula $d = 65t$ gives the distance d that is traveled in t hours at a speed of 65 mph. Suppose you travel at 65 mph for 4 hours. How far have you traveled? We substitute 4 for t and carry out the calculation. $d = 65 \cdot 4 = 260$ You have traveled 260 miles.	5. Using the formula $d = 65t$, find the distance traveled at 65 mph for 3 hours. A. 185 miles B. 195 miles C. 205 miles D. 225 miles
To solve a formula for a given letter, identify the letter and: 1. Multiply on both sides to clear the fractions or decimals, if necessary. 2. If parentheses occur, multiply to remove them using the distributive law. 3. Collect like terms on each side, if necessary. This may require factoring if a variable is in more than one term. 4. Using the addition principle, get all terms with the letter to be solved for on one side of the equation and all other terms on the other side. 5. Collect like terms again, if necessary. 6. Solve for the letter in question using the multiplication principle.	Solve for b: $A = \dfrac{a+b}{2}$. $A = \dfrac{a+b}{2}$ $2 \cdot A = 2\left(\dfrac{a+b}{2}\right)$ $2A = a + b$ $2A - a = b$	6. Solve for h: $A = \dfrac{1}{2}bh$. A. $h = \dfrac{A}{2b}$ B. $h = \dfrac{b}{2A}$ C. $h = \dfrac{2b}{A}$ D. $h = \dfrac{2A}{b}$

Objective [1.3a] Solve applied problems by translating to equations.

Brief Procedure	Example	Practice Exercise
Use the five-step problem solving process. 1. *Familiarize* yourself with the problem situation. 2. *Translate* the problem to an equation. 3. *Solve* the equation. 4. *Check* the answer in the original problem. 5. *State* the answer to the problem clearly.	A 12-ft pipe is cut into three pieces. The second piece is three times as long as the first. The third piece is twice as long as the first. How long is each piece? 1. *Familiarize.* Let x = the length of the first piece of pipe. Then $3x$ = the length of the second piece and $2x$ = the length of the third piece. 2. *Translate.* We use the fact that the sum of the lengths is 12 feet. $$\begin{array}{ccccc}\text{Length} && \text{length} \\ \text{of first} & \text{plus} & \text{of second} & \text{plus} \\ \text{piece} && \text{piece} \\ \downarrow & \downarrow & \downarrow & \downarrow \\ x & + & 3x & + \end{array}$$ $$\begin{array}{ccc}\text{length} \\ \text{of third} & \text{is} & \text{total} \\ \text{piece} && \text{length} \\ \downarrow & \downarrow & \downarrow \\ 2x & = & 12 \end{array}$$ 3. *Solve.* We solve the equation. $$x + 3x + 2x = 12$$ $$6x = 12$$ $$\frac{6x}{6} = \frac{12}{6}$$ $$x = 2$$ If $x = 2$, then $3x = 3 \cdot 2$, or 6, and $2x = 2 \cdot 2$, or 4. 4. *Check.* The second piece, 6 ft, is three times as long as the first, 2 ft, and the third piece, 4 ft, is twice as long as the first. Also, the lengths total 2 ft + 6 ft + 4 ft, or 12 ft. The answer checks. 5. *State.* The first piece of pipe is 2 ft long, the second piece is 6 ft, and the third piece is 4 ft.	7. The perimeter of a rectangular rug is 40 ft. The width is 4 ft less than the length. Find the dimensions of the rug. A. The width is 8 ft. B. The width is 10 ft. C. The width is 12 ft. D. The width is 16 ft.

Objective [1.3b] Solve basic motion problems.		
Brief Procedure	Example	Practice Exercise
Use the motion formula, $d = rt$, and the five-step problem solving process.	An airplane that travels 425 mph in still air encounters a 25-mph headwind. How long will it take to travel 600 mi into the wind? 1. *Familiarize.* We let $t =$ the number of hours it will take the plane to travel 600 mi into the wind. The plane's speed flying into the wind is $425 - 25$, or 400 mph. 2. *Translate.* We use the motion formula $d = rt$ and substitute 600 for d and 400 for r. $$d = rt$$ $$600 = 400 \cdot t$$ 3. *Solve.* We solve the equation. $$600 = 400t$$ $$\frac{600}{400} = \frac{400t}{400}$$ $$1.5 = t$$ 4. *Check.* At a speed of 400 mph, in a time of 1.5 hr the plane would travel $400(1.5)$, or 600 mi. The answer checks. 5. *State.* It will take 1.5 hr to travel 600 mi into the headwind.	8. A boat travels at a rate of 16 km/h in still water. If a river's current moves at a rate of 4 km/h, how long will it take the boat to travel 60 km downstream? A. 3 hr B. 3.75 hr C. 5 hr D. 15 hr

Objective [1.4a] Determine whether a given number is a solution of an inequality.		
Brief Procedure	Example	Practice Exercise
Substitute the given number for the variable and determine if a true inequality results.	Determine whether each number is a solution of $y \leq -4$. a) 2 b) -4 a) Since $2 \leq -4$ is false, 2 is not a solution. b) Since $-4 \leq -4$ is true, -4 is a solution.	9. Determine whether -3 is a solution of $x \geq -5$. A. Yes B. No

Objective [1.4b] Write interval notation for the solution set or graph of an inequality.

Brief Procedure	Example	Practice Exercise
To indicate that a solution set contains all the points in the interval from a to b, write (a, b). The parentheses indicate that neither a nor b is in the solution set. Use a bracket to signify that an endpoint is included. For example, $[a, b) = \{x \mid a \le x < b\}$. Use the symbols $-\infty$ and ∞ to indicate that an interval extends without bound to the left or to the right, respectively.	Write interval notation for the set or graph. a) $\{x \mid -3 < x \le 2\}$ b) a) The set contains all real numbers from -3 to 2 along with the right endpoint 2, so we write $(-3, 2]$. b) The set contains all real numbers less than 1, so we write $(-\infty, 1)$.	10. Write interval notation for the set $\{x \mid x \ge 2.6\}$. A. $(-\infty, 2.6)$ B. $(-\infty, 2.6]$ C. $(2.6, \infty)$ D. $[2.6, \infty)$

Objective [1.4c] Solve an inequality using the addition and multiplication principles and then graph the inequality.

Brief Procedure	Example	Practice Exercise
First use the addition principle to isolate the term that contains the variable. Then use the multiplication principle to get the variable by itself. Keep in mind that the inequality symbol must be reversed when the multiplication principle is used to multiply by a negative number on both sides of the inequality. Then graph the solution set on the number line.	Solve: $6y + 5 \ge 3y - 1$. $$6y + 5 \ge 3y - 1$$ $$6y + 5 - 3y \ge 3y - 1 - 3y$$ $$3y + 5 \ge -1$$ $$3y + 5 - 5 \ge -1 - 5$$ $$3y \ge -6$$ $$\frac{3y}{3} \ge \frac{-6}{3}$$ $$y \ge -2$$ The solution set is $\{y \mid y \ge -2\}$, or $[-2, \infty)$. We graph the solution set. 	11. Solve: $8y - 7 > 5y + 2$. A. $\{y \mid y < -3\}$ B. $\{y \mid y > -3\}$ C. $\{y \mid y > \dfrac{9}{13}\}$ D. $\{y \mid y > 3\}$

Objective [1.4d] Solve applied problems by translating to inequalities.		
Brief Procedure	Example	Practice Exercise
Use the five-step problem solving process.	The perimeter of a rectangular patio is not to exceed 60 ft. The length is to be twice the width. What widths will meet these conditions? 1. *Familiarize.* Recall that the formula for the perimeter P of a rectangle is $P = 2l + 2w$, where l is the length and w is the width. Since the length is twice the width, we have $l = 2w$ and then $2l + 2w = 2 \cdot 2w + 2w = 4w + 2w = 6w$. 2. *Translate.* We reword the problem and translate. $\underbrace{\text{Perimeter}} \quad \underbrace{\substack{\text{is less than} \\ \text{or equal to}}} \quad \underbrace{\text{60 ft.}}$ $\quad\downarrow \qquad\qquad \downarrow \qquad\qquad \downarrow$ $\quad 6w \qquad\qquad \leq \qquad\qquad 60$ 3. *Solve.* We solve the inequality. $6w \leq 60$ $\dfrac{6w}{6} \leq \dfrac{60}{6}$ $w \leq 10$ 4. *Check.* We can obtain a partial check by substituting a number less than or equal to 10 for w. For example, for $w = 9$, we have $l = 2 \cdot 9$, or 18 and $2l + 2w = 2 \cdot 18 + 2 \cdot 9 = 54 \leq 60$. The result is probably correct. 5. *State.* Widths less than or equal to 10 ft will meet the given conditions.	12. Kelly's scores on the first three tests in her physics class are 79, 84, and 68. Determine all scores on the fourth test that will yield an average test score of at least 80. A. Scores of 88 or higher B. Scores of 89 or higher C. Scores of 91 or higher D. Scores of 94 or higher

Objective [1.5a] Find the intersection of two sets. Solve and graph conjunctions of inequalities.		
Brief Procedure	Example	Practice Exercise
The intersection of two sets A and B, denoted $A \cap B$, is the set of all numbers that are common to A and B.	Find the intersection: $\{-4, -2, 0, 2, 4\} \cap \{-2, -1, 0, 1, 2\}$. The numbers -2, 0, and 2 are common to the two sets, so the intersection is $\{-2, 0, 2\}$.	13. Find the intersection: $\{0, 3, 4, 9\} \cap \{-3, 0, 4, 8\}$. A. $\{0\}$ B. $\{3\}$ C. $\{0, 3\}$ D. $\{0, 4\}$

Objective [1.5a] (continued)		
Brief Procedure	Example	Practice Exercise
To solve a conjunction of inequalities, use the addition and multiplication principles to solve both parts of the inequality. The solution set of the conjunction is the intersection of the individual solution sets. The solution set can then be graphed on the number line.	Solve and graph: a) $-1 < 2x - 3$ *and* $2x - 3 < 9$; b) $4x + 10 > -14$ *and* $3x - 4 \le 2$. a) $-1 < 2x - 3$ *and* $2x - 3 < 9$ We can combine the parts of this conjunction into a single inequality. $\quad -1 < 2x - 3 < 9$ $\quad\quad 2 < 2x < 12$ $\quad\quad 1 < x < 6$ The solution set is $\{x \vert 1 < x < 6\}$, or $(1,6)$. We graph the solution set. b) The parts of this conjunction cannot be combined into a single inequality, so we solve each part separately. $\quad 4x + 10 > -14$ *and* $3x - 4 \le 2$ $\quad\quad\quad 4x > -24$ *and* $\quad\quad 3x \le 6$ $\quad\quad\quad\; x > -6$ *and* $\quad\quad\; x \le 2$ Now we find the intersection of the solution sets: $\{x \vert x > -6\} \cap \{x \vert x \le 2\} =$ $\{x \vert -6 < x \le 2\}$. The solution set is $\{x \vert -6 < x \le 2\}$, or $(-6, 2]$. We graph the solution set.	14. Solve: $-4 \le 5x + 6 < 11$. A. $\left\{ x \Big\vert \dfrac{2}{5} \le x < \dfrac{17}{5} \right\}$, or $\left[\dfrac{2}{5}, \dfrac{17}{5} \right)$ B. $\left\{ x \Big\vert \dfrac{2}{5} \le x < 1 \right\}$, or $\left[\dfrac{2}{5}, 1 \right)$ C. $\{x \vert -2 \le x < 1\}$, or $[-2, 1)$ D. $\left\{ x \Big\vert -2 \le x < \dfrac{17}{5} \right\}$, or $\left[-2, \dfrac{17}{5} \right)$

Objective [1.5b] Find the union of two sets. Solve and graph disjunctions of inequalities.		
Brief Procedure	Example	Practice Exercise
The union of two sets A and B, denoted $A \cup B$, is the collection of elements belonging to A and/or B.	Find the union: $\{1, 3, 5\} \cup \{1, 5, 6\}$. The numbers in either or both sets are 1, 3, 5, and 6, so the union is $\{1, 3, 5, 6\}$.	15. Find the union: $\quad \{-4, 2, 6\} \cap \{-3, 0, 2, 6\}$. A. $\{2, 6\}$ B. $\{-4, 0, 2, 6\}$ C. $\{-4, -3, 2, 6\}$ D. $\{-4, -3, 0, 2, 6\}$

Objective [1.5b] (continued)		
Brief Procedure	Example	Practice Exercise
To solve a disjunction of inequalities, use the addition and multiplication principles to solve each inequality separately, retaining the word *or*. The solution set of the disjunction is the union of the individual solution sets. The solution set can then be graphed on the number line.	Solve and graph: $3x + 1 \leq -8$ *or* $4x + 1 > 5$. $$3x + 1 \leq -8 \text{ or } 4x + 1 > 5$$ $$3x \leq -9 \text{ or } \qquad 4x > 4$$ $$x \leq -3 \text{ or } \qquad x > 1$$ Now find the union of the solution sets: $$\{x \mid x < -3\} \cup \{x \mid x > 1\} =$$ $$\{x \mid x \leq -3 \text{ or } x > 1\}.$$ The solution set is $\{x \mid x \leq -3 \text{ or } x > 1\}$, or $(-\infty, -3] \cup (1, \infty)$. We graph the solution set.	16. Solve: $x + 4 < 2$ *or* $2x + 3 \geq 7$. A. $\emptyset$ B. $(-2, 2]$ C. $(-\infty, -2) \cup [2, \infty)$ D. $(-\infty, -2) \cup [5, \infty)$

Objective [1.5c] Solve applied problems involving conjunctions and disjunctions of inequalities.		
Brief Procedure	Example	Practice Exercise
Use the five-step problem solving process.	The equation $P = 1 + \dfrac{d}{33}$ gives the pressure P, in atmospheres (atm) at a depth of d feet in the sea. For what depths d is the pressure at least 2 atm and at most 6 atm? 1. *Familiarize.* We will use the given formula, $P = 1 + \dfrac{d}{33}$. 2. *Translate.* We want to find the depths for which the pressure is greater than or equal to 2 *and* less than or equal to 6, so we have $$2 \leq 1 + \frac{d}{33} \leq 6.$$ 3. *Solve.* We solve the inequality. $$2 \leq 1 + \frac{d}{33} \leq 6$$ $$66 \leq 33 + d \leq 198$$ $$33 \leq d \leq 165$$ 4. *Check.* A partial check can be done by substituting some values of d in the formula. 5. *State.* The pressure is at least 2 atm and at most 6 atm for depths d, in feet, such that $\{d \mid 33 \leq d \leq 165\}$.	17. The formula $F = 1.8C + 32$ can be used to convert Celsius temperatures C to Fahrenheit temperatures F. For what Celsius temperatures are the corresponding Fahrenheit temperatures between 32° and 212°? A. $0° < C < 100°$ B. $0° < C < 141°$ C. $35° < C < 100°$ D. $35° < C < 141°$

Objective [1.6a] Simplify expressions containing absolute-value symbols.

Brief Procedure	Example	Practice Exercise
Use the properties of absolute value: For any real numbers a and b, a) $\lvert ab \rvert = \lvert a \rvert \cdot \lvert b \rvert$. (The absolute value of a product is the product of the absolute values.) b) $\left\lvert \dfrac{a}{b} \right\rvert = \dfrac{\lvert a \rvert}{\lvert b \rvert}$, provided that $b \neq 0$. (The absolute value of a quotient is the quotient of the absolute values.) c) $\lvert -a \rvert = \lvert a \rvert$. (The absolute value of the opposite of a number is the same as the absolute value of the number.)	Simplify: a) $\lvert -2z \rvert$; b) $\left\lvert \dfrac{5}{x} \right\rvert$. a) $\lvert -2z \rvert = \lvert -2 \rvert \cdot \lvert z \rvert = 2\lvert z \rvert$. b) $\left\lvert \dfrac{5}{x} \right\rvert = \dfrac{\lvert 5 \rvert}{\lvert x \rvert} = \dfrac{5}{\lvert x \rvert}$	18. Simplify: $\lvert -1.8y \rvert$. A. $-1.8y$ B. $-1.8\lvert y \rvert$ C. $1.8y$ D. $1.8\lvert y \rvert$

Objective [1.6b] Find the distance between two points on the number line.

Brief Procedure	Example	Practice Exercise
For any real numbers a and b, the distance between them is $\lvert a - b \rvert$.	Find the distance between -5 and -13 on the number line. $\lvert -5-(-13) \rvert = \lvert -5+13 \rvert = \lvert 8 \rvert = 8$	19. Find the distance between -4 and 7 on the number line. A. 3 B. 4 C. 11 D. 15

Objective [1.6c] Solve equations with absolute-value expressions.

Brief Procedure	Example	Practice Exercise
Use the absolute-value principle. For any positive number p and any algebraic expression X: a) The solutions of $\lvert X \rvert = p$ are those numbers that satisfy $X = -p$ or $X = p$. b) The equation $\lvert X \rvert = 0$ is equivalent to the equation $X = 0$. c) The equation $\lvert X \rvert = -p$ has no solution.	Solve: $\lvert x - 4 \rvert = 3$. $x - 4 = -3 \ or \ x - 4 = 3$ $x = 1 \quad or \quad x = 7$ The solution set is $\{1, 7\}$.	20. Solve: $\lvert 3x - 1 \rvert = 5$. A. $\{2\}$ B. $\left\{ -\dfrac{4}{3}, 2 \right\}$ C. $\left(-\dfrac{4}{3}, 2 \right)$ D. $\{-2, 2\}$

Objective [1.6d] Solve equations with two absolute-value expressions.		
Brief Procedure	Example	Practice Exercise
Consider $|a| = |b|$. This means that a and b are the same distance from 0. Thus, they are the same number or they are opposites, so we have $a = b$ or $a = -b$.	Solve: $|3x - 4| = |x + 8|$. $3x - 4 = x + 8$ or $3x - 4 = -(x+8)$ $2x - 4 = 8$ or $3x - 4 = -x - 8$ $2x = 12$ or $4x - 4 = -8$ $x = 6$ or $4x = -4$ $x = 6$ or $x = -1$ The solution set if $\{-1, 6\}$.	21. Solve: $|2x + 1| = |x + 5|$. A. $\{-2, 4\}$ B. $\left\{2, \dfrac{4}{3}\right\}$ C. $\{-2, 6\}$ D. $\left\{-2, -\dfrac{4}{3}\right\}$

Objective [1.6e] Solve inequalities with absolute-value expressions.		
Brief Procedure	Example	Practice Exercise
For any positive number p and any algebraic expression X: a) The solutions of $|X| < p$ are those numbers that satisfy $-p < X < p$. b) The solutions of $|X| > p$ are those numbers that satisfy $X < -p$ or $X > p$. Similar statements hold for inequalities with $\leq$ or $\geq$.	Solve: a) $|5x + 3| < 2$; b) $|x + 3| \geq 1$. a) $\quad |5x + 3| < 2$ $-2 < 5x + 3 < 2$ $-5 < 5x < -1$ $-1 < x < -\dfrac{1}{5}$ The solution set is $\left\{x \middle| -1 < x < -\dfrac{1}{5}\right\}$, or $\left(-1, -\dfrac{1}{5}\right)$. b) $\quad x + 3 \leq -1$ or $x + 3 \geq 1$ $x \leq -4$ or $x \geq -2$ The solution set is $\{x | x \leq -4 \text{ or } x \geq -2\}$, or $(-\infty, -4] \cup [-2, \infty)$.	22. Solve: $|3x + 2| > 8$. A. $(-\infty, -2) \cup (2, \infty)$ B. $\left(-\infty, -\dfrac{10}{3}\right) \cup \left(-\dfrac{10}{3}, \infty\right)$ C. $\left(-\infty, -\dfrac{10}{3}\right) \cup (2, \infty)$ D. $\left(-\dfrac{10}{3}, 2\right)$

Chapter 2 Review

Objective [2.1a] Plot points associated with ordered pairs of numbers.

Brief Procedure	Example	Practice Exercise
Given a point (a, b), start at the origin and move a units right or left depending on whether a is positive or negative. Then move b units up or down depending on whether b is positive or negative. Make a dot and label the point.	Plot the point $(3, -2)$. The first coordinate is positive so, starting at the origin, move 3 units to the right. The second coordinate is negative, so we then move down 2 units.	1. Which point is $(-1, 4)$? A. A B. B C. C D. D

Objective [2.1b] Determine whether an ordered pair of numbers is a solution of an equation.

Brief Procedure	Example	Practice Exercise
Substitute coordinates of the ordered pair for the variables, using the first number to replace the variable that occurs first alphabetically. If a true equation results, the pair is a solution.	Determine whether $(-2, 2)$ is a solution of $2b - a = 6$. We substitute -2 for a and 2 for b. $$\begin{array}{c\|c} 2b - a = 6 \\ \hline 2 \cdot 2 - (-2) \ ? \ 6 \\ 4 + 2 \\ 6 & \text{TRUE} \end{array}$$ Since $6 = 6$ is true, $(-2, 2)$ is a solution of the equation.	2. Determine whether $(-4, 1)$ is a solution of $n - m = -5$. A. Yes B. No

Objective [2.1c] Graph linear equations using tables.

Brief Procedure	Example	Practice Exercise
1. Select a value for one variable and calculate the corresponding value of the other variable. Form an ordered pair using alphabetical order as indicated by the variables. 2. Repeat step (1) to obtain at least two other ordered pairs. Two points are essential. A third point serves as a check. 3. Plot the ordered pairs and draw a straight line passing through the points.	Graph $2x + 3y = 6$. Calculating ordered pairs is usually easiest when y is isolated on one side of the equation, so we solve for y first. $$2x + 3y = 6$$ $$3y = -2x + 6$$ $$\frac{1}{3} \cdot 3y = \frac{1}{3}\left(-2x + 6\right)$$ $$y = -\frac{2}{3}x + 2$$ We now find 3 pairs of solutions, using multiples of 3 to avoid fractions. | x	y
---	---
0	2
-3	4
3	0 | We plot the points, draw the line, and label the graph. 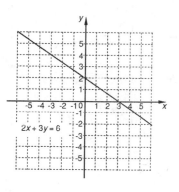	3. Graph $x - 2y = 4$. A. 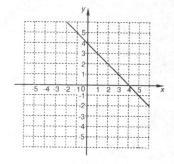 B. 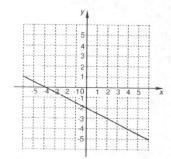 C. 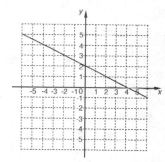 D. 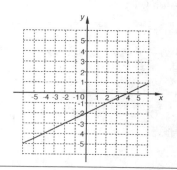

Objective [2.1d] Graph nonlinear equations using tables.

Brief Procedure	Example	Practice Exercise
Select numbers for x and find the corresponding y-values. Plot these points. Find enough points so that the shape of the graph is clear. Then draw the graph.	Graph $y = x^2 - 2x - 3$. Choose some values for x, find the corresponding y-values, plot points, and draw the graph. For $x = 1, y = 1^2 - 2 \cdot 1 - 3 = -4$. For $x = -1, y = (-1)^2 - 2(-1) - 3 = 0$. For $x = 0, y = 0^2 - 2 \cdot 0 - 3 = -3$. For $x = 2, y = 2^2 - 2 \cdot 2 - 3 = -3$. For $x = 3, y = 3^2 - 2 \cdot 3 - 3 = 0$.	4. Graph: $y = x^2 + 2x + 1$.

$$\begin{array}{c|c} x & y \\ \hline 1 & -4 \\ -1 & 0 \\ 0 & -3 \\ 2 & -3 \\ 3 & 0 \end{array}$$

A.

B.

C.

D.

$y = x^2 - 2x - 3$

Objective [2.2a] Determine whether a correspondence is a function.

Brief Procedure	Example	Practice Exercise

A function is a correspondence between a first set, called the domain, and a second set, called the range, such that each member of the domain corresponds to exactly one member of the range.	Determine whether each correspondence is a function.
	
	a)
	Domain Range
	f: $1 \longrightarrow 3$
	    $2 \longrightarrow -5$
	    $3 \longrightarrow 8$
	    $4 \longrightarrow -4$
	
	b)
	Domain Range
	g: $A \longrightarrow m$
	    $B \longrightarrow s$
	    $C \Big\langle {t \atop w}$
	
	a) f is a function because each member of the domain corresponds to exactly one member of the range.
	b) g is not a function because one member of the domain, C, corresponds to more than one member of the range.
		5. Determine whether the correspondence is a function.
		
		Domain Range
		h: $1, 2 \longrightarrow 7$
		    $3 \longrightarrow 5$
		    $4 \longrightarrow 1$
		
		A. Yes
		
		B. No

Objective [2.2b] Given a function described by an equation, find function values (outputs) for specified values (inputs).

Brief Procedure	Example	Practice Exercise
Evaluate the function for the value of the given input.	Find $f(-1)$ for $f(x) = 2x^2 - 1$. $f(-1) = 2(-1)^2 - 1 = 2 - 1 = 1.$	6. Find $g(2)$ for $g(x) = 3x - 5$. A. -11 B. -2 C. 1 D. 8

Objective [2.2c] Draw the graph of a function.

Brief Procedure	Example	Practice Exercise
Find some function values, plot points, and draw the graph.	Graph: $g(x) = 1 - x^2$. We find some function values, plot points, and draw the graph. $\begin{array}{c\|c} x & g(x) \\ \hline -2 & -3 \\ -1 & 0 \\ 0 & 1 \\ 1 & 0 \\ 2 & -3 \end{array}$ 	7. Graph: $f(x) = x - 1$. A. B. C. D.

	Objective [2.2d] Determine whether a graph is that of a function using the vertical-line test.	
Brief Procedure	Example	Practice Exercise

A graph represents a function if it is impossible to draw a vertical line that intersects the graph more than once. This is the vertical-line test.

Determine whether each is the graph of a function.

a)

b)

a) The graph is that of a function because no vertical line can cross the graph at more than one point. This can be confirmed with a straight edge.

b) The graph is not that of a function because a vertical line can be drawn that crosses the graph more than once.

8. Determine whether the graph is the graph of a function.

A. Yes

B. No

Objective [2.2e] Solve applied problems involving functions and their graphs.

Brief Procedure	Example	Practice Exercise
Read data from the graph.	The graph below shows the number of Americans over age 65 as a function of the year. (The data is projected for 2002-2030.)	9. Use the graph at the left to determine the year in which there will be about 52 million Americans over 65.

The graph below shows the number of Americans over age 65 as a function of the year. (The data is projected for 2002-2030.)

Americans over 65, in millions

Year

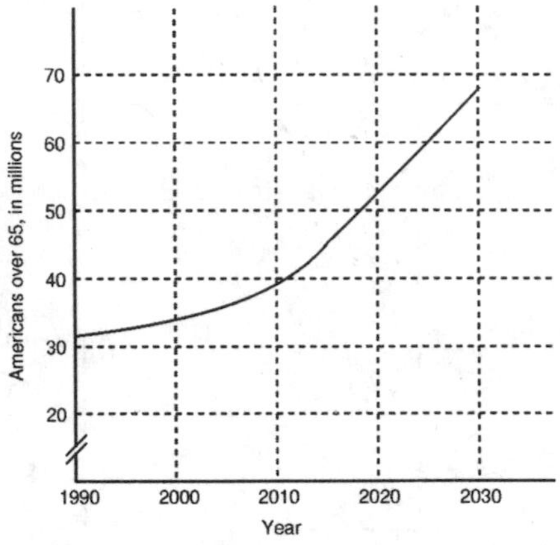

Use the graph to approximate the number of Americans over age 65 in 2000.

Locate 2000 on the horizontal axis, move directly up to the graph, and then across to the vertical axis. We see that the output that corresponds to the input 2000 is about 34, so there will be about 34 million Americans over age 65 in 2000.

9. Use the graph at the left to determine the year in which there will be about 52 million Americans over 65.

A. 2000

B. 2010

C. 2020

D. 2030

Objective [2.3a] Find the domain and the range of a function.

Brief Procedure	Example	Practice Exercise
If the graph of a function is given, the domain is the set of all x-values , or inputs, of points on the graph, and the range is the set of all y-values, or outputs, of the points on the graph. To find the domain of a function given by an equation, find the largest set of real numbers, or inputs, for which function values can be calculated.	a) Find the domain and the range of the function whose graph is shown below. 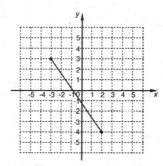 b) Find the domain of $y(x) = \dfrac{3}{x-4}$. a) The x values of the points on the graph extend from -3 to 2, so the domain is $\{x|-3 \le x \le 2\}$, or $[-3, 2]$. The y-values of the points on the graph extend from -4 to 3, so the range is $\{y|-4 \le y \le 3\}$, or $[-4, 3]$. b) Since $\dfrac{3}{x-4}$ cannot be calculated when the denominator, $x - 4$, is 0, we set the denominator equal to 0 and find the number(s) that must be excluded from the domain. $$x - 4 = 0$$ $$x = 4$$ Thus, 4 is not in the domain but all other real numbers are. The domain is $\{x|x$ is a real number and $x \ne 4\}$, or $(-\infty, 4) \cup (4, \infty)$.	10. Find the domain of $g(x) = \dfrac{x-2}{x+3}$. A. $\{x|x$ is a real number and $x \ne 2\}$ B. $\{x|x$ is a real number and $x \ne 3\}$ C. $\{x|x$ is a real number and $x \ne -3\}$ D. $\{x|x$ is a real number and $x \ne -3$ and $x \ne 2\}$

Objective [2.4a] Find the y-intercept of a line from the equation $y = mx + b$ or $f(x) = mx + b$.

Brief Procedure	Example	Practice Exercise
The y-intercept of the graph of $y = mx+b$ or $f(x) = mx+b$ is the point $(0, b)$, or simply b.	Find the y-intercept of $f(x) = -2x + 7$. The function is in the form $f(x) = mx + b$, so the y-intercept is $(0, 7)$, or simply 7.	11. Find the y-intercept of $y = 3x - 5$. A. $(0, -5)$ B. $(0, 5)$ C. $(0, 3)$ D. $\left(0, \dfrac{5}{3}\right)$

Objective [2.4b] Given two points on a line, find the slope; given a linear equation, derive the equivalent slope-intercept equation and determine the slope and the y-intercept.

Brief Procedure	Example	Practice Exercises
The slope of a line containing points (x_1, y_1) and (x_2, y_2) is given by $$m = \frac{\text{rise}}{\text{run}}$$ $$= \frac{\text{the change in } y}{\text{the change in } x}$$ $$= \frac{y_2 - y_1}{x_2 - x_1}.$$	Find the slope, if it exists, of the line containing the points $(-1, 5)$ and $(2, -3)$. Consider (x_1, y_1) to be $(-1, 5)$ and (x_2, y_2) to be $(2, -3)$. $$\text{Slope} = \frac{\text{the change in } y}{\text{the change in } x}$$ $$= \frac{y_2 - y_1}{x_2 - x_1}$$ $$= \frac{-3 - 5}{2 - (-1)}$$ $$= \frac{-8}{3}, \text{ or } -\frac{8}{3}$$ Note that we would have gotten the same result if we had considered (x_1, y_1) to be $(2, -3)$ and (x_2, y_2) to be $(-1, 5)$. We can subtract in either order as long as the x-coordinates are subtracted in the same order in which the y-coordinates are subtracted.	12. Find the slope, if it exists, of the line containing the points $(6, -2)$ and $(8, -1)$. A. -2 B. $-\dfrac{1}{2}$ C. $\dfrac{1}{2}$ D. 2
Given a linear equation, derive the equivalent slope-intercept equation $y = mx + b$ by solving for y. The coefficient of the x-term, m, is the slope of the line. The y-intercept is the point $(0, b)$.	Find the slope and y-intercept of $3x + 4y = 8$. We solve for y to get the equation in the form $y = mx + b$. $$3x + 4y = 8$$ $$4y = -3x + 8$$ $$y = \frac{-3x + 8}{4}$$ $$y = -\frac{3}{4}x + 2$$ The slope is $-\dfrac{3}{4}$, and the y-intercept is $(0, 2)$.	13. Find the slope and y-intercept of $2x - 3y = 12$. A. Slope: $\dfrac{3}{2}$; y-intercept: $(0, 6)$ B. Slope: $\dfrac{2}{3}$; y-intercept: $(0, -4)$ C. Slope: $-\dfrac{2}{3}$; y-intercept: $(0, 4)$ D. Slope: -4; y-intercept: $\left(0, \dfrac{2}{3}\right)$

Objective [2.4c] Solve applied problems involving slope.

Brief Procedure	Example	Practice Exercise
Determine the rise and run, or the change in y and the change in x, and compute the slope, or rate of change.	A road rises 40 m over a horizontal distance of 1250 m. Find the grade of the road. $$\text{Slope} = \frac{\text{rise}}{\text{run}}$$ $$= \frac{40}{1250}$$ $$= 0.032 = 3.2\%$$	14. A set of stairs rises 12 ft over a horizontal distance of 150 ft. Find the grade of the stairs. A. 8% B. 12% C. 12.5% D. 15%

Objective [2.5a] Graph linear equations using intercepts.

Brief Procedure	Example	Practice Exercise
The y-intercept has the form $(0, b)$. To find b, let $x = 0$ and solve for y. The x-intercept has the form $(a, 0)$. To find a, let $y = 0$ and solve for x. To graph using intercepts, find and plot the intercepts and draw the line containing them. As a check that the graph is correct, find a third solution of the equation. If it is on the graph, then the graph is probably correct.	Find the intercepts of $5x - 3y = 15$ and then graph the line. To find the y-intercept, let $x = 0$. Then solve for y. $$5x - 3y = 15$$ $$5 \cdot 0 - 3y = 15$$ $$-3y = 15$$ $$y = -5$$ Thus, $(0, -5)$ is the y-intercept. To find the x-intercept, let $y = 0$. Then solve for x. $$5x - 3y = 15$$ $$5x - 3 \cdot 0 = 15$$ $$5x = 15$$ $$x = 3$$ Thus, $(3, 0)$ is the x-intercept. Plot these points and draw the line. 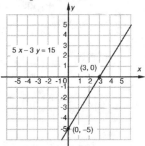 A third point should be used as a check. We substitute any value for x and solve for y. We let $x = 6$. Then $$5x - 3y = 15$$ $$5 \cdot 6 - 3y = 15$$ $$30 - 3y = 15$$ $$-3y = -15$$ $$y = 5$$ The point $(6, 5)$ is on the graph, so the graph is probably correct.	15. Find the intercepts of $2x - y = 4$. Then use the intercepts to graph the equation. A. 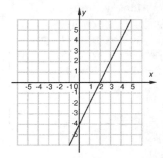 B. 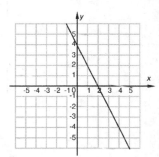 C. 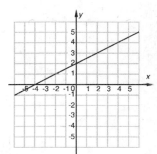 D. 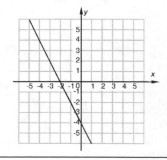

Objective [2.5b] Given a linear equation in slope-intercept form, use the slope and the y-intercept to graph the line.

Brief Procedure	Example	Practice Exercise
First plot the y-intercept. Then move up or down and left or right according to the slope to find another point. Move again from this point or from the y-intercept to find a third point. Then draw the line.	Graph $y = -\dfrac{1}{2}x + 1$ using the slope and y-intercept. First we plot the y-intercept $(0, 1)$. Then we think of the slope as $\dfrac{-1}{2}$. Starting at $(0, 1)$, we find another point by moving 1 unit down (since the numerator is negative and corresponds to the change in y) and 2 units to the right (since the denominator is positive and corresponds to the change in x). We get to the point $(2, 0)$. Now, from $(2, 0)$, move 1 unit down and 2 units to the right again, arriving at the point $(4, -1)$. (Alternatively, we could have returned to the y-intercept, considered the slope as $\dfrac{1}{-2}$, and moved 1 unit up and 2 units to the left to find a third point.) We draw the line through the three points we found. 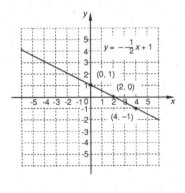	16. Graph $y = \dfrac{2}{3}x - 3$ using the slope and y-intercept. A. 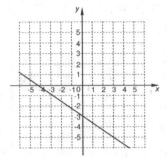 B. 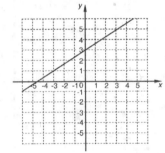 C. 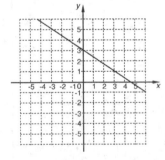 D. 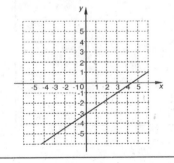

Objective [2.5c] Graph linear equations of the form $x = a$ or $y = b$.		
Brief Procedure	Example	Practice Exercises
The graph of $x = a$ is a vertical line.	Graph $x = 2$. We can think of this equation as $x + 0 \cdot y = 2$. No matter what number we choose for y, x must be 2. We make a table of values and plot and connect the corresponding points. $\begin{array}{c\|c} x & y \\ \hline 2 & -4 \\ 2 & 0 \\ 2 & 3 \end{array}$	17. Graph $x = -3$. A. B. C. D.

Objective [2.5c] (continued)

Brief Procedure	Example	Practice Exercises
The graph of $y = b$ is a horizontal line.	Graph $y = -4$. We can think of this equation as $0 \cdot x + y = -4$. No matter what number we choose for x, y must be -4. We make a table of values and plot and connect the corresponding points. $\begin{array}{c\|c} x & y \\ \hline -2 & -4 \\ 0 & -4 \\ 3 & -4 \end{array}$ 	18. Graph $y = 1$. A. B. C. D.

Objective [2.5d] Given the equations of two lines, determine whether their graphs are parallel or whether they are perpendicular.

Brief Procedure	Example	Practice Exercises
Parallel nonvertical lines have the same slope and different y-intercepts. Parallel vertical lines have equations $x = p$ and $x = q$, where $p \neq q$.	Determine whether the graphs of the lines $y = -2x + 1$ and $4x + 2y = 5$ are parallel. The first equation is in slope-intercept form $(y = mx + b)$, so we see that it has slope -2 and y-intercept $(0,1)$. We solve the second equation for y. $$4x + 2y = 5$$ $$2y = -4x + 5$$ $$y = \frac{1}{2}(-4x + 5)$$ $$y = -2x + \frac{5}{2}$$ Thus, the slope of the second line is -2 and its y-intercept is $\left(0, \frac{5}{2}\right)$. Since the two lines have the same slope, -2, and different y-intercepts, $(0,1)$ and $\left(0, \frac{5}{2}\right)$, they are parallel.	19. Determine whether the graphs of the lines $x + y = 3$ and $x - y = 3$ are parallel. A. Yes B. No
Two nonvertical lines are perpendicular if the product of their slopes is -1. If one line in a pair of perpendicular lines is vertical, then the other is horizontal. That is, two lines with equations $x = a$ and $y = b$ are perpendicular.	Determine whether the graphs of the lines $2x + y = 4$ and $x + 2y = 3$ are perpendicular. We first solve each equation for y in order to determine the slopes. a) $2x + y = 4$ $\quad\quad y = -2x + 4$ b) $x + 2y = 3$ $\quad\quad 2y = -x + 3$ $\quad\quad y = \frac{1}{2}(-x + 3)$ $\quad\quad y = -\frac{1}{2}x + \frac{3}{2}$ The slopes are -2 and $-\frac{1}{2}$. The product of the slopes is $-2\left(-\frac{1}{2}\right) = 1$. Since the product of the slopes is not -1, the lines are not perpendicular.	20. Determine whether the graphs of the lines $3x - 2y = 4$ and $4x + 6y = 3$ are perpendicular. A. Yes B. No

Objective [2.6a] Find an equation of a line when the slope and the y-intercept are given.

Brief Procedure	Example	Practice Exercise
When the slope m and the y-intercept $(0, b)$ of a line are given, find an equation of the line by substituting in the equation $y = mx + b$.	A line has slope -3 and y-intercept $(0,2)$. Find an equation of the line. We substitute -3 for m and 2 for b in the slope-intercept equation. $$y = mx + b$$ $$y = -3x + 2$$	21. A line has slope 4 and y-intercept $(0, -1)$. Find an equation of the line. A. $y = -x + 4$ B. $y = -x - 4$ C. $y = 4x - 1$ D. $y = 4x + 1$

Objective [2.6b] Find an equation of a line when the slope and a point are given.

Brief Procedure	Example	Practice Exercise
To use the point-slope equation $y - y_1 = m(x - x_1)$, substitute the x-and y-coordinates of the given point for x_1 and y_1, respectively, substitute the slope for m, and simplify. To use the slope-intercept equation, $y = mx + b$, substitute the given slope for m and the coordinates of the given point for x and y to find b. Then use the equation $y = mx + b$ again, substituting the given slope for m and the value found for b.	Find an equation of the line with slope -2 that contains the point $(3, -1)$. Using the point-slope equation: Substitute 3 for x_1, -1 for y_1, and -2 for m and simplify. $$y - y_1 = m(x - x_1)$$ $$y - (-1) = -2(x - 3)$$ $$y + 1 = -2x + 6$$ $$y = -2x + 5$$ Using the slope-intercept equation: We know that the slope is -2, so the equation is $y = -2x + b$. Using the point $(3, -1)$, we substitute 3 for x and -1 for y in $y = -2x + b$. $$y = -2x + b$$ $$-1 = -2 \cdot 3 + b$$ $$-1 = -6 + b$$ $$5 = b$$ Then the equation is $y = -2x + 5$.	22. Find an equation of the line with slope 4 that contains the point $(-2, -5)$. A. $y = 4x - 5$ B. $y = 4x + 18$ C. $y = 4x - 2$ D. $y = 4x + 3$

Objective [2.6c] Find an equation of a line when two points are given.

Brief Procedure	Example	Practice Exercise
Use the two given points to find the slope of the line. Then use the point-slope equation or the slope-intercept equation as described in Objective [2.6b].	Find an equation of the line containing the points $(4, 3)$ and $(-2, 5)$. First, we find the slope. $$m = \frac{3-5}{4-(-2)} = \frac{-2}{6} = -\frac{1}{3}$$ Using the point-slope equation: We can use either of the given points for (x_1, y_1). We use $(-2, 5)$ and substitute -2 for x_1, 5 for y_1, and $-\frac{1}{3}$ for m. $$y - y_1 = m(x - x_1)$$ $$y - 5 = -\frac{1}{3}(x - (-2))$$ $$y - 5 = -\frac{1}{3}(x + 2)$$ $$y - 5 = -\frac{1}{3}x - \frac{2}{3}$$ $$y = -\frac{1}{3}x + \frac{13}{3}$$ Using the slope-intercept equation: Since $m = -\frac{1}{3}$, we have $y = -\frac{1}{3}x + b$. Now use either of the given points to find b. We use $(4, 3)$ and substitute 4 for x and 3 for y. $$y = -\frac{1}{3}x + b$$ $$3 = -\frac{1}{3} \cdot 4 + b$$ $$3 = -\frac{4}{3} + b$$ $$\frac{13}{3} = b$$ The equation of the line is $$y = -\frac{1}{3}x + \frac{13}{3}.$$	23. Find an equation of the line containing $(-3, -2)$ and $(3, 4)$. A. $y = x + 1$ B. $y = x - 7$ C. $y = -x + 1$ D. $y = -x - 7$

Objective [2.6d] Given a line and a point not on the given line, find an equation of the line parallel to the line and containing the point, and find an equation of the line perpendicular to the line and containing the point.

Brief Procedure	Example	Practice Exercises
A given line and a line parallel to it have the same slope. Once the slope is determined, use the point-slope equation or the slope-intercept equation as described in Objective [2.6b].	Find an equation of the line containing the point $(-2, 4)$ and parallel to the line $3x + y = 4$. To find the slope of the given line, we first find the slope-intercept equation by solving for y. $$3x + y = 4$$ $$y = -3x + 4$$ Thus, the new line through $(-2, 4)$ must have slope -3. We will use the slope-intercept equation, substituting -3 for m, -2 for x, and 4 for y in $y = mx + b$ and solve for b. $$y = mx + b$$ $$4 = -3(-2) + b$$ $$4 = 6 + b$$ $$-2 = b$$ Finally, we substitute -3 for m and -2 for b in $y = mx + b$ to find the desired equation: $$y = -3x - 2.$$	24. Find an equation of the line containing the point $(1, -3)$ and parallel to the line $4x - 2y = 5$. A. $y = 2x - 5$ B. $y = -2x - 1$ C. $y = 4x - 7$ D. $y = x - 4$
Given a line, the slope of a line perpendicular to it is the opposite of the reciprocal of the slope of the given line. Find the slope of the new line and then use the point-slope equation or the slope-intercept equation as described in Objective [2.6b].	Find an equation of the line containing $(2, -3)$ and perpendicular to the line $x - 2y = 6$. First we find the slope of the given line by solving for y to obtain the slope-intercept equation. $$x - 2y = 6$$ $$-2y = -x + 6$$ $$y = \frac{1}{2}x - 3$$ The slope of the new line through $(2, -3)$ is the opposite of the reciprocal of $\frac{1}{2}$, or -2. We will use the point-slope equation, substituting -2 for m, 2 for x_1, and -3 for y_1 in $y - y_1 = m(x - x_1)$. $$y - y_1 = m(x - x_1)$$ $$y - (-3) = -2(x - 2)$$ $$y + 3 = -2x + 4$$ $$y = -2x + 1$$ The desired equation is $y = -2x + 1$.	25. Find an equation of the line containing the point $(-4, 1)$ and perpendicular to the line $3x + 6y = 5$. A. $y = -\frac{1}{2}x - 1$ B. $y = -2x + 1$ C. $y = 2x + 9$ D. $y = \frac{1}{2}x + 3$

Objective [2.6e] Solve applied problems involving linear functions.		
Brief Procedure	Example	Practice Exercise

Write a linear function that models the situation and use the model to find the desired function values.	Riggins County Cable charges a $40 installation fee and $25 per month for basic service.
	a) Formulate a linear function $C(t)$ for the cost of t months of cable service.
	b) Use the model to determine the cost for 9 months of service.
	
	a) For t months of service the cost is $40 for installation plus $25 per month times the number of months. Thus, we have
	  $C(t) = 40 + 25t$, where $t \geq 0$.
	b) To find the cost for 9 months of service, we find $C(9)$.
	  $C(9) = 40 + 25 \cdot 9 = 265$
	The cost for 9 months of service is $265.
		26. Dorsey plumbing charges $45 for a service call plus $40 per hour. Formulate a linear function $C(t)$ for the cost of t hours of service and use the function to find the cost of a $1\frac{1}{2}$ hour service call.
		A. $85
		B. $105
		C. $135
		D. $145

Chapter 3 Review

Objective [3.1a] Solve a system of two linear equations or two functions by graphing and determine whether a system is consistent or inconsistent and whether the equations in a system are dependent or independent.

Brief Procedure	Example	Practice Exercise
Graph both equations and find the coordinates of the point(s) of intersection, if any exist. If the graphs are parallel lines, there is no point of intersection and, hence, no solution. If the equations have the same graph, there are infinitely many points of intersection and, thus, infinitely many solutions. Otherwise, there is exactly one point of intersection and, hence, exactly one solution. A system of equations that has a solution is consistent. A system that has no solution is inconsistent. A system of two equations that has infinitely many solutions is dependent. A system that has one solution or no solutions is independent.	Solve the system of equations graphically. Then classify the system as consistent or inconsistent and as dependent or independent. $$x - y = 4,$$ $$y = 2x - 5$$ We graph the equations. The point of intersection appears to be $(1, -3)$. This checks in both equations, so it is the solution. The system has one solution, so it is consistent and independent.	1. Solve the system of equations graphically. Then classify the system as consistent or inconsistent and as dependent or independent. $$3x - 2y = 6,$$ $$x - y = 1$$ A. $(4, 3)$; consistent; independent B. $(2, 0)$; consistent; independent C. No solution; inconsistent; independent D. Infinitely many solutions; consistent; dependent

Objective [3.2a] Solve systems of equations in two variables by the substitution method.

Brief Procedure	Example	Practice Exercise
If one equation has a variable alone on one side, substitute for that variable in the other equation, obtaining an equation in one variable. Solve that equation; then substitute in either original equation to find the other variable. If neither equation has a variable alone on one side, solve one equation for one of the variables. Then proceed as described above.	Solve the system $x - 2y = 1,$ (1) $2x - 3y = 3.$ (2) We solve Equation (1) for x, since the coefficient of x is 1 in that equation. $x - 2y = 1$ $x = 2y + 1$ (3) Now substitute for x in Equation (2) and solve for y. $2x - 3y = 3$ $2(2y + 1) - 3y = 3$ $4y + 2 - 3y = 3$ $y + 2 = 3$ $y = 1$ Now substitute 1 for y in Equation (1), (2), or (3) and find x. We choose Equation (3) since it is already solved for x. $x = 2y + 1 = 2 \cdot 1 + 1 = 2 + 1 = 3$ The ordered pair $(3, 1)$ checks in both equations, so it is the solution of the system of equations.	2. Solve the system $x + y = 3,$ $5x + 2y = 3.$ A. The x-value is -1. B. The x-value is 4. C. The x-value is -3. D. The x-value is 1.

Objective [3.2b] Solve applied problems by solving systems of two equations using substitution.

Brief Procedure	Example	Practice Exercise
Use the five-step problem-solving process, translating to a system of two equations.	Two supplementary angle are such that one angle is 20° more than three times the other. Find the measures of the angles. 1. *Familiarize.* Recall that the sum of the measures of supplementary angles is 180°. Let x and y represent the measures of the angles. 2. *Translate.* The sum of the measures is 180°. $x + y = 180$ (continued)	3. The perimeter of a rectangular carpet is 104 ft. The length is 8 ft more than the width. Find the length and width. One of the dimensions is A. 22 ft B. 24 ft C. 28 ft D. 32 ft

Objective [3.2b] (continued)		
Brief Procedure	Example	Practice Exercise
	One angle is 20° more than three times the other. $y = 20 + 3 \cdot x$ We have a system of equations: $x + y = 180,$ (1) $y = 20 + 3x.$ (2) 3. *Solve.* We substitute $20 + 3x$ for y in equation(1). $x + (20 + 3x) = 180$ $4x + 20 = 180$ $4x = 160$ $x = 40$ Now substitute 40 for x in one of the equations and find y. We will use equation (2). $y = 20 + 3 \cdot 40 = 20 + 120 = 140$ 4. *Check.* The sum of the measures is $40° + 140°$, or $180°$. Also, $140°$ is $20°$ more than 3 times $120°$. The answer checks. 5. *State.* The measures of the angles are $40°$ and $140°$.	

Objective [3.3a] Solve systems of equations in two variables by the elimination method.

Brief Procedure	Example	Practice Exercise
If the equations have a pair of terms that are opposites, add the corresponding sides of the equations to eliminate a variable. Solve for that variable. Then substitute in either of the original equations to find the other variable. If there is not a pair of terms that are opposites, multiply one or both equations by appropriate constants to find equivalent equations with a pair of terms that are opposites. Then proceed as described above.	Solve the system $2a - 3b = 7,$ (1) $3a - 2b = 8.$ (2) We could eliminate either a or b. Here we decide to eliminate the a-terms. Multiply Equation (1) by 3 and Equation (2) by -2. Then add and solve for b. $\begin{array}{r} 6a - 9b = 21 \\ -6a + 4b = -16 \\ \hline -5b = 5 \\ b = -1 \end{array}$ (continued)	4. Solve the system $3x + 2y = 5,$ $x - y = 5.$ A. The y-value is -4. B. The y-value is -2. C. The y-value is 2. D. The y-value is 3.

Objective [3.3a] (continued)

Brief Procedure	Example	Practice Exercise
	Next substitute -1 for b in either of the original equations.$$2a - 3b = 7 \quad (1)$$ $$2a - 3(-1) = 7$$ $$2a + 3 = 7$$ $$2a = 4$$ $$a = 2$$ The ordered pair $(2, -1)$ checks in both equations, so it is a solution of the system of equations.	

Objective [3.3b] Solve applied problems by solving systems of two equations using elimination.

Brief Procedure	Example	Practice Exercise
Use the five-step problem solving process, translating to a system of two equations.	Two angles are supplementary. (Supplementary angles are angles whose sum is 180°.) The difference between twice one angle and the other angle is 30°. Find the angles. 1. *Familiarize.* We let x and y represent the angles. 2. *Translate.* We know that the sum of the angles is 180°. This gives us one equation. The sum of the angles is 180°.$$x + y = 180$$ We use the additional information given to translate to a second equation. Twice one angle less the other is 30°.$$2x - y = 30$$ We now have a system of equations:$$x + y = 180$$ $$2x - y = 30.$$ (continued)	5. The sum of two numbers is -3. The sum of twice one number and the other is 4. Find the numbers. A. One number is -10. B. One number is -7. C. One number is -4. D. One number is 4.

Objective [3.3b] (continued)

Brief Procedure	Example	Practice Exercise
	3. *Solve.* We will use the elimination method. First we add the equations to eliminate the y-terms. $x + y = 180$ $\underline{2x - y = 30}$ $3x \quad\;\; = 210$ $\quad\; x = 70$ Now we substitute in one of the original equations to find y. We use the first equation. $x + y = 180$ $70 + y = 180$ $\quad\;\;\; y = 110$ 4. *Check.* The sum of 70° and 110° is 180°. Also, $2 \cdot 70° - 110° = 140° - 110° = 30°$, so the answer checks. 5. *State.* The angles are 70° and 110°.	

Objective [3.4a] Solve applied problems involving total value and mixture using systems of two equations.

Brief Procedure	Example
Use the five-step problem solving process.	Solution A is 40% acid and solution B is 55% acid. How much of each should be used in order to make 100 L of a solution that is 46% acid?

1. *Familiarize.* Let x and y represent the number of liters of 40% and 55% solution to be used, respectively. We organize the given information in a table.

Type of solution	A	B	Mixture
Amount of solution	x	y	100 L
Percent of acid	40%	55%	46%
Amount of acid in solution	40%x	55%y	46% × 100, or 46 L

2. *Translate.* The first row of the table gives us one equation.

$$x + y = 100$$

The last row gives us a second equation.

$$40\%x + 55\%y = 46, \text{ or}$$
$$0.4x + 0.55y = 46$$

After multiplying by 100 on both sides of the second equation to clear decimals, we have the following system of equations.

$$x + \ y \ = 100, \quad (1)$$
$$40x + 55y = 4600 \quad (2)$$

3. *Solve.* We use the elimination method. First multiply Equation (1) by -40 and then add to eliminate the x-terms.

$$-40x - 40y = -4000$$
$$\underline{40x + 55y = 4600}$$
$$15y = 600$$
$$y = 40$$

Now substitute in Equation (1) and solve for x.

$$x + y = 100$$
$$x + 40 = 100$$
$$x = 60$$

4. *Check.* The sum of 60 and 40 is 100. Also, 40% of 60 L is 24 L and 55% of 40 L is 22 L. These add up to 46 L, so the answer checks.

5. *State.* 60 L of solution A and 40 L of solution B should be used.

Practice Exercise

6. There were 220 tickets sold for a school play. The price for students was $3 and it was $7 for non-students. A total of $1080 was collected. How many of each type of ticket were sold?

A. Student: 75, non-student: 145
B. Student: 90, non-student: 130
C. Student: 95, non-student: 125
D. Student: 115, non-student: 105

Objective [3.4b] Solve applied problems involving motion using systems of two equations.

Brief Procedure	Example
Use the five-step problem solving process. It is often convenient to translate to a system of equations.	A canoeist paddled for 1 hr with a 3 mph current. The return trip against the current took 2 hr. Find the speed of the canoe in still water.

1. *Familiarize.* We first make a drawing. Let $d =$ the distance traveled in one direction and let $r =$ the speed of the canoe in still water. When the canoe travels with the current, its speed is $r + 3$ and traveling against the current the speed is $r - 3$.

With the current $\qquad\qquad r + 3$
1 hours $\qquad\qquad d$ miles

Against the current $\qquad\qquad r - 3$
2 hours $\qquad\qquad d$ miles

We can also organize the given information in a table.

$$d \;=\; r \;\cdot\; t$$

	Distance	Speed	Time
With current	d	$r + 3$	1
Against current	d	$r - 3$	2

2. *Translate.* Using $d = rt$, we get an equation from each row of the table.
$$d = (r + 3)1, \qquad (1)$$
$$d = (r - 3)2 \qquad (2)$$

3. *Solve.* We use the substitution method, substituting $(r - 3)2$ for d in Equation (1).
$$(r - 3)2 = (r + 3)1$$
$$2r - 6 = r + 3$$
$$r - 6 = 3$$
$$r = 9$$

4. *Check.* When $r = 9$, then $r + 3 = 12$ and $12 \cdot 1 = 12$, the distance traveled with the current. When $r = 9$, then $r - 3 = 6$ and $6 \cdot 2 = 12$, the distance traveled against the current. Since the distances are the same, the answer checks.

5. *State.* The speed of the canoe in still water is 9 mph.

Practice Exercise

7. A train leaves a station and travels west at 80 mph. One hour later a second train leaves the same station and travels west on a parallel track at 100 mph. When will it overtake the first train?
A. 4 hr after the first train leaves
B. 5 hr after the first train leaves
C. 6 hr after the first train leaves
D. 8 hr after the first train leaves

Objective [3.5a] Solve systems of three equations in three variables.		
Brief Procedure	Example	Practice Exercise

Brief Procedure

1. Write all equations in the standard form $Ax + By + Cz = D$.
2. Clear any decimals or fractions.
3. Choose a variable to eliminate. Then use *any* two of the three equations to get an equation in two variables.
4. Next, use a different pair of equations and get another equation in *the same two variables*. That is, eliminate the same variable that you did in step (3).
5. Solve the resulting system (pair) of equations. That will give two of the numbers.
6. Then use any of the original three equations to find the third number.

Example

Solve:

$$x - y - z = -2, \quad (1)$$
$$2x + 3y + z = 3, \quad (2)$$
$$5x - 2y - 2z = -1 \quad (3)$$

The equations are in standard form and do not contain decimals or fractions. We will choose to eliminate z since the z-terms in equations (1) and (2) are opposites. First we add these two equations.

$$x - y - z = -2$$
$$\underline{2x + 3y + z = 3}$$
$$3x + 2y \quad = 1 \quad (4)$$

Next we multiply equation (2) by 2 and add it to equation (3) to eliminate z from another pair of equations.

$$4x + 6y + 2z = 6$$
$$\underline{5x - 2y - 2z = -1}$$
$$9x + 4y \quad = 5 \quad (5)$$

Now we solve the system consisting of equations (4) and (5). We multiply equation (4) by -2 and add.

$$-6x - 4y = -2$$
$$\underline{9x + 4y = 5}$$
$$3x \quad = 3$$
$$x = 1$$

Now use either equation (4) or (5) to find y.

$$3x + 2y = 1 \quad (4)$$
$$3 \cdot 1 + 2y = 1$$
$$3 + 2y = 1$$
$$2y = -2$$
$$y = -1$$

Finally, use one of the original equations to find z.

$$2x + 3y + z = 3 \quad (2)$$
$$2 \cdot 1 + 3(-1) + z = 3$$
$$-1 + z = 3$$
$$z = 4$$

The ordered triple $(1, -1, 4)$ checks in all three equations, so it is the solution of the system of equations.

Practice Exercise

8. Solve:

$$x - y + z = 9,$$
$$2x + y + 2z = 3,$$
$$4x + 2y - 3z = -1$$

A. The y-value is -5.
B. The y-value is -3.
C. The y-value is 1.
D. The y-value is 3.

Objective [3.6a] Solve applied problems using systems of three equations.

Brief Procedure	Example	Practice Exercise
Use the five-step problem solving process, translating to a system of three equations.	In triangle ABC, the measure of angle B is three times that of angle A. The measure of angle C is 40° more than that of angle B. Find the measure of each angle.	9. Maggie, Juliet, and Erik can process 164 telephone orders per day. Maggie and Juliet together can process 109 orders, while Juliet and Erik together can process 116 orders. How many orders can each person process alone?

In triangle ABC, the measure of angle B is three times that of angle A. The measure of angle C is 40° more than that of angle B. Find the measure of each angle.

1. *Familiarize.* Let $x =$ the measure of angle A, $y =$ the measure of angle B, and $z =$ the measure of angle C.

2. *Translate.* The sum of the measures of the angles of a triangle is 180°, so this gives us one equation:

$$x + y + z = 180.$$

We can also translate two statements in the problem directly.

The measure of angle B is   three times   that of angle A.

$$y \; = \; 3 \cdot \; x$$

The measure of angle C is 40°   more than   that of angle B.

$$z \; = \; 40 \; + \; y$$

3. *Solve.* Solving the system of equations, we get (20, 60, 100).

4. *Check.* The sum of the measures is 20° +60° +100°, or 180°. The measure of angle B, 60°, is 3 times the measure of angle A, 20°, and the measure of angle C, 100°, is 40° more than the measure of angle B. The answer checks.

5. *State.* The measure of angle A is 20°, the measure of angle B is 60°, and the measure of angle C is 100°.

9. Maggie, Juliet, and Erik can process 164 telephone orders per day. Maggie and Juliet together can process 109 orders, while Juliet and Erik together can process 116 orders. How many orders can each person process alone?

A. Maggie can process 48 orders alone.

B. Juliet can process 62 orders alone.

C. Erik can process 56 orders alone.

D. Erik can process 60 orders alone.

Objective [3.7a] Determine whether an ordered pair of numbers is a solution of an inequality in two variables.

Brief Procedure	Example	Practice Exercise
Following alphabetical order, substitute the coordinates of the ordered pair in the inequality and determine whether a true inequality results.	Determine whether $(4, -1)$ is a solution of $x + 3y \geq 5$. Use alphabetical order to replace x with 4 and y with -1. $$\begin{array}{c} x + 3y \geq 5 \\ \hline 4 + 3(-1) \ ? \ 5 \\ 4 - 3 \ \Big| \\ 1 \ \Big| \quad \text{FALSE} \end{array}$$ Since $1 \geq 5$ is false, $(4, -1)$ is not a solution.	10. Determine whether $(-2, 5)$ is a solution of $3x + y \leq -1$. A. Yes B. No

Objective [3.7b] Graph linear inequalities in two variables.

Brief Procedure	Example	Practice Exercise
1. Replace the inequality symbol with an equals sign and graph this related equation. 2. If the inequality symbol is < or >, draw the line dashed. If the inequality symbol is ≤ or ≥, draw the line solid. 3. The graph consists of a half-plane, either above or below or left or right of the line, and, if the line is solid, the line as well. To determine which half-plane to shade, choose a point not on the line as a test point. Substitute to find whether that point is a solution of the inequality. If it is, shade the half-plane containing that point. If it is not, shade the half-plane on the opposite side of the line.	Graph: $x - 2y \geq 4$. First graph the line $x - 2y = 4$. The intercepts are $(0, -2)$ and $(4, 0)$. We draw the line solid since the inequality symbol is $\geq$. Next, choose a test point not on the line and determine if it is a solution of the inequality. We choose $(0, 0)$, since it is usually an easy point to use. $$\frac{x - 2y \geq 4}{0 - 2 \cdot 0 \; ? \; 4}$$ $$0 \; | \quad \text{FALSE}$$ Since $(0, 0)$ is not a solution, we shade the half-plane that does not contain $(0, 0)$. 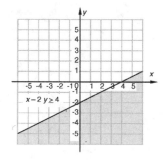	11. Graph $3x + 2y < -6$. A. 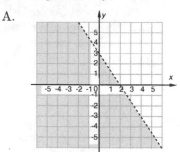 B. 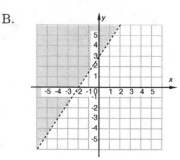 C. 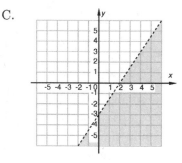 D. 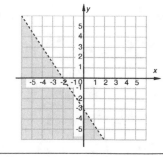

Objective [3.7c] Graph systems of linear inequalities and find coordinates of any vertices.

Brief Procedure	Example	Practice Exercise
Graph each inequality and determine where the graphs overlap, or intersect. The solutions of the system of inequalities are the ordered pairs in this region. To find the vertices, solve systems of equations composed of the appropriate related equations.	Graph the system of inequalities and find the coordinates of any vertices formed. $$x - 2y \geq -2, \quad (1)$$ $$3x - y \leq 4, \quad (2)$$ $$y \geq -1, \quad (3)$$ We graph the lines using solid lines. Indicate the region for each inequality by arrows at the ends of the line. Shade the region of overlap. 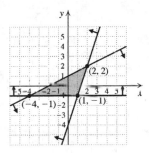 To find the vertices, we solve three different systems of equations. From inequalities (1) and (2) we have $$x - 2y = -2,$$ $$3x - y = 4$$ Solving, we obtain the vertex $(2, 2)$. From inequalities (1) and (3) we have $$x - 2y = -2,$$ $$y = -1$$ Solving, we obtain the vertex $(-4, -1)$. From inequalities (2) and (3) we have $$3x - y = 4,$$ $$y = -1$$ Solving, we obtain the vertex $(1, -1)$.	12. Graph the system of inequalities and find the coordinates of any vertices found. $$x - 2y \leq 4,$$ $$x + y \leq 4,$$ $$x - 1 \geq 0$$ A. One vertex is $(0, -4)$. B. One vertex is $(1, 0)$. C. One vertex is $(1, 3)$. D. One vertex is $(8, -4)$.

Objective [3.8a] Given total-cost and total-revenue functions, find the total-profit function and the break-even point.

Brief Procedure	Example	Practice Exercise
Given a total-cost function $C(x)$ and a total-revenue function $R(x)$, the total-profit function $P(x)$ is given by $P(x) = R(x) - C(x)$. To find the break-even point, solve the system of equations composed of $C(x)$ and $R(x)$.	For the total-cost function $C(x) = 10x + 250,000$ and the total-revenue function $R(x) = 60x$, find (a) the total-profit function and (b) the break-even point. a) Total profit is given by $$P(x) = R(x) - C(x)$$ $$= 60x - (10x + 250,000)$$ $$= 60x - 10x - 250,000$$ $$= 50x - 250,000.$$ b) To find the break-even point we solve the system of equations $C(x) = 10x + 250,000,$ $R(x) = 60x.$ Since both cost and revenue are in dollars and they are equal at the break-even point, the system can be rewritten as $d = 10x + 250,000,$ $d = 60x.$ Then we solve using the substitution method. We substitute $60x$ for d in the first equation and solve for x. $$60x = 10x + 250,000$$ $$50x = 250,000$$ $$x = 5000$$ Now substitute in either equation to find the second coordinate of the break-even point. We will use the second equation. $$d = 60x$$ $$d = 60 \cdot 5000$$ $$d = 300,000$$ The break-even point is $(5000, \$300,000)$.	13. For the total-cost function $C(x) = 15x + 400,000$ and the total-revenue function $R(x) = 55x$, find the total-profit function and the break-even point. A. $P(x) = 400,000 - 40x$ B. $P(x) = 40x + 400,000$ C. The equilibrium point is $(10,000, \$550,000)$. D. The equilibrium point is $(4000, \$220,000)$.

Objective [3.8b] Given supply and demand functions, find the equilibrium point.

Brief Procedure	Example	Practice Exercise
Solve the system of equations composed of the supply and demand functions.	Find the equilibrium point for the demand and supply functions $$D(p) = 5000 - 30p,$$ $$S(p) = 2000 + 10p.$$ Since both demand and supply are *quantities* and they are equal at the equilibrium point, we rewrite the system as $$q = 5000 - 30p;$$ $$q = 2000 + 10p.$$ Then substitute $2000 + 10p$ for q in the first equation and solve for p. $$2000 + 10p = 5000 - 30p$$ $$2000 + 40p = 5000$$ $$40p = 3000$$ $$p = 75$$ The equilibrium price is \$75 per unit. To find the equilibrium quantity, we substitute 75 into either $D(p)$ or $S(p)$. $$S(p) = 2000 + 10(75)$$ $$= 2000 + 750$$ $$= 2750$$ The equilibrium quantity is 2750 units and the equilibrium point is (\$75, 2750).	14. Find the equilibrium point for the demand and supply functions $$D(p) = 900 - 17p,$$ $$S(p) = 150 + 8p.$$ A. (\$30, 390) B. (\$45, 135) C. (\$60, 630) D. (\$125, 1150)

Chapter 4 Review

Objective [4.1a] Identify the degree of each term and the degree of a polynomial; identify terms, coefficients, monomials, binomials, and trinomials; arrange polynomials in ascending or descending order; and identify the leading term, the leading coefficient, and the constant term.		
Brief Procedure	**Example**	**Practice Exercises**
The degree of a term is the sum of the exponents of the variables. The degree of a polynomial is the same as the degree of its term of highest degree.	Identify the degree of each term and the degree of the polynomial: $8x^3 - 15x^2y^3 + 4xy + y^4 - 7$. The degree of $8x^3$ is the exponent of the variable, 3. The degree of $-15x^2y^3$ is the sum of the exponents of the variables, $2 + 3$, or 5. The degree of $4xy$ is the sum of the exponents of the variables, $1 + 1$, or 2. The degree of y^4 is the exponent of the variable, 4. The degree of -7 is the exponent of the variable, 0, since $-7 = -7x^0$. The degree of the term of highest degree is 5, so the degree of the polynomial is 5.	1. Identify the degree of the polynomial: $6a^2b - 4ab + 2b^4 + 10$. A. 2 B. 3 C. 4 D. 10
To identify the terms of a polynomial, rewrite the subtractions in the polynomial as additions. Then each expression being added is a term of the polynomial.	Identify the terms of the polynomial $3y^3 - 2y^2 - 5y + 1$. $3y^3 - 2y^2 - 5y + 1 =$ $\quad 3y^3 + (-2y^2) + (-5y) + 1$ Then the terms are $3y^3$, $-2y^2$, $-5y$, and 1.	2. Identify the terms of the polynomial $-5y^4 + 3y^2 - 2$. A. $5y^4$, $3y^2$, 2 B. $5y^4$, $3y^2$ C. $-5y^4$, $3y^2$ D. $-5y^4$, $3y^2$, -2
The coefficient of a term of a polynomial is the number by which the variable is multiplied.	Identify the coefficients of each term of the polynomial $5y^6 - 10y^2 + 4$. The coefficient of $5y^6$ is 5. The coefficient of $-10y^2$ is -10. The coefficient of 4 is 4.	3. Identify the coefficients of each term of the polynomial $-8x^3 + 4x^2 - 7$. A. -8, 4 B. -8, 4, -7 C. 3, 2 D. 3, 2, 0
A polynomial with just one term is a monomial. A polynomial with just two terms is a binomial. A polynomial with just three terms is a trinomial. Those with more than three terms do not generally have a specific name.	Classify each of the following as a monomial, binomial, trinomial, or none of these. a) $x^2 - 7$ b) $2x^3 - x^2 + 5x + 6$ a) This polynomial has just two terms, so it is a binomial. b) This polynomial has more than three terms, so it is none of these.	4. Classify $-6x^7$ as a monomial, binomial, trinomial, or none of these. A. Monomial B. Binomial C. Trinomial D. None of these

Objective [4.1a] (continued)

Brief Procedure	Example	Practice Exercises
To arrange a polynomial in ascending order, write the terms so that the exponents increase from left to right. To arrange a polynomial in descending order, write the terms so that the exponents decrease from left to right.	Arrange $3t - 4t^2 - 7 + 2t^3$ in ascending order and then in descending order. Ascending order: $-7 + 3t - 4t^2 + 2t^3$ Descending order: $2t^3 - 4t^2 + 3t - 7$	5. Arrange $8 - 3x^2 + 4x^3 - x$ in descending order. A. $8 - x - 3x^2 + 4x^3$ B. $-x - 3x^2 + 4x^3 + 8$ C. $-3x^2 - x + 4x^3 + 8$ D. $4x^3 - 3x^2 - x + 8$
The leading term of a polynomial is the term of highest degree. The leading coefficient is the coefficient of the term of highest degree. The constant term has degree 0.	Identify the leading term, the leading coefficient, and the constant term of $5x^3 - 6x^2y^2 - 4xy^4 + 1$. The degrees of the terms are 3, 4, 5, and 0, respectively. Thus, the term of highest degree is $-4xy^4$, so this is the leading term and the leading coefficient is -4. The term with degree 0 is 1 (or $1 \cdot x^0$), so it is the constant term.	6. Identify the leading term, the leading coefficient, and the constant term of the polynomial $12s^2t + 3s^2t^2 - 4st - 5$. A. $12s^2t$, 12, -5 B. $12s^2t$, 12, 5 C. $3s^2t^2$, 3, 5 D. $3s^2t^2$, 3, -5

Objective [4.1b] Evaluate a polynomial function for given inputs.

Brief Procedure	Example	Practice Exercise
Substitute the given input for each occurrence of the variable and carry out the resulting calculations.	For the polynomial function $P(x) = x^2 - 4x + 5$, find $P(-1)$. $P(-1) = (-1)^2 - 4(-1) + 5$ $= 1 + 4 + 5 = 10$	7. For the polynomial function $P(x) = 2x^2 + x - 8$, find $P(2)$. A. -5 B. -2 C. 2 D. 5

Objective [4.1c] Collect like terms in a polynomial and add polynomials.

Brief Procedure	Example	Practice Exercises
Terms that have the same variable(s) raised to the same power(s) are like terms. The distributive laws allow us to collect like terms by adding or subtracting their coefficients.	Collect like terms: $5x^4 - 6x^2y - 3x^4 + y$. $5x^4 - 6x^2y - 3x^4 + y$ $= (5 - 3)x^4 - 6x^2y + y$ $= 2x^4 - 6x^2y + y$	8. Collect like terms: $4x^3 - 2x^2 + 3x^2 - 5$. A. $7x^3 - 2x^2 - 5$ B. $4x^3 + x^2 - 5$ C. $5x^2 - 5$ D. x^2
To add two polynomials, write a plus sign between them and then collect like terms. The polynomials can also be written with like terms in columns and then added.	Add: $(5x^3 + x - 7) + (2x^3 - 4x^2 + 3)$. $(5x^3 + x - 7) + (2x^3 - 4x^2 + 3)$ $= (5 + 2)x^3 - 4x^2 + x + (-7 + 3)$ $= 7x^3 - 4x^2 + x - 4$	9. Add: $(6x^4y^2 - 5x^2y - 1) + (x^4y^2 + 2x^2 + 3)$. A. $6x^4y^2 - 4x^2y + 2x^2 + 2$ B. $7x^4y^2 - 3x^2 + 2$ C. $7x^4y^2 - 3x^2y + 2$ D. $7x^4y^2 - 5x^2y + 2x^2 + 2$

Objective [4.1d] Find the opposite of a polynomial and subtract polynomials.

Brief Procedure	Example	Practice Exercises

The opposite of a polynomial P can be symbolized $-P$ or by replacing each term with its opposite.	Write two equivalent expressions for the opposite of $2xy - 3xy^2 + y - 5$.
	
	One expression is
	  $-(2xy - 3xy^2 + y - 5)$.
	A second expression is
	  $-2xy + 3xy^2 - y + 5$.
		10. Which is not an expression for the opposite of $x^2 - xy^3 + 4y$?
		A. $-(x^2 - xy^3 + 4y)$
		B. $-x^2 - xy^3 + 4y$
		C. $-x^2 + xy^3 - 4y$

To subtract polynomials, add the opposite of the polynomial being subtracted. Some steps can be skipped if we mentally take the opposite of each term being subtracted and then combine like terms.	Subtract:
	  $(4x^2 - x + 3) - (6x^2 - 4x - 1)$.
	
	  $(4x^2 - x + 3) - (6x^2 - 4x - 1)$
	  $= 4x^2 - x + 3 - 6x^2 + 4x + 1)$
	  $= -2x^2 + 3x + 4$
		11. Subtract:
		  $(x^3 - x + 2) - (5x^3 + x^2 - 8)$.
		A. $-4x^3 + 10$
		B. $-4x^3 + x^2 - x - 6$
		C. $-4x^3 - x^2 - x - 6$
		D. $-4x^3 - x^2 - x + 10$

Objective [4.2a] Multiply any two polynomials.

Brief Procedure	Example	Practice Exercise

Multiply each term of one polynomial by every term of the other and collect like terms, if possible. It is sometimes convenient to write the multiplication in columns.	Multiply.
	  a) $(2x - 7)(x + 3)$
	  b) $(x^2 - 2x + 3)(x - 1)$
	
	a) $(2x - 7)(x + 3)$
	  $= (2x - 7)x + (2x - 7)3$
	  $= 2x \cdot x - 7 \cdot x + 2x \cdot 3 - 7 \cdot 3$
	  $= 2x^2 - 7x + 6x - 21$
	  $= 2x^2 - x - 21$
	
	b) We use columns. First we multiply the top row by -1 and then by x, placing like terms of the product in the same column. Finally we collect like terms.
	
	$\begin{array}{r} x^2 - 2x + 3 \\ x - 1 \\ \hline -\ x^2 + 2x - 3 \\ x^3 - 2x^2 + 3x \\ \hline x^3 - 3x^2 + 5x - 3 \end{array}$
		12. Multiply: $(x^3 - 3x + 1)(x^2 + 4)$.
		A. $x^5 - 3x^3 + x^2$
		B. $x^5 - 12x + 1$
		C. $x^5 + x^3 - 11x^2 + 4$
		D. $x^5 + x^3 + x^2 - 12x + 4$

Objective [4.2b] Use the FOIL method to multiply two binomials.

Brief Procedure	Example	Practice Exercise
To multiply two binomials, $A+B$ and $C+D$, multiply the **F**irst terms AC, the **O**utside terms AD, the **I**nside terms BC, and then the **L**ast terms BD. Then collect like terms, if possible. $(A+B)(C+D) =$ $\quad AC + AD + BC + BD$	Multiply: $(2x + 3y)(x - 4y)$. $(2x + 3y)(x - 4y)$ $\quad$ F $\quad$ O $\quad$ I $\quad$ L $= 2x \cdot x + 2x \cdot (-4y) + 3y \cdot x + 3y \cdot (-4y)$ $= 2x^2 - 8xy + 3xy - 12y^2$ $= 2x^2 - 5xy - 12y^2$	13. Multiply: $(y + 2)(3y - 5)$. A. $3y^2 + y - 10$ B. $3y^2 - 5y - 10$ C. $3y^2 + 6y - 10$ D. $3y^2 - 11y - 10$

Objective [4.2c] Use a rule to square a binomial.

Brief Procedure	Example	Practice Exercise
The square of a binomial is the square of the first term, plus or minus twice the product of the two terms, plus the square of the last term: $(A+B)^2 = A^2 + 2AB + B^2;$ $(A-B)^2 = A^2 - 2AB + B^2.$	Multiply: $(3x - 4)^2$. $(3x - 4)^2$ $= (3x)^2 - 2 \cdot 3x \cdot 4 + 4^2$ $= 9x^2 - 24x + 16$	14. Multiply: $(2x + y)^2$. A. $4x^2 + y^2$ B. $2x^2 + 4xy + y^2$ C. $4x^2 + 2xy + y^2$ D. $4x^2 + 4xy + y^2$

Objective [4.2d] Use a rule to multiply a sum and a difference of the same two terms.

Brief Procedure	Example	Practice Exercise
The product of the sum and the difference of the same two terms is the square of the first term minus the square of the second term: $(A+B)(A-B) = A^2 - B^2.$	Multiply: $(x + 3y)(x - 3y)$. $(x + 3y)(x - 3y) = x^2 - (3y)^2$ $\qquad\qquad\qquad\quad = x^2 - 9y^2$	15. Multiply: $(x + 6)(x - 6)$. A. $x^2 + 12x - 36$ B. $x^2 - 12x - 36$ C. $x^2 + 36$ D. $x^2 - 36$

Objective [4.2e] For functions f described by second-degree polynomials, find and simplify notation like $f(a + h)$ and $f(a + h) - f(a)$.

Brief Procedure	Example	Practice Exercise
Substitute the given input(s) and carry out the resulting computations.	Given $f(x) = x^2 - x + 2$, find and simplify $f(a+4)$ and $f(a+h) - f(a)$. $f(a + 4)$ $= (a+4)^2 - (a+4) + 2$ $= a^2 + 8a + 16 - a - 4 + 2$ $= a^2 + 7a + 14$ $f(a + h) - f(a)$ $= [(a+h)^2 - (a+h) + 2]$ $\qquad -(a^2 - a + 2)$ $= a^2 + 2ah + h^2 - a - h +$ $\qquad 2 - a^2 + a - 2$ $= 2ah + h^2 - h$	16. Given $f(x) = x^2 + 2x - 1$, find and simplify $f(a + h) - f(a)$. A. $2ah + h^2 - 2h$ B. $2ah + h^2 + 2h$ C. $2ah + h^2 + 4a + 2h - 2$ D. $2a^2 + 2ah + h^2 + 4a + 2h - 2$

Objective [4.3a] Factor polynomials whose terms have a common factor.

Brief Procedure	Example	Practice Exercise
Find the largest factor common to all the terms of the polynomial. Then use the distributive law to express the polynomial as a product where one factor is the largest common factor.	Factor $18x^5 - 9x^3 + 27x^2$. Although there are many factors common to the three terms, the *largest* common factor is $9x^2$. $18x^5 - 9x^3 + 27x^2$ $= (9x^2)(2x^3) - (9x^2)(x) + (9x^2)(3)$ $= 9x^2(2x^3 - x + 3)$	17. Factor $24y^8 + 16y^6 - 8y^4$, factoring out the largest common factor. A. $2y(12y^7 + 8y^5 - 4y^3)$ B. $4y^3(6y^5 + 4y^3 - 2y)$ C. $8y^4(3y^4 + 2y^2)$ D. $8y^4(3y^4 + 2y^2 - 1)$

Objective [4.3b] Factor certain polynomials with four terms by grouping.

Brief Procedure	Example	Practice Exercise
Group the terms into two pairs. Factor each group and then factor the common factor out of the resulting expression.	Factor $6x^3 + 9x^2 - 8x - 12$ by grouping. $6x^3 + 9x^2 - 8x - 12$ $= (6x^3 + 9x^2) + (-8x - 12)$ $= 3x^2(2x + 3) - 4(2x + 3)$ $= (3x^2 - 4)(2x + 3)$	18. Factor $x^3 - 3x^2 + 2x - 6$ by grouping. A. One factor is $(x + 2)$. B. One factor is $(x^2 + 2)$. C. One factor is $(x^2 - 3)$. D. One factor is $(x + 3)$.

Objective [4.4a] Factor trinomials of the type $x^2 + bx + c$.

Brief Procedure	Example	Practice Exercise
1. First arrange in descending order. 2. Use a trial-and-error procedure that looks for factors of c whose sum is b. • If c is positive, the signs of the factors are the same as the sign of b. • If c is negative, then one factor is positive and the other is negative. (If the sum of two factors is the opposite of b, changing the sign of each factor will give the desired factors whose sum is b.) 3. Check your result by multiplying.	Factor $x^2 - 2x - 15$. Since the constant term, -15, is negative, we look for a factorization of -15 in which one factor is positive and one factor is negative. The sum of the factors must be the coefficient of the middle term, -2, so the negative factor must have the larger absolute value. The possible pairs of factors that meet these criteria are $1, -15$ and $3, -5$. The numbers we need are 3 and -5. $$x^2 - 2x - 15 = (x+3)(x-5).$$	19. Factor $x^2 - 9x + 8$. A. One factor is $(x+1)$. B. One factor is $(x-1)$. C. One factor is $(x+8)$. D. One factor is $(x-4)$.

Objective [4.5a] Factor trinomials of the type $ax^2 + bx + c, a \neq 1$, by the FOIL method.

Brief Procedure	Example	Practice Exercise
1. Factor out the largest common factor, if one exists. 2. Find the **First** terms whose product is ax^2. 3. Find two **Last** terms whose product is c. 4. Repeat steps (2) and (3) until a combination is found for which the sum of the **O**utside and **I**nside products is bx. 5. Always check by multiplying.	Factor $2y^3 + 5y^2 - 3y$. 1. Factor out the largest common factor, y: $\quad y(2y^2 + 5y - 3)$. Now we factor $2y^2 + 5y - 3$. 2. Because $2y^2$ factors as $2y \cdot y$, we have this possibility for a factorization: $\quad (2y+\quad)(y+\quad)$. 3. There are two pairs of factors of -3 and each can be written in two ways: $\quad 3, -1 \qquad -3, 1$ and $\quad -1, 3 \qquad 1, -3$. 4. From steps (2) and (3) we see that there are 4 possibilities for factorizations. We look for Outer and Inner products for which the sum is the middle term, $5y$. We try some possibilities. $(2y+3)(y-1) = 2y^2 + y - 3$ $(2y-1)(y+3) = 2y^2 + 5y - 3$ The factorization of $2y^2 + 5y - 3$ is $(2y-1)(y+3)$. We must include the common factor to get a factorization of the original trinomial. $2y^3 + 5y^2 - 3y = y(2y-1)(y+3)$	20. Factor $6z^2 + 14z + 4$. A. $(3z+1)(z+2)$ B. $2(3z+1)(z+2)$ C. $(6z+1)(z+6)$ D. $(3z+2)(2z+3)$

Objective [4.5b] Factor trinomials of the type $ax^2 + bx + c, a \neq 1$, by the ac-method.

Brief Procedure	Example	Practice Exercise

1. Factor out the largest common factor.
2. Multiply the leading coefficient a and the constant c.
3. Try to factor the product ac so that the sum of the factors is b. That is, find integers p and q such that $pq = ac$ and $p + q = b$.
4. Split the middle term. That is, write it as a sum using the factors found in step (3).
5. Then factor by grouping.
	Factor $5x^2 + 7x - 6$ by grouping.
	1. There is no common factor (other than 1 or -1).
	2. Multiply the leading coefficient 5 and the constant, -6:
	    $5(-6) = -30$.
	3. Look for a factorization of -30 in which the sum of the factors is the coefficient of the middle term, 7.
	    The numbers we need are 10 and -3.
	4. Split the middle term, writing it as a sum or difference using the factors found in step (3).
	    $7x = 10x - 3x$
	5. Factor by grouping.
	
	$\quad 5x^2 + 7x - 6$
	$= 5x^2 + 10x - 3x - 6$
	$= 5x(x + 2) - 3(x + 2)$
	$= (5x - 3)(x + 2)$
		21. Factor $8x^2 - 2x - 1$ by grouping.
		A. One factor is $(x - 1)$.
		B. One factor is $(2x - 1)$.
		C. One factor is $(4x - 1)$.
		D. One factor is $(8x - 1)$.

Objective [4.6a] Factor trinomial squares.

Brief Procedure	Example	Practice Exercise
Use the following equations: $A^2 + 2AB + B^2 = (A + B)^2$, $A^2 - 2AB + B^2 = (A - B)^2$	Factor $4x^2 - 12xy + 9y^2$. $\quad 4x^2 - 12xy + 9y^2$ $= (2x)^2 - 2 \cdot 2x \cdot 3y + (3y)^2$ $= (2x - 3y)^2$	22. Factor $16x^2 + 8x + 1$. A. $(2x + 1)^2$ B. $(4x + 1)^2$ C. $(8x + 1)^2$ D. $(8x - 1)^2$

Objective [4.6b] Factor differences of squares.		
Brief Procedure	Example	Practice Exercise
Use the equation $A^2 - B^2 = (A+B)(A-B)$.	Factor $t^5 - t$. $$t^5 - t = t(t^4 - 1)$$ $$= t(t^2 + 1)(t^2 - 1)$$ $$= t(t^2 + 1)(t + 1)(t - 1)$$	23. Factor $4a^2 - 9b^2$ completely. A.$(2a - 3b)^2$ B. $(2a + 3b)(2a - 3b)$ C. $(2a + b)(2a - 9b)$ D. $(3b + 2a)(3b - 2a)$

Objective [4.6c] Factor certain polynomials with four terms by grouping and possibly using the factoring of a trinomial square or the difference of squares.		
Brief Procedure	Example	Practice Exercise
Sometimes when factoring by grouping, we get a factor that can be factored further as a difference of squares. Furthermore, we can sometimes factor a polynomial with four terms by grouping the terms as a trinomial square minus a squared term and then factoring as a difference of squares.	Factor completely. a) $x^3 + 3x^2 - x - 3$ b) $a^2 - 8a + 16 - b^2$ a) $\quad x^3 + 3x^2 - x - 3$ $\quad = x^2(x + 3) - (x + 3)$ $\quad = (x^2 - 1)(x + 3)$ $\quad = (x + 1)(x - 1)(x + 3)$ b) $\quad a^2 - 8a + 16 - b^2$ $\quad = (a - 4)^2 - b^2$ $\quad = (a - 4 + b)(a - 4 - b)$	24. Factor completely: $$x^2 - 2x + 1 - 9y^2$$ A. $(x - 1 + 3y)(x - 1 - 3y)$ B. $(x + 1 + 3y)(x + 1 - 3y)$ C. $(x + y)(x - 2y)$ D. $(x - y)(x - 9y)$

Objective [4.6d] Factor sums and differences of cubes.		
Brief Procedure	Example	Practice Exercise
Use the following equations. $A^3 + B^3 =$ $\quad (A + B)(A^2 - AB + B^2)$ $A^3 - B^3 =$ $\quad (A - B)(A^2 + AB + B^2)$	Factor $y^3 - 8z^3$. $$y^3 - 8z^3$$ $$= y^3 - (2z)^3$$ $$= (y - 2z)(y^2 + 2yz + 4z^2)$$	25. Factor: $27m^3 + n^3$. A. $(3m + n)^3$ B. $(3m + n)(9m^2 + 3mn + n^2)$ C. $(3m + n)(9m^2 - 3mn + n^2)$ D. $(3m + n)(9m^2 - 6mn + n^2)$

Objective [4.7a] Factor polynomials completely using any of the methods considered in this chapter.

Brief Procedure	Example	Practice Exercise
a) Always look for a common factor. If there is one, factor out the largest common factor. b) Then look at the number of terms. *Two terms:* Determine whether you have a difference of squares or a sum or difference of cubes. Do not try to factor a sum of squares: $A^2 + B^2$. *Three terms:* Determine whether the trinomial is a square. If it is, factor accordingly. If not, try trial and error, using FOIL or grouping. *Four terms:* Try factoring by grouping. c) *Always factor completely.* If a factor with more than one term can still be factored, you should factor it. When no factor can be factored further, you have finished.	Factor $2y^3 - 12y^2 + 18y$ completely. a) We look for a common factor. $2y^3 - 12y^2 + 18y = 2y(y^2 - 6y + 9)$ b) The factor $y^2 - 6y + 9$ has three terms and is a trinomial square. We factor it. $2y(y^2 - 6y + 9)$ $= 2y(y^2 - 2 \cdot y \cdot 3 + 3^2)$ $= 2y(y - 3)^2$	26. Factor $15x^2 + 5xy - 20y^2$ completely. A. One factor is $(3x + 4y)$. B. One factor is $(3x - 4y)$. C. One factor is $(5x - 5y)$. D. One factor is $(15x + 20y)$.

Objective [4.8a] Solve quadratic and other polynomial equations by first factoring and then using the principle of zero products.

Brief Procedure	Example	Practice Exercise
1. Obtain a 0 on one side of the equation. 2. Factor the other side. 3. Set each factor equal to 0. 4. Solve the resulting equations.	Solve: $x^2 + 2x = 24$. $x^2 + 2x = 24$ $x^2 + 2x - 24 = 0$ $(x + 6)(x - 4) = 0$ $x + 6 = 0 \quad or \quad x - 4 = 0$ $x = -6 \quad or \qquad x = 4$ The solutions are -6 and 4.	27. Solve: $16x^2 = 49$. A. $\dfrac{7}{4}, -\dfrac{7}{4}$ B. $\dfrac{4}{7}, -\dfrac{4}{7}$ C. $7, -7$ D. $4, -4$

Objective [4.8b] Solve applied problems involving quadratic and other polynomial equations that can be solved by factoring.

Brief Procedure	Example	Practice Exercise
Use the five-step problem solving process.	The length of a rectangular rug is 2 ft greater than the width. The area of the rug is 48 ft^2. Find the length and width.	28. The height of a triangle is 4 cm greater than the base. The area is 30 cm^2. Find the height and the base.

Example (continued):

1. *Familiarize.* We make a drawing. Let w = the width of the rug. Then the length is $w + 2$.

$w + 2$

Recall that the area of a rectangle is length × width.

2. *Translate.* We reword the problem.

Length × width is 48 ft^2.

$$(w + 2) \times w = 48$$

3. *Solve.* We solve the equation.

$$(w + 2) \times w = 48$$
$$w^2 + 2w = 48$$
$$w^2 + 2w - 48 = 0$$
$$(w + 8)(w - 6) = 0$$
$$w + 8 = 0 \quad or \quad w - 6 = 0$$
$$w = -8 \quad or \quad w = 6$$

4. *Check.* The width of a rectangle cannot be negative, so -8 cannot be a solution. Suppose the width is 6 ft. Then the length is $6 + 2$, or 8 ft and the area is $6 \cdot 8$, or 48 ft^2. These numbers check in the original problem.

5. *State.* The length is 8 ft and the width is 6 ft.

Practice Exercise (continued):

A. The height is 6 cm.

B. The height is 10 cm.

C. The base is 10 cm.

D. The base is 14 cm.

Chapter 5 Review

Objective [5.1a] Find all numbers for which a rational expression is not defined or that are not in the domain of a rational function.		
Brief Procedure	Example	Practice Exercise
To find the numbers for which a rational expression is undefined or that are not in the domain of a rational function, determine the values of the variable that make the denominator of the expression or function zero.	Find all numbers for which the rational expression $\dfrac{x-2}{x^2-16}$ is undefined. We set the denominator equal to 0 and solve. $$x^2 - 16 = 0$$ $$(x+4)(x-4) = 0$$ $$x+4 = 0 \quad or \quad x-4 = 0$$ $$x = -4 \ or \qquad x = 4$$ The expression is undefined for the numbers -4 and 4. For the rational function $f(x) = \dfrac{x-2}{x^2-16}$, the domain is $\{x \mid x$ is a real number and $x \neq -4$ and $x \neq 4\}$, or $(-\infty, -4) \cup (-4, 4) \cup (4, \infty)$.	1. Find all numbers for which the rational expression $\dfrac{y+3}{y^2+4y-5}$ is undefined. A. -5 B. -3 C. $-5, 1$ D. $-5, -3, 1$

Objective [5.1b] Multiply a rational expression by 1, using an expression like A/A.		
Brief Procedure	Example	Practice Exercise
Multiply the numerators and multiply the denominators.	Multiply: $\dfrac{x+3}{2x-1} \cdot \dfrac{x+2}{x+2}$. $$\dfrac{x+3}{2x-1} \cdot \dfrac{x+2}{x+2} = \dfrac{(x+3)(x+2)}{(2x-1)(x+2)}$$	2. Multiply: $\dfrac{3y}{y-4} \cdot \dfrac{2y}{2y}$. A. $\dfrac{(3y)(2y)}{y-4}$ B. $\dfrac{3y}{(y-4)(2y)}$ C. $\dfrac{2y}{(y-4)(2y)}$ D. $\dfrac{(3y)(2y)}{(y-4)(2y)}$

Objective [5.1c] Simplify rational expressions.

Brief Procedure	Example	Practice Exercise
Factor the numerator and the denominator of the rational expression and remove factors that are common to the numerator and the denominator. These factors of 1 can also be canceled.	Simplify by removing a factor of 1: $\dfrac{6x^2 + 9x}{3x^2 - 3x}$. $$\begin{aligned} \frac{6x^2 + 9x}{3x^2 - 3x} &= \frac{3x(2x + 3)}{3x(x - 1)} \\ &= \frac{3x}{3x} \cdot \frac{2x + 3}{x - 1} \\ &= 1 \cdot \frac{2x + 3}{x - 1} \\ &= \frac{2x + 3}{x - 1} \end{aligned}$$ This could be done using canceling as follows: $$\begin{aligned} \frac{6x^2 + 9x}{3x^2 - 3x} &= \frac{3x(2x + 3)}{3x(x - 1)} \\ &= \frac{\cancel{3x}(2x + 3)}{\cancel{3x}(x - 1)} \\ &= \frac{2x + 3}{x - 1} \end{aligned}$$	3. Simplify by removing a factor of 1: $\dfrac{x^2 + x - 6}{x^2 + 6x + 9}$. A. $\dfrac{x - 6}{6x + 9}$ B. $\dfrac{x - 2}{x + 3}$ C. $-\dfrac{1}{3}$ D. $-\dfrac{2}{3}$

Objective [5.1d] Multiply rational expressions and simplify.

Brief Procedure	Example	Practice Exercise
Multiply the numerators and the denominators and then simplify by removing a factor of 1.	Multiply and simplify: $$\frac{x^2 + 3x - 4}{18} \cdot \frac{6}{x^2 + x - 12}.$$ $$\begin{aligned} &\frac{x^2 + 3x - 4}{18} \cdot \frac{6}{x^2 + x - 12} \\ &= \frac{(x^2 + 3x - 4)6}{18(x^2 + x - 12)} \\ &= \frac{(x + 4)(x - 1)6}{3(6)(x + 4)(x - 3)} \\ &= \frac{(x\cancel{+}4)(x - 1)\cancel{6}}{3(\cancel{6})(x\cancel{+}4)(x - 3)} \\ &= \frac{x - 1}{3(x - 3)} \end{aligned}$$	4. Multiply and simplify: $$\frac{a + 1}{a - 3} \cdot \frac{a^2 + 2a - 15}{a^2 - a - 2}.$$ A. $\dfrac{a + 5}{a - 2}$ B. $\dfrac{a - 5}{a - 2}$ C. $\dfrac{a + 5}{a + 2}$ D. $\dfrac{a - 5}{a + 2}$

Objective [5.1e] Divide rational expressions and simplify.

Brief Procedure	Example	Practice Exercise
Multiply by the reciprocal of the divisor. Then simplify by removing a factor of 1, if possible.	Divide and simplify: $$\frac{y^2 - 4y + 3}{y + 6} \div \frac{2y - 6}{y^2 + 2y - 24}.$$ $$\frac{y^2 - 4y + 3}{y + 6} \div \frac{2y - 6}{y^2 + 2y - 24}$$ $$= \frac{y^2 - 4y + 3}{y + 6} \cdot \frac{y^2 + 2y - 24}{2y - 6}$$ $$= \frac{(y^2 - 4y + 3)(y^2 + 2y - 24)}{(y + 6)(2y - 6)}$$ $$= \frac{(y - 1)(y - 3)(y + 6)(y - 4)}{(y + 6)(2)(y - 3)}$$ $$= \frac{(y - 1)(y\!\!\!\diagup\!\!-3)(y\!\!\!+\!\!\!6)(y - 4)}{(y\!\!\!+\!\!\!6)(2)(y\!\!\!\diagup\!\!-3)}$$ $$= \frac{(y - 1)(y - 4)}{2}$$	5. Divide and simplify: $$\frac{x^2 - 9}{5} \div \frac{x + 3}{x - 5}.$$ A. $x(x - 3)$ B. $-\dfrac{3(x^2 - 9)}{25}$ C. $\dfrac{(x - 3)(x - 5)}{5}$ D. $\dfrac{(x + 3)(x - 5)}{5}$

Objective [5.2a] Find the LCM of several algebraic expressions by factoring.

Brief Procedure	Example	Practice Exercise
Factor each expression and use each factor the greatest number of times it occurs in any one factorization.	Find the LCM of $5x - 5y$ and $x^2 - 2xy + y^2$. $5x - 5y = 5(x - y)$ $x^2 - 2xy + y^2 = (x - y)(x - y)$ The LCM is $5(x - y)(x - y)$.	6. Find the LCM of $y^2 - 9$ and $y^2 + y - 6$. A. $(y + 3)(y - 3)(y - 2)$ B. $(y + 3)(y - 3)(y + 2)$ C. $(y + 3)(y + 3)(y - 3)(y - 2)$ D. $(y + 3)(y - 3)(y - 3)(y - 2)$

Objective [5.2b] Add and subtract rational expressions.

Brief Procedure	Example	Practice Exercise
To add or subtract when the denominators are the same, add or subtract the numerators and keep the same denominator. To add or subtract when when the denominators are different: 1. Find the LCM of the denominators. This is the least common denominator (LCD). 2. For each rational expression find an equivalent expression with the LCD. To do so, multiply by 1 using an expression for 1 made up of factors of the LCD that are missing from the original denominator. 3. Add or subtract the numerators. Write the sum or difference over the LCD. 4. Simplify, if possible.	Subtract: $\dfrac{x-3}{x+5} - \dfrac{x-2}{x+1}$. The LCD is $(x+5)(x+1)$. $\dfrac{x-3}{x+5} - \dfrac{x-2}{x+1}$ $= \dfrac{x-3}{x+5} \cdot \dfrac{x+1}{x+1} - \dfrac{x-2}{x+1} \cdot \dfrac{x+5}{x+5}$ $= \dfrac{(x-3)(x+1)}{(x+5)(x+1)} - \dfrac{(x-2)(x+5)}{(x+1)(x+5)}$ $= \dfrac{x^2-2x-3}{(x+5)(x+1)} - \dfrac{x^2+3x-10}{(x+5)(x+1)}$ $= \dfrac{x^2-2x-3-(x^2+3x-10)}{(x+5)(x+1)}$ $= \dfrac{x^2-2x-3-x^2-3x+10}{(x+5)(x+1)}$ $= \dfrac{-5x+7}{(x+5)(x+1)}$	7. Add: $\dfrac{3}{x^2-3x-4} + \dfrac{5}{x^2+3x+2}$ A. $\dfrac{8}{(x+1)(x-4)(x+2)}$ B. $\dfrac{3x+6}{(x+1)(x-4)(x+2)}$ C. $\dfrac{5x-20}{(x+1)(x-4)(x+2)}$ D. $\dfrac{8x-14}{(x+1)(x-4)(x+2)}$

Objective [5.2c] Simplify combined additions and subtractions of rational expressions.

Brief Procedure	Example	Practice Exercise
Add and subtract as indicated and then simplify, if possible.	Perform the indicated operations and simplify, if possible: $$\frac{4a}{a^2 - 4} - \frac{3}{a - 2} + \frac{5}{a}.$$ The LCD is $a(a + 2)(a - 2)$. $$\frac{4a}{(a+2)(a-2)} \cdot \frac{a}{a} -$$ $$\frac{3}{a-2} \cdot \frac{a(a+2)}{a(a+2)} +$$ $$\frac{5}{a} \cdot \frac{(a+2)(a-2)}{(a+2)(a-2)}$$ $$= \frac{4a^2}{a(a+2)(a-2)} -$$ $$\frac{3a(a+2)}{a(a+2)(a-2)} +$$ $$\frac{5(a+2)(a-2)}{a(a+2)(a-2)}$$ $$= \frac{4a^2}{a(a+2)(a-2)} -$$ $$\frac{3a^2 + 6a}{a(a+2)(a-2)} +$$ $$\frac{5(a^2 - 4)}{a(a+2)(a-2)}$$ $$= \frac{4a^2 - (3a^2 + 6a) + 5a^2 - 20}{a(a+2)(a-2)}$$ $$= \frac{4a^2 - 3a^2 - 6a + 5a^2 - 20}{a(a+2)(a-2)}$$ $$= \frac{6a^2 - 6a - 20}{a(a+2)(a-2)}$$	8. Perform the indicated operations and simplify, if possible: $$\frac{3y}{y^2 + y - 20} + \frac{2}{y + 5} - \frac{3}{y - 4}.$$ A. $\dfrac{-2y - 7}{(y+5)(y-4)}$ B. $\dfrac{-2y - 23}{(y+5)(y-4)}$ C. $\dfrac{2y - 7}{(y+5)(y-4)}$ D. $\dfrac{2y - 23}{(y+5)(y-4)}$

Objective [5.3a] Divide a polynomial by a monomial.

Brief Procedure	Example	Practice Exercise
Divide the coefficients and then divide the variables using the quotient rule for exponents.	Divide: $(6x^3 - 8x^2 + 15x) \div (3x)$. $$\frac{6x^3 - 8x^2 + 15x}{3x}$$ $$= \frac{6x^3}{3x} - \frac{8x^2}{3x} + \frac{15x}{3x}$$ $$= \frac{6}{3}x^{3-1} - \frac{8}{3}x^{2-1} + \frac{15}{3}$$ $$= 2x^2 - \frac{8}{3}x + 5$$	9. Divide: $(4y^2 - 5y + 12) \div 4$. A. $y^2 - 5y + 12$ B. $y^2 - \dfrac{5}{4}y + 12$ C. $y^2 - \dfrac{5}{4}y + 3$ D. $4y^2 - 5y + 3$

Objective [5.3b] Divide a polynomial by a divisor that is not a monomial, and if there is a remainder, express the result in two ways.

Brief Procedure	Example	Practice Exercise
Use long division by repeating the following procedure until the degree of the remainder is less than the degree of the divisor. 1. Divide, 2. Multiply, 3. Subtract, and 4. Bring down the next term. Express the remainder as the difference in the last step of the division preceded by "R" or in terms of a rational expression with the numerator being the difference in the last step of the division and the denominator being the divisor.	Divide $x^2 - 3x + 7$ by $x + 1$. $$\begin{array}{r} x - 4 \\ x+1\overline{\smash{\big)}\,x^2- 3x + 7} \\ \underline{x^2+\ x} \\ -4x + 7 \\ \underline{-4x - 4} \\ 11 \end{array}$$ The answer is $x - 4$, R 11, or $x - 4 + \dfrac{11}{x + 1}$.	10. Divide: $(x^2 - 8x + 5) \div (x - 2)$. A. $x - 10 + \dfrac{25}{x - 2}$ B. $x - 10 + \dfrac{-15}{x - 2}$ C. $x - 6 + \dfrac{-17}{x - 2}$ D. $x - 6 + \dfrac{-7}{x - 2}$

Objective [5.3c] Use synthetic division to divide a polynomial by a binomial of the type $x - a$.

Brief Procedure	Example	Practice Exercise
Synthetic division is a method of dividing a polynomial by a divisor of the form $x - a$ in which the variables are not written and we add instead of subtracting. If the dividend has missing terms, 0's must be written for their coefficients.	Use synthetic division to divide: $(x^3 - 3x + 1) \div (x + 2)$. There is no x^2-term, so we must write 0 for its coefficient. Note that $x+2 = x - (-2)$. $$\begin{array}{r|rrrr} -2 & 1 & 0 & -3 & 1 \\ & & -2 & 4 & -2 \\ \hline & 1 & -2 & 1 & -1 \end{array}$$ The answer is $x^2 - 2x + 1$, R -1, or $x^2 - 2x + 1 + \dfrac{-1}{x + 2}$.	11. Use synthetic division to divide: $(2x^3 - x^2 + 3x - 8) \div (x - 1)$. A. $2x^2 - 3x + 6 + \dfrac{-14}{x - 1}$ B. $2x^2 + x + 4 + \dfrac{-4}{x - 1}$ C. $2x^2 - x + 4 + \dfrac{4}{x - 1}$ D. $2x^2 + 2x + 5 + \dfrac{-1}{x - 1}$

Objective [5.4a] Simplify complex rational expressions.

Brief Procedure	Example	Practice Exercise
To simplify by multiplying by the LCM of all the denominators: 1. First, find the LCM of all the denominators of all the rational expressions occurring *within* both the numerator and the denominator of the (original) complex rational expression. 2. Then multiply by 1 using LCM/LCM. 3. If possible, simplify. To simplify by adding or subtracting in the numerator and in the denominator: 1. Add or subtract, as necessary, to get a single rational expression in the numerator. 2. Add or subtract, as necessary, to get a single rational expression in the denominator. 3. Divide the numerator by the denominator. 4. If possible, simplify.	Simplify: $\dfrac{1-\dfrac{1}{x}}{1-\dfrac{1}{x^2}}$. Using the first method described at the left, we first observe that the LCM of the denominators within the numerator and the denominator is x^2. We multiply by 1 using x^2/x^2. $\dfrac{1-\dfrac{1}{x}}{1-\dfrac{1}{x^2}} \cdot \dfrac{x^2}{x^2}$ $= \dfrac{\left(1-\dfrac{1}{x}\right)x^2}{\left(1-\dfrac{1}{x^2}\right)x^2}$ $= \dfrac{1\cdot x^2 - \dfrac{1}{x}\cdot x^2}{1\cdot x^2 - \dfrac{1}{x^2}\cdot x^2}$ $= \dfrac{x^2-x}{x^2-1}$ $= \dfrac{x(x-1)}{(x+1)(x-1)}$ $= \dfrac{x(x\!\!-\!\!1)}{(x+1)(x\!\!-\!\!1)}$ $= \dfrac{x}{x+1}$ (continued)	12. Simplify: $\dfrac{\dfrac{3}{y}+\dfrac{1}{y}}{y-\dfrac{y}{3}}$. A. $\dfrac{20}{9}$ B. $\dfrac{10}{9}$ C. $\dfrac{6}{y}$ D. $\dfrac{6}{y^2}$

Objective [5.4a] (continued)		
Brief Procedure	Example	Practice Exercise
	Using the second method, we first subtract in the numerator and in the denominator. $$\frac{1 - \dfrac{1}{x}}{1 - \dfrac{1}{x^2}}$$ $$= \frac{1 \cdot \dfrac{x}{x} - \dfrac{1}{x}}{1 \cdot \dfrac{x^2}{x^2} - \dfrac{1}{x^2}}$$ $$= \frac{\dfrac{x}{x} - \dfrac{1}{x}}{\dfrac{x^2}{x^2} - \dfrac{1}{x^2}}$$ $$= \frac{\dfrac{x-1}{x}}{\dfrac{x^2-1}{x^2}}$$ $$= \frac{x-1}{x} \cdot \frac{x^2}{x^2-1}$$ $$= \frac{(x-1)(x)(x)}{x(x+1)(x-1)}$$ $$= \frac{(x-1)(x)(x)}{x(x+1)(x-1)}$$ $$= \frac{x}{x+1}$$	

Objective [5.5a] Solve rational equations.

Brief Procedure	Example	Practice Exercise
First multiply on both sides of the equation by the LCM of all the denominators to clear fractions. Then solve the resulting equation. Since this equation might have solutions that are not solutions of the original equation, the possible solutions *must* be checked in the *original* equation.	Solve: $\dfrac{2x+1}{x-2} = \dfrac{x-1}{3x+2}$. The LCM of the denominators is $(x-2)(3x+2)$. We multiply by the LCM on both sides. $$\frac{2x+1}{x-2} = \frac{x-1}{3x+2}$$ $$(x-2)(3x+2) \cdot \frac{2x+1}{x-2} =$$ $$(x-2)(3x+2) \cdot \frac{x-1}{3x+2}$$ $$(3x+2)(2x+1) = (x-2)(x-1)$$ $$6x^2 + 7x + 2 = x^2 - 3x + 2$$ $$5x^2 + 10x = 0$$ $$5x(x+2) = 0$$ $$5x = 0 \ \ or \ \ x+2 = 0$$ $$x = 0 \ \ or \ \ \ \ \ x = -2$$ Both numbers check. The solutions are 0 and -2.	13. Solve: $x - \dfrac{8}{x} = 2$. A. -2 B. 4 C. $-2, 4$ D. $-2, 4, 8$

Objective [5.6a] Solve work problems and certain basic problems using rational equations.		
Brief Procedure	Example	Practice Exercise
Use the five-step problem solving process. Apply the work principle in the Translate step: Suppose $a =$ the time it takes A to do a job, $b =$ the time it takes B to do the same job, and $t =$ the time it takes them to do the job working together. Then $$\frac{t}{a} + \frac{t}{b} = 1, \text{ or}$$ $$\frac{1}{a} + \frac{1}{b} = \frac{1}{t}.$$	Todd can mow the lawn in 3 hr. It takes Steve 4 hr to do the same job. How long would it take them, working together, to mow the lawn? 1. *Familiarize.* Let $t =$ the time it takes Todd and Steve to mow the lawn, working together. 2. *Translate.* We substitute 3 for a and 4 for b in the work principle. $$\frac{t}{a} + \frac{t}{b} = 1$$ $$\frac{t}{3} + \frac{t}{4} = 1$$ 3. *Solve.* We solve the equation. $$\frac{t}{3} + \frac{t}{4} = 1, \text{LCM is } 12$$ $$12\left(\frac{t}{3} + \frac{t}{4}\right) = 12 \cdot 1$$ $$12 \cdot \frac{t}{3} + 12 \cdot \frac{t}{4} = 12$$ $$4t + 3t = 12$$ $$7t = 12$$ $$t = \frac{12}{7}$$ 4. *Check.* In 12/7 hr, Todd does $\frac{12/7}{3}$, or $\frac{4}{7}$ of the job and Steve does $\frac{12/7}{4}$, or $\frac{3}{7}$ of the job. Together they do $\frac{4}{7} + \frac{3}{7}$, or 1 entire job. The answer checks. 5. *State.* Is takes $\frac{12}{7}$ hr, or $1\frac{5}{7}$ hr, for Todd and Steve to mow the lawn together.	14. Libby can paint a room in 6 hr. It takes Amelia 8 hr to paint the same room. How long would it take them to paint the room, working together? A. $3\frac{3}{7}$ hr B. $5\frac{2}{7}$ hr C. $5\frac{5}{7}$ hr D. 7 hr

Objective [5.6b] Solve applied problems involving proportions.

Brief Procedure	Example	Practice Exercise
Use the five-step problem solving process.	One number is 3 more than another. The quotient of the larger number divided by the smaller is $\frac{3}{2}$. Find the numbers. 1. *Familiarize.* Let $x =$ the smaller number. Then $x + 3 =$ the larger number and the quotient of the larger divided by the smaller is $\frac{x+3}{x}$. 2. *Translate.* $\underbrace{\text{The quotient}}_{\dfrac{x+3}{x}}$ $\underset{=}{\text{is}}$ $\underset{\dfrac{3}{2}}{\dfrac{3}{2}}$. 3. *Solve.* We solve the equation. $$\frac{x+3}{x} = \frac{3}{2}$$ $$2x \cdot \frac{x+3}{x} = 2x \cdot \frac{3}{2}$$ $$2(x+3) = 3x$$ $$2x + 6 = 3x$$ $$6 = x$$ If $x = 6$, then $x + 3 = 6 + 3$, or 9. 4. *Check.* The larger number, 9, is 3 more than the smaller number, 6. Also $\frac{9}{6} = \frac{3}{2}$, so the numbers check. 5. *State.* The numbers are 6 and 9.	15. Jeremy can read 6 pages of his history textbook in 20 min. At this rate, how many pages can he read in 50 min? A. 13 B. 15 C. 18 D. 20

Objective [5.6c] Solve motion problems using rational equations.	
Brief Procedure	**Example**
Use the five-step problem solving process, applying the motion formula, $d = rt$, in the Translate step.	An airplane flies 630 mi with the wind in the same time that it takes to fly 495 mi against the wind. The speed of the plane in still air is 250 mph. Find the speed of the wind. 1. *Familiarize.* We first make a drawing. Let $w =$ the speed of the wind and $t =$ the time. Then we organize the information in a table. With wind $250 + w$ 630 mi 495 mi $250 - w$ Against wind <table><tr><td></td><td>Distance</td><td>Speed</td><td>Time</td></tr><tr><td>With wind</td><td>630</td><td>$250 + w$</td><td>t</td></tr><tr><td>Against wind</td><td>495</td><td>$250 - w$</td><td>t</td></tr></table> 2. *Translate.* Using $t = d/r$, each row of the table yields an equation. $$t = \frac{630}{250 + w} \text{ and } t = \frac{495}{250 - w}$$ 3. *Solve.* We substitute $\frac{495}{250 - w}$ for t in the first equation and solve. $$\frac{495}{250 - w} = \frac{630}{250 + w}$$ $$(250 - w)(250 + w) \cdot \frac{495}{250 - w} = (250 - w)(250 + w) \cdot \frac{630}{250 + w}$$ $$(250 + w)495 = (250 - w)630$$ $$123,750 + 495w = 157,500 - 630w$$ $$1125w = 33,750$$ $$w = 30$$ 4. *Check.* With the wind, the speed of the plane is $250 + 30$, or 280 mph. To travel 630 mi at this speed takes 630/280, or 2.25 hr. Against the wind, the speed of the plane is $250 - 30$, or 220 mph. To travel 495 mi at this speed takes 495/220, or 2.25 hr. Since the times are the same, the answer checks. 5. *State.* The speed of the wind is 30 mph
	Practice Exercise
	16. A passenger car travels 10 km/h faster than a delivery van. While the car travels 240 km, the van travels 200 km. Find their speeds. A. The speed of the car is 45 km/h. B. The speed of the car is 50 km/h. C. The speed of the car is 60 km/h. D. The speed of the car is 65 km/h.

Objective [5.7a] Solve a formula for a letter.

Brief Procedure	Example	Practice Exercise
Identify the letter and: 1. Multiply on both sides to clear fractions or decimals, if necessary. 2. Multiply to remove parentheses, if necessary. 3. Get all terms with the letter to be solved for on one side of the equation and all other terms on the other side using the addition principle. 4. Factor out the unknown, if necessary. 5. Solve for the letter in question, using the multiplication principle.	Solve $S = \frac{n}{2}(a+l)$ for l. $$S = \frac{n}{2}(a+l)$$ $$2S = n(a+l)$$ $$2S = an + ln$$ $$2S - an = ln$$ $$\frac{2S-an}{n} = l, \text{ or}$$ $$\frac{2S}{n} - a = l$$	17. Solve $f = \frac{kMm}{d^2}$ for M. A. $M = fd^2km$ B. $M = \frac{fkm}{d^2}$ C. $M = \frac{fd^2}{km}$ D. $M = \frac{f}{d^2km}$

Objective [5.8a] Find an equation of direct variation given a pair of values of the variables.

Brief Procedure	Example	Practice Exercise
An equation of direct variation has the form $y = kx$, where k is a positive constant. Substitute the given values in this equation to find k.	Find an equation of variation in which y varies directly as x and $y = 20$ when $x = 4$. We substitute to find k: $$y = kx$$ $$20 = k \cdot 4$$ $$5 = k$$ Then the equation of variation is $y = 5x$.	18. Find an equation of variation in which y varies directly as x and $y = 3$ when $x = 2$. A. $y = \frac{2}{3}x$ B. $y = \frac{3}{2}x$ C. $y = 5x$ D. $y = 6x$

Objective [5.8b] Solve applied problems involving direct variation.

Brief Procedure	Example	Practice Exercise
Find an equation of variation and then use that equation to find the desired information.	The interest I earned in 1 yr on a fixed principal varies directly as the interest rate r. An investment earns $56.25 at an interest rate of 3.75%. How much will the investment earn at a rate of 4.5%?	19. The amount of Melissa's paycheck P varies directly as the number H of hours worked. For working 16 hr, her pay is $132. Find her pay for 28 hr of work.
	First find an equation of variation.	A. $224
	$$I = kr$$	B. $231
	$$56.25 = k \cdot 0.0375$$	C. $242
	$$\frac{56.25}{0.0375} = k$$	D. $256
	$$1500 = k$$ The equation of variation is $I = 1500r$.	
	Now use the equation to find the interest earned when the interest rate is 4.5%.	
	$$I = 1500r$$ $$I = 1500(0.045)$$ $$I = 67.50$$	
	When the interest rate is 4.5%, the investment earns $67.50.	

Objective [5.8c] Find an equation of inverse variation given a pair of values of the variables.

Brief Procedure	Example	Practice Exercise
An equation of inverse variation is of the form $y = k/x$, where k is a positive constant. Substitute the given values in the equation to find k.	Find an equation of variation in which y varies inversely as x and $y = 10$ when $x = 0.5$.	20. Find an equation of variation in which y varies inversely as x and $y = 12$ when $x = 3$.
	We substitute to find k.	A. $y = \dfrac{1}{36x}$
	$$y = \frac{k}{x}$$	B. $y = \dfrac{1}{4x}$
	$$10 = \frac{k}{0.5}$$	C. $y = \dfrac{4}{x}$
	$$5 = k$$	D. $y = \dfrac{36}{x}$
	The equation of variation is $y = \dfrac{5}{x}$.	

Objective [5.8d] Solve applied problems involving inverse variation.

Brief Procedure	Example	Practice Exercise
Find an equation of variation and then use that equation to find the desired information.	The time t required to drive a fixed distance varies inversely as the speed r. It takes 4 hr at 60 mph to drive a fixed distance. How long would it take at 50 mph? First find an equation of variation. $$t = \frac{k}{r}$$ $$4 = \frac{k}{60}$$ $$240 = k$$ The equation is $t = \dfrac{240}{r}$. Now use the equation to find the time required to travel the fixed distance at 50 mph. $$t = \frac{240}{r}$$ $$t = \frac{240}{50}$$ $$t = 4.8$$ It would take 4.8 hr to travel the fixed distance at a speed of 50 mph.	21. It takes 4 days for 2 people to paint a house. How long will it take 3 people to do the job? A. 2 days B. $2\dfrac{2}{3}$ days C. 3 days D. $3\dfrac{1}{3}$ days

Objective [5.8e] Find an equation of other kinds of variation given values of the variables.

Brief Procedure	Example	Practice Exercise
y varies directly as the nth power of x if there is some positive constant k such that $y = kx^n$. y varies inversely as the nth power of x if there is some positive constant k such that $y = \dfrac{k}{x^n}$. y varies jointly as x and z if there is some positive constant k such that $y = kxz$.	Find an equation of variation in which y varies jointly as x and the square of z and inversely as w and $y = 15$ when $x = 2, z = 5,$ and $w = 10$. We substitute to find k. $$y = k \cdot \frac{xz^2}{w}$$ $$15 = k \cdot \frac{2 \cdot 5^2}{10}$$ $$15 = k \cdot \frac{50}{10}$$ $$15 = k \cdot 5$$ $$3 = k$$ Thus, $y = 3 \cdot \dfrac{xz^2}{w}$.	22. Find an equation of variation in which y varies directly as the square of x and $y = 20$ when $x = 2$. A. $y = \dfrac{1}{5}x^2$ B. $y = \dfrac{1}{4}x^2$ C. $y = 5x^2$ D. $y = 10x^2$

Objective [5.8f] Solve applied problems involving other kinds of variation.		
Brief Procedure	Example	Practice Exercise
Find an equation of variation and then use that equation to find the desired information.	The distance s that an object falls when dropped from some point above the ground varies directly as the square of the time t that it falls. If the object falls 44.1 m in 3 sec, how far will the object fall in 5 sec? First find an equation of variation. $$s = kt^2$$ $$44.1 = k \cdot 3^2$$ $$44.1 = k \cdot 9$$ $$4.9 = k$$ The equation is $s = 4.9t^2$. Now use the equation to find the distance the object will fall in 5 sec. $$s = 4.9(5)^2$$ $$s = 122.5$$ The object will fall 122.5 m in 5 sec.	23. The surface area of a cube varies directly as the square of the length of a side. If the surface area is 24 cm^2 when the length of a side is 2 cm, what is the surface area when the length of a side is 5 cm? A. 30 cm^2 B. 60 cm^2 C. 120 cm^2 D. 150 cm^2

Chapter 6 Review

Objective [6.1a] Find principal square roots and their opposites, approximate square roots, find outputs of square-root functions, graph square-root functions, and find the domains of square-root functions.

Brief Procedure	Example	Practice Exercises
The principal square root of a number n, denoted $\sqrt{n}$, is the positive square root of the number. The opposite of the principal square root of a number n is denoted $-\sqrt{n}$.	Find each of the following. a) $\sqrt{144}$ b) $-\sqrt{49}$ a) The number 144 has two square roots, 12 and -12. The notation $\sqrt{144}$ denotes the principal, or positive, square root so $\sqrt{144} = 12$. b) $\sqrt{49}$ represents the positive square root of 49, or 7, and $-\sqrt{49}$ represents the opposite of that number. Thus, $-\sqrt{49} = -7$.	1. Find $\sqrt{81}$. A. -81 B. 81 C. -9 D. 9
To approximate square roots, use a calculator with a square-root key. Round to the desired number of decimal places.	Use a calculator to approximate each of the following square roots to three decimal places. a) $\sqrt{17}$ b) $-\sqrt{104.2}$ a) Using a calculator with a 10-digit readout, we get $$\sqrt{17} \approx 4.123105626 \approx 4.123.$$ b) Using a calculator with a 10-digit readout, we get $$-\sqrt{104.2} \approx -10.20784012 \approx -10.208.$$	2. Use a calculator to approximate $-\sqrt{70}$ to three decimal places. A. -8.367 B. -8.366 C. 8.366 D. 8.367

Objective [6.1a] (continued)		
Brief Procedure	Example	Practice Exercises
To find an output of a square root function, substitute an input and carry out the resulting calculation. To graph a square-root function, find several input/output pairs, plot the corresponding points, and connect them with a smooth curve.	For $f(x) = 2\sqrt{x+3}$, find $f(-3)$, $f(1)$, and $f(3)$. Then graph the function. We substitute to find the function values. $f(-3) = 2\sqrt{-3+3} = 2\sqrt{0} = 2 \cdot 0 = 0$ $f(1) = 2\sqrt{1+3} = 2\sqrt{4} = 2 \cdot 2 = 4$ $f(3) = 2\sqrt{3+3} = 2\sqrt{6} \approx 4.899$ To graph the function we plot the points $(-3, 0)$, $(1, 4)$, and $(3, 4.899)$ and connect them with a smooth curve. 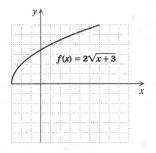	3. For $f(x) = \sqrt{2x-1}$, find $f(5)$. A. Not a real number B. 3 C. $\sqrt{8}$ D. $\sqrt{11}$
To find the domain of a square-root function $f(x)$, find the set of all x-values for which the radicand of the function is nonnegative.	Find the domain of $f(x) = \sqrt{3-x}$. We find the set of all x-values for which $3 - x \geq 0$. We solve as follows. $$3 - x \geq 0$$ $$3 \geq x$$ The domain of $f = \{x \mid x \leq 3\}$, or $(-\infty, 3]$.	4. Find the domain of $f(x) = \sqrt{2x-2}$. A. $\{x \mid x \leq 2\}$ B. $\{x \mid x \leq 1\}$ C. $\{x \mid x \geq -1\}$ D. $\{x \mid x \geq 1\}$

Objective [6.1b] Simplify radical expressions with perfect-square radicands.		
Brief Procedure	Example	Practice Exercise
For any real number a, $\sqrt{a^2} = \lvert a \rvert$. The principal (nonnegative) square root of a^2 is the absolute value of a.	Simplify each of the following. a) $\sqrt{(-8)^2}$ b) $\sqrt{36y^2}$ c) $\sqrt{x^2 - 4x + 4}$ a) $\sqrt{(-8)^2} = \lvert -8 \rvert = 8$ b) $\sqrt{36y^2} = \sqrt{(6y)^2} = \lvert 6y \rvert = \lvert 6 \rvert \cdot \lvert y \rvert = 6\lvert y \rvert$ c) $\sqrt{x^2 - 4x + 4} = \sqrt{(x-2)^2} = \lvert x - 2 \rvert$	5. Simplify $\sqrt{81n^2}$. A. $-9n$ B. $9n$ C. $9\lvert n \rvert$ D. $\lvert 9 \rvert \cdot n$

Objective [6.1c] Find cube roots, simplifying certain expressions, and find outputs of cube-root functions.

Brief Procedure	Example	Practice Exercises
The number c is the cube root of a if its third power is a - that is, if $c^3 = a$. The symbol $\sqrt[3]{a}$ represents the cube root of a. Every real number has exactly one cube root in the system of real numbers.	Find the following. a) $\sqrt[3]{27}$ b) $\sqrt[3]{-8}$ c) $\sqrt[3]{y^3}$ a) $\sqrt[3]{27} = 3$ because $3^3 = 3 \cdot 3 \cdot 3 = 27$. b) $\sqrt[3]{-8} = -2$ because $(-2)^3 = (-2)(-2)(-2) = -8$. c) $\sqrt[3]{y^3} = y$ because $y \cdot y \cdot y = y^3$.	6. Find $\sqrt[3]{-125}$. A. -5 B. -11 C. -25 D. 5
To find an output of a cube-root function, substitute an input and carry out the resulting calculation.	For $f(x) = \sqrt[3]{x-5}$, find $f(-4)$, $f(5)$, and $f(13)$. We substitute to find the function values. a) $f(-4) = \sqrt[3]{-4-5} = \sqrt[3]{-9} \approx -2.080$ b) $f(5) = \sqrt[3]{5-5} = \sqrt[3]{0} = 0$ c) $f(13) = \sqrt[3]{13-5} = \sqrt[3]{8} = 2$	7. For $g(x) = \sqrt[3]{x+3}$, find $g(-4)$. A. -1 B. 1 C. $\sqrt[3]{7}$ D. Not a real number

Objective [6.1d] Simplify expressions involving odd and even roots.

Brief Procedure	Example	Practice Exercise
For any real number a: a) $\sqrt[k]{a^k} = \|a\|$ when k is an even natural number. We use absolute value when k is even unless a is nonnegative. b) $\sqrt[k]{a^k} = a$ when k is an odd natural number greater than 1. We do not use absolute value when k is odd.	FInd the following. a) $\sqrt[5]{-32x^5}$ b) $\sqrt[4]{81a^4}$ a) Absolute value signs are not needed when we find odd roots. $\sqrt[5]{-32x^5} = \sqrt[5]{(-2x)^5} = -2x$ b) We need to use absolute value signs because a variable is involved. $\sqrt[4]{81a^4} = \sqrt[4]{(3a)^4} = \|3a\| = \|3\| \cdot \|a\| = 3\|a\|$	8. Find $\sqrt[5]{-y^5}$. A. $\|y\|$ B. y C. $-y$ D. $5y$

Objective [6.2a] Write expressions with or without rational exponents, and simplify, if possible.

Brief Procedure	Example	Practice Exercise
For any natural numbers m and n ($n \neq 1$) and any nonnegative real number a, $a^{m/n}$ means $\sqrt[n]{a^m}$, or $(\sqrt[n]{a})^m$. When $m = 1$, we have $a^{1/n} = \sqrt[n]{a}$.	a) Rewrite $x^{1/6}$ without a rational exponent. b) Rewrite $(\sqrt[3]{4xy^2})^4$ with a rational exponent. a) Recall that $a^{1/n}$ means $\sqrt[n]{a}$. Then $x^{1/6} = \sqrt[6]{x}$. b) Recall that $(\sqrt[n]{a})^m$ means $a^{m/n}$. Then $(\sqrt[3]{4xy^2})^4 = (4xy^2)^{4/3}$.	9. Rewrite $x^{5/6}$ without a rational exponent. A. $\sqrt{x^{5/6}}$ B. $\sqrt[5]{x^6}$ C. $\sqrt[6]{x^5}$ D. $\sqrt[6]{x}$

Objective [6.2b] Write expressions without negative exponents, and simplify, if possible.

Brief Procedure	Example	Practice Exercise
For any rational number m/n and any positive real number a, $a^{-m/n}$ means $\dfrac{1}{a^{m/n}}$. That is, $a^{m/n}$ and $a^{-m/n}$ are reciprocals.	Rewrite with positive exponents and simplify, if possible. a) $8^{-2/3}$ b) $\left(\dfrac{2x}{y}\right)^{-3/2}$ a) Recall that $a^{-m/n}$ means $\dfrac{1}{a^{m/n}}$. Then $8^{-2/3} = \dfrac{1}{8^{2/3}} = \dfrac{1}{(\sqrt[3]{8})^2} = \dfrac{1}{2^2} = \dfrac{1}{4}$. b) Since $\left(\dfrac{a}{b}\right)^{-n} = \left(\dfrac{b}{a}\right)^{n}$, then $\left(\dfrac{2x}{y}\right)^{-3/2} = \left(\dfrac{y}{2x}\right)^{3/2}$.	10. Rewrite $4^{-5/2}$ with a positive exponent and simplify, if possible. A. $\dfrac{1}{32}$ B. $-\dfrac{1}{32}$ C. 32 D. -32

Objective [6.2c] Use the laws of exponents with rational exponents.

Brief Procedure	Example	Practice Exercise
The laws that hold for integer exponents hold for rational-number exponents as well. 1. $a^m \cdot a^n = a^{m+n}$ 2. $\dfrac{a^m}{a^n} = a^{m-n}$ 3. $(a^m)^n = a^{m \cdot n}$ 4. $(ab)^m = a^m b^m$ 5. $\left(\dfrac{a}{b}\right)^n = \dfrac{a^n}{b^n}$	Use the laws of exponents to simplify. a) $2^{1/4} \cdot 2^{1/2}$ b) $\dfrac{y^{1/3}}{y^{5/3}}$ c) $(x^{3/5})^{5/6}$ d) $(a^{1/4}b^{-2/3})^{1/7}$ e) $\left(\dfrac{w}{z^{1/3}}\right)^{2/5}$ a) We add the exponents. $2^{1/4} \cdot 2^{1/2} = 2^{1/4+1/2} = 2^{1/4+2/4} = 2^{3/4}$ b) We subtract the exponents. $\dfrac{y^{1/3}}{y^{5/3}} = y^{1/3-5/3} = y^{-4/3} = \dfrac{1}{y^{4/3}}$ c) We multiply exponents. $(x^{3/5})^{5/6} = x^{3/5 \cdot 5/6} = x^{15/30} = x^{1/2}$ d) We raise each factor to the 1/7 power and then multiply exponents. $(a^{1/4}b^{-2/3})^{1/7} = (a^{1/4})^{1/7}(b^{-2/3})^{1/7} = a^{1/28}b^{-2/21} = \dfrac{a^{1/28}}{b^{2/21}}$ e) We raise both the numerator and the denominator to the 2/5 power. $\left(\dfrac{w}{z^{1/3}}\right)^{2/5} = \dfrac{w^{2/5}}{(z^{1/3})^{2/5}} = \dfrac{w^{2/5}}{z^{2/15}}$	11. Use the laws of exponents to simplify $(x^{3/2}y^{1/5})^{5/6}$. A. $x^{5/4}y^{1/5}$ B. $x^{5/4}y^{1/6}$ C. $x^{15/2}y^{1/5}$ D. $x^{3/2}y^{1/6}$

Objective [6.2d] Use rational exponents to simplify radical expressions.

Brief Procedure	Example	Practice Exercise
1. Convert radical expressions to exponential expressions. 2. Use arithmetic and the laws of exponents to simplify. 3. Convert back to radical notation when appropriate. (This procedure works only when all expressions under radicals are nonnegative since rational exponents are not defined otherwise. No absolute-value signs will be needed.)	a) Use rational exponents to simplify $\sqrt[6]{a^4b^2}$. b) Use rational exponents to write a single radical expression for $\sqrt{3}\sqrt[3]{4}$. $a)$ $\sqrt[6]{a^4b^2} = (a^4b^2)^{1/6}$ $\qquad = a^{4/6}b^{2/6}$ $\qquad = a^{2/3}b^{1/3}$ $\qquad = (a^2b)^{1/3}$ $\qquad = \sqrt[3]{a^2b}$ $b)$ $\sqrt{3}\sqrt[3]{4} = 3^{1/2} \cdot 4^{1/3}$ $\qquad = 3^{3/6} \cdot 4^{2/6}$ $\qquad = (3^3 \cdot 4^2)^{1/6}$ $\qquad = \sqrt[6]{3^3 \cdot 4^2}$ $\qquad = \sqrt[6]{432}$	12. Use rational exponents to simplify $\sqrt[8]{x^2y^6}$. A. $\sqrt[6]{xy^4}$ B. $\sqrt[8]{xy^3}$ C. $\sqrt[4]{xy^6}$ D. $\sqrt[4]{xy^3}$

Objective [6.3a] Multiply and simplify radical expressions.

Brief Procedure	Example	Practice Exercise
For any nonnegative real numbers a and b and any index k, $$\sqrt[k]{a} \cdot \sqrt[k]{b} = \sqrt[k]{a \cdot b}.$$ (To multiply, multiply the radicands.) To simplify a product we use this rule in reverse, taking the root of each factor separately. A radical expression with index k is simplified when its radicand has no factors that are perfect kth powers.	Multiply and simplify. Assume that all expressions under radicals represent nonnegative numbers. a) $\sqrt{6}\sqrt{15}$ b) $\sqrt[3]{9xy}\sqrt[3]{6y^2}$ a) $\sqrt{6}\sqrt{15} = \sqrt{6 \cdot 15} = \sqrt{2 \cdot 3 \cdot 3 \cdot 5} = 3\sqrt{10}$ b) $\sqrt[3]{9xy}\sqrt[3]{6y^2} = \sqrt[3]{9xy \cdot 6y^2}$ $\qquad = \sqrt[3]{54xy^3}$ $\qquad = \sqrt[3]{27y^3 \cdot 2x}$ $\qquad = \sqrt[3]{27y^3}\sqrt[3]{2x}$ $\qquad = 3y\sqrt[3]{2x}$	13. Multiply and simplify. Assume that all expressions under radicals represent nonnegative numbers. $$\sqrt{10n}\sqrt{15n}$$ A. $10n\sqrt{5}$ B. $5\sqrt{6n}$ C. $5n$ D. $5n\sqrt{6}$

Objective [6.3b] Divide and simplify radical expressions.

Brief Procedure	Example	Practice Exercise
For any nonnegative number a, any positive number b, and any index k, $$\frac{\sqrt[k]{a}}{\sqrt[k]{b}} = \sqrt[k]{\frac{a}{b}}.$$ (To divide, divide the radicands.) We can reverse this rule to simplify a quotient, taking the roots of the numerator and of the denominator separately.	a) Divide and simplify. Assume that all expressions under radicals represent positive numbers. $$\frac{\sqrt{40x^5}}{\sqrt{10x}}$$ b) Simplify: $\sqrt[3]{\dfrac{8y^4}{27x^3}}$. a) $\dfrac{\sqrt{40x^5}}{\sqrt{10x}} = \sqrt{\dfrac{40x^5}{10x}} = \sqrt{4x^4} = 2x^2$ b) $\sqrt[3]{\dfrac{8y^4}{27x^3}} = \dfrac{\sqrt[3]{8y^4}}{\sqrt[3]{27x^3}} = \dfrac{\sqrt[3]{8y^3 \cdot y}}{\sqrt[3]{27x^3}} =$ $\dfrac{\sqrt[3]{8y^3}\,\sqrt[3]{y}}{\sqrt[3]{27x^3}} = \dfrac{2y\,\sqrt[3]{y}}{3x}$	14. Divide and simplify. Assume that all expressions under radicals represent positive numbers. $$\frac{\sqrt{28x}}{\sqrt{7}}$$ A. $2x$ B. $4x$ C. $2\sqrt{x}$ D. $4\sqrt{x}$

Objective [6.4a] Add or subtract with radical notation and simplify.

Brief Procedure	Example	Practice Exercise
Use the distributive laws to collect like radicals (terms with the same radicand). Sometimes radical terms must be simplified before like radicals can be identified.	Add: $5\sqrt{2} + 4\sqrt{18}$. $\begin{aligned}5\sqrt{2} + 4\sqrt{18} &= 5\sqrt{2} + 4\sqrt{9 \cdot 2} \\ &= 5\sqrt{2} + 4\sqrt{9}\sqrt{2} \\ &= 5\sqrt{2} + 4 \cdot 3\sqrt{2} \\ &= 5\sqrt{2} + 12\sqrt{2} \\ &= (5 + 12)\sqrt{2} \\ &= 17\sqrt{2}\end{aligned}$	15. Subtract: $6\sqrt{3} - \sqrt{48}$ A. $2\sqrt{3}$ B. $4\sqrt{3}$ C. $8\sqrt{3}$ D. $10\sqrt{3}$

Objective [6.4b] Multiply expressions involving radicals in which some factors contain more than one term.

Brief Procedure	Example	Practice Exercise
Use the procedures for multiplying polynomials.	Multiply: $(2 - \sqrt{5})(3 + 4\sqrt{5})$. We use FOIL. $\begin{aligned}&(2 - \sqrt{5})(3 + 4\sqrt{5}) \\ &= 2 \cdot 3 + 2 \cdot 4\sqrt{5} - \sqrt{5} \cdot 3 - \sqrt{5} \cdot 4\sqrt{5} \\ &= 6 + 8\sqrt{5} - 3\sqrt{5} - 4 \cdot 5 \\ &= 6 + 8\sqrt{5} - 3\sqrt{5} - 20 \\ &= -14 + 5\sqrt{5}\end{aligned}$	16. Multiply: $(\sqrt{a} - 7)^2$. A. $a - 49$ B. $a^2 - 49$ C. $a - 14\sqrt{a} + 49$ D. $a^2 - 14\sqrt{a} + 49$

Objective [6.5a] Rationalize the denominator of a radical expression having one term in the denominator.

Brief Procedure	Example	Practice Exercise
Multiply by 1 so that the denominator will be a perfect square.	Rationalize the denominator. a) $\sqrt{\dfrac{5}{6}}$ b) $\dfrac{\sqrt{x}}{\sqrt{3}}$ a) We multiply by 1, using $\sqrt{6}/\sqrt{6}$ for 1. $$\sqrt{\dfrac{5}{6}} = \dfrac{\sqrt{5}}{\sqrt{6}}$$ $$= \dfrac{\sqrt{5}}{\sqrt{6}} \cdot \dfrac{\sqrt{6}}{\sqrt{6}}$$ $$= \dfrac{\sqrt{30}}{\sqrt{36}}$$ $$= \dfrac{\sqrt{30}}{6}$$ b) We multiply by 1, using $\sqrt{3}/\sqrt{3}$ for 1. $$\dfrac{\sqrt{x}}{\sqrt{3}} = \dfrac{\sqrt{x}}{\sqrt{3}} \cdot \dfrac{\sqrt{3}}{\sqrt{3}}$$ $$= \dfrac{\sqrt{3x}}{\sqrt{9}} = \dfrac{\sqrt{3x}}{3}$$	17. Rationalize the denominator: $$\dfrac{\sqrt{5}}{\sqrt{11}}.$$ A. $\dfrac{\sqrt{5}}{11}$ B. $\dfrac{\sqrt{55}}{11}$ C. $\dfrac{5}{11}$ D. $\dfrac{5}{\sqrt{11}}$

Objective [6.5b] Rationalize the denominator of a radical expression having two terms in the denominator.

Brief Procedure	Example	Practice Exercise
Multiply by 1 using the conjugate of the denominator for the numerator and denominator of the expression for 1. (Some examples of conjugates are $\sqrt{a}+\sqrt{b}$ and $\sqrt{a}-\sqrt{b}$, $c+\sqrt{d}$ and $c-\sqrt{d}$, and $\sqrt{m}-n$ and $\sqrt{m}+n$.)	Rationalize the denominator: $$\dfrac{3-\sqrt{5}}{1+\sqrt{6}}.$$ $$\dfrac{3-\sqrt{5}}{1+\sqrt{6}}$$ $$= \dfrac{3-\sqrt{5}}{1+\sqrt{6}} \cdot \dfrac{1-\sqrt{6}}{1-\sqrt{6}}$$ $$= \dfrac{(3-\sqrt{5})(1-\sqrt{6})}{(1+\sqrt{6})(1-\sqrt{6})}$$ $$= \dfrac{3-3\sqrt{6}-\sqrt{5}+\sqrt{5}\sqrt{6}}{1-(\sqrt{6})^2}$$ $$= \dfrac{3-3\sqrt{6}-\sqrt{5}+\sqrt{30}}{1-6}$$ $$= \dfrac{3-3\sqrt{6}-\sqrt{5}+\sqrt{30}}{-5}, \text{ or}$$ $$-\dfrac{3-3\sqrt{6}-\sqrt{5}+\sqrt{30}}{5}$$	18. Rationalize the denominator: $$\dfrac{3}{1-\sqrt{x}}.$$ A. $\dfrac{3}{1+\sqrt{x}}$ B. $\dfrac{3+3\sqrt{x}}{1-x}$ C. $\dfrac{3}{1-x}$ D. $\dfrac{3}{1+x}$

Objective [6.6a] Solve radical equations with one radical term.		
Brief Procedure	Example	Practice Exercise
First isolate the radical term on one side of the equation. Then use the principle of powers: For any natural number n, if an equation $a = b$ is true, then $a^n = b^n$ is true. The principle of powers does not always give an equivalent equation, so the possible solutions must be checked in the original equation.	Solve: $x = 3 + \sqrt{x-1}$. First we subtract 3 on both sides to isolate the radical. $$x = 3 + \sqrt{x-1}$$ $$x - 3 = \sqrt{x-1}$$ $$(x-3)^2 = (\sqrt{x-1})^2$$ $$x^2 - 6x + 9 = x - 1$$ $$x^2 - 7x + 10 = 0$$ $$(x-2)(x-5) = 0$$ $$x - 2 = 0 \ \ or \ \ x - 5 = 0$$ $$x = 2 \ \ or \ \ \ \ x = 5$$ We check each possible solution. Check: For 2: $\dfrac{x = 3 + \sqrt{x-1}}{2 \ ? \ 3 + \sqrt{2-1}}$ $3 + \sqrt{1}$ $3 + 1$ 4 FALSE For 5: $\dfrac{x = 3 + \sqrt{x-1}}{5 \ \vert \ 3 + \sqrt{5-1}}$ $3 + \sqrt{4}$ $3 + 2$ 5 TRUE The number 5 checks, but 2 does not. Thus, the solution is 5.	19. Solve: $\sqrt{3x+7} = \sqrt{4x+1}$. A. 6 B. 8 C. 6, 8 D. No solution

Objective [6.6b] Solve radical equations with two radical terms.

Brief Procedure	Example	Practice Exercise
1. Isolate one of the radical terms. 2. Use the principle of powers. 3. If a radical term remains, perform steps (1) and (2) again. 4. Solve the equation. 5. Check the possible solutions.	Solve: $1 = \sqrt{x+9} - \sqrt{x}$. $$1 = \sqrt{x+9} - \sqrt{x}$$ $$\sqrt{x} + 1 = \sqrt{x+9}$$ $$(\sqrt{x}+1)^2 = (\sqrt{x+9})^2$$ $$x + 2\sqrt{x} + 1 = x + 9$$ $$2\sqrt{x} = 8$$ $$\sqrt{x} = 4$$ $$(\sqrt{x})^2 = 4^2$$ $$x = 16$$ The number 16 checks. It is the solution.	20. Solve: $\sqrt{x+3} - \sqrt{x-2} = 1$. A. 1 B. 4 C. 6 D. No solution

Objective [6.6c] Solve applied problems involving radical equations.

Brief Procedure	Example	Practice Exercise
Substitute in a formula and then solve the resulting radical equation.	At a height of h meters, a person can see V kilometers to the horizon, where $V = 3.5\sqrt{h}$. Martin can see 53.2 km to the horizon from the top of a cliff. What is the altitude of Martin's eyes? We substitute 53.2 for V in the equation $V = 3.5\sqrt{h}$ and solve for h. $$53.2 = 3.5\sqrt{h}$$ $$\frac{53.2}{3.5} = \sqrt{h}$$ $$15.2 = \sqrt{h}$$ $$(15.2)^2 = (\sqrt{h})^2$$ $$231.04 = h$$ The altitude of Martin's eyes is about 231 m.	21. A passenger can see 301 km to the horizon through an airplane window. What is the altitude of the passenger's eyes? A. 1053.5 m B. 3529 m C. 5226.4 m D. 7396 m

Objective [6.7a] Solve applied problems involving the Pythagorean theorem and powers and roots.		
Brief Procedure	Example	Practice Exercise
Use the Pythagorean theorem, $a^2 + b^2 = c^2$, where a and b are the lengths of the legs of a right triangle and c is the length of the hypotenuse.	Find the length of a diagonal of a square whose sides are 8 yd long. We first make a drawing. We label the diagonal d. We know that $8^2 + 8^2 = d^2$. We solve this equation. $$8^2 + 8^2 = d^2$$ $$64 + 64 = d^2$$ $$128 = d^2$$ $$\sqrt{128} = d$$ $$11.314 \approx d$$ The length of a diagonal is $\sqrt{128} \approx 11.314$ yd.	22. How long is a guy wire reaching from the top of a 10-ft pole to a point on the ground 7 ft from the pole? A. About 7.141 ft B. About 10.049 ft C. About 12.207 ft D. About 15.811 ft

Objective [6.8a] Express imaginary numbers as bi, where b is a nonzero real number, and complex numbers as $a + bi$, where a and b are real numbers.		
Brief Procedure	Example	Practice Exercise
The number i is defined to be $\sqrt{-1}$. Use this to simplify the square roots of negative numbers, writing them in the form bi.	Express in terms of i. a) $\sqrt{-5}$ b) $\sqrt{-25}$ c) $-\sqrt{-32}$ a) $\sqrt{-5} = \sqrt{-1 \cdot 5} = \sqrt{-1} \cdot \sqrt{5} = i\sqrt{5}$, or $\sqrt{5}i$ b) $\sqrt{-25} = \sqrt{-1 \cdot 25} = \sqrt{-1} \cdot \sqrt{25} = i \cdot 5 = 5i$ c) $-\sqrt{-32} = -\sqrt{-1 \cdot 32} = -\sqrt{-1} \cdot \sqrt{32} = -i \cdot 4\sqrt{2} = -4\sqrt{2}i$	23. Express $\sqrt{-8}$ in terms of i. A. $-4\sqrt{2}i$ B. $-2\sqrt{2}i$ C. $2\sqrt{2}i$ D. $4\sqrt{2}i$

Objective [6.8b] Add and subtract complex numbers.		
Brief Procedure	Example	Practice Exercise
Add and subtract complex numbers as we do binomials with real-number coefficients by collecting like terms.	Subtract: $(5-4i)-(2-i)$. $(5-4i)-(2-i)$ $= (5-2)+[-4-(-1)]i$ $= 3-3i$	24. Add: $(3+7i)+(2-5i)$. A. $1+12i$ B. $5+12i$ C. $3+2i$ D. $5+2i$

Objective [6.8c] Multiply complex numbers.		
Brief Procedure	Example	Practice Exercise
We multiply in much the same way we multiply real numbers and polynomials. Keep in mind that $\sqrt{a}\sqrt{b} \neq \sqrt{ab}$ when a and b are negative numbers. In this situation, $\sqrt{a}$ and $\sqrt{b}$ must be written in terms of i before the multiplication is carried out.	Multiply. a) $\sqrt{-4}\sqrt{-25}$ b) $(2-3i)(1+4i)$ a) We express each number in terms of i first. $\sqrt{-4}\sqrt{-25} = \sqrt{-1}\cdot\sqrt{4}\cdot\sqrt{-1}\cdot\sqrt{25}$ $= i\cdot 2\cdot i\cdot 5$ $= i^2\cdot 10$ $= -1\cdot 10$ $= -10$ b) We use FOIL. $(2-3i)(1+4i)$ $= 2+8i-3i-12i^2$ $= 2+8i-3i-12(-1)$ $= 2+8i-3i+12$ $= 14+5i$	25. Multiply: $(3+2i)^2$. A. $5+12i$ B. $13+12i$ C. $5+6i$ D. $13+6i$

Objective [6.8d] Write expressions involving powers of i in the form $a+bi$.		
Brief Procedure	Example	Practice Exercise
Express the given power in terms of i^2 and then simplify.	Simplify. a) i^{20} b) i^{38} c) i^{27} a) $i^{20} = (i^2)^{10} = (-1)^{10} = 1$ b) $i^{38} = (i^2)^{19} = (-1)^{19} = -1$ c) $i^{27} = i^{26}\cdot i = (i^2)^{13}\cdot i = (-1)^{13}\cdot i = -1\cdot i = -i$	26. Simplify i^{45}. A. $-i$ B. i C. -1 D. 1

Objective [6.8e] Find conjugates of complex numbers and divide complex numbers.

Brief Procedure	Example	Practice Exercise
The conjugate of a complex number $a+bi$ is $a-bi$, and the conjugate of $a - bi$ is $a + bi$. To divide complex numbers, multiply by 1 using the conjugate of the divisor, or the denominator, in the symbol for 1.	Divide and simplify to the form $a+bi$: $\dfrac{5-i}{4+3i}$. The conjugate of the denominator is $4 - 3i$, so we multiply by 1 using $\dfrac{4-3i}{4-3i}$. $\dfrac{5-i}{4+3i}$ $= \dfrac{5-i}{4+3i} \cdot \dfrac{4-3i}{4-3i}$ $= \dfrac{20 - 15i - 4i + 3i^2}{16 - 9i^2}$ $= \dfrac{20 - 19i + 3(-1)}{16 - 9(-1)}$ $= \dfrac{20 - 19i - 3}{16 + 9}$ $= \dfrac{17 - 19i}{25}$ $= \dfrac{17}{25} - \dfrac{19}{25}i$	27. Divide and simplify to the form $a + bi$: $\dfrac{6 + 5i}{3 - i}$. A. $\dfrac{23}{8} + \dfrac{9}{8}i$ B. $\dfrac{23}{10} + \dfrac{9}{10}i$ C. $\dfrac{13}{8} + \dfrac{21}{8}i$ D. $\dfrac{13}{10} + \dfrac{21}{10}i$

Objective [6.8f] Determine whether a given complex number is a solution of an equation.

Brief Procedure	Example	Practice Exercise
Substitute the complex number in the equation and determine whether the result is a true equation.	Determine whether $-1 - 2i$ is a solution of the equation $x^2 + 2x + 5 = 0$. We substitute $-1 - 2i$ for x in the equation. $x^2 + 2x + 5 = 0$ $(-1 - 2i)^2 + 2(-1 - 2i) + 5 \; ? \; 0$ $1 + 4i + 4i^2 - 2 - 4i + 5 \mid 0$ $1 + 4i - 4 - 2 - 4i + 5$ $(1 - 4 - 2 + 5) + (4i - 4i)$ $0 + 0i$ $0 \mid 0$ TRUE We have a true equation, so $-1 - 2i$ is a solution.	28. Determine whether $3i$ is a solution of the equation $x^2 + 9 = 0$. A. Yes B. No

Chapter 7 Review

Objective [7.1a] Solve quadratic equations using the principle of square roots and find the x-intercepts of the graph of a related function.

Brief Procedure	Example	Practice Exercises
The equation $x^2 = d$ has two real-number solutions when $d > 0$. The solutions are $\sqrt{d}$ and $-\sqrt{d}$. The equation $x^2 = 0$ has 0 as its only solution. The equation $x^2 = d$ has two imaginary-number solutions when $d < 0$.	Solve: $3x^2 = 15$. $$3x^2 = 15$$ $$x^2 = 5$$ $$x = \sqrt{5} \text{ or } x = -\sqrt{5}$$ The solutions are $\sqrt{5}$ and $-\sqrt{5}$.	1. Solve: $3x^2 - 2 = 0$. A. $\sqrt{2}, -\sqrt{2}$ B. $\sqrt{3}, -\sqrt{3}$ C. $\dfrac{\sqrt{6}}{3}, -\dfrac{\sqrt{6}}{3}$ D. $\dfrac{\sqrt{6}}{2}, -\dfrac{\sqrt{6}}{2}$
The solutions of a quadratic equation are the first coordinates of the x-intercepts of the related function.	a) Solve: $x^2 - 2x + 1 = 5$. b) Find the x-intercepts of $f(x) = (x-1)^2 - 5$. a) $x^2 - 2x + 1 = 5$ $\quad (x-1)^2 = 5$ $x - 1 = \sqrt{5} \quad$ or $\quad x - 1 = -\sqrt{5}$ $\quad x = 1 + \sqrt{5}$ or $\quad x = 1 - \sqrt{5}$ The solutions are $1 + \sqrt{5}$ and $1 - \sqrt{5}$. b) The x-intercepts of $f(x) = (x-1)^2 - 5$ are $(1 - \sqrt{5}, 0)$ and $(1 + \sqrt{5}, 0)$.	2. Find the x-intercepts of $f(x) = (x+3)^2 - 7$. One intercept is A. $(-7 + \sqrt{3}, 0)$ B. $(7 - \sqrt{3}, 0)$ C. $(-3 - \sqrt{7}, 0)$ D. $(3 + \sqrt{7}, 0)$

Objective [7.1b] Solve quadratic equations by completing the square.

Brief Procedure	Example	Practice Exercise
1. If $a \neq 1$, multiply by $1/a$ so that the x^2-coefficient is 1. 2. If the x^2-coefficient is 1, add so that the equation is in the form $x^2 + bx = -c$, or $x^2 + \dfrac{b}{a}x = -\dfrac{c}{a}$ if step (1) has been applied. 3. Take half of the x-coefficient and square it. Add the result on both sides of the equation. 4. Express the side with the variables as the square of a binomial. 5. Use the principle of square roots and complete the solution.	Solve: $2x^2 + 2x - 3 = 0$ by completing the square. First, we multiply by $\dfrac{1}{2}$ on both sides of the equation to make the x^2-coefficient 1. $$2x^2 + 2x - 3 = 0$$ $$\tfrac{1}{2}(2x^2 + 2x - 3) = \tfrac{1}{2} \cdot 0$$ $$x^2 + x - \tfrac{3}{2} = 0$$ $$x^2 + x \quad\;\; = \tfrac{3}{2}$$ Now we add $\left(\dfrac{b}{2}\right)^2$, or $\left(\dfrac{1}{2}\right)^2$, or $\dfrac{1}{4}$ on both sides. $$x^2 + x + \tfrac{1}{4} = \tfrac{3}{2} + \tfrac{1}{4}$$ $$\left(x + \tfrac{1}{2}\right)^2 = \tfrac{7}{4}$$ $$x + \tfrac{1}{2} = \tfrac{\sqrt{7}}{2} \; or \; x + \tfrac{1}{2} = -\tfrac{\sqrt{7}}{2}$$ $$x = -\tfrac{1}{2} + \tfrac{\sqrt{7}}{2} \; or \; x = -\tfrac{1}{2} - \tfrac{\sqrt{7}}{2}$$ The solutions are $\dfrac{-1 \pm \sqrt{7}}{2}$.	3. Solve: $x^2 + 2x - 5 = 0$. A. $1, -3$ B. $-1 \pm \sqrt{5}$ C. $-1 \pm \sqrt{6}$ D. $-1 \pm \sqrt{7}$

Objective [7.1c] Solve applied problems using quadratic equations.		
Brief Procedure	Example	Practice Exercise
Use the principle of square roots to solve the appropriate equation.	The function $s(t) = 16t^2$ is used to approximate the distance s, in feet, that an object falls freely from rest in t seconds. An object is dropped from the top of a 1214 ft high building. How long will it take the object to reach the ground? We substitute 1214 for $s(t)$ and solve for t. $$1214 = 16t^2$$ $$\frac{1214}{16} = t^2$$ $$75.875 = t^2$$ $$\sqrt{75.875} = t$$ $$8.7 \approx t$$ We took the positive square root since time cannot be negative in this application. It would take the object about 8.7 sec to reach the ground.	4. The Chrysler Building in New York is 1046 ft tall. How long would it take an object to fall to the ground from the top? A. About 7.9 sec B. About 8.1 sec C. About 8.2 sec D. About 8.5 sec

Objective [7.2a] Solve quadratic equations using the quadratic formula, and approximate solutions using a calculator.

Brief Procedure	Example	Practice Exercise
The solutions of the equation $ax^2 + bx + c = 0$ are given by the formula $$x = \frac{-b \pm \sqrt{b^2 - 4ac}}{2a}.$$ We can use a calculator to find the approximate value of solutions found using the quadratic formula.	Solve $x^2 + 4x = 3$. Give the exact solution and approximate the solution to three decimal places. First we find standard form and determine a, b, and c. $$x^2 + 4x - 3 = 0$$ $$a = 1, b = 4, c = -3$$ Then we use the quadratic formula. $$x = \frac{-b \pm \sqrt{b^2 - 4ac}}{2a}$$ $$x = \frac{-4 \pm \sqrt{4^2 - 4 \cdot 1 \cdot (-3)}}{2 \cdot 1}$$ $$x = \frac{-4 \pm \sqrt{16 + 12}}{2} = \frac{-4 \pm \sqrt{28}}{2}$$ $$x = \frac{-4 \pm \sqrt{4 \cdot 7}}{2} = \frac{-4 \pm \sqrt{4}\sqrt{7}}{2}$$ $$x = \frac{-4 \pm 2\sqrt{7}}{2} = \frac{2(-2 \pm \sqrt{7})}{2 \cdot 1}$$ $$x = \frac{2}{2} \cdot \frac{-2 \pm \sqrt{7}}{1} = -2 \pm \sqrt{7}$$ The exact solutions are $-2 + \sqrt{7}$ and $-2 - \sqrt{7}$, or $-2 \pm \sqrt{7}$. Using a calculator and rounding to the nearest tenth, we have $$-2 + \sqrt{7} \approx 0.6457513111 \approx 0.6$$ and $$-2 - \sqrt{7} \approx -4.645751311 \approx -4.6.$$ The approximate solutions are 0.6 and -4.6.	5. Solve $2x^2 - 3x - 7 = 0$ using the quadratic formula. A. $\dfrac{-3 \pm \sqrt{65}}{4}$ B. $\dfrac{-3 \pm \sqrt{65}}{2}$ C. $\dfrac{3 \pm \sqrt{65}}{4}$ D. $\dfrac{3 \pm \sqrt{65}}{2}$

Objective [7.3a] Solve applied problems involving quadratic equations.		
Brief Procedure	Example	Practice Exercise
Use the five-step problem solving process.	The width of a rectangle is 5 m less than the length. The area is 66 m². Find the length and the width. 1. *Familiarize.* We first make a drawing. Let l = the length. Then $l - 5$ = the width. $$\boxed{\quad 66 \text{ m}^2 \quad}\; l-5$$ $$l$$ 2. *Translate.* Recall that the area of a rectangle is length × width. Thus, we have $$l(l-5) = 66.$$ 3. *Solve.* $$l(l-5) = 66$$ $$l^2 - 5l = 66$$ $$l^2 - 5l - 66 = 0$$ $$(l-11)(l+6) = 0$$ $$l-11 = 0 \quad or \quad l+6 = 0$$ $$l = 11 \quad or \quad l = -6$$ 4. *Check.* Length cannot be negative, so −6 is not a solution. If $l = 11$, then $l-5 = 11-5 = 6$ and the area is $11 \cdot 6$, or 66 m². This checks. 5. *State.* The length is 11 m and the width is 6 m.	6. The speed of a boat in still water is 10 km/h. The boat travels 24 km upstream and 24 km downstream in a total time of 5 hr. What is the speed of the stream? A. 2 km/h B. 3 km/h C. 4 km/h D. 6 km/h

Objective [7.3b] Solve a formula for a given letter.		
Brief Procedure	**Example**	**Practice Exercise**
Use an appropriate equation-solving technique to get the letter alone on one side of the equation.	Solve $m^2 + n^2 = r^2$ for n. $$m^2 + n^2 = r^2$$ $$n^2 = r^2 - m^2$$ $$n = \sqrt{r^2 - m^2}$$	7. Solve $A = cd^2$ for d. A. $d = \dfrac{A}{c}$ B. $d = \sqrt{Ac}$ C. $d = \dfrac{c}{A}$ D. $d = \sqrt{\dfrac{A}{c}}$

Objective [7.4a] Determine the nature of the solutions of a quadratic equation.		
Brief Procedure	**Example**	**Practice Exercise**
For a quadratic equation $ax^2 + bx + c = 0$, the expression $b^2 - 4ac$ is the discriminant. If $b^2 - 4ac = 0$, the equation has only one solution and it is a real number. If $b^2 - 4ac > 0$, the equation has two different real-number solutions. And if $b^2 - 4ac < 0$, the equation has two different nonreal complex-number solutions. They are complex conjugates.	Determine the nature of the solutions of the equation. a) $x^2 - 5x + 4 = 0$ b) $4x^2 + 12x + 9 = 0$ c) $x^2 + 2x + 6 = 0$ a) We have $a = 1$, $b = -5$, and $c = 4$. Then $b^2 - 4ac = (-5)^2 - 4 \cdot 1 \cdot 4 = 9$. Since the discriminant is positive, there are two different real-number solutions. b) We have $a = 4$, $b = 12$, and $c = 9$. Then $b^2 - 4ac = 12^2 - 4 \cdot 4 \cdot 9 = 0$. Since the discriminant is 0, there is only one solution and it is a real number. c) We have $a = 1$, $b = 2$, and $c = 6$. Then $b^2 - 4ac = 2^2 - 4 \cdot 1 \cdot 6 = -20$. Since the discriminant is negative, there are two different nonreal complex-number solutions.	8. Determine the nature of the solutions of $2x^2 - 3x - 1 = 0$. A. Only one real-number solution B. Two real-number solutions C. Two nonreal complex-number solutions

Objective [7.4b] Write a quadratic equation having two numbers specified as solutions.

Brief Procedure	Example	Practice Exercise
Use the principle of zero products in reverse.	Write a quadratic equation whose solutions are -3 and $\frac{1}{2}$. If the solutions are -3 and $\frac{1}{2}$, we have: $$x = -3 \; or \qquad x = \frac{1}{2}$$ $$x + 3 = 0 \quad or \; x - \frac{1}{2} = 0$$ $$x + 3 = 0 \quad or \; 2x - 1 = 0$$ Now we use the principle of zero products in reverse. $$(x + 3)(2x - 1) = 0$$ $$2x^2 + 5x - 3 = 0$$	9. Write a quadratic equation whose solutions are 5 and -1. A. $x^2 - 4x - 5 = 0$ B. $x^2 + 6x + 5 = 0$ C. $x^2 + 4x - 5 = 0$ D. $x^2 - 6x + 5 = 0$

Objective [7.4c] Solve equations that are quadratic in form.

Brief Procedure	Example	Practice Exercise
Make a substitution that reduces the given equation to a quadratic equation. Solve first for the new variable and then substitute again and solve for the original variable.	Solve: $x - 2\sqrt{x} - 3 = 0$. Let $u = \sqrt{x}$. Then $u^2 = x$. We substitute u for $\sqrt{x}$ and u^2 for x. $$u^2 - 2u - 3 = 0$$ $$(u - 3)(u + 1) = 0$$ $$u = 3 \; or \; u = -1$$ Now we substitute $\sqrt{x}$ for u and solve for x. $$\sqrt{x} = 3 \; or \; \sqrt{x} = -1$$ Squaring both sides of the first equation, we get $x = 9$ and 9 checks. Since the principal square root cannot be negative, the second equation has no solution. If we failed to observe this and squared both sides of the equation, we would get $x = 1$. This number does not check. The solution is 9.	10. Solve: $x^4 - 11x^2 + 18 = 0$. A. 2, 9 B. ± 2, ± 9 C. $\sqrt{2}$, 3 D. $\pm\sqrt{2}$, ± 3

Objective [7.5a] Graph quadratic functions of the type $f(x) = ax^2$ and then label the vertex and the line of symmetry.

Brief Procedure	Example	Practice Exercise
The graph of $f(x) = ax^2$, or $y = ax^2$, is a parabola with $x = 0$ as its line of symmetry; its vertex is the origin. For $a > 0$, the parabola opens up; for $a < 0$, the parabola opens down. If $|a|$ is greater than 1, the parabola is narrower than $y = x^2$. If $|a|$ is between 0 and 1, the parabola is wider than $y = x^2$. Plot some points on either side of the vertex and connect them with a smooth curve.	Graph $f(x) = -x^2$. The graph of $f(x) = -x^2$ is a parabola with $x = 0$ as its line of symmetry and the origin (0, 0) as its vertex. It has the same shape as $y = x^2$. We choose some values for x, find the corresponding y-values, plot these points, and connect them with a smooth curve. <table><tr><th>x</th><th>$f(x) = -x^2$</th></tr><tr><td>-2</td><td>-4</td></tr><tr><td>-1</td><td>-1</td></tr><tr><td>0</td><td>0</td></tr><tr><td>1</td><td>-1</td></tr><tr><td>2</td><td>-4</td></tr></table> 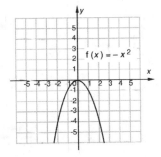	11. Graph: $f(x) = 2x^2$. A. 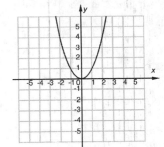 B. 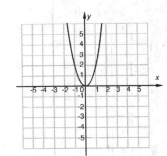 C. 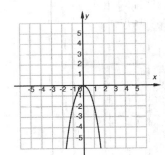 D. 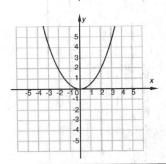

Objective [7.5b] Graph quadratic functions of the type $f(x) = a(x-h)^2$ and then label the vertex and the line of symmetry.

Brief Procedure	Example	Practice Exercise
The graph of $f(x) = a(x-h)^2$ has the same shape as the graph of $y = ax^2$. If h is positive, the graph of $y = ax^2$ is shifted h units to the right. If h is negative, the graph of $y = ax^2$ is shifted $|h|$ units to the left. The vertex is $(h, 0)$ and the line of symmetry is $x = h$. Plot some points on either side of the vertex and connect them with a smooth curve.	Graph $f(x) = 2(x-1)^2$. The graph of $f(x) = 2(x-1)^2$ has the same shape as $y = 2x^2$ but shifted 1 unit to the right. The vertex is $(1, 0)$ and the line of symmetry is $x = 1$. We choose some values for x, find the corresponding y-values, plot these points, and connect them with a smooth curve. 	x	$f(x) = 2(x-1)^2$	 |---|---| 	-1	8	 	0	2	 	1	0	 	2	2	 	3	8	 	12. Graph: $f(x) = -(x+2)^2$. A. B. C. D.

Objective [7.5c] Graph quadratic functions of the type $f(x) = a(x-h)^2 + k$, finding the vertex, the line of symmetry, and the maximum or minimum y-value.

Brief Procedure	Example	Practice Exercise
The graph of $f(x) = a(x-h)^2 + k$ has the same shape as the graph of $y = a(x-h)^2$. If k is positive, the graph of $y = a(x-h)^2$ is shifted k units up. If k is negative, the graph of $y = a(x-h)^2$ is shifted $|k|$ units down. The vertex is (h, k) and the line of symmetry is $x = h$. For $a > 0$, k is the minimum function value. For $a < 0$, k is the maximum function value. Plot some points on either side of the vertex and connect them with a smooth curve.	Graph $f(x) = (x-2)^2 - 1$. Find the vertex, the line of symmetry, and the maximum or minimum y-value. The graph of $f(x) = (x-2)^2 - 1$ has the same shape as $y = (x-2)^2$ but shifted 1 unit down. The vertex is $(2, -1)$, the line of symmetry is $x = 2$, and -1 is the minimum function value. We compute a few points as needed. 	x	$f(x) = (x-2)^2 - 1$	 |---|---| 	0	3	 	1	0	 	2	-1	 	3	0	 	4	3	 	13. Graph: $f(x) = -3(x+1)^2 - 2$. Find the vertex, the line of symmetry, and the maximum or minimum y-value. A. The minimum function value is -2. B. The minimum function value is -3. C. The maximum function value is -1. D. The maximum function value is -2.

Objective [7.6a] For a quadratic function, find the vertex, the line of symmetry, and the maximum or minimum value, and graph the function.

Brief Procedure	Example	Practice Exercise
Given a quadratic function $f(x) = ax^2 + bx + c$, complete the square to obtain an equivalent function of the form $f(x) = a(x-h)^2 + k$. Then find the vertex, the line of symmetry, and the maximum or minimum value, and graph the function using the techniques of Section 7.5. The coordinates of the vertex are also given by $\left(-\dfrac{b}{2a}, f\left(-\dfrac{b}{2a}\right)\right)$ and the line of symmetry is $x = -\dfrac{b}{2a}$.	For $f(x) = 2x^2 - 4x + 4$, find the vertex, the line of symmetry, and the minimum value. The graph the function. $f(x) = 2x^2 - 4x + 4 = 2(x^2 - 2x) + 4$ First we complete the square inside the parentheses. We take half the x-coefficient and square it: $\dfrac{-2}{2} = -1$ and $(-1)^2 = 1$. Then we add 0, or $1 - 1$ inside the parentheses. $$\begin{aligned} f(x) &= 2(x^2 - 2x + 0) + 4 \\ &= 2(x^2 - 2x + 1 - 1) + 4 \\ &= 2(x^2 - 2x + 1) - 2 \cdot 1 + 4 \\ &= 2(x-1)^2 + 2 \end{aligned}$$ The vertex is (1, 2) and the line of symmetry is $x = 1$. The coefficient of x^2, 2, is positive so the graph opens up and 2 is the minimum function value. We find some points on both sides of the vertex and graph the parabola. We could have also found the vertex and line of symmetry as follows: $$-\frac{b}{2a} = -\frac{-4}{2 \cdot 2} = 1$$ $$f(1) = 2 \cdot 1^2 - 4 \cdot 1 + 4 = 2$$ Thus the vertex is (1, 2) and the line of symmetry is $x = 1$. <table><tr><td>x</td><td>$f(x)$</td></tr><tr><td>0</td><td>4</td></tr><tr><td>1</td><td>2</td></tr><tr><td>2</td><td>4</td></tr></table> 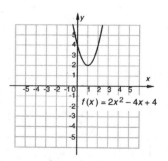	14. For $f(x) = 3x^2 + 12x + 8$, find the vertex, the line of symmetry, and the minimum value. Then graph the function A. The vertex is $(-2, -4)$. B. The vertex is $(2, 46)$. C. The vertex is $(-4, 10)$. D. The vertex is $(-1, 1)$.

Objective [7.6b] Find the intercepts of a quadratic function.

Brief Procedure	Example	Practice Exercise
Given a quadratic function $f(x) = ax^2 + bx + c$, the second coordinate of the y-intercept is $f(0)$, or c. Thus, the y-intercept is $(0, c)$. The first coordinates of the x-intercepts are the solutions of $f(x) = 0$.	Find the intercepts of $f(x) = x^2 - 3x - 1$. Since $f(0) = 0^2 - 3 \cdot 0 - 1 = -1$, the y-intercept is $(0, -1)$. To find the x-intercepts, we solve $x^2 - 3x - 1 = 0$. Using the quadratic formula, we get $x = \dfrac{3 \pm \sqrt{13}}{2}$. Thus, the x-intercepts are $\left(\dfrac{3 - \sqrt{13}}{2}, 0\right)$ and $\left(\dfrac{3 + \sqrt{13}}{2}, 0\right)$, or approximately $(-0.303, 0)$ and $(3.303, 0)$.	15. Find the intercepts of $f(x) = -x^2 + 4x + 3$. One of the intercepts is A. $(3, 0)$ B. $(2 - \sqrt{7}, 0)$ C. $(0, 2 + \sqrt{7})$ D. $(-2 - \sqrt{7}, 0)$

Objective [7.7a] Solve maximum-minimum problems involving quadratic functions.

Brief Procedure	Example	Practice Exercise
Use the five-step problem solving process. Translate the problem to a quadratic function. Then find the maximum or minimum value of the function.	A gardener has 40 ft of fencing. What are the dimensions of the largest rectangular garden plot that can be enclosed with the fencing? 1. *Familiarize.* Let $l =$ the length of the garden and $w =$ the width. Recall that the formula for the perimeter of a rectangle with length l and width w is $P = 2l + 2w$ and the area is given by $A = l \cdot w$. 2. *Translate.* We have two equations. $\quad 2l + 2w = 40,$ $\quad A = l \cdot w$ We use these equations to express A as a function of either l or w. To express A in terms of w, we first solve the first equation for l. $\quad 2l + 2w = 40$ $\quad\quad 2l = 40 - 2w$ $\quad\quad l = 20 - w$ Next we substitute $20 - w$ for l in the second equation to get a quadratic function. $\quad A = lw = (20 - w)w$ $\quad\quad = 20w - w^2$ $\quad\quad = -w^2 + 20w$ (continued)	16. What is the minimum product of two numbers whose difference is 8? A. -12 B. -16 C. -20 D. -24

Objective [7.7a] (continued)		
Brief Procedure	Example	Practice Exercise
	3. *Carry out.* We find the vertex of the quadratic function. The first coordinate is $-\dfrac{b}{2a} = -\dfrac{20}{2(-1)} =$ 10. The second coordinate is found by substituting in the quadratic function. $\quad -w^2 + 20w$ $= -(10)^2 + 20(10)$ $= -100 + 200$ $= 100$ The vertex is (10, 100). Since the w^2-coefficient is negative, the function has a maximum value, 100. 4. *Check.* We could calculate some function values for values of w less than 10 and for values of w greater than 10 and determine if 100 is greater than all of these. We could also use the graph of the function to check that 100 is the maximum value. The answer checks. 5. *State.* The largest garden that can be enclosed is 10 ft by 10 ft.	

Objective [7.7b] Fit a quadratic function to a set of data to form a mathematical model, and solve related applied problems.

Brief Procedure	Example	Practice Exercise
After determining that a quadratic function fits a set of data, find the coefficients of the quadratic function $f(x) = ax^2 + bx + c$ by using three data points to obtain and solve a system of three equations in the three variables a, b, and c. The quadratic function that is found using this procedure can then be used to solve applied problems.	Find a quadratic function $f(x) = ax^2 + bx + c$ that fits the data points $(-1, 6)$, $(1, 4)$, and $(3, 18)$. Then find $f(-2)$. We are looking for a quadratic function $f(x) = ax^2 + bx + c$. We use the data points and substitute. $$6 = a(-1)^2 + b(-1) + c,$$ $$4 = a \cdot 1^2 + b \cdot 1 + c,$$ $$18 = a \cdot 3^2 + b \cdot 3 + c$$ After simplifying we have $$6 = a - b + c,$$ $$4 = a + b + c,$$ $$18 = 9a + 3b + c$$ Solving this system of equations, we get $(2, -1, 3)$, so the function is $f(x) = 2x^2 - x + 3$. Now we find $f(-2)$: $f(-2) = 2(-2)^2 - (-2) + 3 = 8 + 2 + 3 = 13$.	17. Fit a quadratic function $f(x) = ax^2 + bx + c$ to the data points $(-1, 11)$, $(0, 7)$, and $(2, -7)$. Then find $f(-5)$. A. -17 B. -12 C. 3 D. 7

Objective [7.8a] Solve quadratic and other polynomial inequalities.

Brief Procedure	Example	Practice Exercise
1. Get 0 on one side, set the expression on the other side equal to 0, and solve to find the intercepts. 2. Use the numbers found in step (1) to divide the number line into intervals. 3. Substitute a number from each interval into the related function. If the function value is positive, then the expression will be positive for all numbers in the interval. If the function value is negative, then the expression will be negative for all numbers in the interval. 4. Select the intervals for which the inequality is satisfied and write set-builder or interval notation for the solution set.	Solve: $x^2 + 2x - 8 \leq 0$. The solutions of $x^2 + 2x - 8 = 0$, or $(x + 4)(x - 2) = 0$, are -4 and 2. They divide the number line into three intervals. We try a test number in each interval in the function $f(x) = x^2 + 2x - 8$. A: Test -5, $f(-5) =$ $\quad (-5)^2 + 2(-5) - 8 = 7 > 0$ B: Test 0, $f(0) = 0^2 + 2 \cdot 0 - 8 =$ $\quad -8 < 0$ C: Test 3, $f(3) = 3^2 + 2 \cdot 3 - 8 = 7 > 0$ The function values are negative in interval B. Since the inequality symbol is $\leq$, we also include the endpoints of the interval. The solution set is $\{x \mid -4 \leq x \leq 2\}$, or $[-4, 2]$.	18. Solve: $x^2 + 4x - 5 > 0$. A. $(-\infty, -5) \cup (1, \infty)$ B. $(-\infty, -1) \cup (5, \infty)$ C. $(-5, 1)$ D. $(-1, 5)$

Objective [7.8b] Solve rational inequalities.		
Brief Procedure	Example	Practice Exercise

Brief Procedure	Example	Practice Exercise
1. Change the inequality symbol to an equals sign and solve the related equation. 2. Find the numbers for which any rational expression in the inequality is not defined. 3. Use the numbers found in steps (1) and (2) to divide the number line into intervals. 4. Substitute a number from each interval into the inequality. If the number is a solution, then the interval to which it belongs is part of the solution set. 5. Select the intervals for which the inequality is satisfied and write set-builder or interval notation for the solution set.	Solve: $\dfrac{x-1}{x+5} \le 3$. First we solve the related equation. $$\dfrac{x-1}{x+5} = 3$$ $$(x+5) \cdot \dfrac{x-1}{x+5} = (x+5) \cdot 3$$ $$x - 1 = 3x + 15$$ $$-16 = 2x$$ $$-8 = x$$ We also find the number that makes the denominator equal to 0. $$x + 5 = 0$$ $$x = -5$$ Now use the numbers -8 and -5 to divide the number line into intervals. We try test numbers in each interval to see if each satisfies the original inequality. A: Test -9, $$\dfrac{x-1}{x+5} \le 3$$ $$\begin{array}{c|c} \dfrac{-9-1}{-9+5} \ ?\ 3 & \\ \dfrac{-10}{-4} & \\ \dfrac{5}{2} & \text{TRUE} \end{array}$$ Interval A is part of the solution set. <div align="center">(continued)</div>	19. Solve: $\dfrac{3x}{x-1} \le 2$. A. $\{x \mid x \le 2 \ or \ x > 1\}$ B. $\{x \mid x \le 2 \ or \ x \ge 1\}$ C. $\{x \mid -2 < x \le 1\}$ D. $\{x \mid -2 \le x < 1\}$

Objective [7.8b] (continued)		
Brief Procedure	Example	Practice Exercise
	B: Test -6, $$\frac{x-1}{x+5} \leq 3$$ $$\frac{-6-1}{-6+5} \; ? \; 3$$ $$\frac{-7}{-1}$$ $7 \quad$ FALSE Interval B is not part of the solution set. C: Test 0, $$\frac{x-1}{x+5} \leq 3$$ $$\frac{0-1}{0+5} \; ? \; 3$$ $-\dfrac{1}{5} \quad$ TRUE Interval C is part of the solution set. We have seen that the solution set includes intervals A and C. The inequality symbol is $\leq$, so we include the solution of the related equation, -8. The number -5 is not in the solution set because it is not an allowable replacement for x. The solution set is $\{x \mid x \leq -8 \; or \; x > -5\}$, or $(-\infty, -8] \cup (-5, \infty)$.	

Chapter 8 Review

Objective [8.1a] Graph exponential equations and functions.

Brief Procedure	Example	Practice Exercise
Compute some function values, plot points, and connect them with a smooth curve.	Graph $f(x) = 3^x$. We compute some function values and list the results in a table. $f(-2) = 3^{-2} = \dfrac{1}{3^2} = \dfrac{1}{9}$ $f(-1) = 3^{-1} = \dfrac{1}{3}$ $f(0) = 3^0 = 1$ $f(1) = 3^1 = 3$ $f(2) = 3^2 = 9$	1. Graph: $f(x) = 2^x$. A. B. C. D.

Table and graph for the example:

x	$f(x)$
-2	$\dfrac{1}{9}$
-1	$\dfrac{1}{3}$
0	1
1	3
2	9

Now plot the points $(x, f(x))$ and connect them with a smooth curve.

$f(x) = 3^x$

Objective [8.1b] Graph exponential equations in which x and y have been interchanged.		
Brief Procedure	Example	Practice Exercise
Find some ordered pairs by choosing values for y and then computing the corresponding x values. Plot these points and connect them with a smooth curve.	Graph $x = 4^y$. For $y = -2, x = 4^{-2} = \dfrac{1}{4^2} = \dfrac{1}{16}$. For $y = -1, x = 4^{-1} = \dfrac{1}{4}$. For $y = 0, x = 4^0 = 1$. For $y = 1, x = 4^1 = 4$. For $y = 2, x = 4^2 = 16$.	2. Graph: $x = 2^y$. A. 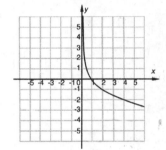

$$\begin{array}{c|c} x & y \\ \hline \dfrac{1}{16} & -2 \\ \dfrac{1}{4} & -1 \\ 1 & 0 \\ 4 & 1 \\ 16 & 2 \end{array}$$

Now we plot these points and connect them with a smooth curve.

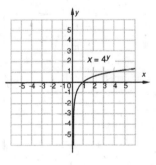

B.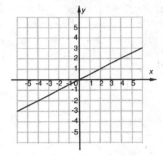

C.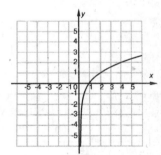

D.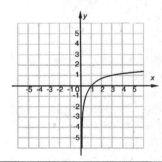

Objective [8.1c] Solve applied problems involving applications of exponential functions and their graphs.		
Brief Procedure	Example	Practice Exercise
Substitute to evaluate the function for desired values of the variable. The function can also be graphed, if desired.	An office machine is purchased for $3600. Its value each year is about 75% of the value the preceding year. Its value after t years is given by the exponential function $$V(t) = \$3600(0.75)^t.$$ a) Find the value of the machine after 3 years. b) Graph the function. a) $V(3) = \$3600(0.75)^3 = \$1518.75$ b) We use the function value found in part(a) and compute others as well to draw the graph.	3. Suppose $5000 is invested at 4% interest, compounded annually. The amount in the account after t years is given by the exponential function $A(t) = 5000(1.04)^t$. Find the amount in the account after 5 years. A. $5624.32 B. $5849.29 C. $6083.26 D. $6326.60

Objective [8.2a] Find the inverse of a relation if it is described as a set of ordered pairs or as an equation.		
Brief Procedure	Example	Practice Exercise
If a relation is described as a set of ordered pairs, interchanging the coordinates produces the inverse relation. If a relation is defined by an equation, interchanging the variables produces an equation of the inverse relation.	a) Find the inverse of the relation $\{(-1,3),(2,-5),(6,10)\}$. b) Find an equation of the inverse of the relation $y = 4x - 5$. a) We interchange the coordinates. The inverse of the given relation is $\{(3,-1),(-5,2),(10,6)\}$. b) We interchange x and y. The equation of the inverse of the given relation is $x = 4y - 5$.	4. Find an equation of the inverse of the relation $y = -x + 7$. A. $x = -y + 7$ B. $-x = y + 7$ C. $-x = -y + 7$ D. $x - 7 = y$

Objective [8.2b] Given a function, determine whether it is one-to-one and has an inverse that is a function.

Brief Procedure	Example	Practice Exercise
If no horizontal line intersects the graph of a function more than once, the function is one-to-one and therefore its inverse is a function. This is called the horizontal-line test.	Determine whether each function is one-to-one and thus has an inverse that is also a function. a) $f(x) = x - 1$ b) $f(x) = -x^2$ a) The graph of $f(x) = x - 1$ is shown below. No horizontal line crosses the graph more than once, so the function is one-to-one and has an inverse that is a function. 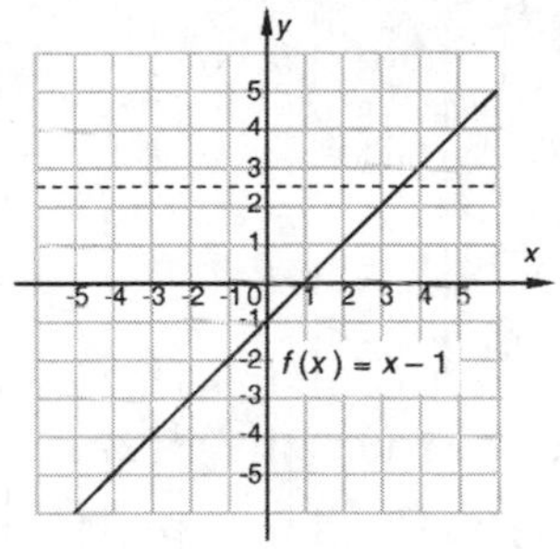 b) The graph of $f(x) = -x^2$ is shown below. There are many horizontal lines that cross the graph more than once, so the function is not one-to-one and does not have an inverse that is a function. 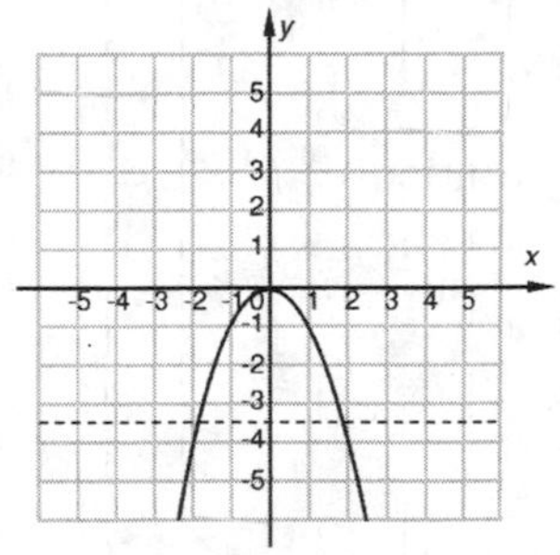 	5. Determine whether the function $f(x) = 5^x$ is one-to-one. A. Yes B. No

Objective [8.2c] Find a formula for the inverse of a function, if it exists, and graph inverse relations and functions.

Brief Procedure	Example	Practice Exercise
If a function f is one-to-one, a formula for its inverse f^{-1} can be found as follows: 1. Replace $f(x)$ with y. 2. Interchange x and y. 3. Solve for y. 4. Replace y with $f^{-1}(x)$.	Determine whether the function $f(x) = 2x + 1$ is one-to-one. If it is, find a formula for its inverse. The graph of $f(x) = 2x + 1$ is shown below. It passes the horizontal-line test, so it is one-to-one. 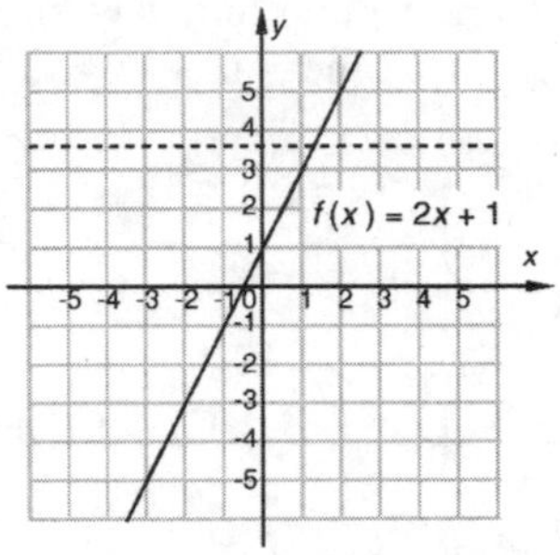 Now we find a formula for $f^{-1}(x)$. 1. Replace $f(x)$ with y: $y = 2x + 1$ 2. Interchange x and y: $x = 2y + 1$ 3. Solve for y: $$x - 1 = 2y$$ $$\frac{x-1}{2} = y$$ 4. Replace y with $f^{-1}(x)$: $$f^{-1}(x) = \frac{x-1}{2}$$ (continued)	6. Determine whether the function $g(x) = 5 - x$ is one-to-one. If it is, find a formula for its inverse. A. Not one-to-one B. $g^{-1}(x) = 5 + x$ C. $g^{-1}(x) = x - 5$ D. $g^{-1}(x) = 5 - x$

Objective [8.2c] (continued)		
Brief Procedure	**Example**	**Practice Exercise**
The graph of f^{-1} is the reflection of the graph of f across the line $y = x$. The graph of f^{-1} can also be drawn by finding a formula for f^{-1} and plotting points.	Graph the one-to-one function $g(x) = x + 2$ and its inverse using the same set of axes. We graph $g(x) = x + 2$ and then we draw its reflection across the line $y = x$. 	7. Graph the one-to-one function $f(x) = 3x - 1$ and its inverse using the same set of axes. A. B. C. D.

Objective [8.2d] Find the composition of functions and express certain functions as a composition of functions.

Brief Procedure	Example	Practice Exercises
The composite function $f \circ g$, the composition of f and g, is defined as $f \circ g(x) = f(g(x))$, or $(f \circ g)(x) = f[g(x)]$.	Given $f(x) = x + 1$ and $g(x) = x^2$, find $f \circ g(x)$ and $g \circ f(x)$. $$f \circ g(x) = f(g(x))$$ $$= f(x^2)$$ $$= x^2 + 1$$ $$g \circ f(x) = g(f(x))$$ $$= g(x + 1)$$ $$= (x + 1)^2$$ $$= x^2 + 2x + 1$$	8. Given $f(x) = 4x$ and $g(x) = 3x - 2$, find $g \circ f(x)$. A. $7x - 2$ B. $12x - 2$ C. $12x - 8$ D. $12x^2 - 8x$
To express a function as a composition of functions, examine the given function and determine how it is formed. There is usually more than one way to express the composition.	Find $f(x)$ and $g(x)$ such that $h(x) = f \circ g(x)$: $h(x) = \sqrt{x+1}$. Two functions that can be used are $f(x) = \sqrt{x}$ and $g(x) = x + 1$. There are other correct answers.	9. Find $f(x)$ and $g(x)$ such that $h(x) = f \circ g(x)$: $h(x) = \dfrac{1}{2x - 3}$. A. $f(x) = \dfrac{1}{x}$, $g(x) = 2x - 3$ B. $f(x) = 2x - 3$, $g(x) = \dfrac{1}{x}$ C. $f(x) = \dfrac{1}{2x}$, $g(x) = -\dfrac{1}{3}$ D. $f(x) = \dfrac{1}{2x}$, $g(x) = x - 3$

Objective [8.2e] Determine whether a function is an inverse by checking its composition with the original function.

Brief Procedure	Example	Practice Exercise
If a function f is one-to-one, then f^{-1} is the unique function for which $f^{-1} \circ f(x) = x$ and $f \circ f^{-1}(x) = x$.	Let $f(x) = x - 2$. Use composition to show that $f^{-1}(x) = x + 2$. $$f^{-1} \circ f(x) = f^{-1}(f(x))$$ $$= f^{-1}(x - 2)$$ $$= (x - 2) + 2$$ $$= x$$ $$f \circ f^{-1}(x) = f(f^{-1}(x))$$ $$= f(x + 2)$$ $$= (x + 2) - 2$$ $$= x$$ Since $f^{-1} \circ f(x) = x$ and $f \circ f^{-1}(x) = x$, then $f^{-1}(x) = x + 2$.	10. Let $f(x) = \dfrac{x - 1}{2}$. Use composition to determine whether it is true that $f^{-1}(x) = 1 - 2x$. A. Yes B. No

Objective [8.3a] Graph logarithmic functions.		
Brief Procedure	**Example**	**Practice Exercise**
For a logarithmic function $y = \log_a x$, write an equivalent equation, $a^y = x$, choose some y-values, find the corresponding x-values, plot points, and connect them with a smooth curve.	Graph $y = f(x) = \log_4 x$. The equation $y = \log_4 x$ is equivalent to $4^y = x$. For $y = -2$, $x = 4^{-2} = \dfrac{1}{4^2} = \dfrac{1}{16}$. For $y = -1$, $x = 4^{-1} = \frac{1}{4}$. For $y = 0$, $x = 4^0 = 1$. For $y = 1$, $x = 4^1 = 4$. For $y = 2$, $x = 4^2 = 16$. <table><tr><th>x</th><th>y</th></tr><tr><td>$\frac{1}{16}$</td><td>-2</td></tr><tr><td>$\frac{1}{4}$</td><td>-1</td></tr><tr><td>1</td><td>0</td></tr><tr><td>4</td><td>1</td></tr><tr><td>16</td><td>2</td></tr></table> Now we plot these points and connect them with a smooth curve. 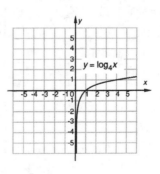	11. Graph: $y = \log_2 x$. A. 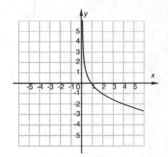 B. 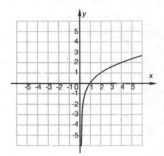 C. 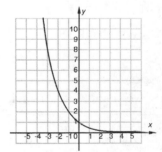 D. 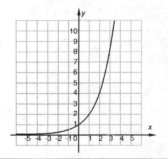

Objective [8.3b] Convert from exponential equations to logarithmic equations and from logarithmic equations to exponential equations.

Brief Procedure	Example	Practice Exercise
$a^y = x \Rightarrow y = \log_a x;$ $y = \log_a x \Rightarrow a^y = x$	a) Convert $2^3 = 8$ to a logarithmic equation. b) Convert $y = \log_a 5$ to an exponential equation. a) The exponent is the logarithm. The base remains the base. $\quad 2^3 = 8 \Rightarrow 3 = \log_2 8$ b) The logarithm is the exponent. The base does not change. $\quad y = \log_a 5 \Rightarrow a^y = 5$	12. Convert $m = \log_3 n$ to an exponential equation. A. $n^3 = m$ B. $m^3 = n$ C. $3^n = m$ D. $3^m = n$

Objective [8.3c] Solve logarithmic equations.

Brief Procedure	Example	Practice Exercise
Some logarithmic equations can be solved by first converting them to exponential equations.	Solve $\log_x 25 = 2$. $\quad \log_x 25 = 2$ $\quad\quad x^2 = 25$ $\quad x = 5 \text{ or } x = -5$ 5 is a solution since $\log_5 25 = 2$, or $5^2 = 25$. However, -5 is not a solution because all logarithmic bases must be positive. That is, $\log_{-5} 25$ is not defined.	13. Solve $\log_3 x = -2$. A. $\dfrac{1}{8}$ B. $\dfrac{1}{9}$ C. -9 D. $-\dfrac{1}{9}$

Objective [8.3d] Find common logarithms on a calculator.

Brief Procedure	Example	Practice Exercise
Enter the appropriate keystrokes for the calculator being used and round to the desired number of decimal places.	Find log 8349, to four decimal places, on a calculator. Using a scientific calculator or a graphing calculator, we find log 8349 $\approx$ 3.9216.	14. Find log 0.0043, to four decimal places, on a calculator. A. -2.3665 B. -1.3665 C. 1.0100 D. 3.3459

Objective [8.4a] Express the logarithm of a product as a sum of logarithms, and conversely.

Brief Procedure	Example	Practice Exercise
The Product Rule For any positive numbers M and N, $\log_a(M{\cdot}N)=\log_a M+\log_a N$. (The logarithm of a product is the sum of the logarithms of the factors. The number a can be any logarithm base.)	a) Express $\log_3(6\cdot 8)$ as a sum of logarithms. b) Express $\log_b A+\log_b C$ as a single logarithm. a) $\log_3(6\cdot 8)=\log_3 6+\log_3 8$ b) $\log_b A+\log_b C=\log_b AC$	15. Express $\log_a YZ$ as a sum of logarithms. A. $\log_a Y + Z$ B. $\log_a(Y+Z)$ C. $\log_a Y + \log_a Z$ D. $Y + \log_a Z$

Objective [8.4b] Express the logarithm of a power as a product.

Brief Procedure	Example	Practice Exercise
The Power Rule For any positive number M and any real number k, $\log_a M^k = k\cdot\log_a M$. (The logarithm of a power of M is the exponent times the logarithm of M. The number a can be any logarithm base.)	Express $\log_m \sqrt[3]{2}$ as a product. $\log_m \sqrt[3]{2} = \log_m 2^{1/3}$ $\phantom{\log_m \sqrt[3]{2}} = \dfrac{1}{3}\log_m 2$	16. Express $\log_n 5^4$ as a product. A. $\log_n(5\cdot 4)$ B. $4\log_n 5$ C. $5\log_n 4$ D. $\log_n 4 \cdot \log_n 5$

Objective [8.4c] Express the logarithm of a quotient as a difference of logarithms, and conversely.

Brief Procedure	Example	Practice Exercise
The Quotient Rule For any positive numbers M and N, $\log_a \dfrac{M}{N} = \log_a M - \log_a N$. (The logarithm of a quotient is the logarithm of the numerator minus the logarithm of the denominator. The number a can be any logarithm base.)	a) Express $\log_5 \dfrac{a}{b}$ as a difference of logarithms. b) Express $\log_m 4 - \log_m 7$ as a single logarithm. a) $\log_5 \dfrac{a}{b} = \log_5 a - \log_5 b$ b) $\log_m 4 - \log_m 7 = \log_m \dfrac{4}{7}$	17. Express $\log_2 5 - \log_2 4$ as a single logarithm. A. $\log_2 1$ B. $\log_2(5\cdot 4)$ C. $\dfrac{\log_2 5}{\log_2 4}$ D. $\log_2 \dfrac{5}{4}$

Objective [8.4d] Convert from logarithms of products, quotients, and powers to expressions in terms of individual logarithms, and conversely.

Brief Procedure	Example	Practice Exercise
Use the product, power, and quotient rules.	a) Express $\log_a \dfrac{x^2 y}{z^3}$ in terms of logarithms of $x, y,$ and z. b) Express $4\log_a x - \dfrac{1}{2}\log_a y$ as a single logarithm. a) $\quad \log_a \dfrac{x^2 y}{z^3}$ $\quad = \log_a (x^2 y) - \log_a z^3$ $\quad = \log_a x^2 + \log_a y - \log_a z^3$ $\quad = 2\log_a x + \log_a y - 3\log_a z$ b) $\quad 4\log_a x - \dfrac{1}{2}\log_a y$ $\quad = \log_a x^4 - \log_a y^{1/2}$ $\quad = \log_a \dfrac{x^4}{y^{1/2}},$ or $\quad \log_a \dfrac{x^4}{\sqrt{y}}$	18. Express $\log_a \sqrt[4]{\dfrac{x}{y^2}}$ in terms of logarithms of x and y. A. $\dfrac{1}{4}\log_a x - \dfrac{1}{2}\log_a y$ B. $4\log_a x - 8\log_a y$ C. $4\log_a x - \dfrac{1}{2}\log_a y$ D. $\log_a x^{1/4} - 2\log_a y$

Objective [8.4e] Simplify expressions of the type $\log_a a^k$.

Brief Procedure	Example	Practice Exercise
For any base a, $\quad \log_a a^k = k.$ (The logarithm, base a, of a to a power is the power.)	Simplify $\log_b b^{-3}$. $\quad \log_b b^{-3} = -3$	19. Simplify $\log_5 5^8$. A. 1 B. 5 C. 8 D. 5^8

Objective [8.5a] Find logarithms or powers, base e, using a calculator.

Brief Procedure	Example	Practice Exercise
Enter the appropriate keystrokes for the calculator being used and round to the desired number of decimal places.	Find $\ln 0.23765$, to four decimal places, on a calculator. $\quad \ln 0.23765 \approx -1.4370$	20. Find $\ln 141.37$, to four decimal places, on a calculator. A. 2.1504 B. 4.9514 C. 5.0017 D. -3.1639

Objective [8.5b] Use the change-of-base formula to find logarithms to bases other than e or 10.		
Brief Procedure	**Example**	**Practice Exercise**
The Change-of-Base Formula For any logarithm bases a and b and any positive number M, $$\log_b M = \frac{\log_a M}{\log_a b}.$$	Find $\log_5 9$ using the change-of-base formula. We can use either common logarithms or natural logarithms. We will use common logarithms. $$\log_5 9 = \frac{\log 9}{\log 5}$$ $$\approx 1.3652$$	21. Find $\log_3 21$ using the change-of-base formula. A. 0.3608 B. 2.7712 C. 5.0317 D. 7

Objective [8.5c] Graph exponential and logarithmic functions, base e.		
Brief Procedure	**Example**	**Practice Exercise**
Use a calculator to find function values, plot points, and connect them with a smooth curve.	Graph: a) $f(x) = e^{x+1}$ b) $g(x) = \ln x + 2$ a) <table><tr><td>x</td><td>$f(x)$</td></tr><tr><td>-2</td><td>0.4</td></tr><tr><td>-1</td><td>1</td></tr><tr><td>0</td><td>2.7</td></tr><tr><td>1</td><td>7.4</td></tr></table> $f(x) = e^{x+1}$	22. Graph $f(x) = e^x - 1$. A. B. C. D.

(continued)

Objective [8.5c] (continued)

Brief Procedure	Example	Practice Exercise
	b) 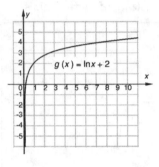	

x	$g(x)$
0.1	-0.3
0.2	0.4
0.5	1.3
1	2
3	3.1
5	3.6
8	4.1

$g(x) = \ln x + 2$

Objective [8.6a] Solve exponential equations.

Brief Procedure	Example	Practice Exercise
When we can write both sides of the equation as a power of the same number, we use the following property: For any $a > 0, a \neq 1$, $\quad a^x = a^y \Rightarrow x = y.$ When we cannot write both sides of the equation as a power of the same number, we can take the common or natural logarithm on both sides.	Solve: a) $3^{x-1} = 27$ $\quad$ b)$4^x = 9$ a) $\quad 3^{x-1} = 27$ $\qquad 3^{x-1} = 3^3$ Since the bases are the same, the exponents must be the same. $\qquad x - 1 = 3$ $\qquad\quad x = 4$ The solution is 4. b) $\qquad 4^x = 9$ $\qquad \ln 4^x = \ln 9$ $\qquad x \ln 4 = \ln 9$ $\qquad x = \dfrac{\ln 9}{\ln 4}$ $\qquad x \approx 1.5850$ The solution is 1.5850.	23. Solve $2^{3x} = 16$. A. -2 B. 4 C. $-\dfrac{1}{3}$ D. $\dfrac{4}{3}$

Objective [8.6b] Solve logarithmic equations.		
Brief Procedure	Example	Practice Exercise
To solve a logarithmic equation, first try to obtain a single logarithmic expression on one side and then write and solve an equivalent exponential equation.	Solve $\log x + \log(x+9) = 1$. $\log x + \log(x+9) = 1$ $\log_{10}[x(x+9)] = 1$ $x(x+9) = 10^1$ $x^2 + 9x = 10$ $x^2 + 9x - 10 = 0$ $(x+10)(x-1) = 0$ $x+10 = 0 \quad or \ x-1 = 0$ $x = -10 \ or \quad x = 1$ The number -10 does not check, but 1 does. The solution is 1.	24. Solve $\log_2(3x-4) = 3$. A. $\dfrac{4}{3}$ B. $\dfrac{10}{3}$ C. 4 D. 8

Objective [8.7a] Solve applied problems involving logarithmic functions.		
Brief Procedure	Example	Practice Exercise
Substitute into a formula or function to find the desired information.	The loudness L, in decibels (dB), of a sound is given by $$L = 10 \cdot \log \frac{I}{I_0},$$ where I is the intensity of the sound in watts per square meter (W/m²) and $I_0 = 10^{-12}$ W/m². Suppose the intensity of a power tool is 10^3 W/m². How loud is this sound level, in decibels? We substitute in the formula and carry out the resulting computation. $L = 10 \cdot \log \dfrac{I}{I_0}$ $= 10 \cdot \log \dfrac{10^{-3}}{10^{-12}}$ $= 10 \cdot \log 10^9$ $= 10 \cdot 9$ $= 90$ The volume is 90 dB.	25. What is the intensity of a sound that measures 110 dB? A. 10^{-1} W/m² B. 130 W/m² C. 10^3 W/m² D. 2.4×10^{-2} W/m²

Objective [8.7b] Solve applied problems involving exponential functions.

Brief Procedure	Example	Practice Exercise
Substitute into a formula or function to find the desired information.	In 1999 the population of Springdale was 120,000 and the exponential growth rate was 0.3% per year. Find the exponential growth function and then find the population in 2005. We substitute 120,000 for P_0 and 0.3%, or 0.003, for k in the exponential growth function. $$P(t) = P_0 e^{kt}$$ $$P(t) = 120,000e^{0.003t}$$ This function gives the population t years after 1999. In 2005, $t = 2005 - 1999$, or 6, so to find the population in 2005 we find $P(6)$. $$P(6) = 120,000e^{0.003(6)}$$ $$\approx 122,180$$ The population will be about 122,180 in 2005.	26. Suppose an amount of money P_0 is invested in a savings account at interest rate k, compounded continuously. Then the balance $P(t)$, after t years, is given by the exponential growth model $P(t) = P_0 e^{kt}$. If \$2400 is invested at 5%, compounded continuously, how much is in the account after 3 years? A. \$2436.27 B. \$2788.40 C. \$6329.18 D. \$10,756.05

Chapter 9 Review

Objective [9.1a] Graph parabolas.

Brief Procedure	Example	Practice Exercise
To graph an equation of the type $y = ax^2 + bx + c$: 1. Find the vertex (h, k) either by completing the square to find an equivalent equation $y = a(x - h)^2 + k$, or by using $-b/(2a)$ to find the x-coordinate and substituting to find the y-coordinate. 2. Choose other values for x on each side of the vertex, and compute the corresponding y-values. 3. The graph opens up for $a > 0$ and down for $a < 0$. To graph an equation of the type $x = ay^2 + by + c$: 1. Find the vertex (h, k) either by completing the square to find an equivalent equation $x = a(y - k)^2 + h$, or by using $-b/(2a)$ to find the y-coordinate and substituting to find the x-coordinate. 2. Choose other values for y that are above and below the vertex, and compute the corresponding x-values. 3. The graph opens to the right if $a > 0$ and to the left if $a < 0$.	Graph $x = y^2 - 2y + 3$. First we find the vertex: $$-\frac{b}{2a} = -\frac{-2}{2 \cdot 1} = 1$$ $$x = 1^2 - 2 \cdot 1 + 3 = 2$$ The vertex is (2, 1). Now we choose some y-values above and below the vertex and compute the corresponding x-values. The graph opens to the right, because the coefficient of y^2, 1, is positive. $\begin{array}{c\|c} x & y \\ \hline 2 & 1 \\ 6 & -1 \\ 3 & 0 \\ 3 & 2 \\ 6 & 3 \end{array}$ 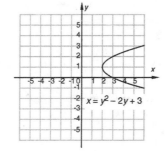	1. Graph: $x = 2y^2 - 4y + 1$. A. 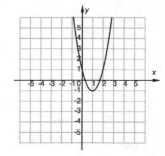 B. 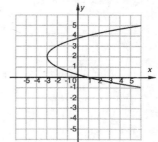 C. 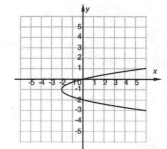 D. 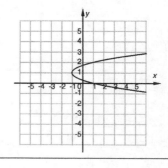

Objective [9.1b] Use the distance formula to find the distance between two points whose coordinates
are known.

Brief Procedure	Example	Practice Exercise
The Distance Formula The distance between any two points (x_1, y_1) and (x_2, y_2) is given by $d = \sqrt{(x_2 - x_1)^2 + (y_2 - y_1)^2}$.	Find the distance between $(-1, 2)$ and $(3, -4)$. Give an exact answer and an approximation to three decimal points. $d = \sqrt{[3 - (-1)]^2 + (-4 - 2)^2}$ $= \sqrt{4^2 + (-6)^2}$ $= \sqrt{52}$ ≈ 7.211 The distance is $\sqrt{52}$ or approximately 7.211.	2. Find the distance between $(5, 1)$ and $(-2, 4)$. A. $\sqrt{18}$ B. $\sqrt{20}$ C. $\sqrt{58}$ D. $\sqrt{74}$

Objective [9.1c] Use the midpoint formula to find the midpoint of a segment when the coordinates
of its endpoints are known.

Brief Procedure	Example	Practice Exercise
The Midpoint Formula If the endpoints of a segment are (x_1, y_1) and (x_2, y_2), then the coordinates of the midpoint are $\left(\dfrac{x_1 + x_2}{2}, \dfrac{y_1 + y_2}{2} \right)$. (To locate the midpoint, determine the average of the x-coordinates and the average of the y-coordinates.)	Find the midpoint of the segment with endpoints $(-1, 6)$ and $(3, -2)$. We have $\left(\dfrac{-1 + 3}{2}, \dfrac{6 + (-2)}{2} \right)$, or $\left(\dfrac{2}{2}, \dfrac{4}{2} \right)$, or $(1, 2)$.	3. Find the midpoint of the segment with endpoints $(5, -3)$ and $(1, -5)$. A. $(3, -4)$ B. $(1, -2)$ C. $(2, 1)$ D. $(-2, -1)$

Brief Procedure	Example	Practice Exercises

Objective [9.1d] Given an equation of a circle, find its center and radius and graph it; and given the center and radius of a circle, write an equation of the circle and graph the circle.

For a circle with an equation of the form $x^2 + y^2 = r^2$, the center is $(0, 0)$ and the radius is r.

For a circle with an equation of the form $(x - h)^2 + (y - k)^2 = r^2$, the center is (h, k) and the radius is r. This is the standard form of the equation of a circle.

It might be necessary to complete the square with the x^2- and x-terms and/or the y^2- and y-terms in order to find the standard form of the equation.

Find the center and the radius of the circle $(x - 1)^2 + (y + 2)^2 = 9$. Then graph the circle.

First we write an equivalent equation in standard form:
$$(x - 1)^2 + [y - (-2)]^2 = 3^2.$$
The center is $(1, -2)$ and the radius is 3.

To graph the circle we locate the center and then use a compass to graph the points 3 units from the center.

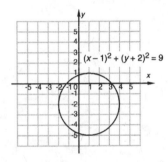

4. Find the center and the radius of the circle $(x + 3)^2 + (y - 2)^2 = 4$. Then graph the circle.

A.
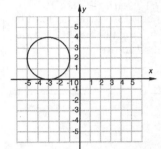

B.
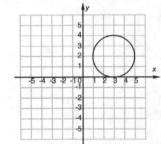

C.
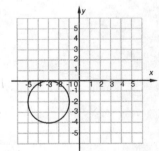

D.
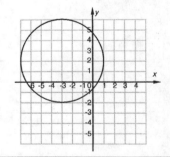

Objective [9.1d] (continued)		
Brief Procedure	Example	Practice Exercises
Given the center and radius of a circle, substitute in the standard form of the equation of a circle with center (h, k) and radius r to write an equation of the circle. The circle can be graphed as described above.	Write an equation of the circle with center $(-3, 4)$ and radius $\sqrt{5}$. We substitute -3 for h, 4 for k, and $\sqrt{5}$ for r in the standard form of the equation. $$(x - h)^2 + (y - k)^2 = r^2$$ $$[x - (-3)]^2 + (y - 4)^2 = (\sqrt{5})^2$$ $$(x + 3)^2 + (y - 4)^2 = 5$$	5. Write an equation of the circle with center $(1, -5)$ and radius 3. A. $(x - 1)^2 + (y - 5)^2 = 9$ B. $(x + 1)^2 + (y + 5)^2 = 9$ C. $(x - 1)^2 + (y + 5)^2 = 9$ D. $(x - 1)^2 + (y + 5)^2 = 3$

Objective [9.2a] Graph the standard form of the equation of an ellipse.		
Brief Procedure	Example	Practice Exercise
An ellipse with an equation of the form $\dfrac{x^2}{a^2} + \dfrac{y^2}{b^2} = 1$, $a, b > 0$, $a \neq b$, has x-intercepts $(-a, 0)$ and $(a, 0)$ and y-intercepts $(0, -b)$ and $(0, b)$. This equation is said to be in standard form. To graph such an ellipse, plot the intercepts and connect them with an oval-shaped curve.	Graph: a) $4x^2 + y^2 = 16$ b) $\dfrac{(x-2)^2}{9} + \dfrac{(y+1)^2}{4} = 1$ a) We multiply by $\dfrac{1}{16}$ on both sides to obtain the standard form of the equation. $$\frac{1}{16}(4x^2 + y^2) = \frac{1}{16}(16)$$ $$\frac{1}{16}(4x^2) + \frac{1}{16}(y^2) = 1$$ $$\frac{x^2}{4} + \frac{y^2}{16} = 1$$ $$\frac{x^2}{2^2} + \frac{y^2}{4^2} = 1$$ We see that $a = 2$ and $b = 4$. Then the x-intercepts are $(-2, 0)$ and $(2, 0)$, and the y-intercepts are $(0, -4)$ and $(0, 4)$. We plot the intercepts and connect them with an oval-shaped curve. 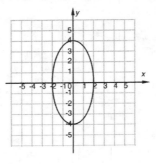 (continued)	6. Graph $9x^2 + 16y^2 = 144$. A. 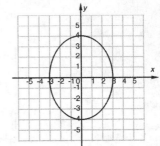 B. 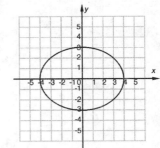 C. 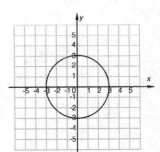 D. 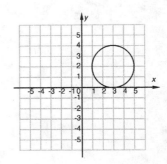

Objective [9.2a] (continued)

Brief Procedure	Example	Practice Exercise
	b) We write the equation in standard form: $$\frac{(x-2)^2}{3^2} + \frac{[y-(-1)]^2}{2^2} = 1$$ We see that the center is $(2,-1)$ and the vertices are $(2-3,-1)$ and $(2+3,-1)$, or $(-1,-1)$ and $(5,-1)$. Two other points on the graph are $(2,-1-2)$ and $(2,-1+2)$, or $(2,-3)$ and $(2,1)$. $$\frac{(x-2)^2}{9} + \frac{(y+1)^2}{4} = 1$$	

Objective [9.3a] Graph the standard form of the equation of a hyperbola.

Brief Procedure	Example	Practice Exercise
A hyperbola with an equation of the form $\dfrac{x^2}{a^2} - \dfrac{y^2}{b^2} = 1$ has its center at the origin and a horizontal axis. A hyperbola with an equation of the form $\dfrac{y^2}{b^2} - \dfrac{x^2}{a^2} = 1$ has its center at the origin and a vertical axis. In either case, the asymptotes of the hyperbola are $y = \dfrac{b}{a}x$ and $y = -\dfrac{b}{a}x$.	Graph $\dfrac{y^2}{9} - \dfrac{x^2}{4} = 1$. First we write the standard form of the equation: $$\frac{y^2}{3^2} - \frac{x^2}{2^2} = 1.$$ Then $b = 3$ and $a = 2$. The asymptotes are $y = \dfrac{3}{2}x$ and $y = -\dfrac{3}{2}x$. Now we substitute 0 for x and solve for y to find the y-intercepts. $$\frac{y^2}{9} - \frac{0^2}{4} = 1$$ $$\frac{y^2}{9} = 1$$ $$y^2 = 9$$ $$y = \pm 3$$ The y-intercepts are $(0, -3)$ and $(0, 3)$. We sketch the asymptotes and plot the intercepts. Then we draw a smooth curve through each intercept that approaches the asymptotes closely. $$\frac{y^2}{9} - \frac{x^2}{4} = 1$$ 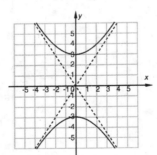	7. Graph $\dfrac{x^2}{1} - \dfrac{y^2}{9} = 1$. A. 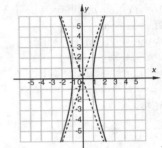 B. 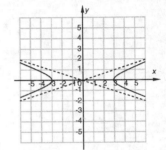 C. 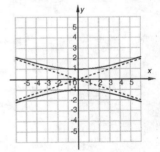 D. 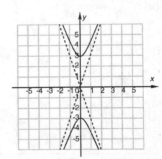

Objective [9.3b] Graph equations (nonstandard form) of hyperbolas.

Brief Procedure	Example	Practice Exercise
Equations of hyperbolas of the form $xy = c$, where c is a nonzero constant, have the x- and y-axes as asymptotes. To graph such an equation, solve for y, find and plot some ordered pairs, and draw two smooth curves that approach the asymptotes.	Graph $xy = -4$. First we solve for y: $y = -4/x$. Now we find some ordered pairs, plot them, and sketch the hyperbola. Note that x cannot be 0. <table><tr><td>x</td><td>y</td></tr><tr><td>-4</td><td>1</td></tr><tr><td>-2</td><td>2</td></tr><tr><td>-1</td><td>4</td></tr><tr><td>1</td><td>-4</td></tr><tr><td>2</td><td>-2</td></tr><tr><td>4</td><td>-1</td></tr></table> 	8. Graph $xy = 6$. A. B. C. D.

Objective [9.4a] Solve systems of equations where at least one equation is nonlinear.		
Brief Procedure	Example	Practice Exercise
A system of equations composed of one linear equation and one nonlinear equation can be solved using the substitution method. Either the substitution method or the elimination method can be used to solve a system composed of two second-degree equations.	Solve: $y^2 = x + 3$, $\quad y = x + 1$. We use the substitution method. First we substitute $x + 1$ for y in the first equation and solve for x. $$y^2 = x + 3$$ $$(x+1)^2 = x + 3$$ $$x^2 + 2x + 1 = x + 3$$ $$x^2 + x - 2 = 0$$ $$(x+2)(x-1) = 0$$ $$x + 2 = 0 \quad or \ x - 1 = 0$$ $$x = -2 \ or \qquad x = 1$$ Now substitute these values for x in the second equation and find the corresponding y-values. $$\text{For } x = -2 : y = -2 + 1$$ $$y = -1$$ $$\text{For } x = 1 : y = 1 + 1$$ $$y = 2$$ The ordered pairs $(-2, -1)$ and $(1, 2)$ check. They are the solutions.	9. Solve: $x^2 + y^2 = 13$, $\qquad 3x^2 - y^2 = 3$. A. There is exactly one solution. B. There are exactly two solutions. C. There are exactly three solutions. D. There are exactly four solutions.

Objective [9.4b] Solve applied problems involving nonlinear systems.		
Brief Procedure	Example	Practice Exercise
Use the five-step problem-solving process.	A rectangular rug has an area of 54 ft^2 and a perimeter of 30 ft. Find its dimensions. 1. *Familiarize.* We make a drawing. We let l = the length of the rug and w = the width. $$\boxed{\begin{array}{c} \\ 54 \text{ ft}^2 \\ \\ \end{array}}\ \ w$$ $$l$$ 2. *Translate.* Perimeter: $2l + 2w = 30$ Area: $lw = 54$ 3. *Solve.* We solve the second equation for l: $l = 54/w$. Then substitute $54/w$ for l in the first equation and solve for w. $$2\left(\frac{54}{w}\right) + 2w = 30$$ $$\frac{108}{w} + 2w = 30$$ $$108 + 2w^2 = 30w$$ $$2w^2 - 30w + 108 = 0$$ $$w^2 - 15w + 54 = 0$$ $$(w - 6)(w - 9) = 0$$ $$w - 6 = 0 \ \ or \ \ w - 9 = 0$$ $$w = 6 \ \ or \ \ \ \ \ \ w = 9$$ If $w = 6$, then $l = 54/w = 54/6 =$ 9. If $w = 9$, then $l = 54/w = 54/9 = 6$. Since length is generally considered to be greater than width, we have $l = 9$ and $w = 6$. 4. *Check.* If $l = 9$ and $w = 6$, then the perimeter is $2 \cdot 9 + 2 \cdot 6$, or 30, and the area is $9 \cdot 6$, or 54. The numbers check. 5. *State.* The length of the rectangle is 9 ft, and the width is 6 ft.	10. The area of a rectangle is 12 m^2, and the length of a diagonal is $\sqrt{40}$ m. Find the dimensions. A. The length is 12 m. B. The length is 6 m. C. The length is 4 m. D. The length is 3 m.

CHAPTER REVIEW ANSWERS

Chapter R

1. A 2. B 3. A 4. A 5. D 6. A 7. A 8. C
9. D 10. C 11. B 12. D 13. D 14. D 15. B
16. B 17. D 18. B 19. D 20. B 21. B 22. C
23. C 24. A 25. C 26. C 27. D 28. A 29. D
30. A 31. B 32. D 33. D 34. B 35. C 36. A
37. C

Chapter 1

1. B 2. C 3. B 4. D 5. B 6. D 7. A 8. A
9. A 10. D 11. D 12. B 13. D 14. C 15. D
16. C 17. A 18. D 19. C 20. B 21. A 22. C

Chapter 2

1. A 2. B 3. D 4. D 5. A 6. C 7. B 8. A
9. C 10. C 11. A 12. C 13. B 14. A 15. A
16. D 17. A 18. D 19. B 20. A 21. C 22. D
23. A 24. A 25. C 26. B

Chapter 3

1. A 2. A 3. A 4. B 5. A 6. D 7. B 8. A
9. A 10. A 11. D 12. C 13. C 14. A

Chapter 4

1. C 2. D 3. B 4. A 5. D 6. D 7. C 8. B
9. D 10. B 11. D 12. D 13. A 14. D 15. D
16. B 17. D 18. B 19. B 20. B 21. B 22. B
23. B 24. A 25. C 26. A 27. A 28. B

Chapter 5

1. C 2. D 3. B 4. A 5. C 6. A 7. D 8. D
9. C 10. D 11. B 12. D 13. C 14. A 15. B
16. C 17. C 18. B 19. B 20. D 21. B 22. C
23. D

Chapter 6

1. D 2. A 3. B 4. D 5. C 6. A 7. A 8. C
9. C 10. A 11. B 12. D 13. D 14. C 15. A
16. C 17. B 18. B 19. A 20. C 21. D 22. C
23. C 24. D 25. A 26. B 27. D 28. A

Chapter 7

1. C 2. C 3. C 4. B 5. C 6. A 7. D 8. B
9. A 10. D 11. B 12. C 13. D 14. A 15. B
16. B 17. D 18. A 19. D

Chapter 8

1. B 2. C 3. C 4. A 5. A 6. D 7. A 8. B
9. A 10. B 11. B 12. D 13. B 14. A 15. C
16. B 17. D 18. A 19. C 20. B 21. B 22. C
23. D 24. C 25. A 26. B

Chapter 9

1. D 2. C 3. A 4. A 5. C 6. B 7. A 8. D
9. D 10. B